P-95

The English Family 1450–1700

Themes in British Social History

edited by Dr J. Stevenson

This series covers the most important aspects of British social history from the renaissance to the present day. Topics include education, poverty, health, religion, leisure, crime and popular protest, some of which are treated in more than one volume. The books are written for undergraduates, postgraduates and the general reader, and each volume combines a general approach to the subject with the primary research of the author.

The English Family
1450–1700

Ralph A. Houlbrooke

Longman
London and New York

Longman Group Limited
Longman House, Burnt Mill, Harlow
Essex CM20 2JE, England
Associated companies throughout the world

Published in the United States of America
by Longman Inc., New York

© Longman Group Limited 1984

First published 1984
Second impression 1985
Third impression 1986

Birtish Library Cataloguing in Publication Data
Houlbrooke, Ralph A.
  The English family 1450–1700. – (Themes in
British social history)
  1. Family – England – History
  I. Title   II. Series
  306.8′5′0942   HQ615

ISBN 0-582-49045-6

Library of Congress Cataloguing in Publication Data
Houlbrooke, Ralph A. (Ralph Anthony), 1944–
  The English family, 1450–1700.

  (Themes in British social history)
  Bibliography: p.
  Includes index.
  1. Family – England – History – 15th century.
2. Family – England – History – 16th century. 3. Family –
England – History – 17th century. I. Title. II. Series.
HQ615.H68 1984   306.8′5′0942   83-22283
ISBN 0-582-49045-6 (pbk.)

Set in 10/11 pt Linotron 202 Times Roman
Produced by Longman Group (FE) Ltd
Printed in Hong Kong

Contents

Acknowledgements

My interest in the early modern family was first aroused some sixteen years ago by reading the vivid testimony of witnesses in matrimonial and testamentary cases heard by the consistory court of Norwich. Since 1975 I have taught a course concerned with 'The Family in Early Modern England'. It was the preparation and teaching of this course, and the wider reading these entailed, which emboldened me to seize the opportunity of writing this book. The latter I owe to John Stevenson, and the accomplishment of the task has been assisted by his subsequent confidence, patience and good humour. I have often felt like an explorer who sets out on a small raft to chart a swift and turbulent river, and I hope that the result conveys something of the exhilaration as well as the perils of the enterprise. Keith Wrightson has been the most thorough and constructive critic of the penultimate version of the text, though by no means all his suggestions were adopted in the final draft. His encouragement was very important to me both at the inception of the project and during the last round of revision. David Palliser, Barry Coward, Chris Chalklin and Anthony Fletcher have also read the typescript, and I am grateful to the first two for their helpful suggestions. I am indebted to all those undergraduates who have over the years studied the life of the family with me, but particularly to the authors of dissertations. Amongst the latter, Felicity Becker (now Wakeling), Cheryl Croydon, David Missen, Gill Silvester and Stephen Taylor have taught me most, and I thank the first three for allowing me to cite their unpublished work in this book. Other friends or colleagues, Grenville Astill, Martin Ingram, Martin Jones and Mary Prior, have given me the same kind permission. Cedric Brown, Jane Gardner, Philippa Hardman, Brian Kemp, Peter Laslett, David Levine, Alan Macfarlane, Bill Sheils, Barry Stapleton, Richard Wall, and Professors Alan Wardman and E. A. Wrigley have all supplied important information, which I was, alas, not always able to use. Particularly fruitful discussions took place in seminars to which I was invited by Cedric Brown, Anthony Fletcher and Keith Thomas. Visits to libraries and archives have been facilitated by the generous assistance given by the Research Board of Reading

University. The staffs of the Berkshire, Devon, Greater London, Norfolk and Norwich and Somerset Record Offices, and Miss Pamela Stewart, formerly Assistant Diocesan and Cathedral Archivist at Salisbury, have given me their friendly cooperation. I am especially grateful to Mr Robin Bush of the Somerset Record Office for introducing me to the incomparable autobiography of John Cannon and to Mr Edward Carson and Mr Graham Smith for allowing me to copy a microfilm of the original manuscript. The quest for printed material of the period has been greatly assisted by the presence in the Reading University Library of Lady Stenton's small but choice collection of books bearing on the lives of women. Here I found a copy of the 1623 edition of William Whateley's *Bride Bush*, whose title page reminds his readers that some have found marriage 'a little hell'. Nothing could have been further from my own experience, and my wife's encouragement has been very important to me, especially during the work of cutting successive drafts, a task to which, so far as I am concerned, Whateley's metaphor is far more appropriate. Finally I would like to thank my typist, Mrs Bogue, for coping so cheerfully with the results of this process.

Whiteknights, November 1983 R.A.H.

For Margaret, Tom and Sarah

Chapter 1

Introduction

Marriage and parenthood are enduring facts of human existence, but over the centuries their character has changed. What were the most important elements in this process and how were they connected? In answering these questions, historians have found it difficult to reach agreement. Economic, religious, institutional and demographic developments have each been given the foremost place by different writers. It has also proved difficult to decide exactly how these developments affected the emotional climate of family life. Did they, as some have believed, transfer to the elementary family primary loyalties previously focused on the community or a larger group of kinsfolk? Did they strengthen the ties of affection binding its members together?

The period between the fifteenth and eighteenth centuries, the period, that is to say, when 'modern' Europe is supposed to have been born, has long been of great interest to historians of family life. The idea that the Protestant reformers took a much more positive view of the conjugal partnership than had the medieval Catholic Church is a very old one. More recently it has been argued that on both sides of the post-Reformation religious divide there was a new stress on the moral formation of the child and a new interest in the early development of personality. In England, the seventeenth century brought a shift of power from the monarchy, the relaxation of tension after the period of religious conflict, and the rise of toleration and scepticism, all allegedly reflected within the families of the wealthy and educated in a gradual growth of individual freedom and a new respect for personal preference. Spontaneous affection began to replace instilled obedience as the main cohesive force within the elementary family. Meanwhile, it is argued, lordship, the local community and wider kinship ties had been eroded by political centralisation and the growth of the market economy.[1]

Other writers, however, have long stressed what they believed to have been the negative effects of economic change, in particular the weakening of household or family organisation in agriculture and industry. The growth of poverty, seen as a consequence either of rapid demographic expansion or the development of capitalism, or of both, has been described as deeply corrosive of family life among lower social groups.[2] The importance of other developments sketched in the last paragraphs, in some cases their very existence, has recently been questioned. Different historians have claimed that Protestant teaching concerning the family was essentially unoriginal, that wider kinship ties had long been relatively weak among the great majority of the population, that strong conjugal and parental affection had existed both as ideals and in practice well before the close of the Middle Ages, and that supposed advances in individual freedom were relatively insignificant.[3]

This book, then, attempts to survey a subject and a period which have recently given rise to lively controversy. Expressed attitudes and expectations are its central themes, but institutional, economic and demographic patterns and changes will be taken into account. The rest of this introduction will deal briefly with the evidence which historians of the family during this period have used, and touch on some of the approaches they have followed. Then, the concern of Chapter 2 will be to isolate certain enduring features of English family life and the most important forces of change. It will make as concisely as possible a number of basic points, many of which will subsequently be discussed more fully. Thereafter discussion will focus in successive chapters upon the relations between the elementary family and kinsfolk outside it, and upon certain major phases in the family life cycle.

The evidence

The historian of the family can draw on a rich variety of sources. But these sources present him with considerable problems of balance and interpretation, for they are uneven in both their social and their temporal coverage. These points need to be developed and emphasised before we consider the approaches so far pursued in investigating the history of the family.

Individual visibility in historical records of this period depends to a great extent upon wealth, social status and the literacy which was connected with them. The most useful source materials bearing on family life may be divided into five main categories. The first embraces correspondence, biographies and diaries, the second those documents which concern the settlement or transmission of property and skills: wills, marriage agreements, family settlements, deeds, leases, surrenders, and indentures of apprenticeship. A third consists of the records of litigation, a fourth certain records of correctional or administrative action concerning individuals such as judicial proceedings against offenders and orders and agreements arising out of the administration of the Poor Law. The fifth resulted from administrative processes designed to cover all the people in certain communities or categories. Such were parish registers, lists of inhabitants and tax assessments. The last two allow us to penetrate much further down the social scale than the first three, but are also more impersonal. The greater part of the material in the first category, the most informative and readily accessible, was produced by the landed gentry and the commercial and professional classes. The second and third categories catch very much larger numbers of people in a light which is often brilliant though restricted to certain critical moments of the family life cycle, such as courtship and the eve of death. But the majority of them were people of substance. The most daunting obstacle in the way of writing a history of the family is that our direct knowledge of personal attitudes and expectations is so largely limited to those expressed by the propertied and articulate. The recorded behaviour of much larger groups of people can be subjected to quantitative analysis, but our interpretation of the assumptions which underlay that behaviour is all too often heavily dependent on inference and conjecture.

The people of the sixteenth and seventeenth centuries, their attitudes and opinions, the pattern of their lives, and even their physical appearance, are all much more familiar to us than are those of their ancestors. The techniques of realistic portraiture, first widely employed in the sixteenth century, bring many of them vividly before us. Sometimes we see them depicted in family groups. In the field of funerary art, the new realism made more vivid an already established form of portrayal. The fashion for painting living families, on the other hand, was slow to develop, though there are some outstanding sixteenth-century examples of family groups. Thomas More, in the earliest and most famous, had Holbein record his household's devotion to classical learning (*c.* 1528).[4] The picture of the family of Lord Cobham, now at Longleat (1567), was perhaps the first to show a brood of small children, the fruit of a happy and fecund marriage.

All the sources already distinguished as the ones most useful for the study of the family either originated or greatly. increased in volume during the sixteenth and seventeenth centuries. Biographies, autobiographies and diaries were different manifestations of the urge to record the individual's experience.[5] This was stimulated by Renaissance humanism, by the opportunities for choice offered by an era of religious conflict, intellectual turmoil and widening horizons, and by the desire of pious people to record God's mercies and come to terms with his judgements. The rough-hewn blocks of personal testimony incorporated in John Foxe's massive martyrology (1563)[6] probably popularised the notion that the experiences of ordinary people were worth recording and prepared the way for the autobiographical efflorescence of the seventeenth century. Several individuals used their diaries as private confessionals; a handful of them, including Samuel Pepys, greatest of English diarists, sought to present a complete picture of themselves, a counterpart in words of the painter's self-portrait. The fifteenth and early sixteenth centuries produced some of the most outstanding of all English letter collections, yet many more survive from the second half of our period. The growth of literacy and the improvement of postal services facilitated correspondence. The increasing readiness of members of the propertied classes to write rather than dictate their letters made possible a new epistolary privacy. This in turn encouraged a loosening of formalities, a fuller expression of intimate feelings and a more discursive treatment of personal pleasures.

Various types of administrative record of vital importance to the historian of the family began to be kept for the first time after 1500. The maintenance of parish registers of births, marriages and deaths was ordered in 1538. The earliest surviving lists and enumerations of the members of individual communities were drawn up during the sixteenth century for a number of fiscal and administrative purposes.

Literary evidence, too, survives in much greater bulk from the sixteenth and seventeenth centuries, largely because of the growing use of the printing press, which by making reading matter more readily available probably facilitated the spread of literacy and enhanced the demand for its own products. The literature of Christian counsel, that is books concerned with the Christian's duties, especially in the domestic sphere, burgeoned to satisfy the appetite of a literate lay audience. A series of such works flowed from the pens of Protestant ministers, most of them married, in the century after the Reformation. Other views of familial relationships found expression in a rich flowering of imaginative literature.

The relative paucity of material surviving from before the sixteenth century creates serious problems for the historian of the family. The greater impersonality of some types of record, the absence of others, make sentiments and expectations harder to assess. Some historians associate the flowering of new forms of evidence with a general transformation of sensibilities. Others, however, believe that changes in the source material merely obscure a fundamental continuity of attitudes and expectations.

Approaches to the history of the English family*

Many different methods and approaches lie behind the attempts made in recent years to write a 'total' history of the institution of the family in England and elsewhere. Any useful scheme of classification will inevitably be somewhat rough and ready. But the history of law and ideas, psychohistory, economic history, sociology, anthropology and historical demography have all contributed in varying measures.

* The numbers in parentheses in this section refer to items in the select bibliography.

The study of the history of individual families, particularly by means of genealogical investigation, long antedated the idea of writing a history of 'the family'. The domestic life of certain families and periods has been studied by a long line of scholars, many of them women, whose main aim was to present a vivid picture of those things which seemed most characteristic and significant in the records they examined. It is to such authors that we owe lively accounts of the Verney, Oxinden, Blundell and Johnson families. Such accounts often include selections from family correspondence. On a much grander scale is the edition of the Lisle Letters, recently completed by Muriel St Clare Byrne, which includes a series of learned and penetrating essays on marriage, service and education in the early Tudor period. Among more general surveys one may mention Elizabeth Godfrey's *Home Life under the Stuarts, 1603–1649* (1925). Its robustly old-fashioned defence of carefully arranged marriages still bears reading today. Mercenary matches, she pointed out, had not been abolished by 'our modern English notions of absolute freedom of choice and the paramount claims of falling in love which the modern novel has erected into a new gospel . . .'.[7]

No English legal historian of the first rank devoted himself primarily to the period between the fifteenth and eighteenth centuries. The chapters on family law in F. W. Maitland's classic work (121) remain indispensable to students of this as of previous periods. Various aspects of the development of family law during this era were dealt with by such Victorian or early twentieth-century historians as C. S. Kenny (70), G. E. Howard (57), L. Dibdin and C. E. H. Chadwyck Healey (69). In the last forty years the most important contribution to our understanding of family law during this period has perhaps been made by economic historians concerned with the means of transmission of property from one generation to the next as an element in the changing fortunes of the nobility, gentry and peasantry. Some courts whose work was particularly important in the life of the family have also been studied. They include those charged with the supervision of wards and orphans (108, 111, 106). Studies of the ecclesiastical courts, particularly by R. H. Helmholz, have thrown much light on courtship, marriage and divorce (56).

The laws governing family life are by no means identical with its guiding ideals. The development of such ideals has been traced by many scholars, particularly those whose interests spanned the frontier between literature and history. Protestantism, and especially puritanism, have long been assigned an important role in this development, particularly by historians working on the copious literature of advice and guidance. 'It has often been said', D. Townshend wrote as long ago as 1897, 'that we owe our English ideal of family life and domestic affection to the teachings of the Puritan party.'[8] C. L. Powell and L. L. Schücking (72) were among the scholars who developed this theme. Both relied primarily upon literary sources:

works of Christian counsel as well as plays, poetry and novels with a didactic purpose. Powell also tried to set the literary ideals alongside the development of the law. But neither author enquired at all closely how far literature either reflected or shaped actual practice, despite the fact that this was Powell's avowed aim and Schücking's description of his work as a 'social study from the literary sources'. The idea that there was a distinctive and innovative Protestant or 'puritan' doctrine of marriage put their evidence under severe strain. Powell claimed, for instance, that Catholic writers had regarded marriage as a necessary evil for the propagation of the race even though they had extolled it at great length.[9] Schücking, despite his title *The Puritan Family*, had to admit that in matters of practical piety the main division lay not between 'Anglicans' and 'Sectaries' but between the pious and the children of the world. He even speculated that the roots of distinctively English attitudes to the family might be traced back long before the Reformation, but did not follow this suggestion very far. In his view, 'puritan' ideals embraced by the bourgeoisie in the end profoundly modified the coarser and more cynical attitudes of the aristocracy, though this contrast between 'bourgeois' and 'aristocratic' ideals was assumed rather than demonstrated.[10] A number of other writers have developed the idea of the supposedly distinctive contribution of Protestantism. But it has recently been called in question in articles by Kathleen Davies (68) and Margo Todd (76); the former emphasised the degree of continuity between medieval and Protestant teaching, the latter the contribution made by humanism.

Religious change was assigned a major role in the most influential of all recent studies of familial ideals, *Centuries of Childhood*, by P. Ariès (1962). Churchmen, he argued, were increasingly concerned from the later Middle Ages onwards, but especially during the Counter-Reformation, to mould the minds of the young. They therefore played a leading part in developing a new awareness of the characteristics which differentiate children from adults and in reducing the indifference with which small children had hitherto been regarded. Ariès took up an already current but somewhat nebulous idea that older children were treated like 'little adults' in early modern times[11] and expressed it with a new vigour. He used what at first looked like a wealth of convincing evidence from literature and art and related his central theme to developments in education and the nuclear family. Yet Ariès ignored, or dismissed as irrelevant, much medieval evidence of solicitude for children and awareness of their distinctive characteristics. The portrayal of children was only one of the areas affected by the development in art of naturalism and a secular spirit; the later Middle Ages saw not only adults and small children, but also men and women, increasingly differentiated by their dress. Yet Ariès failed to take full account of these facts. He repeatedly ripped evidence from its proper context, failed to consider how typical it was, and confused prescription with practice.[12]

Ariès seemed at first to have revealed the existence of an emotional climate completely different from our own. Certain features of his approach foreshadowed the methods of 'psychohistory'. Psychohistorians have sought to uncover the unspoken assumptions of the dead, their hidden fears and sorrows, by inference, the analysis of imagery, the identification of significant silences and omissions, and the sifting of explicit statements to exclude what seemed to be merely conventional or otherwise irrelevant for their purposes. Such methods have led to the rejection of much evidence which might be considered important by more conventional historians and of apparently obvious or reasonable explanations and hypotheses in favour of others more ingenious but often less convincing. Psychohistorians have also tried to assess the influence of customs, conventions and ideals on the personality of individuals. Such efforts arouse serious misgivings. First, because there is disagreement on this subject even among those practitioners who can examine living people. Secondly, because psychohistorians have necessarily concentrated upon certain features of the environment of which evidence survives at the expense of others which, though inadequately documented, may have been just as important. The most important essay in psychohistory so far published, *The History of Childhood* edited by Lloyd de Mause (1974), is open to a number of these criticisms, even though many of the individual contributions to it are relatively conventional in their approach and fit in somewhat uneasily with its main thesis. This is that over the past two millennia relations between parents and children have been gradually improved by the achievement of greater parental empathy. Parents who had themselves suffered from orthodox methods of rearing slowly changed the ways in which they brought up their own children. Parental neglect, child abuse and infanticide, allegedly common in antiquity, gradually declined in subsequent centuries. The child ceased to be regarded with indifference or hostility and became instead a being to be moulded by increasingly subtle and delicate means. Finally, in the most progressive families of today, parents have abandoned the attempt to form the child, instead responding to its needs and developing interests. Such a thesis can only be maintained by means of fairly ruthless selection of evidence and a blurring of the distinction between orthodox practices which parents genuinely if mistakenly thought to be good for their children and those which were condemned at the time and resorted to as a result of harsh necessity or parental inadequacy or perversity.

Criticism of psychohistorians' unwarranted assumptions, manipulation of evidence and excessive respect for controversial theories does not imply the rejection of all attempts to penetrate the emotional world of our ancestors. Their direct personal testimony can be analysed to good effect if it is handled with caution. Alan Macfarlane used an exceptionally full and intimate diary to open up the mental world of the seventeenth-century clergyman Ralph

Josselin (38). The early modern documents which most closely resemble the files of a modern psychiatrist are the case books of the astrological physician Richard Napier (1559–1634), well employed by Michael MacDonald in his study of anxiety, distress and mental illness in early seventeenth-century England (110).

The role of the family and its different members in productive processes, the transfer of resources through marriage and inheritance and the part played by the latter in the formation and maintenance of socio-economic groups are all topics whose importance has long been appreciated by economic historians. Awareness of the economic context has on the other hand made possible a more realistic appreciation of the influence of ideas.

In a classic study of the working life of women (67), Alice Clark pictured most households in Tudor England as units of production based on the closely integrated partnership of man and wife. Concentration of ownership of the means of production in fewer hands and the growth of larger enterprises undermined this domestic economy by forcing men to work outside their homes. Since men's wages were commonly inadequate to maintain their families as well as themselves, wives were forced to enter the labour market in large numbers, but their earning power was far less than that of men, and this exposure produced a sharper deterioration in their position than in that of their husbands. Clark exaggerated the extent of the decline of productive domestic partnership during this period, even though she made important distinctions between the experiences of different socio-economic groups. But some of the questions which she posed have still to be fully answered, though there is an excellent discussion of the economic roles of family members in Charles Phythian-Adams's recent study of early sixteenth-century Coventry (42).

The labour of children and adolescents was exploited by means of apprenticeship and service, respectively the subjects of an old study by J. Dunlop and R. D. Denman (95) and a new one by Anne Kussmaul (96). The latter not only traces the evolution of the institution but sets it in its demographic, agricultural and regional contexts, building here on the work of other historians in related fields.

The part played by marriage and inheritance in the development of socio-economic groups has been the subject of much thorough study. The immensely complex subject of the development of the family settlement has attracted a great deal of attention since Sir John Habakkuk published his seminal article on eighteenth-century marriage settlements in 1950 (117). Among the many distinguished scholars who have advanced understanding of family settlements since then have been K. B. McFarlane (120), J. P. Cooper (116), M. E. Finch (26), Lawrence Stone (31) and L. Bonfield (113). The major questions with which they have been concerned have sometimes been the subject of disagreement. To what extent did the basic aims of landowners change? What effects did various forms of settlement have in safeguarding the integrity of estates? How swift and how widespread was the adoption of new forms of settlement? How important were the effects on family fortunes of such other factors as personal competence, parental affection for younger sons and daughters, and demographic facts such as fertility and the succession of minor heirs?

Among the historians who have followed the fortunes of smaller rural landholders, Joan Thirsk (122), Margaret Spufford (45), Cicely Howell (116), Rosamund Faith (115) and Zvi Razi (43) have been especially concerned with the family and the transmission of property. (The last two have focused their attention on the later medieval period, but their findings have important implications for subsequent centuries.) In her article on 'Industries in the Countryside' (122) Joan Thirsk demonstrated how the reduction in the size of holdings by gavelkind encouraged the development of by-employments. Abundant common resources facilitated the continued practice of partible inheritance, a point also made in Margaret Spufford's *Contrasting Communities* (45). This demonstrates the strength of Cambridgeshire landholders' concern to provide for children other than the heir, even when primogeniture was the rule, which led them to place excessive burdens on their holdings, or even to break them up. This concern also emerges clearly from Zvi Razi's account of fourteenth-century Halesowen (43), the most outstanding of recent studies of the late medieval peasantry. Razi and Howell have shown that the late medieval decline and stagnation of population enabled the more prosperous peasants to accumulate more land. Cicely Howell's study of Kibworth Harcourt in Leicestershire (116) shows that in the sixteenth and seventeenth centuries such men were far better placed than their poorer neighbours to reconcile the integrity of their holdings and adequate provision, increasingly in the shape of money portions, for non-inheriting children.

Historical sociologists and anthropologists have been especially interested in family forms and the ways in which these have influenced law, custom, the performance of mutual services and residential arrangements. Sociologists have long been disposed to see the emergence of the nuclear family as a comparatively recent development. Nineteenth-century writers such as Morgan posited the primeval dominance of tribes or clans.[13] The French sociologist Frédéric Le Play identified two major historical family forms: the patriarchal, in which all sons had remained together after marriage, and the stem, in which only one son in each generation inherited and was able to marry. In the stem family, other siblings were entitled to support from the patrimony so long as they remained unmarried, but if they wished to found a family of their own they had to move away.[14] The study of law and custom in operation was one way of testing Le Play's model. A pioneer of this sort of study was George Homans, who aimed to consider the social order of the thirteenth-century village (28) as if it were that of 'an island in Melanesia' described by an anthropologist. Homans discerned in medieval England two basic family forms: the stem family, and the joint family, in which each son was entitled to a share of the paternal holding. The former, by forcing younger sons to leave home if they wished to marry, prepared the way for the future development of a more fluid society. But the notions of birthright and family attachment to the soil exercised strong influence over Homans's work. The social importance of different inheritance customs in the early modern period has been underlined by such economic historians as Joan Thirsk and Margaret Spufford (122, 45). In 1978, Alan Macfarlane insisted upon the antiquity of individual rights of possession and freedom of alienation in England (15) and made a forceful attack upon the concepts of family ownership and birthright which had been called in question by F. W. Maitland some eighty years before. More recently, however, Zvi Razi has emphasised the strength of feeling in favour of expectant heirs and of the sense of obligation both towards non-inheriting children and 'retired' parents which existed in late medieval Halesowen (50).

The degree of interaction between kindred and the services they performed for one another were among the subjects of Alan Macfarlane's study of Ralph Josselin (38), and his chapter on 'The Relative Importance of Kin and Neighbours' has been one of the most influential recent essays in historical sociology. Investigation of these matters on a larger scale has formed an important part of community studies by Richard Smith (51), Zvi Razi (50), Miranda Chaytor (49), Keith Wrightson and David Levine (46). Most of this work has suggested that kinship ties outside the nuclear family were comparatively weak; on this point the strongest dissenting opinions have been those of Razi and Chaytor.

The study of household structure offered a third avenue of approach to the history of family forms. The exploitation of early community censuses or population listings has been Peter Laslett's major contribution to historical sociology since 1963. He has demonstrated in a series of articles (13, 14) the overwhelming preponderance of nuclear family households in England since at least the later sixteenth century. Subsequent analysis of the earliest urban census by Charles Phythian-Adams (42) has shown that this was well established in Coventry by the 1520s. The fact that a high proportion of families were broken by death or 'reconstructed' by remarriage is evident from some of Laslett's studies and has recently been underlined by Miranda Chaytor's description of Ryton (Co. Durham) in the late sixteenth century (49). In his study of *Family Structure in Nineteenth Century Lancashire* (1972), Michael Anderson used census material to analyse household structure and also drew on a variety of other sources to assess the extent of co-operation between kinsfolk. His work is of major interest to historians of pre-industrial

England both because it turns traditional sociological orthodoxy on its head by suggesting that the industrial revolution might actually have strengthened kinship ties and because it contains a bold and vigorous provisional sketch of English kinship between the seventeenth and twentieth centuries.

Demographic developments are of the utmost interest to the economic historian and the historical sociologist, though the connections between population trends, the conventions governing family and household formation and economic developments have only recently begun to become clearer. This has resulted from the resumption of advances in historical demography whose major achievements remained until recently those of John Rickman (1771–1840), pioneer of English parish register analysis.[15] Rickman's work demonstrated considerable growth in the English population between the sixteenth and nineteenth centuries, especially in the eighteenth, but the respective roles of fertility and mortality in this increase remained subjects of speculation and controversy down to the early 1980s. Aggregative analysis of the totals of vital events listed in parish registers, the basis for many important and useful local studies, could demonstrate the existence of certain population trends and of crises of mortality, but could not fully explain long-term population movements. The perfection in the 1950s of a new technique, 'family reconstitution', essentially the collation of the dates of all relevant vital events of a couple and their children, permitted a much wider range of questions to be asked about levels of mortality and life expectancy, ages at and duration of marriage, and intervals between births and marital fertility. Perhaps the most important single result of its application has been to demonstrate that the age at marriage in pre-industrial England was relatively high for both sexes. Pioneering family reconstitution studies of the parish of Colyton (Devon) and the British nobility were carried out by Prof. E. A. Wrigley (22, 92) and T. H. Hollingsworth (10, 11) respectively. For over twenty years the Cambridge Group for the History of Population and Social Structure has played the chief part in supervising and co-ordinating English demographic studies. The Group's most ambitious publication so far, *The Population History of England 1541–1871* (1981), employs a new technique, aggregative back projection. The computations involved run backwards from a point at which the size and age structure of the population are known from a reliable census (in this case that of 1871) and use quinquennial totals of vital events in a sample of parish registers (404 in this case) as the basis for national estimates. It has permitted the calculation not only of national population totals during the period since registration began but also of birth, marriage and death rates and of the proportion of the population which remained unmarried. It has demonstrated more fully than ever before the importance of nuptiality in helping to determine population levels and has established fairly conclusively that rising fertility bore a far larger share of the responsibility for the dramatic growth of the population in the eighteenth century than falling mortality.

Parish registers have been by far the most important source for demographic studies, but marriage licences have also been used to calculate ages at marriage, particularly by R. B. Outhwaite (60) and V. B. Elliott (61). The analysis of early censuses and population listings has helped to set high ages of marriage in their social context by demonstrating the predominance of nuclear family households and the employment of considerable proportions of adolescents and young adults in household service. Until recently, the possibilities of carrying out detailed demographic work on the period before the inception of parish registers were discounted. But now Zvi Razi has used a particularly informative set of fourteenth-century manorial court rolls as the basis for a form of partial family reconstitution, yielding estimates of changing levels of nuptiality, mortality and life expectancy, and of numbers of children surviving to adulthood (43). The importance of late fourteenth-century poll-tax records as a demographic source has long been known: Richard Smith has subjected them to more thorough and sophisticated analysis in order to gain a fuller knowledge of household structure, sex ratios and proportions married and single (64).

The findings of the historical demographers have been called in question on at least four grounds.[16] The first and most fundamental of these is that the sources used are hopelessly unreliable. Secondly, since only a small minority of families can be reconstituted, the results of reconstitution may be unrepresentative of the experience of the majority of the population. It has been argued, thirdly, that the historical demographers have presented averages, 'meaningless means', which conceal important social, geographical and even temporal variations. Failure to set data in their economic and social context has hindered the convincing explanation of demographic phenomena. There is something in all these criticisms. But the development and refinement of tests of plausibility and means of detecting and compensating for defective registration have been major objectives of the historical demographers. The other points can perhaps best be answered by saying that the demographers see themselves as being merely in the early stages of a great co-operative endeavour, in which the essential first step is to establish the broad outlines of the picture yielded by their most important sources before investigating in greater detail the problems of representativeness, variation and context. To some extent aggregative methods can be used as a check on the results of family reconstitution. Such a comparison helped to lead Professor Wrigley to a revised estimate of the importance of family limitation in seventeenth-century Colyton (93).

The effort to place demographic findings in their social and economic context has now begun. One example is the correlation of nuptiality statistics with wage series in the *Population History of England*. But significant social and geographical variations and the reasons for them can only be revealed by careful local study. The contrasting experiences of four communities form the basis of David Levine's essay on *Family Formation in an Age of Nascent Capitalism* (1977). One of its major themes is the way in which the age and incidence of marriage fluctuated in response to the availability of employment, which in turn depended on the changing character of local agriculture and the vicissitudes of rural industry. Another is the strong likelihood that a high proportion of illegitimate births resulted from the frustration of marriage plans by unforeseen misfortunes, especially dearth or slump. A number of other studies of rural communities by Zvi Razi (43), Margaret Spufford (45), Victor Skipp (44), Keith Wrightson and David Levine (46) have drawn attention to the links between demographic developments, social structure, economic resources and (in varying degrees) the machinery of social control. So far the most ambitious attempt to assess and explain demographic developments in a major city has been Roger Finlay's monograph on London between 1580 and 1650 (8). Besides under-lining the long appreciated fact that immigration was essential to sustain London's rapid growth, Finlay brings out the contrasts in fertility and mortality between richer and poorer parts of the city, and suggests that at least in its more favoured quarters, residential stability may have been greater than is often supposed.

It will already have become obvious how far the various approaches here distinguished for analytical purposes have intermin-gled and overlapped in practice. Recent historians of the family have attempted to pursue several different approaches. Alan Macfarlane's study of the family life of Ralph Josselin, based on that seventeenth-century clergyman's exceptionally full and revealing diary (38), is not simply the work of historical anthropology which its title claims it to be. In its careful tabulation of births, deaths and miscarriages and its discussion of the evidence of maternal breastfeeding, it makes a small but useful contribution to historical demography. In some ways the most satisfying part of the whole book is an essay in what has been dubbed 'Household Economics', a detailed study of Josselin's income and expenditure and the accumulation and distribution of his prop-erty. Finally, his exploration of attitudes and emotions might be called 'psychohistorical', though its conclusions are a good deal more modest and more securely based on solid evidence than those of many ventures in that genre.

A multi-faceted account of family life has been attempted in some studies of social groups and classes. Lawrence Stone examined the family relationships of the nobility from all the angles so far distin-guished here in the course of a much wider study of the attitudes, behaviour and fortunes of a social class (31). Stone's use of demo-graphic data was especially important. He was by no means the first to attempt to incorporate such information in a study of this type. Sylvia Thrupp (32) and K. B. McFarlane (120) had done so in their work on late medieval London merchants and English nobility. But more copious documentation and a shorter time span enabled Stone to give a fuller statistical picture of the demography of the Elizabethan and early Stuart peerage. More recently, Randolph Trumbach drew on Hollingsworth's labours in his study of aristocratic kinship and domestic relations in the eighteenth century (33). Trumbach also contributed to legal history in his valuable account of family settlements and exploited sociological and anthropological research in an analysis of kinship. A great range of intimate sources went into the painting of his vivid picture of aristocratic ideals and attitudes, and he showed himself an unusually cautious and sensitive psychohistorian in his account of improved infant and child care among the nobility, perhaps the best part of his book.

The first attempt to write a 'total' history of the English family in the early modern period was Lawrence Stone's *The Family, Sex and Marriage in England 1500–1800* (1977). This maintains that the nuclear family became very much more important, relationships within it more intense. The core of Stone's subject lay in the 'very significant changes over time' which 'took place in the Early Modern period in family functions, in emotional relationships, in character formation, in attitudes towards and the practice of sexuality, and towards the number of children born and the care taken, within marriage, over their subsequent preservation'. Stone proposed to tackle these major changes from six points of view: biological, sociological, political, economic, psychological and sexual. Stone's work has proved deservedly popular. The grandeur of his central theme, the sustained vigour and elegance of his writing, and the great range of materials laid under contribution, all make this an exciting and readable book. It has acted as a powerful stimulus to discussion and research, and there is much of lasting value in its portrayal of the domestic life of the nobility and gentry between 1650 and 1800.

Yet hardly any aspect of Stone's enterprise has escaped severe criticism. Six important points develop naturally from the foregoing discussion of methods and approaches. First, the degree of change which took place in thinking about conjugal and parental responsibilities and in the importance of affection within the family is exaggerated. Secondly, the correspondence between official doctrines and actual practice, and consequently the speed with which changes in the former affected the latter, are overestimated. Thirdly, particular effects of ideals, practices and experience upon the individual personality are far too confidently asserted, and the controversial or hypothetical character of much psychological theory is ignored. Of all Stone's major approaches, the economic is perhaps the sketchiest, and the enormous range of familial economic forms and of differences in the extent to which family members fulfilled economically productive roles is insufficiently emphasised. Fifthly, assertions of the importance of wider kindred in late medieval England are based on long exploded sociological myths: they fly in face of the facts that there were no clearly defined groups of kinsfolk or obligations towards them. Finally, demographic statistics tend to be interpreted in the most pessimistic fashion, which gives an exaggerated impression of the transience of family ties and the neglect of infants. Furthermore, inferences concerning the onset of contraceptive practices among the upper classes appear to be based on extremely flimsy evidence.

Other broad points can be made. The impression of change over time is exaggerated by failure to pay attention to the likelihood that the character of the source material changed much more radically than the feelings and attitudes reflected in it. Much evidence of love, affection and the bitterness of loss dating from the first half of Stone's period has simply been ignored. The criticisms concerning the assumed relationship between ideals and practice, the perpetuation of sociological myths and the use of evidence strike at the very heart of Stone's scheme of successive family types, the open lineage family, the restricted patriarchal nuclear family, and the closed domesticated nuclear family, which forms the spine of his book. The whole scheme exaggerates the speed, extent and uniformity of change, even with all the qualifications which Stone attaches to it. One cannot but agree with his own admission that 'any generalisation on these complex and obscure subjects inevitably runs into the objection that any behavioural model of change over time imposes an artificial schematisation on a chaotic and ambiguous reality'.[17]

It will be a long time before another work on the history of the family is attempted which matches Stone's in its scope and scale. Meanwhile there is much to be done. The systematic exploration and analysis of the intimate records of the literate and articulate has only begun. The vast archives of central and local courts have yet to yield up many if not most of their secrets. Demographic studies have just come of age, and the minute examination of local communities by means of record linkage is still in its infancy. The next few decades will see great advances in our understanding of past relationships between individual, family and community.

This book rests, in varying degrees, on the work of all the historians mentioned in this introduction. It has been shaped by the assumption that though the surviving evidence of past ideas and attitudes offers a useful entry into the study of the development of the family, all the approaches so far outlined need to be taken into account. In view of the wide differences of existing scholarly opinion, and the amount of important work currently in progress, many of its conclusions can only be provisional. Intended as an introductory survey, it does not, however, pretend to offer only a neutral summary of opposing views. Rather does it argue that the elementary or nuclear family typically occupied a central place in the life and aspirations of the individual between 1450 and 1700 as it still does today. It suggests, furthermore, that the momentous developments of this period, though certainly affecting family life, brought no fundamental changes in familial forms, functions and ideals.

Notes and references

1. See especially **C. L. Powell**, *English Domestic Relations, 1487–1653*, Columbia UP, New York, 1917; **L. L. Schücking**, *The Puritan Family: A Social Study from the Literary Sources*, Routledge & Kegan Paul, London, 1969 (first German edn 1929); **P. Ariès**, *Centuries of Childhood*, Jonathan Cape, London, 1962 (trans. from French edn of 1960); **M. E. James**, *Family, Lineage and Civil Society: A Study of Society, Politics and Mentality in the Durham Region 1500–1640*, Clarendon Press, Oxford, 1974; **L. Stone**, *The Family, Sex and Marriage in England 1500–1800*, Weidenfeld & Nicolson, London, 1977.
2. **A. Clark**, *Working Life of Women in the Seventeenth Century*, George Routledge & Sons, London, 1919, pp. 8–13, 64–92, 145–9.
3. See especially **K. M. Davies**, 'Continuity and Change in Literary Advice on Marriage', in **R. B. Outhwaite** (ed.), *Marriage and Society, Studies in the Social History of Marriage*, Europa Publications, London, 1981, pp. 58–80; **A. Macfarlane**, *The Origins of English Individualism: The Family, Property and Social Transition*, Basil Blackwell, Oxford, 1978; **A. Macfarlane**, review of Stone, *op. cit.*, in *History and Theory*, **18** (1979) 103–26; **F. Mount**, *The Subversive Family: An Alternative History of Love and Marriage*, Jonathan Cape, London, 1982.
4. **A. Lewi**, *The Thomas More Family Group*, HMSO, London, 1974, esp. pp. 3–4.
5. **P. Delany**, *British Autobiography in the Seventeenth Century*, Routledge & Kegan Paul, London, 1969; **A. Macfarlane**, *The Family Life of Ralph Josselin, a Seventeenth-Century Clergyman: An Essay in Historical Anthropology*, Cambridge UP, 1970, pp. 3–9.
6. **J. Pratt** (ed.), *The Acts and Monuments of John Foxe*, The Religious Tract Society, London, 1877.
7. **E. Godfrey**, *Home Life under the Stuarts, 1603–1649*, S. Paul, London, 1925, p. 113.
8. **D. Townshend**, *Life and Letters of Mr Endymion Porter: Sometime Gentleman of the Bedchamber to King Charles the First*, T. Fisher Unwin, London, 1897, p. x.
9. Powell, *op. cit.*, pp. 119–29.
10. Schücking, *op. cit.*, pp. xiii–xv, 6–7, 18–20, 129–44.
11. **I.** and **P. Opie** (eds.), *Oxford Dictionary of Nursery Rhymes*, Clarendon Press, Oxford, 1951, pp. 4–5.
12. For cogent and effective criticism of the work of Ariès, see **A. Wilson**, 'The Infancy of the History of Childhood: An Appraisal of Philippe Ariès', *History and Theory*, **19** (1980), 132–53, and Mount, *op. cit.*, pp. 104–7, 141–7, 149–50.
13. **L. H. Morgan**, *Ancient Society*, New York, 1877.

14. **F. Le Play**, *La Réforme Sociale*, Paris, 1864. Le Play's ideas are discussed by **J.-L. Flandrin**, *Families in Former Times: Kinship, Household and Sexuality*, Cambridge UP, 1979, pp. 50–3; **P. Laslett**, 'Introduction: The History of the Family', in **P. Laslett** and **R. Wall** (eds.), *Household and Family in Past Time*, Cambridge UP, 1972, pp. 16–23.
15. For assessment of Rickman's work, see **E. A. Wrigley** and **R. S. Schofield**, *The Population History of England 1541–1871. A Reconstruction*, Edward Arnold, London, 1981, esp. pp. 2–4, 624–30.
16. See for example **M. Anderson**, *Approaches to the History of the Western Family 1500–1914*, Macmillan, London and Basingstoke, 1980, pp. 27–38.
17. Stone, *op. cit.*, p. 14.

Chapter 2

Enduring patterns and forces of change

Certain major features of English family life, many of them shared with neighbouring countries in north-western Europe, were already established in the Middle Ages. But it is clear that major forces of change have also been at work. The aim of this second chapter, then, is to sketch some of the enduring patterns of English family life and identify the more important forces of change which have influenced them.

Enduring patterns

Six hundred years ago the nuclear family was the basic element in English society as it still is today. In the absence of clearly defined larger groups of relatives, the individual's primary loyalties focused on his elementary family, even though links with other kinsfolk could be both materially and emotionally significant. Since at least the beginning of the sixteenth century and probably long before, the household based on a nuclear family has been by far the commonest type of residential unit in England. Throughout our period the nuclear family had certain special functions. The family was upheld, its life influenced, by religion, literature, law, custom and a variety of exterior social pressures. Religious teaching provided an ideal picture of family relationships. The rights and duties of family members were set out in laws and customs. In practice there was an immense diversity in family life patterns within a complex social structure. Social status, material resources and means of livelihood influenced household size and structure, the ability of the family to perform its basic functions, and relations both among its members and between them and other kinsfolk. The first section of this chapter will develop these points in greater detail.

The word 'family' is most commonly used today to refer to the 'nuclear' or 'elementary' group of parents and children. It can also denote all an individual's relatives by blood or marriage, or, thirdly, all those descended from a common ancestor who share the same surname. The subject of this book is the family in the first sense.

The predominant usage of today is of comparatively recent origin. During our period 'family' denoted above all the body of persons living in one house or under one head, including children, kinsfolk and servants. But within the household the closest of relationships was that between man and wife, as Sir Thomas Smith recognised in about 1565: 'The naturalest and first coniunction of two towards the making of a further societie of continuance is of the husband & of the wife . . . . And without this societie of man, and woman, the kinde of man could not long endure.'[1] Husband and wife had certain responsibilities towards both children and servants, who were in turn bound to obey them. But though servants and children might be members of the same 'family', the bases of their membership, the extent of their duties to the heads of the hosehold, their claims upon them, and the duration of their residence, were completely different, and recognised to be so.

There was no well-defined group of kinsmen larger than the elementary family to which most individuals owed loyalty. Men's strongest personal obligations, legal, customary and moral, were to spouse and children. They generally recognised, for example, their moral obligation to leave the bulk of their property to their wives and offspring, to whom it would descend by the laws and customs of inheritance if they made no dispositions of their own. Dynastic sentiment and awareness of one's lineage played little part in the lives of the great majority of the population. Ties with relatives by marriage and maternal kinsfolk were often stronger than those with paternal kindred.

To deny the existence of loyalties to a clearly defined larger body of kinsfolk is not to claim that relationships outside the nuclear core were unimportant. Each individual who married belonged to at least two nuclear families in the course of his life: his family of origin and his family of marriage. After marriage, each partner retained links with surviving members of his or her nuclear family of origin and gained a new secondary attachment to his or her spouse's family, in which he or she would be accepted as 'son' or 'daughter'. At any given moment, each nuclear family was linked by birth or marriage to a number of others. Personal ties outside the nuclear family were usually concentrated within the ring of grandparents, uncles, aunts, nephews, nieces and in-laws, though their strength and significance depended in each case on social status, geography, the accidents of mortality, personal preferences and calculations of mutual advantage. In general the wealthy and literate probably found it easier and more profitable to maintain kinship links than did the rest of the population. Further down the social scale their importance was probably greatest in those areas where inheritance customs, shared natural resources or growing industries allowed people to make a livelihood near the place where they had grown up. Kinship varied in its strength both socially and geographically. But it would be a mistake to think of the nuclear family as being strongest and most cohesive when its connections with kinsfolk outside it were weakest. The contrary could sometimes be true, for kinsfolk might help a family to surmount economic difficulties, or act to assuage internal strife by timely advice or pressure.

Most English households seem to have been based on nuclear families in the second half of our period. Analysis of sixty-one population lists or censuses (mostly of individual parishes) dating from the late sixteenth to the early nineteenth century has shown that over 70 per cent of households covered were based on elementary families of two generations. Under 6 per cent of households contained three generations, and very few contained two married couples. A very small proportion of households contained identifiable kinsfolk who did not belong to the nuclear family of marriage of the household head, and the majority of these were parents or parents-in-law, siblings (presumably unmarried or separated) and grandchildren. The preponderance of the nuclear family household appears even more marked in the earliest local census so far analysed, drawn up at Coventry in 1523. Only 1 per cent of all households contained adult relatives of any sort; only 3 in 1,302 were of more than two generations. Finally, a list of some 51,000 living and dead people of the predominantly rural archdeaconry of Stafford drawn up for religious purposes about 10 years after the Coventry census, tends to underline the residential and emotional autonomy of the nuclear family. Only about 10 per cent of the family groups listed contain relatives of the head of the family other than spouses or children: most of these are parents, many of them already dead. Only two entries go back beyond dead parents, and none contain people who are clearly servants or apprentices. The Coventry and Staffordshire evidence points to the likelihood that the predominance of the nuclear household had already been established well before 1500. Analysis of poll-tax lists has suggested that it existed in the late fourteenth century.[2]

Inherited conventions and economic arrangements which discouraged more than one couple from living in the same household tended to delay marriage long beyond the age of sexual maturity. Not until after a period of paid employment, apprenticeship, inheritance or a combination of all three did a young couple have the wherewithal to establish a household. Among the bulk of the population the average age of marriage lay in the middle or late twenties. This seems to have been well established by the second half of the sixteenth century, and it was perhaps widely prevalent in the fourteenth, though on this point there is a disagreement. But among the upper classes the early marriage of heirs and heiresses to protect or further family interests remained common far longer. At this social level the boarding of young married people in their parents' houses was fairly widespread.

The elementary family had recognised special functions and

purposes upon which there was a wide measure of agreement among contemporaries, though there might be differences of emphasis, for example between clerical and lay writers. Procreation, the first purpose of marriage, embraced parents' duty to bring up their children and to provide so far as lay in their power for their subsequent 'advancement' through education, service, apprenticeship and marriage. Marriage also provided a legitimate channel for the satisfaction of sexual desire. It was a lifelong, indissoluble partnership of husband and wife for mutual support in sickness and health. The duty of support was fulfilled by means of the property and skills brought to the union by both partners. A division of tasks between husband and wife was envisaged, but these often overlapped.

Affection and obedience were the bases for the performance of familial duties. Mutual love was described as the basis of marriage in both religious and secular literature. Parental affection, and the instinct to protect and nourish children, were held to be natural, strong and deeply implanted. But it was widely recognised that conjugal love often perished or failed to develop. When love turned sour, antipathy was the stronger, and marriage could be a 'little hell'.[3] Parental love was held to be much stronger than filial, and reluctance to help parents in old age was allegedly widespread.

The family was held together not only by affection, but also by obedience to superior authority and divine commandment. Obedience to both parents and husbands was enjoined by Scripture. The family was seen as a monarchy. The authority of human fathers, indeed of all temporal rulers, rested on that of God the Father.

God was an infinitely loving father. The fact that he so often punished his children justified and reinforced the conviction that the truly solicitous human father must not flinch from the duty of corrective punishment set out in Scripture. 'For whom the Lord loveth he chasteneth, and scourgeth every son whom he receiveth.'[4] Human suffering was part of the divine plan, and the Christian had to try to accept with patience even bereavement, the worst of afflictions. Death was the constant companion of life, especially in its first year. Many of the children born never reached maturity, marriages were much more likely to be cut short in youth or middle age than they are today, and the experience of losing a parent in childhood or adolescence was common. A high proportion of all marriages were remarriages. Death was double-faced. To the survivor it might seem a trial or a punishment, but for those who died in Christ it was the gateway to everlasting bliss. These convictions strongly influenced people's bearing in the face of bereavement and the way they referred to it. But in practice, as contemporary observers knew full well, the experience of loss was often bitter and hard to accept. The difficulty of matching the conduct of Job was recognised.

Christian teaching was designed both to strengthen the family and enhance its significance while also tempering the intensity of the emotions experienced within it. Potent rites accompanied the major events in the family cycle. Ideally, religion bound members of families closer together. But the Christian's love of God was to be greater than the strongest of his earthly affections. A current of suspicion of the most intense earthly pleasures, especially physical love, ran through Christian writings. It is impossible to say how widespread effective understanding and acceptance of Christian teaching were. Such teaching provided the only comprehensive synthesis of thought concerning the family for most of our period, and shaped and coloured much of the evidence coming down to us from the articulate and literate. Other influences were however at work. In romantic literature, for example, ancient quasi-pagan and classical elements mingled with Christian tenets.

The life of the family was also regulated and influenced by various interlocking laws and customs. The common law of England, largely developed in the courts of strong medieval kings, underpinned the husband's power and authority. During marriage, it regarded the wife as being almost completely subject to her husband. Her goods became his, and provided she bore him a child, he had a life estate in all her lands, while the widow was entitled to only a third of her husband's lands. The wife might forfeit widowhood property rights by adultery, but not the husband. The courts would punish a man for killing or maiming his wife, but his right to chastise her survived throughout this period. The protection given to children against parental violence was even less satisfactory. As late as the eighteenth century misadventure was considered the appropriate verdict to return when a child or apprentice died as a result of 'moderate' correction.[5] Married parents were hardly ever punished for deaths of children occurring in the vulnerable first year of life. Rules originally designed to uphold the interests of the Anglo-Norman crown governed succession to real property. The most important was male primogeniture.

The Church in its teaching and law took account of areas of family life barely touched by the common law and was in some respects readier to protect the interests of women and children. It had made free and mutual consent a condition of the validity of marriages. The church courts granted separations for cruelty and infidelity and when necessary ordered restoration of the conjugal rights of bed and board. Succession to movable goods was usually their concern, and some local customs guaranteed a man's widow and children shares in these goods. Until the sixteenth century the courts imposed penance on parents guilty of infanticide and made orders for the maintenance of illegitimate children.

The courts of manors and boroughs supervised succession to tenements subject to their jurisdiction. The customs they upheld in the absence of individual dispositions sometimes divided a man's land among all his sons or made exceptionally generous provisions for widows. London made its own arrangements to safeguard the rights of freemen's widows and orphans.

The law was not static. Two important examples of developments affecting the family may be given. The Court of Chancery protected uses and trusts designed to make more secure provision for wives, widows and younger sons. It became the chief court concerned with orphan heirs. At the local level the responsibilities of the justices of the peace expanded in the later sixteenth century to include orders for the maintenance of bastards and the punishment of their parents as well as supervision of a new system of poor relief based on local rates.

The family was subject to greater outside scrutiny than it is today. A concept of privacy certainly existed, and both law and social convention discouraged prying and snooping.[6] Yet the simple internal layout and relatively insubstantial construction of the majority of dwellings, high housing densities along the streets of bigger villages and towns, and the widespread employment of servants all made it more difficult to hide what went on in the 'private' domain. Personal misconduct such as fornication and adultery was punished as criminal, particularly by the church courts, which received presentments based on 'common fame'. Communities also had their own informal means of punishing unacceptable conduct, such as hounding by boys with sticks and stones, 'rough music' and the skimmington ride. But the degree of supervision was far from uniform. Tightest in well-governed corporate towns, close in nucleated villages, it was comparatively loose in the scattered woodland and upland settlements where family and household enjoyed most autonomy. Let us not exaggerate the power of external pressures to mould the internal life of the family. Its distribution of effective power often failed to correspond with the stereotypes upheld by society. Contemporaries were well aware that women often had more forceful characters than their husbands, and that many of them had an important or even decisive say in the disposal of their husbands' property. All but the most serious conflicts which arose in families were also settled within them, without the intervention of external agencies.

Social and economic status exerted a powerful influence over the character of family life. The thin crust of society was composed of those exempt from menial toil, the peerage and gentry, who probably never comprised more than about 2 per cent of the total population. The wealthier landowners lived a partly urban, partly rural life. The great majority of English people lived in the countryside. Broadly speaking, substantial non-gentle landholders and farmers were covered by the contemporary term 'yeomen', middling and small farmers were called 'husbandmen', while those chiefly dependent on wages were called 'labourers' or 'cottagers'. Rural craftsmen, many of whom were also farmers, spanned a spectrum of wealth which touched the yeomanry at the top, and the labouring class at the bottom.[7]

The highest ranks of urban society were largely filled with merchants, many of them as rich as gentlemen. Their wealth was less illustrious and less secure, but the great expansion of trade increased their numbers, importance and confidence. Below them were to be found three broad groups, in descending order of wealth and status: independent craftsmen and lesser traders, journeymen and labourers. The majority of urban householders were probably employees rather than masters even in the early sixteenth century. The subsequent growth of centralised production in certain industries both urban and rural would greatly increase the numbers of employed workers.[8]

The professions embraced huge differences in wealth and status and spanned the division between town and countryside. They included the Church, the law, the administrative service of the Crown and greater landowners, the armed forces, medicine and teaching. Most were expanding during this period, though at different rates. The law was the most respected and lucrative of the professions, and many of its more eminent practitioners, largely recruited from the gentry, combined the tenure of legal office with the ownership of a country estate. Indeed the edges of the concept of gentility gradually became more blurred as a 'liberal' occupation and appropriate education and tastes came to be regarded as qualifications even without the support of a substantial estate.

Of all the social developments of this period perhaps the most striking was the growth in the numbers of poor people. The statistician Gregory King believed that a majority of the population were unable to make ends meet in 1688. They included not only 'paupers' but large numbers of at least partially employed people such as common soldiers and seamen and 'labouring people and outservants'.[9]

Some of the most obvious ways in which social status affected the life of the family stand out from population listings. The biggest households were at the top of the social scale, the smallest at the bottom. The mean household size among building workers, the poorest group of Coventry householders in 1523, and of paupers in a large sample of later pre-industrial censuses, was between three and four people. Coventry merchant households contained a mean number of 7.4 persons; those of gentry in listed communities 6.63. (Gregory King, however, credited even 'mere' gentry with an average number of 8 household members, knights with 13, peers with 40, and the size of the greater households may well have declined during our period.)[10]

The size of households largely depended on whether or not they contained other people besides a nuclear family. Pre-industrial community censuses show that the employment of servants was closely associated with social status. The percentages of households containing them grew smaller towards the bottom of the social scale. The presence of servants influenced the life of the family in many ways. The more numerous servants were, the wider the range of intimate tasks they performed, the greater the constraints imposed by the need to maintain deference and decorum. The local censuses also reveal, not surprisingly, that gentry households were much more likely to contain kinsfolk than were those of farmers.

The numbers of children living at home naturally varied from one household to another, but it is as yet impossible to generalise about the connections, if any, between social status and the size of the group of co-resident children. One might have expected to find that the richest people, who presumably enjoyed the most salubrious living conditions, had the largest numbers of children living with them. This was indeed the case at Coventry in 1523. But the average number of children in gentry families covered by samples of later pre-industrial censuses was smaller than in the households of certain groups of lower social status, including husbandmen.[11] Under the Tudors and Stuarts the gentry usually had their infants fed by wet-nurses, many of them non-resident; they often sent them to live with grandparents when quite small, and commonly despatched them to another household or to boarding school before they reached adolescence. So it should not surprise us if indeed they had relatively few children living with them at any one time. Further down the social scale, the age of departure from home doubtless depended on the need or ability of parents to use their children's labour, the availability of employment, local opportunities for earning while remaining at home, and the accessibility of schools. All these might vary between town and countryside and from one part of the country to another. The connections between fertility, child mortality and social status have yet to be worked out in detail, although infant mortality was almost certainly higher among the wet-nursed offspring of the upper classes than in the majority of families where children were suckled by their own mothers.

The factors governing the length of children's sojourn with their parents remain obscure. But it is clear that their advancement depended upon their parents' substance, status and useful contacts. Education cost money and meant forgoing children's labour. Among the wealthier classes, financial dependence on parents commonly survived physical separation and lasted much longer than it did further down the social scale. Parents' ability to give help enabled them to exercise much greater influence over their children's choices of calling and marriage partner than was possible for poorer people. This picture is complicated by the operation of inheritance. Primogeniture, which influenced the family strategies of many farmers and even ambitious townsmen as well as gentlemen, sharply differentiated the careers of heirs from their younger brothers. The prospects of the latter were generally more precarious, their need for self-reliance greater. Their chances of remaining in their class of birth or of achieving their own heirs' return to it depended upon skill, enterprise and, in many cases, a readiness to delay marriage.

The part played by family members in the care of the old also depended in part on social position. The wealthy might have children living with them but could if need be pay servants to look after them. It may have been in the middle ranks of society that the assistance of children was most important. People commonly had a child still living with them when they crossed the threshold of old age, and the final years of widowed decrepitude might be spent under the roof of a married son or daughter.[12] The poor stood least chance of having children living near who were able to help them if they survived till old age. The elderly and aged poor always bulked largest among the recipients of municipal and parochial relief.

The matrimonial partnership brought together material and personal resources. The former had the greatest relative importance at the upper levels of the social scale, the latter at the lower, but most gentlemen hoped to marry competent housewives, while even poor girls were expected to bring their husbands a portion. The roles of husband and wife were different but complementary. They were most closely integrated on small farms, in shops and the workshops of some types of craftsmen. Economic partnership was looser in that growing proportion of households whose dependence on wages forced the husband to work away from the home. Among professional men the domestic sphere was often completely divorced from work for a livelihood. Among the gentry neither partner worked for a living, but both often needed to co-operate in the oversight of the family's affairs and the defence of its interests: the wife might need to perform 'masculine' tasks in time of crisis, especially in the first half of our period. The nature of a marriage's economic basis strongly flavoured the companionship of husband and wife. At one end of the spectrum were the small farmer and his wife, most of whose time together was spent in toil in a shared enterprise which must nearly always have been in the forefront of their minds. At the other end we find a bureaucrat like Samuel Pepys, whose wife was the companion of his leisure hours, and whose office and home were close but separate worlds.

The major forces of change

The first section of this chapter underlined the enduring importance of the nuclear family in England, outlined its special functions, and singled out certain major continuing influences on the cohesion and effectiveness of the family group and the perceptions, expectations and attitudes of the individuals who composed it. This second section will identify some of the linked developments which in the course of our period most obviously shaped the material and ideological environments within which the family must be studied.

This period witnessed considerable demographic and economic expansion. For much of the time, however, particularly during the period's middle two quarters, the former outran the latter, so that, even though many benefited from increasing agricultural and industrial output and the expansion of trade, they were greatly outnumbered by the growing legions of the poor. Geographically, economic and demographic growth were unevenly spread. Both were most spectacular in London, which achieved during this period a position of unprecedented importance in English economic and social life. Political developments, notably the growth of effective government in the sixteenth century and the constitutional changes of the seventeenth, influenced both the course of economic expansion and the reception of new or unfamiliar ideas. Foremost among the vehicles of the latter were the Protestant Reformation, Renaissance humanism and the Scientific Revolution. The dissemination of ideas was promoted during this period by the linked growths of a national market and of literacy, assisted by the printing press. The following section will suggest some of the ways in which these various developments may have influenced family life.

Of all those developments which acted from without upon the life of the family, the changing balance between population and resources affected the largest numbers of individuals in the most visible fashion. Following a period of stagnation, a hesitant growth of English population began after 1470 from a probable level of a little over 2 million, which gathered strength in the early sixteenth century. It then grew to 3 million by 1550, over 4 million by 1600, and by the 1650s was fluctuating around $5\frac{1}{4}$ million, according to the most recent estimates. Thereafter, it fell gently and remained below 5 million for much of the late seventeenth century. Fertility and mortality were the major determinants of population levels. Probably the declining virulence and reduced geographical spread of bubonic plague were the most important causes of the initial recovery of population from about 1470. The later sixteenth-century growth rates were due to a combination of high but falling fertility and low mortality. Thereafter, fertility fell and mortality rose through the first half of the seventeenth century. Then, mortality remained high until the later 1680s, but fertility made a sharp recovery from about 1670. Fertility was influenced above all by changes in the timing and incidence of marriage, which seem in turn to have occurred in response to the developing economic situation, especially trends in real wages.[13] But though it seems fair to conclude that a process of adjustment was taking place by means of individual or group decisions, it is important to realise that changes in behaviour were relatively slow to take effect. Thus, as has already been mentioned, the population went on rising long after fertility had begun to fall in the later sixteenth century, with serious consequences for wage rates and the living standards of a large proportion of the population.

The great mortalities of the fourteenth century and the subsequent stagnation of population made it much easier to rent land, and, raising the demand for labour, increased wages. The resumed growth of population, outstripping that of the economy, set these developments into reverse. The ranks of landless labourers were swelled by men unable to find holdings or driven off the land by the scissors of rising rents and prices. During the sixteenth century, England gradually came to terms with the need to succour a massive and growing number of poor people. Relief would ultimately help to maintain countless fragile households. But many of the parochial ratepayers on whom the burden of relief fell became determined to do what they could to prevent a growth in the numbers of resident poor by limiting settlement by outsiders, which in turn reduced wage-earners' chances of marriage.

Redistribution of population took place as well as growth. Areas which had previously been thinly settled, such as forests and uplands, supported rapidly increasing numbers, and many towns attracted a swelling stream of immigrants. In both town and countryside the numbers of craftsmen grew rapidly. The fact that an increasing proportion of the population needed to buy its food stimulated internal trade. The expansion of demand and the growth of trade encouraged specialised production.

Between 1500 and 1700, the numbers of town and city dwellers grew faster than the total national population. This growth was uneven. In the provinces a number of towns failed to keep pace with national growth, though some leapt ahead of it and others sprang into existence for the first time. Urbanisation was above all due to the expansion of London. Five per cent of the country's population lived there in 1600, over 10 per cent in 1700.[14] London owed its phenomenal growth to the expansion of international and internal trade, the development of its own industries, and the services it offered the upper classes. They flocked to seek education and advancement, prosecute litigation, enjoy leisure and purchase luxuries.

Their high mortality made all towns dependent upon immigration to maintain their populations, let alone increase them. Between 1580 and 1650 London probably absorbed half the natural increase of the country's population; thereafter its sink of death temporarily checked national growth altogether. The survivors of about one in eight English births became Londoners at some stage of their lives between 1580 and 1650, of one in six between 1650 and 1750. By 1650, English population may have been near the level of its medieval peak. Massive absorption of rural immigrants by the urban sector was one of the more important features differentiating the experience of the early seventeenth-century countryside from that of the fourteenth. There was now less need for the prosperous landholder to establish sons on the land: a portion saved from the profits of the booming market in agricultural produce could be used to secure entry to a trade or profession.[15]

London's increasing influence facilitated the growth of a national market, and not in commodities alone. A national marriage market provided a much wider choice of eligible partners. The upper classes were most affected, but the influx of enterprising young people of both sexes to enter service or apprenticeships in the capital had consequences similar in character if proportionally smaller among a much larger group. In the second half of our period the majority of London marriage partners were immigrants. The capital, with its lion's share of England's printing presses and its concentration of merchants, clergy and professional laity, also strengthened its position as the country's leading market of ideas. Such theoretically subject groups as servants and women became much more literate in London than they were elsewhere.[16]

But it would be hard to demonstrate the existence of a distinctively new 'metropolitan' pattern of family life. Rather was the capital distinguished by the wide variety of patterns found within its boundaries. Residential stability and life expectancy were far higher among the more prosperous central parishes than they were in the suburbs where disease culled the poor, including many immigrants. Sexual laxity and vice may have been rife in certain parts of the capital, as contemporaries believed, but its parish registers suggest that ante-nuptial fornication and illegitimate births were less common than in rural England. Migrant female servants tended to get married late, presumably after saving a portion, with men of a similar age. Wealthy London-born girls were married early to men much older than themselves, a pattern which strengthened domestic patriarchy.[17]

Strong and effective government by the Tudors underpinned many of the economic and social developments so far touched on. The curbing by the monarchy of the habit of violence was a gradual process whose origins long antedated this period, but it was accelerated by the Tudor peace. The settlement of disputes by force grew rarer. Armed conflict gave way to litigation. In those remoter and more lawless parts of the country where blood kinship had played a part in individual security, its importance diminished. No longer did the members of gentry families have to work together to organise the armed defence of their interests as had the Pastons and the Plumptons in the fifteenth century. Internal peace was one of the prerequisites of the development of a national marriage market, as the use of matches to gain powerful local allies became less important.

Civil peace and the refinement of manners went hand in hand. Already in the Middle Ages the knightly code had, at least in theory, added gentleness and courtesy to the warrior virtues. In the late four-teenth century, a French gentleman, the Chevalier de La Tour Landry (the Knight of the Tower), had told his daughters that whereas 'moyen people' chastised their wives with blows, gentle-women ought to be corrected 'by fayre semblaunt and by curtosye'. Concern for civility and decorum, within the family as without, made violence and open discord increasingly unacceptable. On balance the softening of manners, spreading gradually down the social scale, improved women's security and social position by slowly removing those crude and brutal forms of pressure which put them most clearly at a disadvantage in dealing with men, even though disapproval of conjugal altercation forced the wife to control her tongue as well as restraining the husband's desire to use his palm or fist.[18]

The growth of peace and order which was assisted by stronger government had many beneficial consequences. But in one major respect Tudor rule weighed heavily upon the landed classes. This was the more vigorous exploitation of the Crown's feudal prerogatives of wardship and marriage, treated primarily as sources of revenue, and commonly sold to individuals who had little concern for the interests of the family. Fear of feudal exploitation was a major reason for continuing to arrange children's marriages early even after the decline of civil violence. Gradually, however, the administration of these prerogatives was modified, especially by reforms introduced under James I, so as to allow relatives better opportunity to purchase wards. The relaxation of pressure probably made parents readier to accept greater individual freedom of choice.[19]

It was the support given by the Tudor monarchy which ensured the official triumph of the Reformation in England. Protestantism, it is widely claimed, affected both the theory and the practice of family life. The reformers denied that marriage was inferior to celi-bacy. Higher value was assigned to companionship as an end of marriage. Let us not forget that the Catholic Church had also held matrimony in very high honour and esteem, and had greatly valued matrimonial affection. Many Protestants continued to value the gift of chastity because it allowed the individual greater freedom from worldly cares. There is little to show that the married lives of the great majority were much affected either by the Catholic assertion of the ideal superiority of celibacy or its abandonment. The chief importance of the latter was that it allowed the marriage of the clergy. Many of the most outstanding exponents and practitioners of the Christian married life were henceforth found among these men. But in their way of life they were very far from being a homogeneous group, and the extent to which the 'spiritualisation' of the household among the laity was inspired by clerical example remains obscure.

Protestantism is also claimed to have given the household much greater importance in religious life, particularly in prayer and religious instruction. But the roots of household piety can be traced far back into the Middle Ages. One of its features was the sanctification of meal times through prayer and devotional reading. The fullest late-medieval vernacular exposition of the Ten Commandments endorsed St Augustine's saying that each man should perform the bishop's office of teaching and correction in his own household.[20] The parental blessing, so frequently requested and bestowed in fifteenth-century letters, underlined the fact that father and mother were God's representatives within the family. Protestant ministers repeatedly bewailed the slowness with which their ideal of domestic christianisation was being realised. In their eyes the role of the household was important but still ancillary to that of the Church in which the Christian community showed its unity in prayer. The ministry of the Word, including the more thorough catechising of the young, remained with the clergy first and foremost. The household was most important in religious life, both before and after the Reformation, among dissident minorities (Lollards, Separatists and Catholic recusants) who had withdrawn partially or completely from common worship.

Some believe that Protestantism gave husbands and parents greater authority over wives and children, though obedience to superiors within the family rested on the same texts after the Reformation as it had done beforehand. Others have claimed that it did something to raise the status of wives by underlining the husbandly duties of fidelity and tender consideration, by insisting on the importance of the mother's educational responsibilities, and by making women their husbands' deputies in the religious life of the family. In the first two respects, Protestant teaching was not substantially new. Those who wrote on the third point tended to hedge their remarks with important qualifications. A third view, first expressed during the Reformation, has stressed Protestantism's subversive potential. By emphasising the importance of individual faith and understanding, by asserting the priesthood of all believers, and by insisting that the Scriptures were the property of all Christians, the Reformers tended to encourage the use of individual judgement, as their opponents claimed. But heads of families on *both* sides of the religious divide found themselves confronted by the religious dissidence of wives and children in an epoch of confessional strife. Subordinate family members who espoused Protestantism or radical sectarian beliefs were better placed to find religious fulfilment outside the family because dissident congregations were more numerous and more accessible to them. But Protestantism and the sects both threw their weight behind the traditional authority of husbands and parents within their own ranks.

So far as family life is concerned, the Reformation is perhaps best viewed as a phase of intensified effort in a long struggle to inculcate Christian beliefs and attitudes. The christianisation of the family should ideally have enhanced the level of mutual solicitude and the sense of common purpose among its members. The most intimate documents left by the pious, such as autobiographies, letters and diaries, show that religion could indeed heighten the sense of mutual duty, check impulses to anger, prompt efforts at reconciliation, and bring members of families together in moments of great emotional intensity. But it could also buttress petty domestic tyranny and shackle daily life with an arid routine of observance. Families, like communities and individuals, differed greatly in their ability to assimilate religion; perhaps only a minority ever did so more than superficially.

The Reformation was indebted to humanism and intertwined with it. Yet the close relationship was fraught with tensions, even though the cheerful, positive and practical tone of much Protestant writing on family life conveys the flavour of humanist influence. Humanism was tinged with an optimism concerning human character and potential which was at odds with the deep Augustinian pessimism so central to Reformation thought. Again, humanism, even in its Christian form, was heavily indebted to the literature of pagan antiquity not only for style and manner of presentation, but also for much of its practical ethics. Medieval Catholic doctrine had stressed the innate depravity of the infant. The humanists, drawing on classical teaching, thought of it as morally neutral and apt to learn, or even essentially good. But it had to be protected from evil or contaminating influences. This task was to start with maternal breastfeeding, the need for which was asserted with a new confidence and vigour, and was to be continued by close parental involvement in the child's education. Humanist optimism concerning the child's nature tempered the corrective emphasis of the existing educational orthodoxy. Erasmus wrote about marriage in his enormously influential *Colloquies* in a markedly secular tone. He depicted its delights with enthusiasm but also handled the tensions to which it gives rise with frankness, subtlety and realism. The healing 'medicine' of sexual intercourse was mentioned with none of the reservations or suspicions so evident in much medieval Catholic discussion. But the loving companionship of marriage was a union of minds and spirits as well as bodies. The Renaissance mounted the first serious attack on the medieval belief in women's natural inferiority in intellect and virtue and their physiological imperfection. Female learning, it was claimed, could create a new bond between husbands and wives.[21]

Humanist celebration of earthly affections was uninhibited and positive. Medieval letters had emphasised the distance between superiors and subordinates within the family. The humanists revived the simpler epistolary forms of antiquity, and encouraged in letter-writers the cultivation of an easy, intimate style, and the expression of individual feelings of affection. Funeral inscriptions became another vehicle for their expression. Writers of epitaphs of the new type recalled the dead person's virtues in a characteristically humanist belief that all sorts of men and women might in some aspect of their lives set an example worthy to be followed. Among these virtues, domestic and familial ones came to bulk increasingly large. Writers celebrated the love between husband and wife, parents and children, and (harking back to a theme prominent in antiquity) expressed the deep pain of loss.[22]

Both Protestantism and humanism contributed to the very considerable expansion of educational facilities which took place in England during the sixteenth and early seventeenth centuries. In the eyes of its supporters and propagandists, a principal aim of this expansion was to make the individual a better member of the Christian commonwealth by instilling a fuller understanding of his duty to God and his prince. At the very moment when Tudor central and local government stood on the verge of their most dramatic expansion, the humanist Sir Thomas Elyot supplied in *The Gouernour* (1531) a highly attractive image of the inferior magistrate and the honourable character of his responsibilities. Humanism promoted the ideal of a gentleman who was scholar as well as warrior and helped to draw the gentry into the spreading web of Tudor administration. Protestantism had a wider popular impact than humanism. There is abundant evidence that very humble people were often fired with the desire to learn to read so that they might explore the Scriptures themselves. But such individuals were nevertheless a small minority among the social groups to which they belonged. There was perhaps a remarkable expansion of literacy in Tudor and early Stuart England, certainly an improvement in its quality, but their effects on the lower strata of society were limited. Educational achievement depended very largely upon material incentives and opportunities. Administration, adjudication, exposition, persuasion: these were the tasks of the 'gouernour' in local and national government and in parliament: the necessary skills were supposedly nurtured by a broad classical education such as Elyot outlined. The ability to hold one's own in an age of litigation depended upon knowledge of the law. Participation in trade, business and the increasingly complex tasks of parochial government demanded the ability to read and write. A substantial proportion of the population lacked the opportunities to acquire much education as well as the incentives to do so. The small farmer or labourer could not usually forgo the help of his children after it became useful to him; he could barely afford even the small sums commonly necessary to acquire a schooling. As a result the improvement of educational attainments was socially limited. Advances were most marked among those who participated in the developing market economy: yeomen, tradesmen and craftsmen. They were far more limited among husbandmen and labourers.[23]

In the course of the four centuries after the Reformation, the educational role of the household would shrink and that of the school would expand. In the sixteenth century we can discern the first phase of this process, as the gentry increasingly looked to the free schools rather than magnate households for their sons' education.[24] What happened in the middling ranks of society is more obscure. Perhaps school education replaced household service to some extent in the pre-apprenticeship phase of late childhood. The period spent in school may also have grown longer when the age of entry into apprenticeship rose in certain occupations. In so far as an extension of schooling took place, it represented a substitution of one form of tutelage for another, not a lengthening of childhood.[25] The austere, rough and competitive environment of the school was thought to aid the maturing process.

From our standpoint, political upheaval seems to dominate the seventeenth century as religious controversy had overshadowed the sixteenth. The profound crisis of government which took place in the mid-seventeenth century shook both Church and Monarchy to their foundations. Since the government of the family was seen as a monarchy which, like its counterpart in the state, was underpinned by God's Word, it was natural to believe that religious and political convulsions in the state could not but have repercussions in the family. It is hardly surprising that some contemporaries should have claimed that these predictions had been fulfilled and that the events of the civil war and its aftermath had destroyed discipline and obedience, or, alternatively, that they had led to a beneficial relaxation of domestic manners. Almost certainly they exaggerated the effects of the crisis. In the first place it is questionable how far the reality of family life had ever matched the ideal of domestic monarchy save in the best-regulated households. Many men had allegedly failed to control their wives or even stood in awe of them. Complaints of the irreverence of the young towards their elders can be found throughout the Middle Ages. Even some of the better-documented changes associated with the crisis had been in train long beforehand. A relaxation of epistolary forms of address, which was perhaps accompanied by a similar change in the rules of deportment, can certainly be traced to the sixteenth century. An undeniable landmark in the history of the upper-class family was the abolition of feudal wardship in 1646, confirmed in 1660. But changes in its mode of administration had removed its worst abuses in James I's reign. Some of the most striking developments of the crisis did not have a wide or enduring influence. The collapse of censorship allowed subterranean currents of hostility to many institutions, including both property and marriage, to bubble to the surface, but there is little to show that many people's attitudes or behaviour were influenced by these ideas.

More enduring was the secularisation of thought which the final collapse of religious unity facilitated. This was most obvious in the investigation of the origins and foundation of earthly power which the political upheavals stimulated. Political theory now broke away from its scriptural moorings, and the work of Hobbes and Locke was marked by its coolly secular tone and its advancement of expediency and utility as the chief criteria by which to judge political structures. Locke argued that God's commandment to honour father and mother could not be applied, as it customarily had been, to subjects' duty of obedience to their secular rulers. The authority of parents and monarchs were quite different in nature. Some conservative political theorists had conceded that political authority was based on a contract, but likened this to the contract between man and wife, which bound the latter to permanent obedience. Locke, this time quietly disregarding Scripture, argued that both the terms and the duration of the marriage contract might be altered by mutual consent.[26]

The scientific revolution of the seventeenth century, and especially the idea that God governed the physical universe through immutable natural laws, also contributed powerfully to the secularisation of the climate of thought. Acceptance of the existence of natural laws made it increasingly difficult to attribute the individual's misfortunes to immediate divine intervention. Locke believed, unlike many of his puritan contemporaries, that God should be presented to the small child as a nebulous but above all beneficent Supreme Being.[27] At first, no mention was to be made of divine punishment. Men's conceptions of the Heavenly Father and of human fathers were interdependent. If the punitive aspect of God's nature was to be played down, there seemed the less justification for severity on the part of earthly parents. The scientific revolution and the concept of natural laws also reinforced the determination to conquer disease through experiment and investigation rather than accept it as an aspect of divine corrective activity. The conviction that long-established practice could be improved upon or replaced played a major part, between the seventeenth and nineteenth centuries, in reducing mortality in childbed and infancy.

This necessarily brief preliminary survey must end on a cautious note. Economic or demographic developments cannot be weighed in the scales with ideological ones, and the links between them are often hard to trace. Fluctuations in prices, wage rates and the volume of external trade can to some extent be measured, even though much controversy surrounds the data on which such measurements are based. Registered baptisms, marriages and burials can likewise be counted, and plausible hypotheses can be advanced to explain the patterns which such counting reveals. But ideas and attitudes cannot be quantified, nor can their diffusion be measured. Perhaps we are prone to exaggerate the speed of change in this domain. The Reformation and humanist ideals probably affected the quality of conjugal partnership and parenthood among the majority of the population little if at all. It seems very doubtful whether the scientific revolution had much influence on the way most people viewed God and the natural order until after the end of our period. The interaction of material and ideological factors in the lives of individuals during these centuries can rarely be clearly observed. The extent of the unknowable limits the historian of the family to tentative conclusions.

Notes and references

1. **T. Smith**, *De Republica Anglorum. The Maner of Gouernement or policie of the Realme of England*, London, 1583, p. 12.
2. **P. Laslett**, 'Mean Household Size in England since the Sixteenth Century', in **P. Laslett** and **R. Wall** (eds), *Household and Family in Past Time*, Cambridge UP, 1972, pp. 153, 149: **C. Phythian-Adams**, *Desolation of a City: Coventry and the Urban Crisis of the Late Middle Ages*, Cambridge UP, 1979, pp. 94–5; **A. J. Kettle** (ed.), *A List of Families in the Archdeaconry of Stafford, Collections for a History of Staffordshire*, 4th ser., **8** (1976), vii–xi, xiv, xv–xix; **P. Laslett**, *Family Life and Illicit Love in Earlier Generations: Essays in Historical Sociology*, Cambridge UP, 1977, pp. 47–8, citing work by Dr R. M. Smith.
3. **W. Whateley**, *A Bride Bvsh or, A Direction for Married Persons. Plainely describing the duties common to both, and peculiar to each of them. By performing of which, Marriage shall prooue a great helpe to such, as now for want of performing them, doe finde it a little hell*, London, 1623 (first edn 1617); **W. Gouge**, *Of Domesticall Duties Eight Treatises*, London, 1622, pp. 237–8.
4. Hebrews 12 : 6.
5. **J. A. Sharpe**, 'Domestic Homicide in Early Modern England', *Historical Journal*, 24 (1981), 38.
6. **R. Burn**, *The Justice of the Peace and Parish Officer*, 26th edn, London, 1831, Vol. V, p. 685; **B. H. Putnam** (ed.), *Proceedings before the Justices of the Peace in the Fourteenth and Fifteenth Centuries, Edward III to Richard III*, Spottiswoode, Ballantyne, London, 1938, pp. cxviii, 97; **T. Wright**, *A History of Domestic Manners and Sentiments in England during the Middle Ages*, London, 1862, pp. 275–6; **A. V. Judges** (ed.), *The Elizabethan Underworld*, G. Routledge & Sons, London, 1930, p. 245.
7. **L. Stone**, *The Crisis of the Aristocracy, 1558–1641*, Clarendon Press, Oxford, 1965, p. 51; 'Social Mobility in England, 1500–1700', *Past and Present*, 33 (1966), 16–22; **K. Wrightson**, *English Society, 1580–1680*, Hutchinson, London, 1982, p. 35.
8. For the best available description of the social structure of an early Tudor town, see Phythian-Adams, *op. cit.*, Ch. X; **D. C. Coleman**, *Industry in Tudor and Stuart England*, Macmillan, London, 1975, pp. 35–49.
9. **Sir C. Whitworth** (ed.), *Political and Commercial Works of Charles Davenant*, London, 1761, Vol. II, p. 184.
10. Phythian-Adams, *op. cit.*, p. 242; Laslett, 'Mean Household Size', p. 154; Whitworth, *op. cit.*, Vol. II, p. 184; **M. Girouard**, *Life in the English Country House: A Social and Architectural History*, Yale UP, London, 1978, pp. 138–9.

11. Laslett, 'Mean Household Size', p. 154; Phythian-Adams, *op. cit.*, p. 227.

12. Laslett, *Family Life and Illicit Love*, pp. 201–3.

13. **J. Hatcher**, *Plague, Population and the English Economy, 1348–1530*, Macmillan, London, 1977, pp. 63–7, 71; **E. A. Wrigley** and **R. S. Schofield**, *The Population History of England 1541–1871. A Reconstruction*, Edward Arnold, London, 1981, pp. 236–45, 402–30, 472, 528.

14. **P. Clark** and **P. Slack**, *English Towns in Transition, 1500–1700*, Oxford UP, 1976, p. 83; **R. Finlay**, *Population and Metropolis: The Demography of London, 1580–1650*, Cambridge UP, 1981, p. 7.

15. Finlay, *op. cit.*, p. 9; **E. A. Wrigley**, 'A Simple Model of London's Importance in changing English Society and Economy 1650–1750', *Past and Present*, 37 (1967), 49. For the possibility that the English population did not reach its medieval peak level till the eighteenth century, see **D. M. Palliser**, 'Tawney's Century: Brave New World or Malthusian Trap?' *Economic History Review*, 2nd ser., **35** (1982), 342.

16. Finlay, *op. cit.*, p. 138; **D. Cressy**, *Literacy and the Social Order. Reading and Writing in Tudor and Stuart England*, Cambridge UP, 1980, pp. 128–9, 177.

17. Finlay, *op. cit.*, pp. 100–8, 149–50; **V. B. Elliott**, 'Single Women in the London Marriage Market: Age, Status and Mobility, 1598–1619', in **R. B. Outhwaite** (ed.), *Marriage and Society: Studies in the Social History of Marriage*, Europa Publications, London, 1981, pp. 84–5.

18. **N. Elias**, *The History of Manners: The Civilizing Process*, Vol. I, Basil Blackwell, Oxford, 1978, esp. pp. 191–205; **M. Y. Offord** (ed.), *The Book of the Knight of the Tower*, Early English Text Society, supplementary ser., **2** (1971), 37.

19. **H. E. Bell**, *An Introduction to the History and Records of the Court of Wards and Liveries*, Cambridge UP, 1953, pp. 116–17.

20. **P. H. Barnum** (ed.), *Dives and Pauper*, Vol. I, *Early English Text Society* **275, 280** (1976, 1980), Pt. I, 328.

21. **G. Strauss**, *Luther's House of Learning: Indoctrination of the Young in the German Reformation*, Johns Hopkins UP, London, 1978, pp. 53–4; **G. F. Still**, *The History of Paediatrics*, Oxford UP, 1931, p. 33; *The Colloquies of Erasmus*, trans. **C. R. Thompson**, Univ. of Chicago Press, 1965, pp. 114–26, 218–23, 276–85; **I. Maclean**, *The Renaissance Notion of Woman: A Study in the Fortunes of Scholasticism and Medical Science in European Intellectual Life*, Cambridge UP, 1980.

22. My impressions concerning the character of funeral inscriptions are based on the personal examination of large numbers of them scattered through a number of counties. For the inscriptions of antiquity, see **R. Lattimore**, *Themes in Greek and Latin Epitaphs*, Univ. of Illinois Press, Urbana, 1942.

23. Cressy, *op. cit.*, Chs 1 and 6. Contrast **M. Spufford**, 'First Steps in Literacy: the Reading and Writing Experiences of the Humblest Seventeenth-Century Spiritual Autobiographers', *Social History*, **4** (1979), 407–35. Spufford rates the chances of learning to read higher than Cressy but is in broad agreement about the obstacles to further progress.

24. Stone, *Crisis of the Aristocracy*, pp. 208–9.

25. Contrast **P. Ariès**, *Centuries of Childhood*, Jonathan Cape, London, 1962 (trans. from French edn of 1960), pp. 329, 369–71.

26. J. Locke, *The Second Treatise of Government and a Letter Concerning Toleration*, **J. W. Gough** (ed.), Basil Blackwell, Oxford, 1956, pp. 27–42; **M. L. Shanley**, 'Marriage Contract and Social Contract in Seventeenth Century English Political Thought', *Western Political Quarterly*, **32** (1979), 79–91.

27. **K. V. Thomas**, *Religion and the Decline of Magic*, Penguin Books, Harmondsworth, 1973, pp. 126–8, 769–70; **J. Locke**, *Some Thoughts Concerning Education*, 1693, in *The Educational Writings of John Locke*, **J. Axtell** (ed.), Cambridge UP, 1968, pp. 241–2.

Chapter 3

Family and kindred

Types and structures of kinship

Outside his nuclear family of birth or marriage each individual is related to a much larger group of people, the kinsfolk who are the subject of this chapter. In writing of kinship one must distinguish first of all between the relationships of shared blood (consanguineal) and those created by marriage (affinal). The individual shares blood with all those who have an ancestor in common with him. His affinal relationships are established both by his own marriage and by the marriages of his blood relatives. In medieval ecclesiastical law, baptism and confirmation established a third sort of relationship, spiritual kinship, between the individual and his sponsors.

Genealogies, correspondence and personal memoranda suggest that members of the propertied classes took care during this period to maintain a fairly broad knowledge of their kindred, going well beyond those with whom they were on close terms. Apart from sentiment, there were two practical reasons for this. First, by the laws of succession, men's and women's property passed in the absence of other arrangements either to a descendant, or, if none existed, to a collateral relative. In an epoch when the land law was complex and uncertain titles and ingenious claimants abounded, it made sense to know who one's ancestors and collateral kindred were. Secondly, according to the canon law, all three types of kinship limited one's choice of marriage partners. Consanguinity barred marriage between any two individuals up to the fourth degree of kinship. In order to calculate the degrees, one had to go back to the common ancestor of the two. Thus brothers and sisters were related in the first degree, cousins in the second, and so on. An individual and his aunt of the same blood would be related in the second and first degrees. A man joined to a woman by carnal knowledge, whether in marriage or outside it, might not subsequently marry any of her blood as far as the fourth degree. Spiritual kinship barred marriage between those baptised or confirmed on the one hand and their sponsors and the latter's children on the other; also between the parents of those baptised or confirmed and the sponsors. But couples were rarely divorced by the church courts for contravening these regulations, partly because it was difficult to produce witnesses to the remoter prohibited degrees. Henry VIII's matrimonial entanglements and the Reformation led to their curtailment. From 1540, by virtue of a parliamentary statute, spiritual ties and all but the two closest degrees of kinship and affinity ceased to be obstacles to marriage.[1]

Today, sociologists distinguish among a person's kindred those he recognises, and among recognised kindred the 'effective' kin with whom he has social contacts. Within the latter, and closest to him, are the 'intimate' kin with whom he enjoys a close and sustained relationship characterised by regular contact and mutual aid.[2] In medieval and early modern England, kinship recognition and the composition of the fluctuating body of the effective kin were determined, as they still are at present, by individual circumstances and preferences, not by any clear set of rules. Each person in effect stood at the centre of a unique network of kinsfolk which he shared in its entirety with no one else. The absence of rules giving priority to any one group of kindred was matched by the vagueness of English kinship terminology, which for the most part did not distinguish between consanguineal and affinal kin, or, among blood relatives, between those on the father's and those on the mother's side. The word 'cousin' was far wider and vaguer in its use than it is today. Those so addressed included distant affinal relatives on the one hand, nephews and even grandchildren on the other.

Surnames, gradually adopted by most ranks of society during the later Middle Ages, passed from father to son, so that paternal kindred were in general easier to identify than maternal. To be a scion of an ancient family, especially its senior living representative, was a matter of great pride. The bearer of an illustrious name often felt a special solidarity with dead ancestors and descendants yet unborn. Such sentiments often served to dignify, even to endow with an air of altruism, what might otherwise have looked like a rapaciously selfish struggle to extend his lands by rather dubious means. Very many gentlemen genealogists, especially of the sixteenth and seventeenth centuries, celebrated the gradual augmentation of the property of their lines, and the descent of their names and coats of arms through several centuries. Nor was pride of ancestry limited to the gentry alone. Robert Furse, a Devon yeoman who wrote an account of his family in 1593, was able to record ten generations of it before his own. He urged his heirs not to despise their ancestors. Big things had grown from small, and though they had been at first 'but plene and sympell men and wemen and of smalle possessyon and habylyte', gradually, by God's help and their own wisdom and frugality, the family had come to 'myche more possessyones credett and reputasyion then ever anye of them hadde'. The considerable knowledge of ancestry and kindred to be found among the farmers of a prosperous rural community in the seventeenth century is suggested by that treasure house of local genealogical information, Richard Gough's *History of Myddle*.[3]

Belonging to a well-established or famous family was often a matter of pride, but the fact of family membership did not, as some romantic descriptions have suggested, bind kinsmen together in a loyalty to name and blood which transcended the interests of the individual or his nuclear family. In each generation the great bulk of the lands whose accumulation and defence were so lovingly recorded by family chroniclers went to the eldest son. Male primogeniture produced a widening gap between the head of the house and his descendants on the one hand and his younger brothers and their descendants on the other. Many great landowners did provide generously for younger sons, but such provision depended very much on individual affection and preferences, above all on the ability to accumulate resources. Few men were prepared to endow younger sons on a substantial scale if this could only be done by passing to the eldest an inheritance smaller than that which they had themselves entered upon.

In the eyes of many parents, the favoured position of the first-born son carried with it moral and material responsibilities to younger siblings. In about 1465, for example, Agnes Paston made her eldest son's concern for his brethren one of the conditions for the continued bestowal of her blessing on him. She assured him that they would for their part work on his behalf as hard as they could. The fourth duke of Norfolk, writing in 1572, and Sir William Wentworth, in 1604, both in their solemn directions to their heirs laid upon them quasi-paternal responsibilities towards their siblings. Certainly there were conscientious eldest brothers who did their best to further the interests of younger siblings. And in the correspondence of the Paston and Stonor families in the fifteenth century, the Trevelyans in the early sixteenth, we find loyal younger brothers performing useful services in their turn.[4]

But bonds between siblings commonly weakened gradually in the course of time. The deaths of parents removed the strongest link between them, for parents did most to perpetuate a sense of their solidarity by periodically gathering them together under their roof, by reminding them of their mutual obligations, and by passing on to them news of each others' doings. Marriage established a new focus of loyalty, to which attachment to the family of origin took second place. In August 1478 John Paston II wrote to reproach his younger brother John III for failing to alert him to a possible challenge to a piece of family patronage: '. . . I mervayle þat ye sente me no worde ther-off; butt ye haue nowe wyffe and chylder, and so moche to kare fore thatt ye forgete me.' Continuing loyalty to the family of origin tended, not surprisingly, to be strongest among the unmarried. It was not uncommon for childless men to make nephews their heirs. Some, both clerical and lay, sought in their wills to help a larger group of kindred through their munificent benefactions.[5]

The privileged position of the first-born was the source of some bitter resentment, pithily expressed by Thomas Wilson in 1601:

He must have all, and all the rest that which the catt left on the malt heape, perhaps some smale annuytye during his life or what please our elder brother's worship to bestowe upon us if wee please him, and my mistress his wife.[6]

Many eldest sons were aware that their younger siblings harboured what they felt to be an unmerited dislike for them. Sir Christopher Guise (1618–70) complained that younger brothers were often the most unnatural enemies of their own house.[7] The jealousy of George, duke of Clarence, and Thomas, Lord Seymour of Sudeley, towards their elder brothers Edward IV and the duke of Somerset, jealousy which amounted to pathological hatred in the second case, helped to bring about the downfall and death of both these younger brothers. At a later period and a much lower social level, Samuel Pepys felt himself the object of an undeserved resentment on the part of his younger siblings. When in August 1663 some gypsies bade him beware a John and a Thomas, the warning clearly strengthened his existing suspicions of his brothers.[8]

Heirs for their part often behaved in a high-handed, selfish and ungrateful manner towards younger brothers. John Paston I (1421–66) frustrated provisions his father attempted to make for his younger sons William and Clement. William Lord Berkeley (1426–92), although himself childless, ruthlessly pursued his own aggrandisement at the price of an agreement with the Crown which sacrificed the interests of his loyal younger brother. The correspondence of Henry Oxinden of Barham (Kent) in the years before the civil war contains many complaints of his tardy or inadequate discharge of his responsibilities towards his younger siblings. When in 1636 his unmarried brother James sent word from Cambridge that he had been sick, Henry answered that he might stay with him a month or six weeks but also made clear his determination that his brother should not become dependent upon him. His letter stands as a classic expression of a typically English concentration of sentiment upon the newly formed nuclear family at the expense of claims of members of the family of origin.[9]

It is true I doe not desire any more company in my house then my wife, children and servants, yet to doe you a curtesy I shall bee willing of your company during the time aforesaid. I know you are none of them that when they have once gotten into a friend's house continue there without shame or modestie longer then they are wellcome, and in conclusion goe away enemies when they came friends, and I know by this time you have learnt there is a difference betweene Meum and Tuum, not only amongst strangers but amongst friends and Brothers, and that they are men of a senseles disposition that thinke [that] is done toward them out of love is done out of duty.

Below the level of the gentry, primogeniture was weaker, and in some areas of the country custom gave brothers a right to an equal share in a parental holding. But although siblings sometimes held land in common for a period after their parents' deaths, especially in Kent, the heartland of partible inheritance, this situation was in most cases only temporary, for brothers usually allowed themselves to be bought out by one of their number, or divided the land between them. Formal, long-term associations of brothers holding land and other resources in common, such as existed in France and other continental countries, were unknown in England. In forty-six pre-industrial community listings, only 10.1 per cent of households contained resident kin, and of these kinsfolk only one in nine is certainly known to have been a sibling of the household head. Two married brothers are never found in the same household in these lists. Attachments between brothers could be strong. But they did not rest on shared property rights or a sense of family loyalty of the sort so vividly described by the Florentine L. B. Alberti (1404–72) in his dialogue *Della Famiglia*. Instead, they were based on personal preferences, while the antipathies which so often develop between brothers as a result of the competition for parental approval and affection were in many cases reinforced by primogeniture.[10]

Inheritance of the paternal surname encouraged individuals to perceive themselves as members of their fathers' lines, and in nearly every autobiography which includes some survey of the author's ancestry paternal kindred occupy more space than maternal. But this fact by no means always reflects the true configuration of the individual's effective or intimate kin. Connections on the mother's side could be just as important as were those on the father's, sometimes more so. Renowned maternal ancestors were a source of pride, as also were the armorial quarterings achieved by marriage with an heiress. The Yorkshire recusant gentleman Thomas Meynell (1564–1653), for example, recorded that he had received some property by his mother, but that he esteemed even more the five worthy coat armours and as many crests which she had brought with her.[11] When a woman married, although she assumed her husband's name, her links with her kinsmen were by no means severed. Her closest blood relatives often stood ready to assist or advise her, particularly concerning her property rights. An heiress's lands were often used in whole or in part to endow a younger son, and in some families, from the later sixteenth century onwards, sons of heiresses were given their mothers' surnames as Christian names. If an heiress died without bearing her husband a child, her land passed by the common law to one of her blood relatives, not one of her husband's.

The early experience of Simonds D'Ewes (1602–50) furnishes an outstanding example of the strength of links with maternal kindred. In the upper and middle ranks of society women sometimes underwent their early confinements in their parents' homes, and D'Ewes was born in his mother's father's house. When his mother announced his impending arrival to his father, she allegedly told him, presumably in jest, that the child was none of his. Her father, she said, intended to take it. His maternal grandfather greeted D'Ewes's arrival with scarcely less joy than did his parents, and as godfathers, he and his brother gave the boy their family name of Simonds as a Christian name. When the time came for his parents to go home, it proved impossible to carry Simonds on the long journey over bumpy roads without serious threat to his life, and he was instead left in the vicinity of his grandparents' house, where he spent his childhood, growing to love them more than he did his parents.[12] His experience was admittedly a somewhat exceptional one. But it was by no means unusual for maternal kindred to concern themselves in children's welfare and to attempt to safeguard their interests after their mothers' deaths. Bonds with maternal uncles were often strong and enduring.

It is clear, not only that English blood kinship had a bilateral character which sometimes made links with maternal relatives very important, but that affinal relationships made through marriage were often very close and could indeed be the most directly useful ones at certain stages of the individual's life. Men could on occasion see their fathers-in-law as the chief means of their advancement, even as sources of assistance in their disagreements with their own blood relatives, as did German Pole, who married a daughter of the substantial Yorkshire landowner Sir Robert Plumpton. Pole, whose own father had died, told Plumpton in about 1499 that he had no other father but him. In the years before the civil war the Somerset gentleman Amias Bampfield maintained a steady correspondence with his father-in-law John Willoughby of Payhembury in Devon. Willoughby not only took several of Bampfield's children under his own roof but made him loans in money and kind. Bampfield was as he confessed a man of few friends and clearly viewed his father-in-law as his chief source of help and support. The importance of affinal relationships was not restricted to the upper classes. In 1588 the Essex puritan minister Richard Rogers, a joiner's son, listed the loss of friendship among her kindred as one of the sad prospective consequences of his wife's possible death in childbed.[13]

The configuration of the individual's effective and intimate kindred depended a great deal upon his age, personal concerns and other circumstances. In the course of his lifetime, its shape changed considerably, not only as a result of deaths and marriages, but also because of the development of personal needs, preferences and enmities. In the conventional view, the strength of 'natural' affection was intimately connected with closeness of relationship.[14] But this was contrary to common experience. In all save the very closest relationships of all, those between parents and children, husbands and wives, the salient characteristic of effective kinship in England was its fluidity.

The uses of kinship

Kinship was not in our period the mainspring of English politics or the individual's most important source of security. There were some notable political dynasties, the Cecils and the Hydes for example. But political alliances between kinsmen were as fragile and volatile as any other sort, and often flawed by additional suspicions and resentments. The fall of the House of York provides a uniquely spectacular example of the destruction of a family's fortunes through internecine rivalry and hatred, but it would be difficult to cite any bunch of kinsmen which achieved successful political co-operation for more than a few years. Nor did men rely for their physical protection upon any save their very closest relatives within the nuclear family. The days when paternal and maternal kinsmen were entitled to compensation for a man's murder belonged to the remote past. It is true that in dire emergency kinsfolk might sometimes risk their lives for each others' protection. As late as 1617 Nicholas Assheton of Downham in Lancashire recorded in his diary his ride over the Pennines into Wensleydale to help his aunt, whose house had been attacked by an armed band.[15] But this incident was an exceptional one. During our period individual safety normally depended over most of the country not on ties of kinship but upon a close-meshed network of public law-enforcing agencies. When law, order and even central government broke down, as they did in the fifteenth century, men counted for help from outside household and nuclear family upon the basically contractual relationship of lord and man. Nowhere is this fact better illustrated than in the Paston letters. This Norfolk family relied for the defence of its interests in the first place upon the partnerships of husband and wife, father and sons, brother and brother, then upon the help of faithful servants and the good lordship of magnates.

Kinsfolk were often appealed to for aid in the law, to help ensure a speedy or fair hearing of a suit, or even a favourable outcome. But such requests might be framed in such a way as to disclaim any desire to bring undue influence to bear. In 1537, for example, John Whalley, a cousin of Thomas Cromwell's, wrote to Lord Lisle 'only' to seek Lisle's good lordship for his wife's kinsman, that the latter might have judgement 'according unto the law'. It was not of course always possible for a relative to give effectual help, even though he might wish to do so. In 1633, bad news of a young man of his name kept Thomas Knyvett away from the Norfolk Assizes because he was afraid that he would not be able to 'doe him good'. But their expected partiality in favour of the party related to them laid open to challenge kinsfolk who acted as witnesses or compurgators in the church courts or jurors at the common law.[16]

Service and kinship overlapped, but there was a strong sentiment that the two mixed badly. Kinship introduced undesirable complexities, inhibitions on the one hand, excessive expectations on the other, into the relationship of master and servant. William Cecil, Lord Burghley, counselled his son not to employ kinsmen, for they would expect much and do little. The auditor of Henry Lord Berkeley gave him almost exactly the same advice in about 1575. In fact the Berkeleys and other noble families often employed relatives, but many of them were remote kinsmen with slender claims for consideration; few of them bore the family name.[17] Further down the social scale, seventeenth-century diarists seldom recruited servants from among their kindred. In community censuses drawn up between the sixteenth and nineteenth centuries, listed servants seldom bore the same names as the heads of the households in which they served. A sample of 500 apprenticeship indentures enrolled at Norwich, concentrated mainly in the Tudor and early Stuart periods, includes only 18, fewer than 4 per cent, concerning apprentices who had entered the service of masters who bore the same name.[18]

Men were probably readier to bestow places in their gift upon their relatives than they were to employ them as their servants, at any rate when such nomination did not entail the establishment of a working relationship which might be adulterated by kinship. But for a number of reasons the exercise of patronage in favour of kinsfolk was not as extensive as might be expected. In the first place, the moment of vacancy might not coincide with the need for employment. Secondly, the patron had to weigh many other considerations besides kinship in filling the positions in his gift. He might wish to reward loyal services rendered or requite past favour granted. He might need to exploit his patronage for financial gain. Nor must we rule out concern to see the job properly done, which would dictate the choice of the best qualified man.

Much more widespread, at all levels of society, was the use of kinsmen as contacts, brokers and intermediaries, means of finding out about suitable places and of securing the favour of those who had them in their gift. Kinsfolk used for these purposes were sometimes quite distant. Requests for nomination or employment of relatives can be found in most of the letter collections of the period. They abound in the correspondence of an important office holder such as Lord Lisle, Henry VIII's deputy of Calais.[19] The maker of such a request could help a kinsman without impairing the prospective relationship between master and servant. But the use of one's influence to advance a kinsman's career was an investment of credit which would redound to one's advantage if the man did well but which could damage one's future influence if he failed to live up to expectations. Such investment had to be made wisely and was not to be taken for granted. In 1621 Sir Thomas Wentworth administered a sharp rebuke to his cousin Michael, who had complained of his delay in securing a place for his son. The service was not, as Michael had described it 'but an ordinary curtesie amongst comon acquaintance'. Sir Thomas pointed out that his reputation was at risk; he would not 'make a custom to lay [his] discretion and creditt at stake upon the staied and sober carriage of an unexperienced yong man . . .'[20]

Marriage was a major avenue of advancement, and kinsmen were expected to send news of suitable partners and to act as intermediaries in bringing matches about. Thus Thomas Hampton wrote in about 1465 to his cousin Thomas Stonor, asking him to bear in mind the preferment of his daughters. Almost two centuries later, in 1649–50, Thomas Knyvett, looking for a suitable match for his eldest son, was offered help and given useful information by two distant relatives.[21]

Implicit in an effort to advance a kinsman by means of the investment of personal influence was an element of trust, and this was even more obviously important when kinsfolk made loans or acted as sureties for their repayment. Money loans are more prominent in surviving records, but the borrowing of equipment, animals and services may have been just as important. The extent of borrowing from kinsmen varied between socio-economic groups. Between 1558 and 1641, the nobility apparently relied above all upon London moneyed men and scriveners, while much lower down the social scale, in the Essex village of Terling, between 1525 and 1700, only 17 per cent of the loans mentioned in wills were made by the relatives of borrowers. But on the other hand relatives are thought to have been important as lenders or in facilitating the raising of loans in both early sixteenth-century Coventry and seventeenth-century London.[22] A number of diaries and autobiographies mention kinsfolk as an important source of credit. Though kinsmen were sometimes released from repayment in lenders' wills, it was probably expected in the normal course of things, and a relative could be pressing in his requests for it. William Harleston marvelled at the failure of his 'right trusty and well enprovyd' brother-in-law Thomas Stonor (d. 1474) to repay the money he had lent him. He had never had such great need of it, he wrote, 'and þerfor I besech yow fayll me nat now, as ye wyll have eny good turne of me anothyr day'. Moreover interest might be expected in the shape of reciprocal assistance when the need arose. Lord Burghley's advice on the point was quite emphatic:

Neither borrow money of a neighbour or friend [a term which at this period covered relatives] but rather from a mere stranger, where paying for it thou mayest hear no more of it, for otherwise thou shalt eclipse thy credit, lose thy freedom, and yet pay to him as dear as to the other.[23]

Hospitality was an important family duty and pleasure, especially in the middle and upper ranks of society. Relatives often stayed in each others' houses and possession of kinsmen who lived in London or had a residence there could be particularly useful if one had lawsuits to tend or children whom one wished to marry or place in apprenticeship. Especially in the second half of the period, relatives went on impressively long journeys to visit each other. In the summer of 1654, for example, John Evelyn, who lived in Surrey, took his young wife on a long tour, visiting *en route* relatives who lived in Wiltshire and Leicestershire. It was no doubt the case in this period as it still is today that it was at social gatherings, particularly marriages and funerals, that the individual had most clearly the sense of belonging to a family group larger than a simply nuclear or elementary one.[24]

How far loans and hospitality served to alleviate the lot of poorer relatives is an important question which it is hard to answer at present. But there is little evidence that in our period men were prepared to subsidise poorer kindred in the long term. The most generous help given was probably that extended to orphaned nephews and godsons, whose planned duration was more or less strictly limited. Nor does it seem particularly likely that the advent of the Poor Laws in the sixteenth century undermined an earlier readiness to help kindred. Our best available description of an early fourteenth-century village (Halesowen in Worcestershire) provides no ground for supposing that the decline into destitution of the economically feckless or unfortunate had been slowed by the action of relatives. There are one or two indications from early sixteenth-century Coventry of citizens' readiness to help poorer kindred, but these are no more than scraps of evidence. The Poor Law of 1601 laid the obligation to support impotent poor only upon grandparents, parents and children. There was no generally accepted obligation to support or aid siblings, at any rate once portions or legacies had been paid. Among the property-owning classes, ageing spinster sisters were often afforded shelter, though we should not necessarily assume that this went unpaid for, and brothers' willingness to accept the burden of a sister's presence in the house varied greatly. The inheritance customs prevalent in the upper and middling ranks of English society tended to push younger siblings down the social scale. The history of the Isham family of Northamptonshire furnishes an example of what were probably fairly typical attitudes towards socially declining collateral relatives. The great bulk of the property of John Isham (1525–96) continued in the main line of his family. Two younger sons later fell into debt. Their nephew of the senior line and other relatives exacted payment for their financial help; they had to mortgage the annuities their father had left them and ultimately lost them. The majority of their children remained unmarried.[25]

Recognised kin could span a wide social spectrum. John Edwards, candidate for admission to the English College at Rome, testified in

1604 that he counted gentry, merchants and poor men among his relatives. In the village of Terling in Essex the majority of kinship links between householders resident in the parish in 1671 crossed the boundaries of social categories. But recognised were not the same as effective kin. Just how quickly a broad social gulf could come between known kinsfolk is illustrated by the account which Lucy Hutchinson wrote of her father's relatives. He had been a younger brother who had been fortunate enough to inherit most of his eldest brother's wealth and marry well. Of his other brothers, she wrote, 'there remain'd none of them nor their issues when I was born but only three daughters, who bestowed themselves meanely and their generations are worne out except two or three unregarded children'.[26]

Advice was a commodity which kinsmen may have been much readier to give each other than material assistance in money or kind. To give it to a young man was a pleasurable duty. After his first wife's death, in 1480, Sir William Stonor was urged by his uncle William Harleston to take the opportunity to reduce his household. The older man also advised him to limit his ambitions and avoid excessive purchases, lavish building and litigation.[27]

And of certen thynges I wold desire you and pray you in the name of God, that ye wolle not over wissh yow, ner owyr purches yow, ner owyr bild you; for these iij thynges wolle plucke a yongman ryth lowe. Ner medyll with no gret materis in the lawe. For I truste to God to see you the worshipfulest of the Stoners that ever I sawe or shall se be my days.

Failures in duty or 'unnatural' behaviour by one kinsman towards another very often prompted letters of advice from relatives. Quarrels between husband and wife, fears that a second marriage would lead to the neglect of the children of an earlier union, and unfair treatment of younger sons or brothers: all these provoked letters of remonstrance or reminders of family obligations.[28]

The last service which a relative could perform was to assist in the execution of a man's will or, as overseer, supervise its implementation. Testators' widows and children were the people most likely to be chosen to act as executors. The kinsmen outside their nuclear family of marriage most often picked to act as executors or overseers were brothers and brothers-in-law, members of the families of origin of testators and their wives. It was also to brothers and brothers-in-law that widows and widowers most often entrusted the guardianship of their orphaned children.[29] Remoter kinsfolk were relatively seldom given these responsibilities. But in the upper and middle ranks of society a large body of his relatives customarily wore mourning for the deceased, and kinsfolk might also be called upon to act as pallbearers.[30]

The motives which underlay the performance of services by kinsmen were complex and intricately interconnected. They varied greatly from one situation to another and from person to person. Affection, gratitude, a sense of obligation or an expectation of reciprocal benefits: most men were actuated by one of these or a combination of them when they helped a relative in one of the ways outlined above. The expectation of reciprocal favours at some future time was often important. The man who showed ingratitude or failed to fulfil the obligations which relatives were on occasion all too ready to point out to him might reckon that his actions would damage his reputation and make kinsfolk less ready to help him on some subsequent occasion. Men sometimes viewed their kinsfolk with a coolly calculative eye. In 1604, Sir William Wentworth gave his son the following advice[31]:

OF KINSFOLKES esteme the companie of them most thatt be riche, honest and discrete and use them in your causes befor others. If they be porer and yett of a good conscyence and humble regard them well. Yett if anie of all these haue lands or goods ioyning with yow in no case trust them too much, for such occasions brede suits and future enmityes.

But to describe behaviour towards kindred as predominantly calculative would be psychologically naïve. The mixture of beliefs, assumptions, expectations, emotions and impulses which led to action cannot be analysed in most cases. It seems unlikely that people either acted consistently or were usually fully aware why they behaved as they did.

Determinants of the strength of kinship

Ever since late Anglo-Saxon times if not before, kinship ties had been relatively weak in England.[32] Within the country, however, there were considerable variations in their strength, which was chiefly determined by the effectiveness of government, geography, custom and social status. Nowhere in England remained lawless and without effective government longer than the far north, where the Crown had for long periods tolerated the continuance of uniquely strong bonds of kinship or lordship as bulwarks against the Scots. On the wild northern edge of England, kinship groups, the 'surnames', undertook the protection of their members, resorting if need be to the 'deadly feud' against their enemies. The headmen of the surnames pledged their good behaviour to local officials and made agreements with the heads of lowland families who feared their enmity. One of the last of the great Northumberland feuds was settled in 1591 after it had lasted some thirty-six years. The union of the Crowns ushered in a new era. But John Armstrong, a young recusant questioned in 1613 before admission to the English College in Rome, could still claim to have 600 kinsmen of his name and blood dwelling within sixty miles of his Northumberland home. In Cumberland, the power of the surnames endured for a time after 1603. In 1604, the earl of Cumberland, warden of the West March, described the powerlessness of the law in the face of surname loyalty, cemented by endogamy.[33]

On the border, politics reinforced the influence of geographical factors characteristic of large areas of the north. Remoteness, difficult terrain and relatively poor communications strengthened both rivalries and attachments within the region. One consequence of the strong localism of the north was that even noble and gentry families in the region exhibited, as late as the sixteenth century, exceptionally strong geographically endogamous* tendencies. A marked preference for marrying within their own area had two major results. The first was an abnormally high proportion of marriages to relatives. The second was that better opportunities existed here than in most other areas for younger sons of old families to marry well and establish cadet branches. In Tudor Lancashire, we are told, the 'second rank of gentry consisted mainly of cadet branches of leading families'. It has also been suggested (though not as yet conclusively proved, save in respect of a few communities) that in large parts of the north, as perhaps elsewhere in forest and fen, extensive common rights, especially over pasture, facilitated the continued division of holdings among offspring and tended to reinforce kinship ties.[34]

In certain other areas geography or inheritance customs favoured a high degree of endogamy, the proliferation of cadet branches and an awareness of kinship ties. 'All Cornish gentlemen are cousins'; the gentry of that poor and relatively remote peninsular county married among themselves or with the men of Devon, another county where there were large numbers of cadet branches of local families. Kent, another peninsular county, was also the one in all England most famous for its practice of partible inheritance (gavelkind). As late as the mid-seventeenth century, there were nine or ten separate branches of some ancient Kentish lines. The term 'Kentish cousin', meaning a very remote relative, alluded to the exceptionally wide knowledge of kindred common among the gentry of the county. There is some evidence which suggests that the employment of relatives may have been commoner in Kent than elsewhere. But counties of high endogamy and proliferating junior branches were exceptional in Southern and Midland England. In Leicestershire, for example, hardly any of the gentry of the shire belonged to cadet branches even in the fourteenth century.[35]

The growth of towns and cities, especially London, helped to erode local economic autonomy and particularism. But the effects of urban expansion and urban life on kinship ties were mixed. Although

---

* Endogamy is, strictly speaking, marriage within the same tribe or clan. Following Lawrence Stone, I have also used it of marriage within the same social group or geographical area.

those who migrated to towns and cities often had to move a long way from home, the more successful and literate of them often maintained contacts with their kinsfolk and places of origin. For their part, increasing numbers of country dwellers found urban relatives useful as sources of information about possible avenues of advancement for their children and as providers of accommodation during necessary visits. Among female migrants to London who subsequently married there by licence between 1598 and 1619, nearly a third had relatives other than parents living there and nearly a fifth lived with them while there.[36] A much greater variety of employment was available in many towns and cities than in the countryside, so that once established, especially in London, members of a family probably had less incentive to migrate than those born in the country. Between 1660 and 1730 witnesses in church courts living in towns were rather less likely to have moved during their lives than were countrymen. (Mobility also fell during those years in rural areas where industries developed.)[37] On the other hand, urban families suffered from relatively high mortality. This, along with aspirations to landed gentility, the vicissitudes of business and the partible inheritance of movable goods, militated against the survival of urban dynasties. But generous children's and widows' portions also meant that a young man's capital could most readily be built up by marriage into another merchant or business family, which would also extend his range of useful contacts and possible sources of loans, and affinal ties were often very important. Partible inheritance, and the nature of trading enterprises, which often called for a division of tasks performed in different places between two or three men whose mutual trust was based on long knowledge and shared acquaintance, encouraged the setting up of partnerships between brothers, brothers-in-law and even cousins.[38]

Social status was a very important determinant of the strength of kinship. Associated with high social standing were wealth, literacy, leisure and influence. The first three enabled kinsfolk to remain in touch with each other by means of travel, hospitality and writing letters. The individual born into a property-owning family was the likeliest to find among his kinsfolk the knowledge and influence which would enable him to encompass some of his most important goals. Adult life expectation was probably higher among the upper classes than it was in the population at large, and their heirs and daughters married younger, quite often spending the early years of marriage under a parental roof. It was probably in the upper reaches of society that individuals had the best chance of meeting or even living with grandparents, aunts and uncles during the early years of life. In a sample of pre-industrial local population listings, more than a quarter of gentry householders were found to have kinsfolk outside their nuclear families of marriage living with them, just over a sixth of the yeomen and husbandmen, fewer than one in twelve of the labourers and paupers.[39]

At the other end of the social scale from the nobility and gentry were the labouring poor. In this social group, relatively high mortality and a high degree of geographical mobility, necessitated by the search for employment, were not offset by the means of maintaining contact and the inducements for doing so which existed among the upper classes. In between, yeomen and husbandmen tended to be less mobile than the poor. Some holdings were large enough to support a widowed grandparent or parent in addition to a married couple; a few supported for short periods married couples of two generations. In periods of high mortality the remarriages of widowed people with children could lead to the establishment of quite complex households such as have been found at Ryton (Co. Durham) in the 1590s. Smaller landholders often had enough leisure and resources to maintain contacts with kinsfolk over a larger district than the parish in which they lived. But from week to week, unrelated neighbours were probably more important sources of assistance than were kinsfolk save perhaps in upland areas of partible inheritance.[40]

In towns, too, the bonds of kinship were probably strongest at the top of the social scale and weakest at the bottom. In Coventry in the 1520s, for example, relatively low child and adult mortality, much intermarriage, and the maintenance through frequent travel of contacts outside the city, all made for the creation of fairly large networks of kinsfolk among the merchant oligarchy. Among the craftsmen there is some evidence of the establishment by young men just embarking on their careers of households near to where their parents lived. But there are hardly any indications of such close residence among the 'fluid unskilled labour-force'.[41]

One further factor, the settlement of estates, made for a relatively high degree of co-operation among kinsfolk at the upper levels of the social scale. The feoffees or trustees chosen to hold property and assume responsibility for the payment of portions and annuities often included brothers or brothers-in-law. These trusted senior kinsmen gained a certain degree of authority and influence over younger relatives, especially when they were also made guardians. The machinery of family settlements, especially in the second half of our period, made agreement between a number of actual or prospective kinsfolk necessary for both their arrangement and their smooth operation.[42]

It is hard to discern any significant weakening of kinship over the long term during our period, save perhaps in a few geographically restricted areas. More effective government finally undermined the surnames of the far north. Much slower to take effect were the decline of gavelkind in Kent (which had begun well before this period) and the weakening of local loyalties and endogamy in remoter regions. More generally, the slow and uneven decline of customary tenures very gradually reduced the extent of hereditary succession to land. Migration in search of holdings or employment was stimulated by high mortality in the later Middle Ages and the growth of towns and the market economy in the sixteenth century. But from the seventeenth century comes some evidence of declining geographical mobility, partly attributable to settlement regulations and laws.[43] A substantial minority of the English population enjoyed growing affluence during the later sixteenth and seventeenth centuries. Increasing literacy and more secure communications allowed them to maintain improved contact with geographically distant kinsfolk. In this age of growing economic diversity and increasingly varied opportunities for employment, kinsfolk remained very important as sources of information and influence, and a basis for business co-operation. Among the landed classes, harmony among kinsfolk may have been enhanced by the seventeenth-century rise of the strict settlement, which, while safeguarding the prospects of heirs to great estates, made securer provision for widows, younger sons and non-inheriting daughters.

The diversity of individual experience: some examples

The flavour of individual experience of relations with kinsfolk can best be conveyed by some examples. For this purpose, diaries and autobiographies are by far the best sources. Although limited to the last quarter of our period and the upper and middle ranks of society, the most useful of them, of which five have been used here, concern people living in different parts of the country whose social backgrounds, occupations, characters and attitudes varied widely.

The diarist Ralph Josselin (1617–83) was minister of Earl's Colne (Essex) from 1641 till his death. Josselin lost both parents early in life. With no substantial assets save his university education, he was given vital help in the early stages of his career by his paternal uncle Ralph, possibly his godfather, who also stood by him in an inheritance dispute with three other uncles. His one maternal uncle gave him less important aid; he exchanged several visits with another paternal uncle. Though he gave some help to a widowed sister of his own who had children, Josselin otherwise took little interest in his nephews and nieces. His relations with most of his numerous cousins were tenuous, but one of them was steward of the manors of which Josselin held almost all his land. He gave three others financial assistance (one of them, however, unwillingly). Distance made it hard to keep in close touch with his wife's family. But his mother-in-law helped at the birth of the Josselins' first child; his father-in-law lived with them for a while. Relations with a brother, sister and aunt of his wife's were also friendly. The Josselins in turn maintained close contact with their married daughters. Josselin was greatly helped by some kinsfolk. Yet from week to week his relations with those of his neighbours who were also close friends were more important; cumulatively his exchanges with them of loans, gifts, hospitality and help in emergencies were greater than those with his kin.[44]

The autobiographer Alice Thornton (1627–1707) was the daughter of Christopher Wandesford (d. 1640), a Yorkshire gentleman, friend of Sir Thomas Wentworth and briefly his successor as lord deputy of Ireland. Her marriage to William Thornton in 1651 was the price paid for the help of his uncle, who had married a maternal cousin of her father's, in getting the sequestration of the family estates lifted. Alice had a stronger character than her husband's and was a better match than he could normally have expected. These facts influenced the subsequent shape of their kinship network. Alice, who had accepted the match for her family's good, retained close contacts with her blood relatives. She lived in her beloved mother's house for eight years and bore five children there. Her father's sister sheltered her during another pregnancy in 1659–60. Her father's half-brother, who had helped to arrange her marriage, also stood by her in a dispute with her brother over her father's will. Her relations with this brother were cool and distant. But she gave important help to the daughter-in-law of her dearly loved sister Catherine (d. 1645). Her mother's maternal half-brother was later to secure a crown living for her son-in-law. The great majority of her children's godparents were chosen from her side of the family, as were the guardians whom Alice picked for her three young children when she feared death in 1665.[45]

Alice, staunchly loyal to the Church, felt at first a stranger among her husband's kindred, with their papist or presbyterian sympathies. Resentments and suspicions over inheritance inhibited the development of close relations with some of William Thornton's siblings. Yet with two of his brothers-in-law Alice was on friendly terms; both were among her children's godfathers. From the ministry of one of them, John Denton, she derived much comfort. He lived with the Thorntons after his ejection for nonconformity in 1662. After William's death in 1668 a number of his kinsfolk attended his funeral or sent letters of condolence.[46]

In Alice's sad life, overshadowed by repeated bereavements and persistent worries about property, the influence of kinship was all-pervasive, its embrace by turns supportive and suffocating. Some relatives made or helped her make the weightiest decisions of her life and gave her help and support in crises; others, especially her brother, blighted her existence through their greed, envy and ingratitude. Her experience demonstrates how far 'effective' kinship depended on personal temperament and circumstances rather than a sense of loyalty to house or line.

The diarist Oliver Heywood (1630–1702) was a minister near Halifax for most of his adult life, though put out of his living in 1662.

His grandfather, a carpenter, and his father, a weaver and businessman, who lived till Oliver was forty-seven, had both resided near Bolton in Lancashire. Heywood's voluminous diaries and memoranda reveal a strong blend of Christian piety with pride and interest in kindred. When in 1678 he began to meditate one Sunday night on the blessed souls that had gone before him to heaven, he resolved to make a list of his relatives who had died in the Lord. On it he placed six brothers and sisters, a brother-in-law, two nephews and a niece. Among paternal relatives he listed besides his father and grandparents two aunts, a great-uncle and the latter's daughter. (Some time later Heywood noted with sorrow the death of his only surviving paternal uncle.) On his mother's side he included, besides her and his grandmother, four uncles, a cousin's husband and a cousin of his mother's. It was by means of a maternal uncle that Heywood had come to his congregation. Besides his first wife, who had died in 1661, Heywood named her parents. His father-in-law, John Angier, an outstanding puritan minister, had remained in close touch with Heywood after his daughter's death. Heywood's interest in his kindred and knowledge of their doings is also demonstrated by a list of sixty-six descendants of his father which he drew up in 1675. Heywood's numerous preaching journeys across the Pennines helped him to maintain contact with kinsfolk. One of his diaries shows that he saw some three dozen relatives from outside his nuclear families of origin and marriage in the years 1666–73 alone. His writings leave the inescapable impression that he belonged to a kinship network stronger, denser and more extensive than that of his fellow clergyman Ralph Josselin. The frequency of his contacts with relatives may have been due in part to the quasi-itinerant character of his ministry, but his close interest in them may have been characteristic of the north of England.[47]

During the years 1660–69 Samuel Pepys, outstanding diarist and naval administrator, recorded his relations with his kinsfolk in exceptional detail.[48] Some three-quarters of his very extensive recognised kindred were related to him through his father, though Pepys exhibited hardly any dynastic loyalty. His paternal kindred ranged from the nobility to cottagers. But his knowledge of his socially undistinguished maternal relatives was far more restricted, while hardly any of his wife's kinsfolk were known to him. She was the daughter of an impoverished French exile whom Samuel had married for love.

Pepys's respect for kinsfolk depended above all on their status, personal qualities and potential usefulness to himself. During this period of growing wealth and professional success, Pepys drew closer to his richer and better-born relatives, while gradually distancing himself from his poorer kindred. This process was slowed only by Pepys's fitful sense of obligation and his feeling that it was as well to 'keep in with' some of them in case he 'should have occasion to make use of them'.[49]

The diary is an unrivalled source of information about the services kinsmen performed for each other. Pepys's professional advancement was due above all to the earl of Sandwich, his second cousin once removed. His own responses to requests to help place relatives were largely conditioned by his assessment of their ability to do him credit. Pepys found his wife's brother a job with some misgivings; the man's subsequent success made him warmer and more friendly. He was asked for, and gave, help and advice in making a number of matches, including that of a daughter of Lord Sandwich. He was frequently asked for loans, whose advantages and disadvantages were carefully assessed. Pepys gave and received much hospitality. Contact with his relatives was facilitated by the fact that so many of them lived in or near London.[50]

Inheritance was, as so often, a source of bitterness. A childless uncle who died in 1661 left some land in Cambridgeshire to Pepys's father, entailing it upon Samuel. Resultant lawsuits soured the diarist's relations with a number of his paternal relatives. This inheritance may also have contributed to Pepys's poor relations with his siblings, since he failed to fulfil the expectations of assistance which it helped to raise.[51] Pepys's recognised kindred was very extensive. Relatives played an important part in his life. But his attitude towards them was highly calculative. His calculations were tempered by affection and a sense of duty, but his generosity towards those less fortunate than himself was limited: he was determined not to let them become a burden upon him.

The autobiography of John Cannon (b. 1684), at various times exciseman, maltster, schoolmaster and scribe, shall furnish our last example. Both his grandfather and his father were substantial farmers of West Lydford (Somerset). The paternal kindred whom he knew personally were all descendants of his grandfather save one second cousin whom he met by chance. Cannon gave vivid sketches of all his paternal uncles and aunts, but in these there was little affection. His uncle Thomas looked forward eagerly to inheriting his brother's copyhold when Cannon's parents fell ill in 1693, and Cannon later refused to lend him money. Among his numerous paternal cousins, Cannon seems to have had warm feelings for only two. Emotionally, some of his maternal relatives, especially his aunt and godmother Sarah, were far closer to him. Her husband stood ready to help Cannon and his brother and sister when it looked as though their parents might die, and briefly employed Cannon when the latter first left home. Relations with another maternal cousin were also warm and close. But he felt less friendly towards the children of his uncle Thomas, with one of whom he engaged in an inheritance dispute.[52]

Cannon knew a great deal about his relatives, but wrote of the majority of them with detachment or dislike. Nearly all his uncles and aunts had lived within five miles of his parents' home in West

Lydford, yet the amounts of recorded assistance exchanged seem small. Most of Cannon's youthful companions were unrelated to him; his kinsfolk played hardly any part in his entry into the excise service, which enabled him to escape the uncongenial life of a farm manager.

In each of these cases relatives outside their nuclear families of origin played an important part in the lives of the individuals concerned. But there was no sense of exclusive or overriding loyalty to a well-defined body of kinsfolk. The shape and size of the effective kindred varied greatly from one writer to another. Many of the relatives for whom writers felt most affection were maternal or affinal. These examples show that kinsfolk performed a number of services, of which by far the most consistently important was assistance in individual advancement. But readiness to help kinsfolk depended upon character and experience. There was a big difference, for instance, between the generous, impulsive and affectionate Alice Thornton and the ambitious and calculating Samuel Pepys. Close residence, readiness to travel, shared pleasures, perceived mutual usefulness and the survival of older relatives acting as bridges between one individual and another: all these helped to preserve links between kinsfolk. These examples suggest that kinship may have mattered more in the comparatively close-knit and exclusive societies of parts of Lancashire and Yorkshire than it did in Somerset or Essex. Analysis of Pepys's diary tends to support the suggestion that certain features of life in the metropolis favoured the maintenance of ties of kinship; whether the calculative attitudes towards relatives which Pepys displayed were commoner in London than they were elsewhere it is hard to say.

Kindred formed only one of the social networks to which the individual belonged. In the case of Ralph Josselin, probably in that of John Cannon's family too, links with neighbours were of greater significance for most of the time than those with kinsmen. '. . . Kinship grows out in processe of time', wrote Oliver Heywood.[53] Kinship groupings were of their very nature fluid and transitory. A widening economic gap between branches of a family was usually accompanied by a cooling of relations between them. Poor relatives were not generally allowed to become a burden on the more prosperous branches of their kindred. Families were often torn apart more swiftly by rival claims to inherited resources. In all save one of these five cases, relations between kinsfolk were soured by inheritance disputes.

The experiences of these five individuals differed in a number of obvious ways from those which might have been recorded some two centuries earlier. Yet it is hard to point to a change which had much affected the essential character of English kinship.

Notes and references

1. **R. H. Helmholz**, *Marriage Litigation in Medieval England*, Cambridge UP, 1974, pp. 77–87; **R. A. Houlbrooke**, *Church Courts and the People during the English Reformation*, Oxford UP, 1979, pp. 74–5, 84–5; 32 Henry VIII, c. 38.

2. **R. Firth** (ed.), *Two Studies of Kinship in London*, Athlone Press, London, 1956, p. 45.

3. **H. J. Carpenter** (ed.), 'Furse of Moreshead. A Family Record of the Sixteenth Century', *Report and Transactions of the Devonshire Association*, **26** (1894), 170–1; **R. Gough**, *The History of Myddle*, **David Hey** (ed.), Penguin Books, Harmondsworth, 1981.

4. **N. Davis** (ed.), *Paston Letters and Papers of the Fifteenth Century*, Clarendon Press, Oxford, 1971, 1976, Vol. I, pp. 43–4; **N. Williams**, *Thomas Howard, Fourth Duke of Norfolk*, Barrie & Rockliff, London, 1964, pp. 239–43; **J. P. Cooper** (ed.), *Wentworth Papers 1597–1628*, *Camden Society*, 4th ser., **12** (1973), 13, 54–5; **C. L. Kingsford** (ed.), *Stonor Letters and Papers, 1290–1483*, *Camden Society*, 3rd ser., **29–30** (1919), I, 149, 158–9, 161; **W. C.** and **C. E. Trevelyan** (eds), *Trevelyan Papers*, Vol. III, *Camden Society*, old ser., **105** (1872), 6–8, 10.

5. Davis, *op. cit.*, Vol. I, p. 511; **T. Birch**, *The Life of the Honourable Robert Boyle*, London, 1744, pp. 335–7; for examples of childless men at different levels of society who made nephews their heirs, see Gough, *op. cit.*, pp. 184, 194, 197, 202; **T. Fuller**, *History of the Worthies of England*, **J. G. Nichols** (ed.), London, Edinburgh and Perth, 1811, Vol. I, p. 91; monuments to John Truslowe, d. 1593, at Avebury, Wilts, and Sir Thomas Fane, d. 1606, at Hunton, Kent; for benefactions in favour of kindred see esp. **G. D. Squibb**, *Founder's Kin: Privilege and Pedigree*, Clarendon Press, Oxford, 1972, Chs i, ii.

6. **F. J. Fisher** (ed.), *The State of England anno dom. 1600, by Thomas Wilson, Camden Society*, 3rd ser., **52** (1936), 24. (This work is actually headed 1 March 1600, i.e. 1601 N.S.)

7. **G. Davies** (ed.), *Autobiography of Thomas Raymond, and Memoirs of the Family of Guise of Elmore, Gloucestershire, Camden Society*, 3rd ser., **28** (1917), 114.

8. **R. Latham** and **W. Matthews** (eds), *The Diary of Samuel Pepys: a New and Complete Transcription*, G. Bell & Sons, London, 1970–, Vol. IV, p. 284.

9. Davis, *op. cit.*, Vol. I, p. 46; **J. Smyth**, *The Berkeley Manuscripts*, **J. Maclean** (ed.), Bristol and Gloucestershire Archaeological Society, Gloucester, 1883, Vol. II, pp. 129–30, 147–8, 173; **G. W. Bernard**, 'The Fortunes of the Greys, Earls of Kent, in the Early Sixteenth Century', *Historical Journal*, **25** (1982), 680; **D. Gardiner** (ed.), *The Oxinden Letters, 1607–1642*, Constable & Co., London, 1933, pp. 81–2, 102–5, 114–15, 117–23, 181–2, 218–20.

10. **C. W. Chalklin**, *Seventeenth-Century Kent: A Social and Economic History*, Longmans, London, 1965, pp. 56–7; **P. Laslett** and **R. Wall** (eds), *Household and Family in Past Time*, Cambridge UP, 1972, pp. 13–14, 149–50; **G. A. Guarino** (ed.), *The Albertis of Florence: Leon Battista Alberti's Della Famiglia*, Bucknell UP, Lewisburg, 1971, pp. 41, 49–50, 56, 84–5, 89, 94, 193–4.

11. **J. H. Aveling** (ed.), *Recusancy Papers of the Meynell Family, Catholic Record Society*, **56** (1964), 4.

12. **J. O. Halliwell** (ed.), *The Autobiography and Correspondence of Sir Simonds D'Ewes, Bart.*, London, 1845, Vol. I, pp. 2–4, 24–7, 29–31.

13. **T. Stapleton** (ed.), *Plumpton Correspondence, Camden Society*, old ser., **4** (1839), 138–40, 178–81, 211–14; Amias Bampfield to John Willoughby, 4 Sept. 1634, 27 Jan. 1635, 14 Aug. 1636, 28 Aug., 28 Nov. 1637, Taunton, Somerset Record Office, Trevelyan MSS DD/WO/57; **M. M. Knappen** (ed.), *Two Elizabethan Puritan Diaries*, American Society of Church History, Chicago, 1933, pp. 73–4.

14. See e.g. **W. Gouge**, *Of Domesticall Duties, Eight Treatises*, London, 1622, pp. 80–1.

15. **F. R. Raines** (ed.), *The Journal of Nicholas Assheton of Downham, in the County of Lancaster, Esq., for part of the year 1617, and part of the year following, Chetham Society*, 1st ser., **14** (1848), 9–13.

16. **M. St Clare Byrne** (ed.), *The Lisle Letters*, Univ. of Chicago Press, 1981, Vol. IV, 253; **B. Schofield** (ed.), *The Knyvett Letters 1620–1644, Norfolk Record Society*, **20** (1949), 82; **T. Smith,** *De Republica Anglorum. The Maner of Gouernment or policie of the Realme of England*, London, 1583, p. 61.

17. **L. B. Wright** (ed.), *Advice to a Son: Precepts of Lord Burghley, Sir Walter Raleigh, and Francis Osborne*, Cornell UP, Ithaca, 1962, p. 11; Smyth, *op. cit.*, Vol. II, pp. 84, 89, 91, 92, 184, 230, 241, 267, 285–6, 287, 336–7, 377–8.

18. **A. Macfarlane**, *The Family Life of Ralph Josselin, a Seventeenth-Century Clergyman: An Essay in Historical Anthropology*, Cambridge UP, 1970, p. 148 (apparently fairly typical in this respect); **P. Laslett**, 'Mean Household Size in England since the Sixteenth Century', in Laslett and Wall, *op. cit.*, p. 151; **W. M. Rising** and **P. Millican** (comp.), *An Index of Indentures of Norwich Apprentices enrolled with the Norwish Assembly, Norfolk Record Society*, **29** (1959), l–19. See also **V. B. Elliott**, 'Single Women in the London Marriage Market: Age, Status and Mobility, 1598–1619', in **R. B. Outhwaite** (ed.), *Marriage and Society: Studies in the Social History of Marriage*, Europa Publications, London, 1981, p. 93.

19. St Clare Byrne, *op. cit.*, Vol. I, pp. 584–5; Vol. II, pp. 33, 131, 426; Vol. IV, p. 106; Vol. V, p. 15.

20. Cooper, *op. cit.*, pp. 148–50.

21. Kingsford, *op. cit.*, Vol. I, pp. 70–1; Schofield, *op. cit.*, pp. 44–5.

22. **L. Stone**, *The Crisis of the Aristocracy, 1558–1641*, Clarendon Press, Oxford, 1965, pp. 532–8; **M. Chaytor**, 'Household and Kinship: Ryton in the Late Sixteenth and Early Seventeenth Centuries', *History Workshop Journal*, **10** (1980), 38; **K. Wrightson** and **D. Levine**, *Poverty and Piety in an English Village: Terling, 1525–1700*, Academic Press, London, 1979, pp. 100–1; **C. Phythian-Adams**, *Desolation of a City: Coventry and the Urban Crisis of the Late Middle Ages*, Cambridge UP, 1979, p. 150.

23. Kingsford, *op. cit.*, Vol. I, p. 140; Wright, *op. cit.*, p. 12.

24. Raines, *op. cit.*, *passim*; Trevelyan and Trevelyan, *op. cit.*, Vol. III, p. 63; Elliott, *op. cit.*, pp. 93–5; **E. S. de Beer** (ed.), *The Diary of John Evelyn*, Clarendon Press, Oxford, 1955, Vol. III, pp. 98–142.

25. **Z. Razi**, *Life, Marriage and Death in a Medieval Parish: Economy, Society and Demography in Halesowen 1270–1400*, Cambridge UP, 1980, pp. 94–8; 43 Elizabeth I, c. 2; (in **Z. Razi**, 'Family, Land and the Village Community in Later Medieval England', *Past and Present*, **93** (1981), 28, a case of 1365 is cited in which an old man's nephew paid his debts to avoid the forfeiture of his holding. But the young man may have been his heir); Latham and Matthews, *op. cit.*, Vol. V, p. 152; **M. E. Finch**, *The Wealth of Five Northamptonshire Families, 1540–1640*, Northants. Record Society, **19** (1956), 28–30.

26. **A. Kenny** (ed.), *Responsa Scholarum of the English College, Rome. Part One: 1598–1621*, Catholic Record Society, **54** (1962), 146–7; Wrightson and Levine, *op. cit.*, p. 89; **L. Hutchinson**, *Memoirs of the Life of Colonel Hutchinson, with the fragment of an autobiography of Mrs Hutchinson*, **J. Sutherland** (ed.), Oxford UP, 1973, pp. 282–4.

27. Kingsford, *op. cit.*, Vol. II, p. 98.

28. Cooper, *op. cit.*, pp. 94–6; Gardiner, *op. cit.*, pp. 179–80; John Buckland to Edward Phelips, 17 Feb. 1668, Taunton, Somerset Record Office, Phelips MSS DD/PH/224/37.

29. See for example Wrightson and Levine, *op. cit.*, pp. 93–4, 99–100.

30. **R. Trumbach**, *The Rise of the Egalitarian Family: Aristocratic Kinship and Domestic Relations in Eighteenth-Century England*, Academic Press, London, 1978, pp. 33–41; **J. Cannon**, χρονεχα *Seu Annales or Memoirs of the Birth Education Life and Death of Mr Iohn Cannon Sometime Officer of the Excise and Writing Master at Mere Glastonbury & West Lydford in the County of Somersett*, n.d., MS in the Somerset Record Office, Taunton, p. 61; **C. Jackson** (ed.), *The Autobiography of Mrs Alice Thornton, of East Newton, in the County of York*, Surtees Society, **62** (1875), 116.

31. Cooper, *op. cit.*, p. 13.

32. **L. Lancaster**, 'Kinship in Anglo-Saxon Society', *British Journal of Sociology*, **9** (1958), 373–6.

33. **S. J. Watts**, *From Border to Middle Shire: Northumberland 1586–1625*, Leicester UP, 1975, pp. 25–8; Kenny, *op. cit.*, Vol. I, p. 263.

34. **C. Haigh**, *Reformation and Resistance in Tudor Lancashire*, Cambridge UP, 1975, pp. 89–90; **J. Thirsk**, 'The Farming Regions of England', in *The Agrarian History of England and Wales*, IV, *1500–1640*, Cambridge UP, 1967, pp. 8–12, 23–5.

35. **A. L. Rowse**, *Tudor Cornwall: Portrait of a Society*, Jonathan Cape, London, 1941, p. 85; **W. G. Hoskins**, *Devon*, Collins, London, 1954, p. 87; **A. Everitt**, *The Community of Kent and the Great Rebellion*, Leicester UP, 1966, pp. 41–3, 46–8; *Oxford Dictionary of English Proverbs*, **W. G. Smith**, (comp.), 3rd edn, **F. P. Wilson** (ed.), Clarendon Press, Oxford, 1970, p. 420. Sussex was another southern county where intermarriage was common; see Hutchinson, *op. cit.*, p. 282; **A. J. Fletcher**, *A County Community in Peace and War: Sussex 1600–1660*, Longman, London, 1975, pp. 44–8, 53. For information about Leicestershire I am indebted to an unpublished paper by **G. G. Astill**, 'Kinship and County Community: A Characterisation of Gentry Society in Later Medieval England'.

36. **S. L. Thrupp**, *The Merchant Class of Medieval London, 1300–1500*, U. of Chicago Press, 1948, pp. 211–12, 228; Elliott, *op. cit.*, p. 93.

37. **M. Young** and **P. Willmott**, *Family and Kinship in East London*, Penguin Books, Harmondsworth, 1962, pp. 91–3; **P. Clark**, 'Migration in England during the Late Seventeenth and Early Eighteenth Centuries', *Past and Present*, **83** (1979), 65–7; **R. M. Smith**, 'Population and its Geography in England, 1500–1730' in **R. A. Dodgshon** and **R. A. Butlin** (eds), *An Historical Geography of England and Wales*, Academic Press, London, 1978, pp. 226–7.
38. Thrupp, *op. cit.*, pp. 105–7, 191–206, 222–33; **F. F. Foster**, *The Politics of Stability: A Portrait of the Rulers of Elizabethan London*, Royal Historical Society, London, 1977, pp. 98–103; **W. G. Hoskins**, 'The Elizabethan Merchants of Exeter', in **S. T. Bindoff**, **J. Hurstfield** and **C. H. Williams** (eds), *Elizabethan Government and Society. Essays presented to Sir John Neale*, Athlone Press, London, 1961, pp. 164–5; Phythian-Adams, *op. cit.*, pp. 150–1; **A. Hanham** (ed.), *The Cely Letters, 1472–1488, Early English Text Society*, **273** (1975), xi; **B. Winchester**, *Tudor Family Portrait*, Jonathan Cape, London, 1955, pp. 209–38; on the continuing importance of kinship in seventeenth-century London, see **R. Grassby**, 'Social Mobility and Business Enterprise in Seventeenth-century England', in **D. Pennington** and **K. Thomas** (eds), *Puritans and Revolutionaries. Essays in Seventeenth-Century History presented to Christopher Hill*, Clarendon Press, Oxford, 1978, pp. 367–8.
39. Laslett, *op. cit.*, p. 154 (mean proportions).
40. **K. Wrightson**, *English Society, 1580–1680*, Hutchinson, London, 1982, pp. 43–51; **M. E. James**, *Family, Lineage and Civil Society: A Study of Society, Politics and Mentality in the Durham Region 1500–1640*, Clarendon Press, Oxford, 1974, pp. 22–5; Chaytor, *op. cit.*, pp. 38, 45–7.
41. Phythian-Adams, *op. cit.*, pp. 148–57.
42. **M. Slater**, 'The Weightiest Business: Marriage in an Upper-Gentry Family in Seventeenth-Century England', *Past and Present*, **72** (1976), 29; **Sir John Habakkuk**, 'The Rise and Fall of English Landed Families, 1600–1800', *Transactions of the Royal Historical Society*, 5th ser., **29** (1979), 190; Trumbach, *op. cit.*, pp. 70–1.
43. Smith, 'Population and its Geography', pp. 225–6.
44. Macfarlane, *op. cit.*, pp. 113–17, 126–43, 149–60.
45. Jackson, *op. cit.*, pp. 61–2, 78–9, 87–8, 91–6, 119, 123–4, 142, 145, 148, 165, 202, 220, 224–5.
46. *Ibid.*, pp. 131, 152, 157, 165, 168, 175, 213–14, 215, 231–2, 241, 253–4, 357.
47. **J. Horsfall Turner** (ed.), *The Rev. Oliver Heywood, B.A., 1630–1702: his Autobiography, Diaries, Anecdote and Event books*, Brighouse, 1881–85, Vol. I, pp. 17, 20, 33–8, 94–109, 223–300.
48. These remarks about Pepys's kinsfolk are largely based upon an unpublished dissertation written at Reading University by **Felicity Becker** (now Mrs Wakeling), 'Samuel Pepys and his Wider Kindred', 1980.
49. Latham and Matthews, *op. cit.*, Vol. IV, p. 265.
50. *Ibid.*, Vol. III, pp. 185, 205, 226–36; Vol. IV, pp. 19, 21, 154–5, 159–60, 387; Vol. V, p. 286; Vol. VI, pp. 136–7, 158–61, 167, 271, 318, 333.
51. *Ibid.*, Vol. II, pp. 132–8; Vol. III, p. 302; Vol. IV, pp. 28, 33–4, 35, 42–3, 308; Vol. V, p. 91.
52. Cannon, *op. cit*., pp. 7–20, 28, 54–5, 68–9, 129–30, 133, 149.
53. Horsfall Turner, *op. cit.*, Vol. I, p. 17.

Chapter 4

The making of marriage

The age of marriage and its incidence

Among the destitute who found their way to the Spital-House, Robert Copland listed in about 1535 young folk 'that wed or they be wise', borne down by 'House-rent and children and every other thing', unable to get their living and without friends to sustain them.[1] A marriage had to be built on material foundations, whether these were laid by the couple's own efforts or supplied by friends. This convention had probably governed family formation among the bulk of the English people for centuries before Copland wrote. It denied marriage to those without material resources and postponed it for those who were able to accumulate them only slowly. But the help of 'friends' also contributed to the shaping of marriage patterns. When those who had resources died or were ready to transfer sufficient of them to establish a new family, marriage could take place earlier than would otherwise have been possible.

At the beginning of the twentieth century, North-western Europe possessed a distinctive marriage pattern whose two major features were a late age at marriage and a relatively high proportion of individuals who never married at all. Analysis of parish registers suggests that this pattern was already well established for the majority of the population in Elizabethan and Stuart England. Such analysis points to a mean age of marriage for women of about 26, for men one varying between 27 and 29. Amongst those born between the defeat of the Armada and the Popish Plot, the proportion remaining unmarried in their early forties may always have been at least one in six, sometimes more than one in four.[2]

How much further back can this pattern be traced? In one view, a 'non-European' pattern probably prevailed among certain sections of the fourteenth-century population. In the manor of Halesowen (Worcs.), between 1270 and 1348, parents made strenuous efforts to establish their children on the land by purchase, marriage and (despite the fact that primogeniture was the reigning custom) subdivision of holdings. A high proportion of the offspring of the wealthier peasants were married in their parents' lives. Halesowen tenants were apparently ready to marry on inadequate holdings and face hardship rather than remain celibate. Among families reconstitutable from the court rolls, marriage seems commonly to have taken place between eighteen and twenty-two. After the Black Death of 1348, when land became more abundant, the age at marriage may have fallen even further. But rough ages at marriage can be worked out for only a minority of the village population, and at any rate before the plague many sons and daughters of poorer tenants may have married later, some not at all. Furthermore, serious doubts have been expressed concerning the reliability of calculations of marriage age from court rolls.[3]

From other parts of England comes evidence which casts doubt on the prevalence of a 'non-European' marriage pattern either before or after the Black Death. Before it there were considerable numbers of people who held no land at all or held it precariously. High proportions of both sexes seem to have remained unmarried in certain parts of late thirteenth-century Lincolnshire. Analysis of Rutland poll-tax records of 1377 has revealed a proportion of unmarried males in the population similar to that found in later community listings dating from a period when a 'European' marriage pattern is known to have been established. It has also cast doubt on earlier calculations purporting to show that a very high proportion of adult women were married. In early modern England, young adults commonly spent several years in service before marriage. Young servants are found in England in large numbers from the thirteenth century onwards; in Rutland the proportion of households containing servants in 1377 was higher than in later pre-industrial community listings. All this evidence makes one wonder how typical the behaviour of the more visible of the Halesowen landholders was.[4]

Can we account for widespread early entry into marriage among Halesowen peasants and a possible subsequent change of habits between *c.* 1400 and the early sixteenth century? The apparent determination of tenants to establish their children on the land and to marry them as soon as possible might be attributed in large part to the lack of alternative opportunities in a period of land hunger, low wages, small towns and relatively restricted geographical mobility. In the short term, the catastrophic mortalities of the fourteenth century might have brought no change in habits. Later, however, continuing abundance of land and greatly improved real wages may have made the establishment of their children seem less urgent to the more prosperous peasants. Changing patterns of mortality could have played a part. Higher infant mortality reduced the numbers of surviving children and thus also the burden of provision falling upon holdings.[5]

It is possible, then, that the 'European' pattern of marriage revealed by study of the period after *c.* 1540 was not fully established 100 years earlier, or that it became more pronounced during the fifteenth century. Even after the mid-sixteenth century there were enormous variations in the age of first marriage both within and between communities and socio-economic groups which mean averages conceal.

Early marriage was far commoner among the nobility and gentry than it was further down the social scale. The higher a man's social status, the fewer the suitable marriages available to his children, and the possible choice was further restricted in some areas by the geographically endogamous preferences of the nobility and gentry. Children's matches were important means of gaining friends and allies in a man's own region in a time of political uncertainty. A match inimical to the interests of his line might be arranged after his death, which could be early and violent in the later Middle Ages. The Crown and many noblemen possessed rights of feudal wardship and marriage, and wardships were sold in large numbers. It was in the feudal guardian's interest to marry off his ward before the age of majority, in the father's interest to pre-empt possible action by the guardian before his own death. Tudor rule brought internal peace but also, especially from the 1530s onwards, much more systematic exploitation of the Crown's rights of wardship and marriage. The abuses of wardship were bitterly unpopular: Thomas Starkey, Henry Brinkelow and Sir Thomas Smith named loveless marriages among its evil consequences.[6]

Not all children were equally likely to be married early. The danger of an unsuitable match, made through force or enticement, was greater in the case of girls. (The abduction or enticement of heiresses was the subject of a number of medieval and Tudor statutes.) Among sons, there was a big difference between younger brothers and heirs, upon whom the maintenance or enhancement of the family's position chiefly rested. Younger sons (unlike younger daughters, when a man had no sons) did not enter feudal wardship. Only 19 per cent of the eldest sons of British dukes born between 1330 and 1679 remained unmarried at the age of thirty compared with 42 per cent of their younger brothers.[7]

The danger that wardship would lead to unsuitable marriage gradually receded as close relatives received a growing proportion of grants of wards under Elizabeth I. Grants to them were further facilitated by new regulations issued under James I. After the abolition of the Court of Wards in 1646, finally confirmed in 1660, the nobility and gentry could at last feel free of the threat of outside interference with the marriage of their children. Meanwhile the decline of civil violence lessened the need to use marriage for political purposes, and the development of the London season facilitated the growth of a national marriage market. The development of aristocratic social life in London, country houses and fashionable provincial centres allowed young people increasing opportunities to meet, under discreet surveillance, contemporaries of their own rank at such gatherings as dinners, music parties, balls and race meetings. This allowed parents to delay marriages and pay more attention to their children's wishes when planning them. Both developments were gradual, and their scope must not be exaggerated. Nevertheless, between 1600 and 1659 only 12 per cent of peers and their heirs married by the time they were seventeen, compared with 21 per cent between 1540 and 1599. During the seventeenth century, the proportion of the children of the British peerage who remained single also rose, though the significance of the development is not clear. How far was it due to difficulty in finding and financing suitable matches, how far to individual unwillingness to assume the 'yoke of wedlock'?[8]

Early marriage was not entirely restricted to the upper classes in Elizabethan and Stuart England. Matches between children may have been fairly common in Elizabethan Lancashire and Cheshire.[9] The power of lordship, the concern of families to use marriage to secure friends in a comparatively turbulent region and the paucity of suitable partners in geographically isolated communities may have contributed to the continuance of habits which died out more swiftly elsewhere. In 1593, a Devonshire yeoman, Robert Furse, 'havynge a grette care for the prefermente of John Ffurse his sonne and here', and fearing that he might make an unsuitable match, arranged that the nine-year-old boy should marry an heiress at the age of fifteen, though in the event the marriage never took place. Among the merchant class of London, and perhaps of other towns, daughters were commonly married far younger than sons, often when they were still in their teens, until at least the early seventeenth century.[10]

Examples of early marriage are not hard to find in certain areas and social groups. But the evidence so far available suggests that only a very small proportion of the population of Elizabethan England married before the age of twenty. Most of the middling and small property holders of Tudor and Stuart England probably sought to assist their children's material advancement. A girl's marriage prospects depended very largely on the size of her portion. Those who helped to make their children's marriages possible expected to play some part in their arrangement. But Elizabethan and Stuart parents on the whole do not seem to have shared the driving concern to see their offspring settled as soon as possible which had apparently been so common among the landholders of fourteenth-century Halesowen. The bulk of the population had to rely partly or mainly upon their own acquisition of skills or accumulation of resources to build up the wherewithal for marriage. Apprenticeship, the gateway to a craft, usually lasted into the early or middle twenties. Domestic and agricultural service were recognised means of laying up a 'stock or portion': the numbers engaged in them were largest in the 15–24 age-group. Both service and apprenticeship were usually incompatible with marriage, and many young people were unable to set up house immediately after their completion.[11]

It would be wrong to assume that individuals always wanted to marry as soon as possible. It is true that matrimony conferred status and satisfied important sexual and emotional needs. Yet it also marked the assumption of potentially irksome responsibilities. Future labourers and small farmers were often better fed and housed as servants under another man's roof than they ever would be in their own households.[12]

The chances of marriage depended to a large extent upon the availability of suitable partners and prospects of future employment. An imbalance between the sexes in a community created opportunities for the one which was in the minority. The fact that early marriage was common among London girls in the early seventeenth century has been attributed in part to a big surplus of men in the capital. Crises of mortality were commonly followed by a spate of marriages, a high proportion of them remarriages in which the widowed took new partners. These often gave men control of a holding or a workshop earlier than they could otherwise have expected it. Good harvests and prosperity helped to bring marriage plans to fruition, while bad ones, dislocation and slump might force their postponement. Local ages of marriage altered with the rise and decline of rural industry, changing patterns of land use, and the commercialisation of agriculture.[13]

A relationship has been discovered between the known movements of real wage rates and the national incidence and timing of marriage. Both real wages and marriage rates fell sharply during the later sixteenth century, with only one short interruption. The marriage rate revived for a time between 1566 and 1581 in response to a short-lived improvement in real wages. Real wages reached their nadir in the early seventeenth century and began to rise very slowly thereafter. A readjustment of expectations took place only slowly after the long period of falling wages had come to an end, and the rate of marriage went on falling, albeit more unevenly, till after the middle of the century.[14]

Awareness among young people and their parents and kinsfolk of past deterioration in standards of living and fears of future poor prospects may have played some part in the postponement or renunciation of marriage. But it is clear, too, that more formal and direct pressures were brought to bear. Premature marriage was singled out by contemporary commentators as a major cause of social ills. In 1556 the age of twenty-four was fixed for the earliest termination of London apprenticeships in a deliberate attempt to check 'ouer hastie maryages and over sone settyng upp of householdes of and by the youthe', and in 1563 this was prescribed by statute for all cities and corporate towns. In 1583, the pamphleteer Philip Stubbes complained of adolescents who rushed into marriage without thinking how they would support themselves and then built flimsy cottages in which they lived like beggars. An Act of 1589 prohibited the building of cottages without four acres of land to support their occupants. After the terrible crisis of the 1590s, which saw four bad harvests in a row and pushed parliament into giving the Poor Law the shape it would retain for over two centuries, overseers of the poor in a number of counties prevented wage-earners born outside their parishes from settling within them if they intended to marry or had dependent families which might become a burden on the rates. Clergymen apparently co-operated by agreeing not to marry would-be immigrants whom the parishioners were anxious to exclude. Given the high degree of mobility among servants, most of them in their teens and early twenties, these restrictions probably played an important part in reducing the incidence of marriage.[15]

Patterns of matchmaking: arrangement and freedom

In the eyes of the Church, which was chiefly responsible for developing the law and theory of marriage, wedlock was properly a matter of concern not only to those joined together in it, but also to their parents. The medieval Church insisted upon individual consent in marriage, but qualified its insistence by recommending compliance with parental advice and guidance. Protestant writers emphasised that the initiative in making marriages properly belonged to the parents of the parties, but qualified this emphasis by reminding parents that they must consider their children's inclinations.

From the twelfth century onwards, the canon lawyers viewed the consent of the parties as the indispensable core of a valid marriage. The Church upheld the right of individuals to renounce marriages made before the ages of consent (twelve for girls, fourteen for boys). What had long been the conventional wisdom was summed up by Peter Idley in the metrical advice he wrote for his son in the mid-fifteenth century. The marriage of children of tender age and lacking in understanding for the sake of goods and inheritance was to be avoided, for such unions led to subsequent sorrow and strife. The vernacular treatise *Dives and Pauper*, perhaps the most comprehensive and popular late medieval English exposition of the Ten Commandments, insisted that the servant might wed without leave of his lord, the son without leave of his father. Nevertheless, the author added, it was good that in such matters young folk follow the advice of father, mother and friends, unless their counsel was contrary to their duty to God. The Church courts do not seem to have encouraged children to go against their parents' wishes either in making their own matches or breaking those arranged for them. In 1469, for example, the bishop of Norwich examined Margery Paston, who had contracted herself in marriage with the family's loyal and resourceful bailiff, Richard Calle, in the face of her mother's opposition. He reminded her of her birth, kin and friends and pointed out that by refusing their guidance she would forfeit all hope of future help from them. He evidently hoped to be able to find some flaw in their contract, though in the end he was unable to do so.[16]

From the start, Protestant reformers, especially William Tyndale, insisted on the necessity of parental consent. A canon passed by the convocation of Canterbury in 1571 stipulated that marriages were not to be contracted without parental agreement; one of 1604 specified that such agreement was necessary until the age of twenty-one. The writers of domestic counsel assumed that conscientious parents would take the initiative in choosing partners because they knew better than their children what was good for them. Daniel Rogers (1642) criticised those who were content to leave the choice to their children: parents 'should not only hearken to, but runne and ride to seeke out good matches for their children, if any occasion be offered . . .'. The possibility of initiative on the part of young people was not totally excluded, but it was hedged about with qualifications. Children were not so much as to give any liking, much less make any mention of marriage, without the consent of their parents or guardians, insisted Robert Cawdrey (1598).[17]

But although Protestant writers insisted upon the due obedience of children, they also urged proper consideration upon parents. Thomas Becon told children in his *Catechism* (1560) to follow the wise advice of their parents rather than their own impulses and opinions. On the other hand, parents were to place their children in marriage to their profit 'and that with the good-will and consent of the children, to whom the matter chiefly pertain; that the authority of the parents and the consent of the children may go together, and make perfect an holy and blessed marriage'.[18]

In practice, matches ranged across a wide spectrum which ran from the arranged at one end to the completely free at the other. The degree of freedom allowed the individual depended among other things upon his or her sex, prospects of inheritance and social rank. The marriages of substantial landowners were commonly arranged by their parents or guardians with little or no reference to their wishes, especially in the first half of the period. By Elizabeth's reign, the arrangement of matches before the age of consent was almost certainly less common at the upper levels of society than it had been a century earlier. Yet adolescent sons were often given little choice but to comply with their fathers' wishes. Anthony Mildmay, son of Sir Walter, Elizabeth's puritan Chancellor of the Exchequer, would have preferred to travel to get to know the world rather than marry the fourteen-year-old girl his father proposed to him. But Sir Walter told him that if he did not do so, he should never bring any other woman into his house. At this point, Anthony yielded to his father's importunity. Some sons complied more readily with paternal wishes. When John Bruen, later a famous puritan, returned from Oxford in 1579 his father chose and recommended to him the daughter of the mayor of Chester, whom he married in 1580. Bruen's biographer praised his father for choosing him a suitable wife when he was past infancy and had reached years of discretion (he was about nineteen) 'in a seasonable time, without any long delayes'. Bruen himself was commended for receiving his wife from his father's hand with his best affection and 'in all due subjection to his father's choice'.[19]

Matches agreed between parents were sometimes made dependent upon the mutual liking of the parties, and at least a show of courtship arranged. In 1665, for instance, after Lord Sandwich had agreed upon the marriage of his daughter Jemimah to Sir George Carteret's eldest son, Samuel Pepys was entrusted with the delicate task of giving the shy and callow Carteret a crash course in the arts of court-ship. After the young couple's third encounter, Pepys asked Jemimah how she liked young Carteret. Bashfully 'she answered that she could readily obey what her father and mother had done', which, as Pepys commented, was all she could say or he expect. But Mary Boyle, courted by the son of Lord Claneboye in about 1639, showed more spirit than Jemimah Montagu. 'My father and his had, some years before, concluded a match between us, if we liked when we saw one another, and that I was of years of consent; and now he being returned out of France, was by his father's command to come to my father's . . . .' Her father permitted the young man to court her, with a command to Mary to receive him as one designed to be her husband. But this particular project fell through, even though her father pressed her to it, because of Mary's 'extraordinary' aversion to her intended mate.[20]

In the seventeenth century, parents were often ready to allow greater freedom of choice. Matchmaking sometimes assumed the guise of a co-operative venture in which both father and son played their part and had their say. Before Simonds D'Ewes was finally married in 1626, both he and his father were engaged in the search for a suitable match for him. But, since his father was concerned above all with the size of the portion while D'Ewes himself sought a woman of outstanding personal qualities and good birth, it was some time before a wife acceptable to both was found. In Yorkshire on the eve of the civil war it was said to be the common practice (probably among the lesser gentry and yeomen) for the young man's father to write to the girl's father to find out whether his son would be welcome in the house. Daughters' marriages remained subject to a greater degree of parental control than their brothers'. They were thought less capable of judging what was expedient and they were unable to take the initiative in courtship. But they too might be given a wider choice in the seventeenth century. No fewer than four 'Gentlemen of Quality' offered to treat with John Evelyn for marriage to his beloved daughter Mary (d. 1685). (The fact that this Surrey gentleman's daughter attracted the interest of men from Staffordshire and Cheshire reflects the development of a national marriage market.) From among these suitors Evelyn 'Freely gave her her owne Choice, knowing she was discreete'.[21]

Fatherless sons who had attained their majority unmarried, and younger brothers, commonly enjoyed considerable freedom in courtship even among the upper classes, which contrasted with the much more limited opportunities open to the young women who were their social equals. They had to court not only the girls whom they wanted to win, but their parents too. In the course of his efforts to gain the hand of his future wife Margery Brews in 1476–77, John Paston III first won the support of her mother Dame Elizabeth, and the match's successful completion owed much to her influence with her husband. But he also managed to make Margery herself such an advocate for him that she gave her mother no rest with her pleas to help the marriage forward. The courting strategy of the man about town, as described in 1694, bore certain similarities to that followed by John Paston III over 200 years earlier, despite the obvious growth of freedom in the interval. First the prospective lover enquired at a distance of the girl's birth, education and good parts, but more particularly of her portion. Having previously secured an introduction, he was able to ask her to dance at a ball and then to take her sightseeing round London. He wooed her carefully till the time came to accompany her home openly. After putting the question to her, he asked her mother's consent, for the mother was always the first to be consulted in such matters and left 'to mould the Father into a complying temper . . . .'.[22]

This pattern of courtship could lead to conflict between a girl and her parents if they judged the prospective husband unsuitable. It is clear from a large body of evidence that the duty of compliance with parental wishes was never inculcated with uniform success even in wealthy families. There was a widespread belief among would-be marriage partners that freedom of choice was their right. When in 1469 her family put pressure on Margery Paston to break off her match with the bailiff Richard Calle, he wrote to remind her of the curse which the Church laid on those who hindered marriage and to assert his personal merits against the ideal of class endogamy upheld by the Pastons. Just over a century later, in 1575, Stephen Drury wrote to Nathaniel Bacon to explain his manner of proceeding in courtship. Convinced that the couple had the chief part in 'knytting the knotte of wedlocke', their parents only a secondary one, he had first ascertained the feelings of the girl he hoped to marry. In his view the substance of marriage lay in the consent of man and woman, not that of their parents. Apparently the girl's mother had objected to the match on the ground of social disparity. Drury invoked Scripture to dispose of this and other objections. Anyone who forced them to break their match would, he claimed, cause irreparable damage to their consciences.[23]

Young people in the middling ranks of society generally had a wider choice of suitable partners and rather greater freedom than those above them. But here too daughters were subject to greater control than sons. The seventeenth-century godly ministers Adam Martindale, Ralph Josselin and Henry Newcome, men who should have been especially well equipped to inculcate in their children the duty of considering parental wishes, all had sons who failed even to consult them before marrying. On the other hand Josselin tried to persuade one of his daughters to marry a man whom he approved, even though he was ultimately ready to respect her wishes. Martindale moved his daughter from service when she became entangled with an undesirable suitor.[24] The pattern of seeking a girl's goodwill first and then the parents' consent was probably extremely common among middling and small property owners, to judge from both church court depositions and the case books of Richard Napier, the astrological physician, covering the years 1597–1634.[25] But conflict frequently arose. In about 1566, Katherine Imber, a Wiltshire girl, reproached for causing her parents great grief through her disregard of their wishes answered 'that they were to blame so to take it for ther was no remedye therin . . . yf she sholde forsake him' [her suitor] 'she knewe well she sholde displease God . . .'. Initially, at any rate, many people were resolved in true 'romantic' fashion to put personal attachments before their hopes of endowment. In two similar cases from Buckinghamshire (1520) and Norwich (1552), young women were allegedly prepared to forgo paternal goods in order to marry the men they had chosen.[26]

The majority of the population were largely dependent upon their own efforts to accumulate the resources necessary for marriage. Even when parents or other kinsfolk gave some material assistance, it was often insufficient in itself to provide the basis for marriage, which limited their influence over the choice of partner. Furthermore, a substantial proportion of young people (perhaps a half or more in the seventeenth century) had lost one parent or both by the time they got married. The children of the poor and of small property owners frequently met their future partners while they were in service or apprenticeship some distance away from home. At the lower levels of society, young people seem to have enjoyed throughout this period a considerable freedom to meet and mix with members of the opposite sex. During the hours of work, encounters in streets, shops, markets, backyards, lanes and fields seem to have been frequent. In the Lancashire of the 1660s, mixed groups of young people went for rambles together which often ended in an alehouse. Drinking and dancing formed part of many rural festivities. One summer night in 1595, for instance, many young men and women met at the 'dauncinge place' at Uton in Devon to dance by candlelight. Dances like these gave opportunities for close embraces and the 'groping' deplored by contemporary moralists. During the seventeenth century, justices and parish officials did their best to curb abuses associated with the alehouse and the dance, particularly on the Sabbath, but with uneven success. Visits to the houses of sweethearts' masters or parents were a frequently described element of courtship. They were usually, though not always, made by the young man. Such visits followed no set pattern, because the degree to which the older generation were prepared to countenance them or were able to supervise them varied greatly, and thus, as a result, the extent to which couples felt it necessary to conceal them and the parts of the house where they took place. When visits were impossible, courtship was sustained by the exchange of messages and tokens, assurances of love and symbols of mutual commitment.[27]

The length of the period between sexual maturity and the termination of service or apprenticeship meant that courtship was often a protracted process, and that an individual often had a succession of partners. The Lancashire apprentice Roger Lowe engaged with Mary Naylor to be faithful till death while they were walking together in June 1663. Yet the following October he asked Ann Barrow, who was being courted by Mary Naylor's brother, if he could be next in succession 'in case they two should breake of'. In November he recorded that he knew himself 'exceptable with Emm Potter'. He still felt that his vow to Mary Naylor held good, but it was Emm Potter whom Lowe finally married over four years later. John Cannon made a solemn marriage contract in 1706 with his first true love, a servant of his uncle's towards whom he bore 'a fervent Ardour & Earnest'; but later fell in love with a girl of Watlington (Oxon.) to whom he pledged himself in 1709. But 'halting between hope and fear, hope that one of the two strings to my bow would do and Afraid that neither of them would prove faithfull' he went on to further dalliances, making a servant girl pregnant, before he finally married yet another woman in 1714. That the pattern of successive courtship partners was already old is suggested by the numerous medieval and sixteenth-century marriage cases in the church courts in which more than one plaintiff laid claim to the same man or woman.[28]

The criteria of choice

Four main criteria governed the choice of marriage partners during our period: the advancement of the individual or the family, the ideal of parity, the character of the proposed partner, and personal affection or love.

A suitable marriage, especially among the propertied classes, was one which gave the individual and those closest to him potentially useful new kinsmen, and increased the number of people through whom favours might be sought and advancement achieved. 'Good lordship' and help in recovering family lands were among the possible advantages accruing from matches considered by the Paston family, while Alice Wandesford's match with a man of very different religious and political sympathies from her own was made after the civil war in order to free the family's lands from sequestration. The need to use marriage to gain useful allies made for the choice of partners from within one's own region.[29]

Material substance was always a very important consideration. A father's ability to provide for the rest of his children often depended upon his heir's making the most advantageous match available to him. The connection can be seen quite clearly in a document like the will of Thomas Stonor (d. 1431) who wished the proceeds of the sale of his son's marriage to be used to marry his five daughters. In 1644, Anne Murray's mother opposed her marriage to the heir of Lord Howard of Escrick, because the latter needed a bigger portion than Anne's mother could give with her in order to provide for his younger children. A younger brother's best chance of remaining in the class into which he had been born often lay in marriage with an heiress or a widow. When in the early 1660s Samuel Pepys helped his brother Tom in some ultimately abortive matrimonial projects, he judged each proposal primarily in terms of the size of the dowry and the outlay Tom would have to make.[30] The importance of material considerations was generally appreciated by those who entered into marriage. Apprentices or servants in husbandry often chose to marry widows considerably older than themselves as their best or only chance of establishing themselves in business or on the land. Men sometimes deliberately sought wives whose dowries would enable them to discharge debts or mortgages. The prominence of financial criteria, then, was certainly not due only to the arrangement of marriages by parents and kinsfolk; suitors were often keener than their elders in their pursuit of fortunes.[31] Criticisms of the 'mercenary' character of early modern marriage are largely misconceived. Marriage was one of the chief means of securing that 'livelihood' upon whose possession individual and family security and independence chiefly rested before the advent of large-scale salaried employment, insurance or the Welfare State. Yet the excessive pursuit of material gain through marriage was condemned by moralists and a perennial subject of contemporary satire.[32] In the seventeenth century, it is true, there was much complaint among the landed classes that matchmaking was becoming an inordinately mercenary business. But this was largely because the gradual decline of the 'political' considerations of alliance and good lordship seemed to enhance the relative weight of property, which had always been important. At the same time a wider and more sophisticated marriage market was developing.[33]

The ideal of parity between marriage partners was widely emphasised in the literature of counsel. Some writers gave due weight to temperamental compatibility. Similarity of ages was widely thought important. (Though a slight superiority in age on the husband's part was felt to give his authority desirable reinforcement.) Most important of all was parity of rank. The authors of domestic counsel claimed that social disparity between partners would have bad effects on their subsequent relationship and the internal balance of the marriage. If the wife were higher in social status than her husband, she might come in time to despise him and seek to command him, reversing the 'natural' order of things, while a man who chose a wife markedly his social inferior might seek to place her under excessive subjection. Among the upper classes the aim of social endogamy might be waived in the choice of a wife, but much more rarely in that of a husband, save by those women who had been freed to choose for themselves, especially by widowhood. Inevitably noblemen often had to marry their daughters to the sons of the greater gentry, or lesser gentlemen find sons-in-law among the yeomanry. But though gentry and occasionally even noblemen married merchants' daughters for the sake of their dowries, merchants' sons were rarely allowed to marry into the landed classes. Marriage seldom enabled a man to climb from his own class into that of his bride. But it could nevertheless be an important means of social advancement. Heiresses, especially sole heiresses with land, were well qualified to marry into a higher class; when one married into her own, often in return for a generous marriage settlement, the resulting union of two estates greatly enhanced the bridegroom's status. Many noble families owed the achievement of their rank to a series of such matches. In towns, apprentices fairly frequently married their masters' daughters or widows, but such apprentices were often younger sons of families equal or superior to their masters' in social standing.[34]

An estimate of the personal character of proposed marriage partners and their parents played some part in matchmaking throughout this period. John Paston II, in his favourable assessment of his brother John's intended match in 1477, took into account the 'vertuous dysposicion' of his future parents-in-law, which suggested that the maid herself would be virtuous and good. In 1497, Edward Plumpton told his cousin and patron Sir Robert Plumpton that the woman he was courting was 'amyable and good, with great wysdome and womanhead'. Birth and property were important qualifications, but, these provided, what recommended each of these matches was personal character. This, together with the dispositions of parents, also bulked large in the paternal advice on the choice of wives given by two Elizabethan fathers as diverse as Lord Burghley and the Devonshire yeoman Robert Furse. The writers of Christian counsel, especially after the Reformation, naturally saw personal piety as an indispensable quality in a prospective spouse. Riches of mind, in particular the fear of God, wrote Robert Cawdrey, were to be preferred to riches of body or temporal substance. In practice estimates of personal worth were often based on practical considerations of skill and competence, whether within house and kitchen or in running farm or business.[35]

Throughout this period 'love' was widely held to be an essential element in marriage. But the word love had a number of meanings, ranging from friendship to passionate mutual absorption. Furthermore, it was widely believed, especially among the upper classes, that mutual affection could easily develop within marriage between well-matched partners. In this view a strong prior attraction between prospective spouses was inessential. Even at this social level, however, it could be recognised that a basic personal compatibility was a prerequisite for the subsequent development of affection. When in about 1466 Thomas Rokes and Thomas Stonor agreed upon a marriage between two of their children, it was stipulated that the arrangement should be void if the children disagreed when the boy was fourteen and the girl thirteen. Subsequent humanist and Protestant writers from Erasmus onwards laid especial stress on the importance of suitability of temperaments. Jeremy Taylor told parents that they could do 'no injury more afflictive to the children than to join them with cords of a disagreeing affection'. The gradual development of a more careful and leisurely approach to matchmaking allowed such personal incompatibilities to be taken into account more often by the seventeenth century.[36]

The Church's teaching, though often vague on this point, tended to suggest that the origins of married love preceded the union of the couple. Thus William Harrington wrote in his *Commendacions of Matrymony* (c. 1513) that the consent of marriage partners ought to be in their souls by true love.[37] A prior love which was compatible with the other criteria of good marriage was in practice widely welcomed in lay society. Mutual love was among the reasons why John Paston II thought his younger brother's match with Margery Brews in 1477 a good one. In 1504, a prospective suitor for his daughter's hand was recommended to Sir Robert Plumpton. Because of the love and favour he bore her (which she reciprocated), he would be prepared to take less with her than would any man in England of his wealth. At lower social levels, mutual affection was often felt desirable both by prospective partners and those close to them, as is clear from depositions taken in matrimonial cases. Women were often reported to have rejected suitors because they could not love them or feel affection for them. A witness to the marriage contract of Anne Prickett and Henry Jaie, an East Anglian couple, in 1556, thought that 'it was as godlie . . . as ever he was at, sayenge the same was onlie for love of both partes and without corruption'. One father told his daughter and her suitor, 'yf you can be contented to marry for love, thone thother, I am contented, and do grant you my good will'.[38]

Passionate love was widely condemned as irrational and disruptive. According to Peter Idley, expressing a view already old when he wrote in the mid-fifteenth century, its malign influence set a man on fire and deranged his wits. In crude yet vivid verse the author of the mid-Tudor interlude *The Disobedient Child* pictured a 'vehement' love accompanied by 'many smyrkes, and dulsome kysses', and a precipitate marriage followed by poverty, recriminations and vain regrets. Attitudes were nevertheless deeply ambivalent. The Church was hostile to any passionate and exclusive devotion to an earthly creature which might dim the individual's awareness of God. Yet there was a long literary tradition of ardent love, which some authors had largely reconciled with Christian ideals. In Chaucer's *Franklin's Tale*, ardent courtship had introduced a story of matrimonial constancy and forbearance. The second half of our period witnessed a luxuriant growth of the literature of love, notably in Elizabethan lyrical poetry and the French romantic novel. The language of romantic love sometimes coloured even the literature of Christian counsel. Marriage love, wrote Daniel Rogers in 1642,

is oftime a secret worke of God, pitching the heart of one party upon another, for no knowne cause; and therefore where this strong lodestone attracts each to other, no further question need to be made, but such a man and such a womans match were made in heaven, and God hath brought them together.[39]

Among the propertied classes, the language of passionate love can occasionally be found even in letters of the fifteenth century. In 1472, William Stonor was assured by a kinsman that a prospective spouse's motives were not mercenary. On the contrary, tossed by the waves of love, she desired relief as much as a drowning man, but prudence and modesty prevented her from speaking her feelings unless William first took the initiative. Examples of ardent love can also be found in the voluminous Lisle letter collection of the 1530s, though they were not always allowed to blossom into marriage. By the early seventeenth century, the gradual relaxation of the control of marriage had proceeded far enough to allow a more widespread implementation of a long expressed ideal. If she had told the full story of her husband's courtship of her, claimed Lucy Hutchinson, it would have made 'a true history of a more handsome management of love than the best romances describe'. Never had there been 'a passion more ardent and lesse idolatrous; he loved her better than his life, with unexpressible tendernesse and kindnesse, had a most high oblieging esteeme of her, yet still consider'd honour, religion and duty above her'; in this way Lucy reconciled romantic passion with Christian duty. Others of her generation or the one before who saw their courtships in highly romantic terms included Sir Kenelm Digby, Sir Thomas Wentworth, Henry Oxinden and Mary, countess of Warwick.[40]

Cases in the church courts reveal that passionate attachment was a common experience further down the social scale and suggest that the ideal of romantic love was deeply rooted in popular culture in the first half of our period. We read of men and women of the fifteenth and sixteenth centuries who fell ill and almost died of love or even threatened suicide. People were often described as saying that there was only one person they could possibly marry as long as their lives lasted. One girl said that she loved her suitor with all her heart and would never forsake him while the breath were in her belly; another, that she would forsake all other men for the love of her sweetheart and wished herself 100 miles away with him. In the seventeenth century, romantic passion and the thwarting of love matches were common causes of mental instability among the patients of the astrological physician Richard Napier.[41]

Contracts of marriage

Courtship or marriage negotiations often culminated in pledges of mutual acceptance and lasting fidelity which the law called matrimonial contracts. A Buckinghamshire man used the commonest formula, hallowed by long usage and sanctioned by the Church, when in 1521 he told his sweetheart 'I Robert take the Agnes to my weddid wiff for better for worsse and thereto I plyght my traught'. The degree of formality observed varied enormously. Sometimes a clergyman put the question to the parties with a solemnity not much less than that observed in a wedding in church. More often it was asked by parents or masters, sometimes at a 'bankett . . . comonlie called a trothinge feaste' such as was common in Elizabethan Somerset. Yet the words could equally well be spoken in the presence of friends and workmates of the parties, summoned at short notice from their bench, counter or work in the fields. It quite often happened that nobody was present save an eavesdropper, like the harvestman, who, pretending to be asleep during a break in the work, overheard a young Suffolk couple exchange words when the girl brought her man a pot of ale and a halfpenny worth of cake (c. 1517) or the young labourer of Dowland in Devon, who, in bed in his master's gallery one autumn night in 1566, was aroused by the sound of amorous dalliance by the fire in the hall below. Sometimes such pledges went completely unwitnessed.[42]

In the Church's view, full consummation of a marriage was not permissible until after solemnisation in church, preceded by triple banns to ensure adequate publicity for the couple's intentions. At first, however, lay opinion refused to accept that unsolemnised marriages should be considered void. Only slowly did the Church succeed in bringing marriage under its own control. Twelfth-century canon lawyers did not yet feel in a sufficiently strong position to insist that only marriages blessed by a priest should be considered valid, though all others were irregular in the eyes of the Church. The essential criterion adopted for judging the validity of marriages was therefore the open and free expression of consent by both parties, before at least two witnesses, whether it took place in a priest's presence or not.[43]

This principle of mutual consent, easy enough to enunciate, was very often difficult to apply in practice. Had the couple really meant to accept each other as man and wife at once? Or had they made a promise of future performance, analogous to the modern engagement? (The Church reluctantly allowed such contracts to be broken off.) Or again, had they qualified their mutual acceptance with conditions, such as parental consent or an adequate marriage portion? (Such conditional contracts were very common.) The canon lawyers tried to develop rules which would determine the validity of every conceivable formula, but these fearfully complex rules never worked very well. The Catholic Church finally decided in 1563, at the Council of Trent, that only marriages celebrated in the presence of a priest could be considered valid. But the English law escaped reform till 1753, when Lord Hardwicke's Act laid down that a church service, preceded by due formalities, was essential to the validity of a marriage.[44]

By the thirteenth century, however, the English common lawyers had already decided that endowment at the church door, ensuring publicity for a marriage, was a prerequisite for the payment of widow's dower. Between 1300 and 1500, disputes in church courts over unsolemnised contracts of marriage gradually became much less common, probably in large part because the propertied classes had been won round to the view that the formalities demanded by the Church were the best means of ensuring a publicity which helped parents, kindred and neighbours to control the process of marriage. The hardening of opinion against informal and unsupervised contracts may have influenced the way in which ecclesiastical judges enforced the law. Whether this was so or not, they seem to have become in the course of time more and more unwilling to enforce disputed contracts which had not been properly solemnised.[45]

Pious Protestants favoured a solemn betrothal some time before marriage. It allowed the couple to demonstrate their ability to postpone physical gratification and to prepare for marriage both mentally and spiritually. Seventeenth-century puritans who were solemnly contracted before their marriage ceremonies included Richard Baxter, Oliver Heywood and Adam Martindale. But puritan writers of Christian counsel tended either to cut through the complexities of the existing law or demonstrate their ignorance of them. Daniel Rogers, for example, made a clear-cut but misleading distinction between a contract and a marriage. The former was simply a promise of future performance which could be broken off by mutual consent.

Such accounts can only have added to the already widespread confusion and ignorance concerning the technicalities of the law.[46]

How far popular custom at the lower levels of society was influenced either by the elaborate distinctions of the canonists or the pastoral guidance of post-Reformation clergymen is open to question. Witnesses in matrimonial disputes frequently described couples as being 'man and wife before God' even before solemnisation in church had taken place. But this opinion seems very often to have been based on the way they had comported themselves rather than upon any formal, witnessed matrimonial contract.

Many people seem to have regarded matrimonial contracts in a robust, even casual, fashion as agreements which might be terminated by common consent in return for compensation. In 1480, Robert Cely, member of the prominent London merchant family, sought to escape an unsuitable match in this way. In 1519 one Buckinghamshire man offered to 'discharge' a woman from her suitor for a halfpenny worth of ale if she would marry his kinsman instead. The prices of other agreements were £3 (Somerset, c. 1594) and £5 (Wilts., 1598). In the sixteenth century, the common law courts began to offer the remedy of an action for breach of promise of marriage which enabled the successful plaintiff to recover damages. Its availability may have been one reason for the decline in the amount of matrimonial litigation handled by the church courts after the Reformation.[47]

Faced with the complexities of the law, some preferred not to run the risk of binding themselves before they came to church. In about 1521, a London fishmonger's apprentice said he would do as his father had done and never be 'sure' until he came to the church door. A Somerset man insisted in about 1567 that he would 'neuer make contracte before marriedge'. William Gouge, writing in 1622, remarked that very many people thought a contract needless, and utterly neglected it, while the 1686 preface to Henry Swinburne's *Treatise of Spousals* suggests that contracts were 'in great measure worn out of use'.[48]

Throughout this period, private, unwitnessed agreements, unenforceable at law, were probably common, though they may have become more frequent with the enfeeblement of the church courts and their growing reluctance to enforce contracts. Both Roger Lowe, in 1663, and John Cannon, in 1706, made solemn but completely secret engagements with their first true loves. Cannon, with his customary sense of drama, described his as 'binding in the presence of the all seeing God and who only we made our Witness . . .'.[49]

Ante-nuptial consummation and illegitimacy

Although Church, community and the couple themselves expected the process of marrying to be completed by a public ceremony, its indispensable core lay in words of consent which could be exchanged privately. On this law and widespread popular custom agreed. But the Church prohibited sexual relations before the union had been blessed in a nuptial service, and private agreements were vulnerable. These facts help to explain the following superficially puzzling exchange between a Somerset couple, overheard one night in 1562:

'Be not you my wiff? Whie should you refuse me?'

'I am so . . . but what will folkes saye, because I am not maried?'

Very many couples nevertheless entered into sexual relations on the strength of private agreements or promises. These might be highly informal. Round about All Saints' Day in 1567, Richard Thomas of Portbury (Somerset) was sowing wheat together with Maud Methewaye, a maidservant of his father's. He told her that he wished her belly was as big as that of Joan Asheman, a pregnant girl of the parish. If she were with child by him, he would marry her. He 'had carnall knowledge of the sayde Mawde Methewayes bodye at diverse and sondrie times' in the following Christmas holidays. Many young women yielded to even vaguer undertakings or suggestions.[50]

Attitudes to ante-nuptial sexual relations varied from one social group to another and from one century to the next. Intolerance was always strongest among the most substantial property holders.[51] At the upper levels of society marriage usually affected the interests of a number of people besides the couple themselves, and determination to control the process was consequently strong. At the lower levels of society such behaviour was widely tolerated in the first half of our period. But in many communities there was by the early seventeenth century a growing determination to control entry into marriage, especially by the young and poor. One symptom of this determination was support for more severe punishment of ante-nuptial fornication by the church courts. In the 1620s, large numbers of couples already married in church were prosecuted for this offence. Proceedings were in many cases based upon a careful count of the months elapsing between solemnisation in church and the birth of the first child. Measures such as these help to explain why ante-nuptial conceptions diminished during the seventeenth century. The mean average of the proportions of first baptisms occurring within 8 months of marriage in 12 widely scattered parishes was 255 per thousand in 1550–99, 228 in 1600–49 and 162 in 1650–99. (Anticipation of the church ceremony was however almost certainly a good deal commoner than these figures suggest. Many people married in a parish different from that in which they baptised their first child. Chances of conception would have been influenced by the frequency of intercourse, the stage of the woman's menstrual cycle, her state of health, and the efficacy of a range of possible contraceptive measures.)[52]

A major social reason for discouraging ante-nuptial sexual relations was the danger that children would be born out of wedlock if marriage plans were not completed. Secret promises and 'privy contracts' could not be enforced at law. According to Peter Idley, trusting women were sometimes seduced by deceitful men who, while speaking of marriage, had no intention of undertaking it. Other secret promises were given in good faith. But, as Richard Whytforde pointed out, couples often quarrelled after their 'vnlawful pleasure' was past, either because hot love soon grew cold, as the common proverb said, or under their friends' influence, or in greedy hope of a better match. Poor girls were probably the more likely to be abandoned by their lovers. Perhaps unforeseen misfortune was even more important in frustrating marriage plans. Under this heading come the loss of employment or failure to secure it and inability to find a house or holding.[53]

Such tragedies grew more numerous in the wake of general disasters like a run of poor harvests such as that which occurred in the fearful years 1594–97. A third of the bastards known to have been born in the Essex village of Terling in the years between 1570 and 1699 were conceived in the decade between 1597 and 1607. The run of bad harvests produced a marked fall in the number of marriages, and frustrated matrimonial plans probably lay behind many of the bastardy cases which occurred at this time. During the years of predominantly good harvests between 1598 and 1605 there was a boom in weddings. But many young people who consummated their unions without waiting for solemnisation subsequently found themselves without livelihood or accommodation because of the lasting effects of the crisis, particularly the continuing indebtedness and insecurity of small farmers.[54]

The percentages of baptised children described as illegitimate in the registers of a sample of nearly 100 parishes rose to 3.08 and 3.20 in the decades of the 1590s and 1600s respectively. These levels, the highest of our period, were never again attained before 1750.[55] Recorded bastard births grew markedly less frequent during the first half of the seventeenth century. There was a widespread determination among ratepayers to curb the practices likely to result in unwanted and unsupported children, which harmonised with puritan desire for the stricter control of morals. This was not of course everywhere equally marked; much depended upon the character of individual parishes and the degree of control exercised by the more substantial inhabitants. But to an increasing extent young people seem to have become more wary, adjusting themselves to reduced opportunities and the heightened likelihood of punishment for sexual misbehaviour. The latter was due in part to more effective use of the church courts, in part to the extension of the powers of the justices of the peace. A statute of 1576 empowered justices to order the parents of bastard children to maintain them and authorised them to punish the mother and father. Further legislation of 1610 enabled them to order the confinement to the house of correction of the mother of a bastard chargeable to the parish.[56]

Recorded illegitimate births fell to their lowest level during the 1650s. But this fact may be misleading. The registration of baptisms was defective for much of the interregnum. Puritan efforts to impose more effective moral discipline, symbolised by a harsh statute of 1650, were probably hampered by the temporary abolition of the church courts.[57] After the Restoration, the economic climate improved, and the incidence of marriage rose. So too did the illegitimacy ratio, though only very gradually before the end of our period.[58]

Marriage and property: bargains and settlements

The wealthier the parties to a marriage, the more prominent in general was the place occupied in the marriage agreement by property arrangements. Whereas at the lower levels of society simple verbal negotiations and agreements were usually enough to ascertain the economic resources and prospects of the couple and to sort out what each should contribute to the marriage, among the upper classes marriages were the occasion for the making of carefully worded treaties or settlements, which grew more and more elaborate as time went by. It was of course essential to sort out these property arrangements before an irrevocable contract had been exchanged or solemnisation had taken place.

At the heart of the agreement about property which preceded marriage was an exchange of material benefits between the partners or their families. In return for the portion or 'dowry' which the bride brought with her, she gained the right to support from her husband's property for the rest of her life. (In practice, payment of the portion, which represented a considerable outlay for the bride's father, was often spread over a period of years, especially in the first half of the period.) By common law, the widow was entitled to enjoy a third part of her husband's land in dower. In the later Middle Ages, however, it became increasingly common to specify a 'jointure' (lands or income to be held jointly by the husband and wife, and then by the widow alone). Its major advantage was to facilitate planning and diminish the possibilities of dispute by determining in advance exactly what was to be the source of the widow's livelihood. But in the course of time its usual annual value fell below a third of the rental income of the husband's lands. For reasons which are far from clear, the annual income which a given portion would buy diminished sharply, perhaps by as much as a half, between the midsixteenth and the early eighteenth century.[59]

It was expected, especially in the case of heirs and heiresses, that marriage settlements would be made by the fathers of the bride and groom, even though in practice a substantial proportion of men did not live to see their heirs married, especially in the seventeenth century. In the marriage treaty, the groom's father not only made provision for the proper support of his daughter-in-law during her widowhood but also undertook to settle a considerable proportion of his land, to come to his son after his death, and to maintain the newly married couple during his lifetime.[60]

When planning the advancement of his children, a father would commonly try to reconcile his own interests, those of his heir, and those of his non-inheriting children. This could be difficult. The increasing cost of suitable matches for non-inheriting daughters may help to explain why the proportion of women of noble birth who remained unmarried rose sharply during the seventeenth century. If he did not need to use it to pay his debts, a father might hope to use the dowry he received with his heir's wife to assist the advancement of his other children. But the cost of a good marriage for the eldest son, especially to an heiress, might limit what he could do for them. Dynastic ambition did not however necessarily outweigh affection. In about 1600, Catherine Doyly, writing to her brother Sir Henry Neville, mentioned as one of the main disadvantages of a match recently proposed for her son the likelihood that 'greater maintenance' would be expected than she and her husband could afford, 'hauing many other chillderin to prouide for'.[61]

In making marriages, desire to secure the best possible terms often led to long and tortuous negotiations. Sir William Plumpton (1404–80), a hard and canny Yorkshireman, was reminded by his correspondents of the need for greater speed in his matrimonial bargaining, 'for in long tarriing comes mekell letting', as one of them expressively put it. But haste was incompatible with the careful investigation of prospective relatives' intentions, the examination of their deeds or ledgers and viewing of their lands which was often considered desirable. The crucial stages of negotiation could be tough, especially if one found oneself dealing with an unscrupulous negotiator. Roger North dealt as guardian with more than one such. Sir John Knatchbull, for example, demanded for his daughter an annual jointure of a sixth of her portion instead of the going rate of a tenth. Some of his reasons North found highly offensive, 'being insinuations of dishonour, which he would have made up by jointure'.[62]

Lower down the social scale the same process of bargaining went on, but there was probably much greater diversity in the terms of agreements. Endowment might be in money. Even poor girls hoped to bring a portion with them, however small. But dowries were sometimes paid partly or wholly in goods or services. In 1567, Grace Bab, a widow of Highweek (Devon), promised with her daughter twenty nobles in money, a bed, two brazen crocks, two pans, half a dozen pewter vessels and her wedding apparel. In 1593 a man of Tedburn

St Mary (Devon) said he had given his son-in-law, apparently in lieu of dowry, the crops from an acre of ground for a term of years, bearing the costs of ploughing, sowing and harvesting.[63]

Security for widowhood, where this was not assured by manorial custom, was of course an important concern in many negotiations. Surviving settlements show that widows of prosperous husbandmen of Wigston (Leics.) were assured of an estate in a farm towards the end of the sixteenth century, or (in at least one case) the value of the dowry brought to the first husband in the event of remarriage. In 1603, Joan Hedges, a Somerset woman, was told that her prospective husband would assure her of twice as much money as the dowry her father gave with her, whether the latter were £20 or £40. In 1634, after much talk between the parties and their friends, John Tocker of North Molton (Devon) agreed to accept £32 in marriage with Emlyn Nethercott. If he died before her he was to leave her £25 payable in six months or a source of income worth £5 or £6 a year.[64]

Quite often the woman held the land and she and her friends demanded a portion with her prospective husband rather than the other way round. In 1595, for example, John Dasheper of Little-hampton (Devon) offered Elinor Blatchford £20 with his brother Michael and the ploughing of their ground as long as he lived with the couple. Elinor and her mother asked in addition that John pay for the renewal of her mother's lease.[65]

Wedding

The process of courtship and matchmaking was crowned by the solemnisation in church. This was hedged about with a number of regulations. Medieval ecclesiastical legislation had forbidden it during Advent, Lent and Rogationtide, which between them totalled nearly twenty weeks of the year. The seasonal marriage pattern continued to bear the imprint of the Lent and Advent prohibitions for a long time after the Reformation, and there were marked troughs in the celebration of marriages in March till the nineteenth century and (rather less pronounced) in December till the later seventeenth. A third trough in August probably reflected the concentration of effort on the gathering of the harvest. The three peak periods for marriage fell in October–November (by far the biggest), April–June and January–February. The first of these came at a slack time immediately after the harvesting of the crops had been completed; it was particularly marked in the arable areas of England, and corresponded with the most widespread date for the termination of annual contracts of service. May and June were peak months for marriages in the pastoral areas. Here too contracts of service expired after the busiest period of the farmer's year. The large numbers of marriages in January were in great measure due to the postponement of plans on account of Advent.[66]

Medieval ecclesiastical legislation, and a canon passed by Convocation in 1604, laid down that nobody was to be married except in their own parish church or that of their future spouse. The ceremony was to be preceded by the reading, on three separate Sundays or holy days, of banns designed to allow any possible objections to the marriage to be voiced in good time. Dispensations or licences could be obtained which waived the requirement of banns. A remarkable paper written in defence of licences in *c.* 1598 pointed out that they enabled individuals to escape pressure to marry in conformity with the wishes of friends and parents, which was probably one of their major inconveniences in the eyes of their critics. A canon of 1604 stipulated that applicants for licences must enter bond that they had their parents' or guardian's consent, but this was probably enforced with varying degrees of efficiency. The purchase of licences was widespread. Just before the civil war Daniel Rogers wrote regretfully that 'now he is thought but a peasant who declines not this lawful provision of the church'.[67]

Clandestine marriages, i.e. without due publicity or proper authorisation, were performed not only by clergymen who claimed to be independent of episcopal jurisdiction but also, according to a statute of 1696, by ministers who were unbeneficed, of no fixed habitation, or in prison for debt. The marriages they performed were valid, if irregular, and they were evidently prepared to run the risk of punishment which their moonlighting carried with it. Clandestine marriages occasionally took place throughout this period. Sir William Plumpton, for example, who wanted to keep his second marriage secret from his first wife's family, had it celebrated clandestinely in 1451. But during the seventeenth century, prosecutions of participants and celebrants in the church courts grew increasingly common, especially after the civil war. The analysis of parish registers, too, has suggested that clandestinity was most common in the later seventeenth century. There are good reasons for supposing that clandestine ceremonies may indeed have been more popular in the seventeenth century than ever before. They may have enabled many poor people to circumvent ratepayers' efforts to prevent their marriages, and, by allowing them to marry at short notice, to mask the fact of ante-nuptial fornication from prying authorities. Acts of 1695 and 1696 which introduced and enforced the taxation of marriages laid down stiffer penalties for those participating in such ceremonies. They sharply reduced the incidence of irregular marriages, but the problem was not finally dealt with until such unions were at last declared invalid in 1753.[68]

Only a public wedding could meet in full the demands of family, Church and community as well as the needs of the couple who were the central actors. The wedding incorporated a number of elements.

First, the exchange of marriage vows and words of mutual acceptance were the basis of the couple's marriage partnership, which they solemnly undertook to continue through all the vicissitudes of life. Secondly, the man endowed his wife with all his worldly goods and thus undertook the responsibility for her material support. The priest then invoked God's blessing on the marriage. The following feast, more than the rite itself, celebrated the alliance of two families, the increase of amity through the extension of the network of affinal kinship. Whoever paid for the feast (customarily but not always the bride's father), its scale and duration testified to the wealth and good-will of those who had invested in the new marriage. The food and drink, the ribbons, gloves and scarves distributed as favours were symbolic of the new friendship, and to skimp them could be a cause of lasting resentment. The wedding festivities of the wealthy often lasted several days. The poor, who often had few or no relatives to help and attend them, celebrated their weddings as lavishly as they could. In about 1503 the bride of Lewys Mone, a London smith, brought him only an anvil in dowry, and came to her wedding in a borrowed gown and kirtle. But they had wine served in the parish church after the nuptial mass and a dinner at his lodgings. When the sailor Edward Barlow got married far from his boyhood home in 1678, he had a wedding dinner at the King's Head in Deal attended by officers and merchants from his ship, with 'music and wine a-plenty, and good victuals enough . . .'. The climax of the celebrations was the bedding of the couple. The Sarum rite included a priestly blessing of the bridal chamber, and long after the Reformation the pious Alice Thornton was still glad to see her daughter decently bedded. Very often, however, the bedding was a bawdy romp which afforded the onlookers the greatest possible vicarious anticipation of the nuptial pleasures of the married pair while also marking their departure from the peer groups of young bachelors and spinsters. Puritan writers might deplore the waste and profanity which mingled with the wedding celebrations, but the efforts of the godly to impose decorum had achieved only partial success by the 1690s. The festivities might be shorter than hitherto; dinner might be followed by the parson's address in praise of marriage, but then began the dancing which culminated in the uproarious scenes of the bedding and the throwing of the stocking at the bride's nose to see who would be married next.[69]

Conclusion

Contrasts between the marriage patterns of different social groups were always sharp in this period. Though there were members of the upper ranks such as younger sons who were left relatively free to choose their own marriage partners, the wealthiest families were the best placed to dictate or at least to influence their children's matches. The children of the poor, whose dependence on their parents ended soonest, probably tended to lose them earliest, and had least to hope for by inheritance; they enjoyed the greatest freedom from familial supervision. At all levels of society economic considerations perforce bulked large in the choice of partners, and among the upper classes may indeed have become more important with the growth of political security. The viability of the union depended upon the resources (land, money, skill, strength and earning power) which each partner brought to it. But this dependence was not necessarily incompatible with a choice based on love or affection, recognised for centuries as a desirable element in marriage, celebrated in literature and symbolised in the rituals of courtship.

Marriage based on love and free consent was a long-established ideal. But the extent of this freedom depended in practice upon political, economic and social circumstances. A number of developments widened the choice of eligible mates for the members of the upper ranks and made it possible for parents to allow their children more freedom. But the effects of change on the great majority of the rural population were slow, uneven and sometimes adverse. Among the consequences of the way in which the increasing English population outstripped the expansion of the economy between the early sixteenth and mid-seventeenth centuries was that a growing minority had to forgo marriage altogether. Freedom of courtship was reduced by a mixture of informal pressures and institutional measures. The apparently widespread idea that entry into marriage was a prolonged transitional process begun by private agreement and only completed by public rites came under renewed attack. It was in fact far from dead among the people, as big increases in ante-nuptial consummation and illegitimate births from the later seventeenth century onwards were to show. But the atrophy of the old law of matrimonial contracts and its ultimate reform in 1753 completed the rift between law and widespread popular practice across which the medieval canonists had maintained a precarious bridge.

Notes and references

1. **R. Copland**, *The Highway to the Spital-house* (1535–36), in **A. V. Judges** (ed.), *The Elizabethan Underworld*, G. Routledge and Sons, London, 1930, p. 16.
2. **J. Hajnal**, 'European Marriage Patterns in Perspective', in **D. V. Glass** and **D. E. C. Eversley** (eds)., *Population in History: Essays in Historical Demography*, Edward Arnold, London, 1965, pp. 101–43, esp. 101–6, 110–11; **E. A. Wrigley** and **R. S. Schofield**, *The Population History of England, 1541–1871. A Reconstruction*, Edward Arnold, London, 1982, pp. 257–65, 423–4.
3. **Z. Razi**, *Life, Marriage and Death in a Medieval Parish: Economy,*

Society and Demography in Halesowen 1270–1400, Cambridge UP, 1980, pp. 50–64; **A. Macfarlane**, *The Origins of English Individualism: The Family, Property and Social Transition*, Basil Blackwell, Oxford, 1978, p. 158.

4. **R. M. Smith**, 'Some Reflections on the Evidence for the Origins of the "European Marriage Pattern" in England', in **C. C. Harris** (ed.), *The Sociology of the Family: New Directions for Britain*, Sociological Review Monographs, 28, Keele, 1979, pp. 83–4, 100–1, 110, 112; **J. Hatcher**, 'English Serfdom and Villeinage: towards a Reassessment', *Past and Present*, **90** (1981), 25.

5. Razi, *op. cit.*, pp. 130–38, 142–6.

6. **L. Stone**, *The Crisis of the Aristocracy, 1558–1641*, Clarendon Press, Oxford, 1965, pp. 623–4; **J. Hurstfield**, *The Queen's Wards: Wardship and Marriage under Elizabeth I*, Longmans, London, 1958, pp. 3–19, 96–107; **M. J. Hawkins**, 'Royal Wardship in the Seventeenth Century', *Genealogists' Magazine*, **16** (1969), 41–4; **T. Starkey**, *A Dialogue between Reginald Pole and Thomas Lupset*, **K. M. Burton** (ed.), Chatto & Windus, London, 1948, pp. 109–11, 168–9; **H. Brinkelow**, *The Complaynt of Roderyck Mors, c. 1542*, **J. M. Cowper** (ed.), *Early English Text Society*, extra ser., **22** (1874), 18; **T. Smith**, *De Republica Anglorum The Maner of Gouernement or policie of the Realme of England*, London, 1583, pp. 98–101. Starkey and Smith put the arguments for and against the institution, but those against with much more apparent conviction.

7. **E. W. Ives**, ' "Agaynst taking awaye of Women": the Inception and Operation of the Abduction Act of 1487', **E. W. Ives, R. J. Knecht** and **J. J. Scarisbrick** (eds.), *Wealth and Power in Tudor England: Essays presented to S. T. Bindoff*, Athlone Press, London, 1978, pp. 21–44, esp. 22–5; **T. H. Hollingsworth**, 'A Demographic Study of the British Ducal Families', in Glass and Eversley, *op. cit.*, p. 374.

8. **H. E. Bell**, *An Introduction to the History and Records of the Court of Wards and Liveries*, Cambridge UP, 1953, pp. 116–17; Stone, *op. cit.*, pp. 234–50 624–5, 653; *The Family, Sex and Marriage in England 1500–1800*, Wêidenfcld & Nicolson, London, 1977, pp. 316–17; **T. H. Hollingsworth**, 'The Demography of the British Peerage', supplement to *Population Studies*, **18** (1964), 20; **C. L. Kingsford** (ed.), *Stonor Letters and Papers, 1290–1483*, Camden Society, 3rd ser., **29–30** (1919), I, 158.

9. **F. J. Furnivall** (ed.), *Child-marriages, Divorces, and Ratifications . . . in the Diocese of Chester, A. D. 1561–6*, Early English Text Society, orig. ser., **108** (1897); **P. Laslett**, *The World We Have Lost*, Methuen, London, 1965, p. 86, and **C. Haigh**, *Reformation and Resistance in Tudor Lancashire*, Cambridge UP, 1975, pp. 48–9, offer contrasting views of the significance of this evidence.

10. **H. J. Carpenter** (ed.), 'Furse of Moreshead. A Family Record of the Sixteenth Century', *Report and Transactions of the Devonshire Association*, **26** (1894), 181; **S. L. Thrupp**, *The Merchant Class of Medieval London, 1300–1500*, Univ. of Chicago Press, 1948, pp. 193, 196; **V. B. Elliott**, 'Single Women in the London Marriage Market: Age, Status and Mobility, 1598–1619', in **R. B. Outhwaite** (ed.), *Marriage and Society: Studies in the Social History of Marriage*, Europa Publications, London, 1981, pp. 84–7.

11. P. Laslett, *Family Life and Illicit Love in Earlier Generations: Essays in Historical Sociology*, Cambridge UP, 1977, p. 34.

12. K. Wrightson, *English Society, 1580–1680*, Hutchinson, London, 1982, p. 35; A. Macfarlane, *The Family Life of Ralph Josselin, a Seventeenth-Century Clergyman: An Essay in Historical Anthropology*, Cambridge UP, 1970. p. 94; A. Kussmaul, *Servants in Husbandry in Early Modern England*, Cambridge UP, 1981, p. 84.

13. R. Thompson, *Women in Stuart England and America: A Comparative Study*, Routledge & Kegan Paul, London, 1974, Ch. 2, 'The Sex Ratio'; R. Finlay, *Population and Metropolis: The Demography of London, 1580–1650*, Cambridge UP, 1981, p. 140; Wrigley and Schofield, *op. cit.*, pp. 359–63, 368–9, 400–1, 421–2; D. Levine and K. Wrightson, 'The Social Context of Illegitimacy in Early Modern England', in P. Laslett, K. Oosterveen and R. M. Smith (eds.), *Bastardy and its Comparative History*, Edward Arnold, London, 1980, pp. 159–61.

14. Wrigley and Schofield, *op. cit.*, pp. 421–30. But note their warning, pp. 441–2, that the real-wage index is not necessarily an accurate guide to the real income of the population at large. 'Especially in the earlier centuries a large proportion of the population was either not dependent upon wages for income or was dependent upon them only to a limited extent.'

15. *Ibid.*, pp. 417, 421–3, 435; S. Brigden, 'Youth and the English Reformation', *Past and Present*, 95 (1982), 46; 5 Elizabeth I, c. 4, clause 19; Memorandum on the Statute of Artificers, (1573?) in R. H. Tawney and E. Power (eds.), *Tudor Economic Documents*, Longmans, London, 1924, Vol. I, pp. 353–8; F. J. Furnivall (ed.), *Phillip Stubbes's Anatomy of Abuses in England in Shakspere's Youth, A.D. 1583*, London, 1877–82, Vol. I, p. 97; 31 Elizabeth I, c 7; 43 Elizabeth I, c. 2; A. Clark, *Working Life of Women in the Seventeenth Century*, George Routledge & Sons, London, 1919, pp. 80–6; K. Wrightson and D. Levine, *Poverty and Piety in an English Village: Terling, 1525–1700*, Academic Press, London, 1979, pp. 80–1, 133; M. Ingram, 'Spousals Litigation in the English Ecclesiastical Courts *c.* 1350–*c.* 1640', in Outhwaite, *op. cit.*, pp. 55–6.

16. R. H. Helmholz, *Marriage Litigation in Medieval England*, Cambridge UP, 1974, pp. 26–7, 90–3, 98–9; C. N. L. Brooke, 'Marriage and Society in the Central Middle Ages', in Outhwaite, *op. cit.*, pp. 26–8; C. D'Evelyn (ed.), *Peter Idley's Instructions to his Son*, Modern Language Association of America, Boston, 1935, p. 136; P. H. Barnum (ed.), *Dives and Pauper*, Vol. I, *Early English Text Society*, 275, 280 (1976, 1980), Pt. 1, 340; N. Davis (ed.), *Paston Letters and Papers of the Fifteenth Century*, Clarendon Press, Oxford, 1971, 1976, Vol. I, pp. 341–3.

17. W. Tyndale, *The Obedience of a Christen Man*, in *Doctrinal Treatises and Introductions to Different Portions of the Holy Scriptures*, H. Walter (ed.), *Parker Society*, 42 (1848), 169–70; W. H. Frere and W. P. M. Kennedy (eds.), *Visitation Articles and Injunctions of the Period of the Reformation*, Alcuin Club Publications, 14–16 (1910), III, 6; E. Cardwell (ed.), *Synodalia: A Collection of Articles of Religion, Canons and Proceedings of Convocations*, Oxford, 1842, Vol. I, pp. 122, 304–5; D. Rogers, *Matrimoniall Honour: or The Mutuall Crowne and comfort of godly, loyall, and chaste Marriage*, London, 1642, p. 80; Robert

Cawdrey, *A Godlie Forme of Hovseholde Gouernment: for the Ordering of Private Families, according to the Direction of God's Word*, London, 1600, (first edn 1598), p. 352. Not all libraries attribute this work to Cawdrey. It appears under his name in the catalogue of the Bodleian Library, Oxford.

18. **T. Becon**, *The Catechism . . . with other pieces written by him in the Reign of King Edward the Sixth*, **J. Ayre** (ed.), *Parker Society*, **11** (1844), 372.
19. **R. Weigall** (ed.), 'An Elizabethan Gentlewoman. The Journal of Lady Mildmay, circa 1570–1617', *Quarterly Review*, **215** (1911), 122; **F. R. Raines** (ed.), *The Journal of Nicholas Assheton of Downhan, in the County of Lancaster, Esq., for part of the year 1617, and part of the year following*, *Cheltham Society*, old ser., **14** (1848), 22.
20. **R. Latham** and **W. Matthews** (eds), *The Diary of Samuel Pepys: a New and Complete Transcription*, G. Bell & Sons, London, 1970–, Vol. VI, pp. 71, 136–7, 141, 158–9, 161, 167; **T. C. Croker** (ed.), *Autobiography of Mary, Countess of Warwick*, *Percy Society*, **76** (1848), 2–3.
21. **J. O. Halliwell** (ed.), *The Autobiography and Correspondence of Sir Simonds D'Ewes, Bart.*, London, 1845, Vol. I, pp. 308–9; **C. B. Robinson** (ed.), *Rural Economy in Yorkshire in 1641, being the Farming and Account Books of Henry Best, of Elmswell in the East Riding*, Surtees Society, **33** (1857), 116–17; cf. **M. Blundell** (ed.), *Cavalier: Letters of William Blundell to his Friends, 1620–98*, Longmans, Green & Co., London, 1933, p. 131; **E. S. de Beer** (ed.), *The Diary of John Evelyn*, Clarendon Press, Oxford, 1955, Vol. IV, pp. 425–6.
22. **Davis**, *op. cit.*, Vol. I, pp. 662–3; Vol. II, pp. 435–6; *The Ladies' Dictionary*, London, 1694, pp. 492–504.
23. **Davis**, *op. cit.*, Vol. II, pp. 498–500; **A. H. Smith, G. M. Baker** and **R. W. Kenny** (eds), *The Papers of Nathaniel Bacon of Stiffkey, Vol. I, 1556–1577*, Norfolk Record Society, **46** (1979), 146–154, esp. 151.
24. **R. Parkinson** (ed.), *The Life of Adam Martindale, written by himself*, *Chetham Society*, old ser., **4** (1845), 208, 212; Macfarlane, *Family Life of Josselin*, pp. 95–6; **R. Parkinson** (ed.), *The Autobiography of Henry Newcome, M. A.*, *Chetham Society*, old ser., **26–7** (1852). II, 215.
25. Norwich, Norfolk and Norwich Record Office, DEP 3, f. 47; DEP 5A, f. 282ᵛ; DEP 5B, f. 102ᵛ; DEP 6A, ff. 86, 247; **M. MacDonald**, *Mystical Bedlam: Madness, Anxiety, and Healing in Seventeenth-Century England*, Cambridge UP, 1981, p. 94.
26. Trowbridge, Wilts. Record Office, Bishop's Deposition Book 5, f. 91; **E. M. Elvey** (ed.), *The Courts of the Archdeaconry of Buckingham 1483–1523*, Bucks. Record Society, **19** (1975), 310; Norwich, Norfolk and Norwich Record Office, DEP 5B, ff. 95–6.
27. **W. L. Sachse** (ed.), *The Diary of Roger Lowe of Ashton-in-Makerfield, Lancs., 1663–74*, Longmans, Green & Co., London, 1938, pp. 20, 21, 23, 25, 33–4, 46–7, 58, 68, 75, 79; Exeter, Devon Record Office, Chanter 864, ff. 230ᵛ–1; Furnivall, *Stubbes's Anatomy of Abuses*, pp. 146–69; Wrightson and Levine, *op. cit.*, pp. 134–8; **P. Clark**, 'The Alehouse and the Alternative Society', in **D. Pennington** and **K. Thomas** (eds.), *Puritans and Revolutionaries: Essays in Seventeenth-Century History presented to Christopher Hill*, Clarendon Press, Oxford, 1978, pp. 47–72; **C. Hill**, *Society and Puritanism in Pre-Revolutionary England*, Martin Secker & Warburg, London, 1964, pp. 183–94; Norwich,

Norfolk and Norwich Record Office, DEP 5A, ff. 32ᵛ–3; Winchester, Hants. Record Office, CB 6, ff. 19–21, Kussmaul, *op. cit.*, pp. 41–4; **G. R. Quaife**, *Wanton Wenches and Wayward Wives: Peasants and Illicit Sex in Early Seventeenth Century England*, Croom Helm, London, 1979, pp. 59–88; **R. A. Houlbrooke**, *Church Courts and People during the English Reformation*, Oxford UP, 1979, pp. 58–61.

28. **Sachse**, *op. cit.*, pp. 22, 42, 45, 119; **J. Cannon**, χρονεχα *Seu Annales or Memoirs of the Birth Education Life and Death of Mr Iohn Cannon Sometime Officer of the Excise and Writing Master at Mere Glastonbury & West Lydford in the County of Somersett*, n.d., MS in the Somerset Record Office, Taunton, pp. 57, 64, 86–7, 115; Helmholz, *op. cit.*, pp. 57–66; Houlbrooke, *op. cit.*, p. 59.

29. **J. Gairdner** (ed.), *The Paston Letters, 1422–1509 A.D.*, John Grant, Edinburgh, 1910, introductory volume, pp. cclxxiii, cclxxix, ccxcix–ccc, cccvi–vii; Davis, *op. cit.*, Vol. I, pp. 380–1; **C. Jackson** (ed.), *The Autobiography of Mrs Alice Thornton, of East Newton, in the County of York, Surtees Society*, **62** (1875) 61–2; Stone, *Crisis of the Aristocracy*, pp. 623–4.

30. Kingsford, *op. cit.*, Vol. I, pp. 48–9; **J. G. Nichols** (ed.), *The Autobiography of Anne Lady Halkett, Camden Society*, new ser., **13** (1875), 7–8; **J. Smyth**, *The Berkeley Manuscripts*, **J. Maclean** (ed.), Bristol and Gloucestershire Archaeological Society, Gloucester, 1883, Vol. II, p. 252; Latham and Matthews, *op. cit.*, Vol. III, pp. 3, 16, 228, 231; Vol. IV, p. 19.

31. **M. E. Finch**, *The Wealth of Five Northants. Families, 1540–1640, Northants. Record Society*, **19** (1956), 6, 28, 50; **M. Campbell**, *The English Yeoman under Elizabeth and the early Stuarts*, Yale UP, New Haven, 1942, p. 48; **B. Winchester**, *Tudor Family Portrait*, Jonathan Cape, London, 1955, p. 61; **A. Hanham** (ed.), *The Cely Letters, 1472–1488, Early English Text Society*, **273** (1975), 217; *Life of Martindale*, p. 212; **A. Jessopp** (ed.), *The Autobiography of the Hon. Roger North*, David Nutt, London, 1887, pp. 232–5.

32. Rogers, *op. cit.*, p. 13; **F. Mount**, *The Subversive Family: An Alternative History of Love and Marriage*, Jonathan Cape, London, 1982, pp. 66–70; Winchester, *op. cit.*, p. 62.

33. Stone, *Crisis of the Aristocracy*, pp. 617–18, 627–32, 637–49.

34. **W. Gouge**, *Of Domesticall Duties, Eight Treatises*, London, 1622, pp. 188–92; **A. Niccholes**, *A Discourse of Marriage and Wiving, and of the greatest Mystery therein contained: How to choose a good Wife from a bad*, London, 1615, pp. 14–15; **J. P. Cooper** (ed.), *Wentworth Papers 1597–1628, Camden Society*, 4th ser., **12** (1973), 20; Rogers, *op. cit.*, pp. 60–3, 66–7; Cawdrey, *op. cit.*, pp. 148–9; *Ladies' Dictionary*, pp. 87–8; Stone, *Crisis of the Aristocracy*, pp. 192–4, 627–32, 789; *idem, Family, Sex and Marriage*, pp. 60–1; **R. Grassby**, 'English Merchant Capitalism in the Late Seventeenth Century. The Composition of Business Fortunes', *Past and Present*, **46** (1970), 102.

35. Davis, *op. cit.*, Vol. I, p. 500; **T. Stapleton** (ed.), *Plumpton Correspondence, Camden Society*, old ser., **4** (1839) 126; **L. B. Wright** (ed.), *Advice to a Son: Precepts of Lord Burghley, Sir Walter Raleigh, and Francis Osborne*, Cornell UP, Ithaca, 1962, p. 10; Carpenter, *op. cit.*, p. 172; Cooper, *op. cit.*, p. 20; Cawdrey, *op. cit.*, pp. 102–3; **S. Clarke**, *A Collection of the Lives of Ten Eminent Divines*, London, 1662, p. 326;

Ladies' Dictionary, pp. 87–8; **B. Lubbock** (ed.), *Barlow's Journal of his life at sea*, Hurst & Blackett, London, 1934, Vol. II, p. 310; Norwich, Norfolk and Norwich Record Office, DEP 6A, ff. 106^v–7; **R. Davies** (ed.), *The Life of Marmaduke Rawdon of York, Camden Society*, old ser., **85** (1863), 28.

36. **E. A. Parry** (ed.), *Letters from Dorothy Osborne to Sir William Temple, 1652–54*, Sherratt & Hughes, London and Manchester, 1903, p. 33; Kingsford, *op. cit.*, Vol. I, p. 93; *The Colloquies of Erasmus*, Trans. **C. R. Thompson**, Univ. of Chicago Press, 1965, p. 94; **H. Bullinger**, *The Christen State of Matrimonye*, Trans. **M. Coverdale**, London, 1541, p. 20; Niccholes, *op. cit.*, p. 14; **J. Taylor**, *The Rule and Exercises of Holy Living*, Longmans, Green & Co., London, 1926, p. 148.

37. **W. Harrington**, *In This Boke are conteyned the Cōmendacions of Matrymony*, sig. Aiii^v, dated to between 1512 and 1515 by **D. Ramage** in *The Durham Philobiblon*, **1** (1949–55), 69.

38. Davis, *op. cit.*, Vol. I, pp. 381, 500, 591; Stapleton, *op. cit.*, p. 192; Norwich, Norfolk and Norwich Record Office, DEP 6A, f. 131; DEP 5B, ff. 303^v–4.

39. D'Evelyn, *op. cit.*, pp. 100–1; **M. Y. Offord** (ed.), *Book of the Knight of the Tower, Early English Text Society*, Supplementary ser., **2** (1971), 163–76; **T. Ingelend**, *The Disobedient Child*, **J. O. Halliwell** (ed.), *Percy Society*, **75** (1848), 22–3, 33; Rogers, *op. cit.*, pp. 146–8.

40. Kingsford, *op. cit.*, Vol. I, pp. 126–7; **M. St Clare Byrne** (ed.), *The Lisle Letters*, Univ. of Chicago Press, 1981, Vol. I, p. 330, Vol. III, p. 22; **Sir N. H. Nicholas** (ed.), *Private Memoirs of Sir Kenelm Digby*, London, 1827; Cooper *op. cit.*, pp. 324–5; **L. Hutchinson**, *Memoirs of the Life of Colonel Hutchinson, with the fragment of an autobiography of Mrs Hutchinson*, **J. Sutherland** (ed.), Oxford UP, 1973, pp. 27–32; Croker, *op. cit.*, pp. 5–14; **D. Gardiner** (ed.), *The Oxinden Letters, 1607–1642*, Constable & Co., London, 1933, pp. 262–4.

41. Helmholz, *op. cit.*, p. 131; Norwich, Norfolk and Norwich Record Office, DEP 3 f. 11^v; DEP 7C, f. 119; DEP 4B, f. 59; DEP 6A, F. 129^v; Macdonald, *op. cit.*, pp. 88–98.

42. Elvey, *op. cit.*, p. 305; Winchester, Hants. Record Office, CB 44, p. 6; Taunton, Somerset Record Office, D/D/Cd 2, pp. 1–3; D/D/Cd 20, ff. 3–4, 49^v–50; Norwich, Norfolk and Norwich Record Office, ACT 4B, f. 42; Exeter, Devon Record Office, Chanter 864, ff. 276^v–7; Chanter 556, ff. 58–9.

43. Helmholz, *op. cit.*, pp. 26–30; Brooke, *op. cit.*, pp. 26–34; **M. M. Sheehan**, 'The Formation and Stability of Marriage in Fourteenth-Century England: Evidence of an Ely Register'. *Mediaeval Studies*, **33** (1971), 228–31.

44. Helmholz, *op. cit.*, pp. 31–57; Houlbrooke, *op. cit.*, pp. 56–8; Ingram, *op. cit.*, pp. 37–41.

45. **Sir F. Pollock** and **F. W. Maitland**, *The History of English Law before the Time of Edward I*, reprint of 2nd edn of 1898, Cambridge UP, 1968, Vol. II, pp. 374–5; Helmholz, *op. cit.*, pp. 72–3, 166–8; Houlbrooke, *op. cit.*, pp. 64–7; Ingram, *op. cit.*, pp. 42–4, 52–5.

46. **H. Smith**, *A Preparatiue to Marriage. The summe whereof was spoken at a Contract, and inlarged after*, London, 1591, pp. 1–2; **Gouge**, *op. cit.*, pp. 198–203; **J. M. Lloyd Thomas** (ed.), *The Autobiography of Richard Baxter, being the Reliquiae Baxterianae abridged from the folio*

(*1696*), J. M. Dent & Sons, London, 1931, p. 274; **J. Horsfall Turner** (ed.), *The Rev. Oliver Heywood, B. A., 1630–1702: his Autobiography, Diaries, Anecdote and Event books*, Brighouse, 1881–85, Vol. I, p. 62; Parkinson, *Life of Martindale*, p. 72; Rogers, *op. cit.*, pp. 115–18, 120.

47. Helmholz, *op. cit.*, pp. 135–8; Hanham, *op. cit*, p. 75; Elvey, *op. cit.*, p. 300; Taunton, Somerset Record Office, D/D/Cd 18, f. 1ᵛ; Trowbridge, Wilts. Record Office, Bishop's Dep. Bk. 16, f. 92; **S. F. C. Milsom**, *Historical Foundations of the Common Law*, Butterworth, London, 1969, p. 289.

48. Greater London Record Office, DL/C/207, f. 117; Taunton, Somerset Record Office, D/D/Cd 12, unfoliated, suit by E. Watkins; Gouge, *op. cit.*, p. 202; **H. Swinburne**, *A Treatise of Spousals or Matrimonial Contracts*, London, 1686, sig. A2ᵛ. (This work had been written before 1624, the date of Swinburne's death.)

49. D'Evelyn *op. cit.*, pp. 135–6; Sachse, *op. cit.*, p. 22; Cannon, *op. cit.*, p. 64.

50. Taunton, Somerset Record Office, D/D/Cd 12, unfoliated, 2 Nov. 1568, White c. Prickett; 1 Feb. 1569, Methewaye c. Thomas; Quaife, *op. cit.*, p. 62.

51. **M. Slater**, 'The Weightiest Business: Marriage in an Upper-Gentry Family in Seventeenth-Century England', *Past and Present*, **72** (1976), 47: Winchester, *op. cit.*, pp. 85–8.

52. Wrightson and Levine, *op. cit.*, pp. 126–7, 132–3; Ingram, *op. cit.*, p. 54; Reading, Berks. Record Office, D/A/2, c. 70, ff. 80, 87ᵛ; Wrigley and Schofield, *op. cit.*, pp. 190–1, 254; **P. E. H. Hair**, 'Bridal Pregnancy in Rural England in Earlier Centuries', *Population Studies*, **20** (1966), 233–43; 'Bridal Pregnancy in Earlier Rural England further examined', *Population Studies*, **24** (1970), 59–70.

53. D'Evelyn, *op. cit.*, pp. 135–6; **R. Whytforde**, *A Werke for Housholders*, 1530, sig. E iiiᵛ; Razi, *op. cit.*, pp. 66–8; **D. Levine**, *Family Formation in an Age of Nascent Capitalism*, Academic Press, London, 1977, pp. 127–45; Levine and Wrightson, *op. cit.*, pp. 163–75.

54. Wrightson and Levine, *op. cit.*, pp. 127–32.

55. Laslett, *Family Life and Illicit Love*, pp. 113, 125.

56. Ingram, *op. cit.*, p. 54; 18 Elizabeth I, c. 3; 7 James I, c. 4; Levine and Wrightson, *op. cit.*, pp. 170–4.

57. **K. Wrightson**, 'The Nadir of English Illegitimacy in the Seventeenth Century', in Laslett, Oosterveen and Smith, *op. cit.*, pp. 180–6; **K. V. Thomas**, 'The Puritans and Adultery: the Act of 1650 Reconsidered', in Pennington and Thomas, *op. cit.*, pp. 257–8, 263–6.

58. Wrigley and Schofield, *op. cit.*, pp. 266, 425; Laslett, *Family Life and Illicit Love*, pp. 116–17.

59. Smyth, *op. cit.*, Vol. II, pp. 91, 142–5, 172–3, 210–11, 225, 235; **K. B. McFarlane**, *The Nobility of Later Medieval England*, Clarendon Press, Oxford, 1973, pp. 64–7; Stone, *Crisis of the Aristocracy*, pp. 632–4, 637–49; **H. J. Habakkuk**, 'Marriage Settlements in the Eighteenth Century', *Transactions of the Royal Historical Society*, 4th ser., **32** (1950), 21–7; **L. Bonfield**, 'Marriage Settlements, 1660–1740: The Adoption of the Strict Settlement in Kent and Northamptonshire', in Outhwaite, *op. cit.*, p. 106.

60. Stone, *op. cit.*, pp. 633–5.

61. Stone, *Crisis of the Aristocracy*, pp. 175–8, 640; Reading, Berks. Record Office, D/EN, F6/2/8 (from miscellaneous correspondence of Sir Henry Neville).

62. Stapleton, *op. cit.*, pp. 8, 11, 38; Kingsford, *op. cit.*, Vol. I, pp. 124, 126; **J. Shakespeare** and **M. Dowling** (eds.), 'Religion and Politics in Mid-Tudor England through the Eyes of an English Protestant Woman: the Recollections of Rose Hickman', *Bulletin of the Institute of Historical Research*, **55** (1982), 98; **G. Davies** (ed.), *Autobiography of Thomas Raymond, and Memoirs of the Family of Guise of Elmore, Gloucestershire, Camden Society*, 3rd Ser., **28** (1917), 150; Jessopp, *op. cit.*, pp. 205–9.

63. Exeter, Devon Record Office, Chanter 856, ff. 38ᵛ–9; Chanter 864, ff. 1–3, 8ᵛ, 15ᵛ.

64. **W. G. Hoskins**, *The Midland Peasant: The Economic and Social History of a Leicestershire Village*, Macmillan, London, 1957, pp. 123–4; Taunton, Somerset Record Office, D/D/Cd/20, ff. 4ᵛ–5; D/D/Cd 36, 31 Oct. 1604; Exeter, Devon Record Office, Chanter 866, 22 July 1635.

65. Exeter, Devon Record Office, Chanter 864, f. 257.

66. **L. Bradley**, 'An Enquiry into Seasonality in Baptisms, Marriages and Burials', Pt. 1, *Local Population Studies*, **4** (1970), 32–40; Wrigley and Schofield, *op. cit.*, pp. 298–305.

67. **E. Gibson**, *Codex Juris Ecclesiastici Anglicani*, Oxford, 1761, Vol. I, pp. 424–5, 428; **J. Strype**, *The Life and Acts of John Whitgift*, Oxford, 1822, Vol. III, pp. 380–1; Rogers, *op. cit.*, p. 110.

68. Gibson, *op. cit.*, pp. 425–6; 6 & 7 William III, c. 6; 7 & 8 William III, c. 35; 26 George II, c. 33; Stapleton, *op. cit.*, lxxvi; Ingram, *op. cit.*, pp. 56–7; **M. D. W. Jones**, 'The Ecclesiastical Courts before and after the Civil War: The Office Jurisdiction in the Dioceses of Oxford and Peterborough, 1630–75', Oxford Univ. B. Litt. thesis, 1977, Ch. 6; Wrigley and Schofield, *op. cit.*, pp. 27–30.

69. **J. C. Jeaffreson**, *Brides and Bridals*, London, 1872, Vol. I, pp. 231–75; Stone, *Crisis of the Aristocracy*, p. 633; Greater London Record Office, DL/C/207, ff. 70ᵛ–1; Lubbock, *op. cit.*, Vol. II, p. 309; **H. A. Kelly**, *Love and Marriage in the Age of Chaucer*, Cornell UP, Ithaca, 1975, pp. 293–5; Halliwell, *Autobiography of D'Ewes*, Vol. I, pp. 174–5; Jackson, *op. cit.*, pp. 232–3; Gouge, *op. cit.*, pp. 206–7; *Ladies Dictionary*, pp. 504–9.

Chapter 5

Husband and wife

The Christian view of marriage

The partnership of husband and wife had a number of purposes. Christian teaching gave prominence to three of these: the procreation of children, the regulation of sexual activity, and mutual comfort and support. Implicit in the first and the third of these was the acquisition of the means of subsistence for the couple and their children. This responsibility belonged in the first place to the husband, but the wife took a share of varying importance in it. The husband was held to be the superior partner, the wife the subordinate and inferior. According to the most frequently cited Scriptural texts, the wife's foremost duty was obedience, the husband's tender consideration.

The honourable partnership of matrimony was held in high regard. In the eyes of the Roman Catholic Church it was a sacrament. The celibacy of the priesthood might theoretically be superior, but no hint of this superiority marred the highly positive tone of the pastoral guidance for married people contained in such works as *Dives and Pauper* or William Harrington's *Commendacions of Matrymony*. First of all orders to be instituted, the only one preserved during the Flood, marriage had been specially favoured by the Virgin's entry into it and Christ's presence at Cana. The Protestant Reformers, while denying the sacramental status of marriage, insisted that it was an 'honourable estate' no whit inferior to celibacy, which clergy as well as laity might enter. But a number of Protestants recognised that the single life, though certainly not intrinsically superior to matrimony, nevertheless offered those capable of chastity an opportunity to devote themselves more whole-heartedly to God's service.[1]

An unequal partnership

St Paul had told wives to submit to their husbands as unto the Lord, for the husband was the wife's head, as Christ was head of the Church. The medieval scholastic synthesis of Christian theology and Aristotelian scientific ideas drew a sharp distinction between the equality of immortal souls, irrespective of sex, and earthly inequality. Men were stronger and wiser than women. The male was active and formative, the female material and passive. Less fully developed than man, woman was rendered by her predominantly cool and moist humours softer and weaker in body, less able to control her emotions, and therefore naturally unfitted either for heavy work or for public life. In law, as in theology and scientific theory, the woman's position was in many ways inferior. The husband enjoyed legal supremacy over his wife within marriage. He controlled her property, and for many purposes the common law regarded husband and wife as one person. The wife's acknowledgement of her husband's superiority was supposed to be conveyed in humble and respectful forms of address.[2]

The duty of obedience set out in Scripture rested on the wife whether or not she appeared to be superior to her husband in spirit or intelligence. Once convinced of it, the wife would not enquire into the reasons for a husbandly command, much less resist it, but follow where she was led, as the Israelites had followed the cloudy pillar. It was particularly necessary for a wife to accept husbandly reproofs meekly, without grudging or argument. She must bear with her husband's faults, concealing them from public notice as far as possible, accommodate his various moods and quiet his anger by soft and gentle behaviour. On any breach it was up to her to be the first to seek reconciliation.[3]

The rigours of wifely subjection were however mitigated by the separate Scriptural passages which set out husbands' duties. St Peter had called for husbandly understanding and discretion in married life. Men were to honour their wives as weaker vessels and as heirs of grace together with themselves. A number of writers, especially after the Reformation, reminded husbands that they should never insist upon the utmost extent of their authority. Especial care was needed in criticism or reproof, which was only to be given privately and when the wife was in a suitable frame of mind. Men were to be careful not to give trifling, senseless or over-frequent commands, or give them in a hectoring or abrasive manner. Much had to be left to the wife's discretion, and she was to be allured to do what her husband wanted by 'louing perswasions and familiar requests'. Always to stand upon one's authority was the surest way, in the long run, to destroy both love and respect.[4]

The weaker vessel was to be treated with honour. (Reverence and worship were the words used in the tract *Dives and Pauper*.) The metaphor of a precious yet brittle crystal glass appealed to more than one commentator upon St Peter's words. It was upon the frailer sex, Daniel Rogers pointed out, that all the pain and worry of pregnancy, childbirth and motherhood fell. Tact, tenderness and consideration were essential parts of the husband's duty. He was to comfort his wife when she was sad, be patient with her when she was depressed and to try to lighten her labours. He was to praise her virtues and indulge her small vanities. A wife without faults was not to be expected, and to bear with them was part of necessary husbandly discretion. Some writers conceded that occasional matrimonial discord was almost inevitable. Whether it was allowed to fester would depend above all on the husband's skill and judgement. Instead of counting upon the compliance which it was his wife's duty to give, he was to study her character thoroughly and in a measure adapt his own expectations and behaviour to it.[5]

Eve had been made of Adam's rib to be his companion, *Dives and Pauper* pointed out, not of his foot to be his thrall, nor his head to be his master. Many subsequent writers made the same point. The wife's place, though indeed subject and inferior, was, wrote William Gouge, the nearest to equality that might be. Matrimonial subjection, claimed Daniel Rogers, was 'not slavish, but equal and royal'. It was necessary for a man to take his wife into his confidence and sometimes to accept her advice. Many places in Scripture, Peter Idley told his son, showed that women's advice was good and reasonable. Thomas Becon condemned men who ignored what their wives had to say, for women, he pointed out, were often capable of giving better advice than men. Indeed, some writers thought that the wife was bound to admonish her husband when she saw him failing in his duty. Daniel Rogers advised that the wife be consulted in all major and hazardous undertakings such as removal to a remote new home, sudden changes of trade, big investments or borrowings and family settlements.[6]

Christian thought about the relationship between husband and wife, grounded on certain key Scriptural texts, underwent no major change during this period. It is true that after the Reformation some writers discussed the husbandly duty of tender consideration more fully than before, influenced perhaps both by humanist treatment of this topic and their own experience as husbands. But they added little of substance that was not implicit in St Peter's words or in medieval glosses upon them.[7]

In the long run, changing secular conceptions of woman's character and capacity would do more to enhance female rights. But during our period, changes in thinking and theory far outstripped those which took place in practice. Erasmus and Castiglione were among the more important writers of the later Renaissance who used the dialogue form to pit feminist against anti-feminist notions and to suggest that women had equal intelligence and capacity for virtue. Their example may have helped to give polemical argument between the two points of view the great popularity it enjoyed in western Europe in the later sixteenth and early seventeenth centuries. In England the accession of Elizabeth I provided a pretext for defence of female rule, while experience of her reign added considerably to the evidence of female sagacity and virtue in public life. Here some feminist polemical writing of the early seventeenth century appeared under women's names.[8]

Medieval Christian writers, as in the dialogue *Dives and Pauper*, had long since pointed out that women, though naturally less stable and wise than men, were often better by grace because, knowing their own frailty, they were readier to trust in God. Women excelled in some of the gentler virtues. But during the Renaissance writers influenced by Neoplatonic or neo-Stoic thought argued that men and women had identical capacities for virtue. Neo-Stoic psychology in particular stressed the possibility of women's control of their bodily passions through will and reason, thus dissociating the humours from mental behaviour.[9]

From the sixteenth century onwards, a succession of writers, in England as elsewhere, claimed that women's mental abilities, properly developed, were the equal of men's. Women themselves complained of their exclusion from education, devised by men in order to secure their own continued domination, in both *The Woman's Sharpe Revenge* of 1640 and in Hannah Woolley's *The Gentlewoman's Companion* (1675). The conservative feminist Mary Astell argued in *A Serious Proposal to the Ladies* (1697) that women's improvement was frustrated by bad education, custom, and the low and wrong aims proposed to them, especially the attraction of men as an end in itself. Better-educated women would indeed be more interesting companions for their husbands, but above all better fitted for their paramount responsibility, the religious education of their children. So while she sought to free women from the tyranny of fashion and custom, Astell insisted that the family was their proper sphere; they had no business with 'the Pulpit, the Bar or *St. Stephen's Chapel* . . .'. Despite their reiterated demand for better female education, none of the English feminist writers of our period proposed a major extension of woman's role. Women's capacity for virtue might be the equal of men's, but it was to be exercised in different areas. At first, then, changing views of women's capacity were very limited in their impact on familial relationships. Even John Locke, one of the most innovatory and coolly secular English political theorists of his century, defended male supremacy within marriage. It was unavoidable, he thought, that husband and wife should sometimes disagree, and 'it therefore being necessary that the last determination – i.e., the rule – should be placed somewhere, it naturally falls to the man's share, as the abler and the stronger'. Thus while he discarded scripture as the foundation of husbandly authority, Locke disregarded in this context the claims made for women's abilities during the previous century. An equally secular thinker, the marquess of Halifax, told his daughter that 'there is inequality in the sexes, and that for the better economy of the world the men, who were to be the lawgivers, had the larger share of reason bestowed upon them'; he advised her to make the best of what had been settled by law and custom. It was to be a very long time before changes in the latter took place commensurate with the changes in the theoretical view of woman accomplished during this period.[10]

Nowhere did the wife appear more completely subordinate to her husband than in the common law, especially in so far as it related to property. She enjoyed no security whatever against his wasteful dissipation of her movable goods. But her prospective rights limited his freedom to dispose of lands and strengthened her position in the matrimonial partnership. During the marriage, a husband could not legally alienate any land in which his wife had an interest by virtue of dower or jointure beyond his own lifetime without her consent. In February 1648, for example, Sir Robert Pye wrote to his daughter Anne Phelips to remind her that many of her children might be dependent upon her for support and to advise her not to join in an intended conveyance of lands by her husband until other Phelips lands had been secured to her by a settlement. For her part, an heiress could not dispose of her lands during her marriage except in certain towns. But if she bore no child, they would go, not to the widower, but to her next heir, a relative by birth, unless she had passed them to her husband. Even if children were born to her marriage, the heiress might prevent her lands descending to them if she entered her widowhood unfettered by an entail. Not surprisingly, a number of husbands tried, often unsuccessfully, to persuade their wives to forgo their rights as heiresses. In 1608 Edward Herbert's wife refused her husband's suggestion that they settle lands on their children. She would not draw the cradle upon her head, i.e. sacrifice her own interests, especially perhaps her chance of remarriage, to her children.[11]

It was possible to provide the wife with a separate income by means of the marriage settlement. Before their marriage in 1468, William Lord Berkeley bound himself to allow Joan Willoughby to dispose of the profits of seven manors and an annuity of 100 marks, without interference. The most secure device was to appoint trustees to hold property to the wife's use, and such provisions became much commoner in the seventeenth century. As late as 1710, however, one husband, Sir John Guise, bitterly resented them. Originating in the 'folly of parents and distrust of wives' they diminished 'the dignity and authority of a husband'. A guaranteed separate income was a luxury enjoyed only by wives of the propertied classes. But the husband was obliged to maintain his wife, and if he expelled or deserted her might be sued in the ecclesiastical court. Despite the common law, works of Christian counsel taught that in conscience the goods of husbands and wives were common, or for the use of wives as well as husbands. Furthermore, some wives were allowed in practice to trade or sell produce on their own account and to keep or spend the proceeds.[12]

Convention demanded that the wife address her husband with

humility and deference. In this respect the letters which survive from the fifteenth and early sixteenth centuries demonstrate wifely compliance, though their contents are not always wholly consistent with their deferential opening salutations. Later on, the tone of letters became much freer and more intimate. This was due not so much to a changing view of the wife's place as to greater epistolary privacy. As female literacy grew among the propertied classes and the custom of dictation to a clerk declined, so the composition of letters became a more personal and private matter. Further down the social scale, and in conversation, wives customarily addressed their husbands with unbecoming familiarity, according to one early seventeenth-century complaint. Even the affectionate terms (Love, Joy, Dear, Duck, Chick, Pigsnie) were not appropriate in the mouth of a subordinate, let alone those used in anger.[13]

Forms of address provide only one of many examples of the contrast between the ideal of wifely comportment and the way in which, according to contemporary observers, wives actually behaved towards their husbands. This in turn raises the larger question of the degree of correspondence between the model of the conjugal relationship underpinned by religion, science and law and the real balance of power in families. According to Thomas Fuller, more men betrayed their command through their own fondness than ever lost it through their wives' rebellion. But we are told by other writers that many women held themselves to be equal to their husbands and refused to accept management or reproof. Women commonly showed no more respect for their husbands than they did for their servants and insisted on getting their own way with them, so that their menfolk were forced to submit if they wanted outward quiet. Women's will to independence or mastery was a popular literary theme, a constant source of verbal and visual wit. The knight in Chaucer's *Wife of Bath's Tale* had saved his life by discovering what women most desired: the same mastery over their husbands as over their lovers. One popular fifteenth-century song urged husbands to let their wives have their way or risk being undone, while in another a husband made pitiful lament of his wife's beating him if he ventured the slightest complaint of her, and her compelling him to trot by her side when she rode to drink ale. Husband-beating is depicted both on many late medieval misericords and on an early seventeenth-century plasterwork panel at Montacute House in Somerset.[14]

The actual location of power in the relationship of husband and wife depended upon a number of variables, of which individual character and temperament are the hardest to quantify. Age and wealth were also important. One feature of the west European marriage pattern which England shared was that the age gap between spouses was usually small. Although the husband was generally slightly older than his partner, the wife was the older in a substantial minority of cases, especially when a young man married a widow in order to gain access to a workshop or a holding. On the other hand, the daughters of greater landowners and London merchants often married men much older than they were. This could lead to the wife's being treated almost like a child by her husband. When Thomas More sought to mould his first wife to his own tastes by teaching her literature and music and training her to repeat what she had heard in sermons, her frustration found vent in fits of weeping and in banging her head on the floor. In this case a gap of ten years in age between husband and wife clearly influenced their relationship.[15]

In the sections which follow, the extent of marital partnership and co-operation will be explored in four important areas: conjugal love, work, leisure and religion.

Conjugal love

Married love was highly valued by the Christian Churches both before and after the Reformation. It became sinful only when, intemperate and obsessive, it placed a creature in the position which God should have occupied in the heart of the individual. In his *Summa Theologica*, St Thomas Aquinas distinguished the form of marriage, which 'consists in a certain inseparable union of souls, by which husband and wife are pledged by a bond of mutual affection that cannot be sundered' as one of its perfections. The wedding ring was held to be symbolic of true married love. It was without end, like that love, and made of precious metal in token that it should surpass all other human loves. According to the early fifteenth-century tract *Dives and Pauper* the wife was to be the husband's 'felaw in loue [and] helper at nede [and] . . . nest solas in sorwe'. Unless there were a joining of hearts and a knitting of affections together, emphasised the Elizabethan minister Henry Smith, it was not marriage indeed, but only in show and name.[16]

The duty of love was a mutual one, as most writers stressed both before and after the Reformation. Yet it had been the husband whom St Paul had particularly enjoined to love his partner. This was, explained Thomas Gataker (1620), because love went downward while duty came upward. Expounding St Paul's comparison between husbandly love and that of Christ for the Church, Daniel Rogers pointed out that the common duty was to be exercised in a different manner and to a different degree of intensity by each partner. The wife's love, like the light of the moon, was borrowed; love must decend from the husband 'as the oile of *Aarons* head descended downe to his beard, and his cloathing', he wrote.[17]

Secular philosophy and romantic literature, much less inhibited by the framework of Scriptural texts, could much more readily than pastoral and theological treatises recognise conjugal love as a force which might not only modify male supremacy but even in some sense make a man subject to a woman. In Chaucer's *Franklin's Tale*, Arverargus swore to Dorigen upon their marriage that he would never exercise his authority against her will, but obey her in everything as every lover should, keeping only the name of sovereignty, 'for shame of his degree'. In this romantic context it was possible to envisage in the private domain and the emotional life a quite different relationship from the one of male superiority and female subjection presented to the outside world. During Elizabeth's reign, the humanist Sir Thomas Smith described the constitution of the household as an aristocracy, in which each partner had a share in sovereignty. Though God had given the man 'great wit, bigger strength, and more courage to compell the woman to obey by reason or force', he had also given the woman 'bewtie, faire countenaunce, and sweete wordes to make the man to obey her againe for loue . . .'.[18]

Within marriage, according to Christian teaching, following St Paul, each spouse's body belonged to the other, and the satisfaction of the marriage debt was second only to procreation among the legitimate motives for sexual intercourse. There was considerable disagreement among medieval theologians over the degree of sin involved in the satisfaction of one's own urges or the pursuit of sexual pleasure for its own sake. St Thomas Aquinas recognised that physical intercourse was conducive to a 'certain sweet relationship' between spouses, and some moralists distinguished between the man who enjoyed his wife with matrimonial affection and he who took her with impersonal lust. Some humanists, especially Erasmus, took a positive view of intercourse as a means of bringing partners together and strengthening love. They quietly abandoned the medieval Church's elaborate attempts to decide exactly when it was sinful. In these two respects, English Protestants tended to follow them, but they continued to fear that the marriage bed, pure and undefiled when rightly used, might be abused to satisfy brute lust. Both Catholic and Protestant clergy taught the need for moderation, and some Protestants specified periods of abstinence, though their prohibitions were not as extensive or rigorous as those upheld by the medieval Church. How far ecclesiastical precepts affected lay attitudes in this area at any period it is impossible to know. But the distinction between blind lust and true love in intercourse can also be found in secular romantic literature.[19]

For the most vivid evidence of the actual experience of conjugal love we must turn to intimate documents which tell us most about the propertied classes. They survive in greatest quantity from the second half of our period. But the outstanding Paston and Stonor letters of the fifteenth century not only suggest that marriages varied greatly in their quality but also demonstrate the reality of marital love for the more fortunate. There are clear expressions of wifely solicitude, anxiety to hear news, and sadness at being left alone. Spouses sometimes looked forward to talking to each other, and recalled or anticipated the pleasure of being in bed together. Salutations, for reasons already mentioned, tended to be somewhat formal; yet even the churlish John Paston I once addressed his wife as 'Myn owne dere souereyn lady', while his daughter-in-law Margery could abandon convention to call her husband 'Myne owyn swete hert'. By the 1530s, correspondence was more overtly affectionate. Lord and Lady Lisle were to each other 'Mine own sweet heart' and 'My very heart root', and longed for each other's company when they were apart. Both complained of how hard they found it to get to sleep on their own. Lady Lisle begged her husband to write to her in his own hand of secret things, for two lines of his writing would be more comfort to her than a hundred of another man's. In the following decade the correspondence of the staple merchant John Johnson and his wife was characterised by conjugal endearments of great freshness and variety, apparently complete mutual confidence and a shared sense of humour. From the early seventeenth century, the letters of Endymion Porter to his wife Olive alternate between the sublime and the mundane, between remonstrance, appeasement and affectionate effusion, between high seriousness and robust fun. The Norfolk gentleman Thomas Knyvett would wish himself in bed with his 'Sweete Hart & honybloude', or in her 'pretty little Armes'. He would send her 'a kiss an hower long'. He was refreshed by her 'wholsome advise and comfort' and told her '. . . I am nobody without thee, but altogether out of my Ellement, wanting thy companye'. Surviving correspondence of that time is sufficiently abundant to show that in many other marriages expectations were high, emotional demands extensive, mutual involvement deep, and shared interests and sense of humour very important.[20]

Among diarists, Samuel Pepys stands unrivalled in the intimacy of his portrayal of marriage. He delighted to record amorous play, intimate conversations and shared aspirations. In his wife's absences, Pepys was sad and lonely. In October 1662 he blessed God for their increasing happiness together. Pepys was not only convinced of the reality of married love but also aware of the variety of matrimonial experience. In 1663 the Pepyses believed that they enjoyed each other's company better than other couples did. Samuel noted that a couple at a wedding had behaved like people who had married for convenience, with none of the 'kindness nor bridall respect' that there had been in his own marriage. Pepys's adultery does not call this early love in question. Rather does it underline the fact that the Pepyses lacked many of the things which might have helped keep another man in harness when faced with the trying combination of strong sexual drives and wifely illness: children, shared piety, a joint economic enterprise and well-knit groups of kindred on both sides.[21]

The more serious or narrower purposes of other diarists and autobiographers did not allow much space for recording pleasurable intimacies. Yet many of them wrote of their spouses with deep appreciation. Oliver Heywood thought his first partner 'as loving a wife as ever lay in any mans bosome' and claimed that no couple had had 'so much comfort in each other and so little discontent, as we had in that sixe years we were togather' (1655–61). In 1649 Anthony Ashley Cooper smarted under the loss of a wife who had been not only beautiful, pious and wise, but also 'the most sweet, affectionate, and observant wife in the world'.[22] According to Lucy Hutchinson, no man had 'had a greater passion for a woman' than her husband, 'nor a more honourable esteeme of a wife', while Lady Fanshawe, whose husband had fought on the opposite side in the civil war, wrote one of the period's most eloquent descriptions of married happiness:

Glory be to God we never had but one mind throughout our lives, our souls were wrapped up in each other, our aims and designs one, our loves one, and our resentments one. We so studied one the other that we knew each other's mind by our looks; whatever was real happiness, God gave it me in him.[23]

A humbler autobiographer, the seaman Edward Barlow, thought that in his marriage true love had made up for lack of means. Had he married another woman with £1,000 he could never have met with one more deserving his love and respect. The importance in marriage of affection as well as material considerations is evident in some of Richard Gough's comments on seventeenth-century Myddle.[24]

After the mid-sixteenth century, classical and humanist influences made it possible to use funeral inscriptions to express grief and celebrate the personal qualitites of the deceased, purposes to which late medieval funerary art had allowed relatively little scope. Epitaphs now stressed the length of time which husband and wife had spent together, celebrated their mutual love and catalogued the conjugal virtues. Husbands and wives had been dear or most dear to each other, their marriages unions of hearts and souls.[25]

Married love clearly existed in practice and was highly valued as an ideal. We cannot say how typical it was. Perhaps it became commoner among the propertied classes with the gradual extension of freedom of choice in the second half of our period. Yet for some this perhaps brought with it an unsettling rise in expectations which were not always easy to satisfy. Contemporaries were often right in thinking that a strong affection could develop within carefully arranged marriages. It is also impossible to assess the actual degree of mutuality in married love. The spinster Mary Astell, looking with tart detachment at women's experience of marriage at the very end of our period, believed that a man typically gained in his wife a submissive companion whose task it was to make herself agreeable and to heal the wounds he had received from other people's opposition or neglect.[26] The notion that marriage occupies a more central place in the lives of women than those of men, and that they usually invest in it far more patience and tender consideration, is one that has remained popular among feminists down to the present day.

Marriage as economic and social partnership

According to the conventional image, marriage was a partnership in which each member had separate roles, 'the man to get, to trauaile abroad, to defende: the wife, to saue that which is gotten, to tarrie at home to distribute that which commeth of the husbandes labor . . . and to keepe all at home neat and cleane'.[27] The husband enjoyed a superior position as head of the household, and the main responsibility for dealings outside it rested on him. Yet the wife had her own domain, which embraced the kitchen, the garden, the care of small children and the cure of minor ailments. The extent to which this delineation of separate roles mirrored reality varied from one socio-economic group to another. In almost all marriages each sex had an important contribution to make. But in some partnerships these contributions were closely integrated, while in others they were complementary but separate.

Among the nobility and gentry, a husband's major preoccupations included the efficient management and augmentation of his estate. But local administration, politics and the defence of his interests through litigation often necessitated long absences from home, during which, especially before the seventeenth century, he very often went without his wife's company. The multifarious responsibilities of a conscientious gentlewoman were carefully recorded in the diary of Lady Margaret Hoby (1599–1605). In the house she span and wound yarn, dyed wool, mended and sorted linen, carried out a wide variety of kitchen tasks, supervised the making of rushlights, discharged household bills, drew accounts and paid the servants. The garden was her province. She was probably the only readily available source of medical and surgical advice in her neighbourhood, and often tended sick tenants and neighbours. She also took a very close and extensive interest in the running of the estate. The degree of control her husband allowed her in this area may have been due to the fact that she brought it to him. Yet it is also clear from the Paston, Plumpton and Johnson letters that when their husbands were absent, wives were expected to take a major part in estate administration, including the levying of rents, the sale of produce and the making of necessary repairs. Paston and Plumpton wives were actively involved in the defence of estates against attack. Given the weighty responsibilities so often assumed by wives, it is hardly surprising that some of them aspired to take an equal or even dominant part in decision-making. Isabel, wife of the first James Lord Berkeley (c. 1394–1463), went to London to tend their lawsuits while he held Berkeley Castle. Naming those whom he should most distrust, she told him to keep well all about him till she came home and warned him to enter into no negotiations without her. In Elizabeth's reign Lady Katherine Berkeley aimed to rule her husband's affairs both at home and abroad and to be kept fully informed of all their details. When women left home, there was sometimes a partial reversal of roles as husbands temporarily took over the direction of the household and the supervision of domestic staff.[28]

The growth of civil peace, better means of transport, and the improvement of estate management, would all in the long run make it less necessary for wives to remain at home when their husbands went away. More time spent together was accompanied by a more marked restriction of women to their domestic sphere. Yet this trend was temporarily interrupted during and after the civil war, when husbands' enforced absences often placed the burden of estate management in their wives' hands for longer periods than usual. The Norfolk gentleman Thomas Knyvett told his wife: 'I knowe I cannot have a Better steward then thy selfe to mannage our affaiers.' The wives of royalists in prison or exile often came to London to sue for the lifting of sequestrations and the arrangement of terms of composition.[29]

On the farm, the heavier work in the fields belonged primarily to the husband. To the wife, according to an account written in Henry VIII's reign, fell the care of house, children, garden and the yard where cows were milked, pigs and poultry fed, as well as such indoor tasks as spinning and the making of butter and malt. But in time of need her work might include even heavy field tasks such as driving the plough or loading wains. She travelled outside the farm to take corn to the mill and produce to the market, and to buy all things necessary for the household.[30] The male and female spheres, though largely separate, overlapped. This was also true in Lancashire in the 1670s, where, so William Stout recalled, his mother had not only been fully employed in the house and in dressing corn for the market but also in the fields in hay and corn harvests, along with his father and the servants. The critical importance of the housewife's contribution to the farm's economy was brought out by Thomas Tusser's remarks that 'husbandrie weepeth, Where huswiferie sleepeth', and by the comments of Robert Furse on his Devon yeomen ancestors and of Richard Gough on the families of Myddle. Indeed a farmer could hardly do without a wife, for no servant could accomplish her special combination of tasks. Between the farmer and his wife there had to be complete mutual trust and confidence.[31]

When a man combined a craft with the running of his farm, the degree of integration between the tasks performed by different members of the family could be especially close, though this of course depended on the nature and organisation of the process. It was common, for example, for the wives of yeomen and husbandmen who ·were also weavers to be employed in spinning and carding to help keep the loom supplied.[32]

The growth of dependence on wages affected not only the cohesion of the family partnership but also its internal balance. The labouring cottager had to quit his home during the day to work for an employer, leaving his wife on her own to look after house, children and perhaps a smallholding. A readiness on the husband's part to travel in search of seasonal work was a condition of survival for many poor families. In bad times, the distinction between the fruitless quest and the abandonment of wife and children became increasingly blurred, and the wife was often left dependent on her own resources. The smaller the holding, the more important it became for the wife too to be mobilised as a wage-earner. The later medieval period of low population and high demand for labour was particularly favourable to the female worker. Women worked with their sickles at harvest time; some even did heavy work later reserved for men and received men's wages. The growth in the labour supply from the early sixteenth century onwards and the development of agricultural specialisation tended to push women into less skilled and less well-paid work and widened the gap between male and female earnings. The gradual spread of the scythe, for which greater strength was required, reduced women's chances of sharing in the better-paid harvest work. Increasing numbers of poor women in the countryside became dependent on spinning and carding for wages. Those who relied on this sort of work for their living were competing in a swollen market. Their wages were often barely enough for their own subsistence. The couple dependent on wages paid by different employers, with no common assets beyond a hovel and a patch of ground, stood at the opposite end of the rural spectrum from the farmer and his wife working on their holding in closely integrated partnership.[33]

Economic partnership between man and woman grew increasingly precarious towards the lower end of the social scale, yet it was to be found even at its very bottom. A wide variety of criminals relied upon their womenfolk (to whom they were customarily bound in unofficial and often temporary 'marriages') to spy out the land, bring food to their hiding places and to stow stolen goods. Often the woman, more plausible in begging alms, more deft in picking pockets, was the main 'breadwinner' in such partnerships.[34]

It is impossible to generalise about wives' position in towns both because of the enormous variety in the organisation of different trades and industries and because of the paucity of descriptions of their working day. Entry by apprenticeship to all but a tiny minority of skilled crafts was barred to women. On the other hand widows commonly continued their husbands' businesses, at least temporarily, which suggests that they must have gained some understanding of their operation. In early sixteenth-century Oxford, agreements with apprentices were commonly made by husbands and wives together. But how closely were they involved in their husbands' manual work? It may well have fallen to them to see that apprentices were working properly, especially during husbands' temporary absences. In some late medieval towns women seem to have worked as weavers, to judge from a number of prohibitions issued by urban authorities, though it is hard to know how typical such participation was. Some crafts, however, demanded a degree of technical knowledge and skill which only well-educated women whose time was not taken up with the care of house and children would have had the opportunity to acquire. Others, such as the building trades, took husbands away from home.[35]

In urban society the economic co-operation of husband and wife probably came closest to being a full working partnership in small-scale trade, retail shopkeeping and in certain branches of provisioning, particularly brewing and baking. The growth of large-scale breweries would in time reduce women's participation. On the other hand the enormous growth of London, where restrictions on retail trade were relatively weak, and the great growth in the number and variety of shops in towns large and small tended to improve women's opportunities.[36]

Independent or semi-independent craftsmen or retailers were, however, always outnumbered in bigger towns by journeymen and labourers who had to leave home to work. There was no question in their case of couples working together as integrated units of production. A survey of the poor inhabitants of Norwich undertaken in about 1570 demonstrates that both husband and wife had to work if they possibly could in order to avoid destitution; more than 86 per cent of the women listed in the census aged twenty-one or more were employed. But only a small minority of husbands and wives were engaged in similar or complementary work.[37]

The lives of husbands and wives in the burgeoning professional classes tended to conform to the pattern of separate roles. Samuel Pepys's diary gives us an incomparably vivid picture of one professional household, though one somewhat atypical because of Mrs Pepys's childlessness and comparatively small domestic responsibilities. Pepys entered a different world when he shut his office door behind him, and there is little evidence that he discussed his work with his wife Elizabeth. But she was socially useful to him: she helped him entertain his colleagues and superiors and once gave him 'very good and rationall advice' on his behaviour towards his patron Lord Sandwich.[38]

Among the clergy, one of the largest of professional groups, there were considerable differences in life-style. By the end of Elizabeth's reign the great majority of the beneficed men had taken wives. Married men were more likely to have their households run efficiently and to fulfil their duty of hospitality. Well-remunerated clergy were often able to devote themselves to prayer, preaching and pastoral work while their wives looked after the household. In 1588, Richard Rogers, minister at Wethersfield (Essex), reflected that the loss of his wife in childbirth would among other things cause him considerable material loss, and, by involving him in running the household and caring for their children, force him to neglect his

studies. But many clergy were part-time farmers whose wives helped
them work their glebe. In addition wives often helped rural incumbents gather their tithes, sometimes earning in the process the abuse
of unwilling parishioners.[39]

Leisure and social life

Married couples spent a great deal of their leisure together, either
in company or alone, despite the existence of sports and pastimes
proper to each sex and the importance in social life of groups of men
and women friends. (Groups of female 'gossips' could be a potent
force in the life of the local community, and on occasion they co-
operated in order to punish or put pressure on errant men.)[40]
Husbands and wives frequented dances, fairs, plays, alehouses and
taverns together, though the rowdy amusements of the alehouse and
the village green faced increasing hostility during the early seventeenth century from those who were concerned to tighten social
discipline. Those who could afford to do so entertained or visited
their friends. The shared pleasure which an Elizabethan citizen and
his wife derived from giving a good dinner was well portrayed in a
delightful dialogue by Claudius Hollyband, who captured not only
the wife's pride in her cookery but also her affectionate irritation with
her husband ('my lover') for his late arrival with their guests and his
failure to keep their plates full. Food and drink formed the heart of
entertainment, but were often accompanied or followed by dancing
or music. Women often helped to make music as well as listen to it.
The madrigals, lute songs and chamber music which burgeoned in
the sixteenth century were well suited to the needs of small audiences
and domestic gatherings. Samuel Pepys attended a number of mixed
musical parties; one, held in December 1665, brought him into what
he called 'the best company for Musique I ever was in my life'; the
exquisite quality of the singing and the beauty of the ladies combined
to give him intense pleasure. Men and women joined in a number
of indoor games. Card games, played for stakes in the upper ranks
of society by ladies as well as gentlemen, were, despite the disapproval of the pious, widely popular as a pastime both for couples and
for mixed groups. Other diversions suitable for mixed company
included chess, draughts, shuttlecock, telling stories and a variety of
guessing games. Out of doors, women often joined in hunting. The
art of intelligent and amusing conversation in mixed company,
expounded by Castiglione, was one for which an increasing number
of gentlewomen were equipped by a broad general education, wide
reading and varied experience. The Elizabethan musician and autobiographer Thomas Whythorne recalled how a lady whose children
he had taught had discoursed both of religious controversies and
profane matters, of life in country, city and court.[41]

Married people might not wish to spend all their leisure in the company of others. In 1441 the free servants of the bakers of London complained that although most of them were married, they could spend little time at home with their wives. Some of the fuller diaries kept by members of the literate minority in the second half of the period suggest that reading aloud, taking the air and making conversation were the commonest conjugal pastimes. More often than not the husband read to the wife, both perhaps because he could read more fluently and because she could work with her needle while listening. The Elizabethan writer Robert Greene imagined a couple who, to pass the evening together, 'fell to pleasant chatte between them selues, some time discoursing of what came first in their heads, with *Pro & Contra* . . . other while with merie tales, and tending to some good end without either lasciuiousnesse or scurrilitie, thus euer they passed away the night'. Pepys delighted in his conversations with his wife about her clothes, their social advancement, improvements to their house, plans to entertain their friends and their impressions of their acquaintances.[42]

Religion in the life of the married couple

The husband was expected to be the dominant partner in the religious life of the household. There he was bishop. Some early fifteenth-century instructions for a devout and literate householder suggested that at meal times (i.e. when the whole household was gathered together), he should say grace and expound something in English which might edify his wife and the others present. A special intimacy between husband and wife was indicated by the suggestion that he make a cross of five breadcrumbs on the table which she alone could see, though she was not given any special responsibilities. But the author of *Dives and Pauper* made both parents responsible for the religious instruction of their children and in this he was probably setting out the normal practice of pious late medieval families.[43]

Some of the humanists, and, following them, Protestant writers of Christian counsel laid more emphasis on the religious life of the family and household than most of their Catholic predecessors. The husband was the superior partner in religious duties. It was for the husband, wrote Thomas Becon in his *Catechism*, to give his wife such instruction as was necessary for the health of her soul and he cited with approval St Paul's admonition, 'Let the woman learn in silence with all subjection.' But mutual help in spiritual progress was after the Reformation increasingly stressed as the transcendent purpose which gave shape and meaning to the lives of the married couple. Husband and wife were to 'conferre, read, pray, confesse, and give thanks' together; share in the instruction of children and servants; confide their spiritual difficulties to each other, and look to one another for wholesome counsel and admonition.[44]

The regime of regular household prayers, catechising and readings was never generally instituted. Complaints of its neglect, often because of the opposition of husband or wife, were numerous. Even the pious found it a hard struggle to keep religion at the heart of their marriages. To Richard Rogers his private prayers with his wife were a source of great satisfaction, but in February 1589 he had to record sadly that 'the convenant betwixt us in usual privat praying alone and daily stirreinge upp to the practize of godlines is much neglected'. Perhaps it was given to relatively few to experience such moments of ecstasy as those recorded by the nonconformist minister Oliver Heywood, who in March 1678 described the 'meltings of heart' he had had in prayer with his wife. Even he had to admit in October 1679 that God had helped her heart while his was dull and dead.[45]

One responsibility belonged to the wife in the first place, namely the early religious education of children, upon which the reformers laid increased stress. Some writers thought that the wife could assume the conduct of family prayers in her husband's absence, or if he showed himself careless of his duty or incapable of performing it. Even his tacit or grudging permission was enough, in the opinion of Daniel Rogers. If however he utterly refused to allow her to take his place, she must not disobey.[46]

The husband was God's representative in the family, but he was never the wife's only source of guidance. The pious could seek counsel at confession or, after the Reformation, from one of those godly Protestant ministers such as Edward Dering (1540–76), who played a part as spiritual directors of the godly female laity at least as important as that taken by their Catholic predecessors. The importance of the doctrinal guidance and intellectual stimulus which Lady Margaret Hoby derived from her young chaplain Mr Rhodes is amply evident from her diary. Women were among the most attentive listeners to sermons, and in 1650 Sir Ralph Verney believed that 'multitudes' of women had made notes on them. Nor were women always uncritical recipients of what they heard, as William Gouge found to his cost when his remarks on matrimonial property aroused angry reaction from the female members of his London congregation. After the Reformation the Bible assumed increasing importance in the life of the pious lay woman. Literacy was far less widespread among women than among men. But they had shown a remarkable capacity for memorising large chunks of the English Bible even when it had been a proscribed book, and substantial portions of the Scriptures were now incorporated in the Church's cycle of lessons and thus made available to all.[47]

But the Scriptures did not give much guidance to the wife faced with an ungodly husband. St Peter's instruction to wives so to behave themselves that their chaste and reverent behaviour would win the hearts of their husbands even if the latter did not obey God's word did not seem to give much encouragement to overt resistance. Both Catholic and Protestant writers thought that wives should not obey commands directly contrary to God's word. But it was unclear exactly how far legitimate disobedience extended, and advice on this point was sometimes equivocal or even self-contradictory. William Gouge was unusually clear-cut in specifying that the wife should not comply with commands to go to mass or a stage play, play at dice, 'prostitute her body to vncleanness, to goe garishly and whorishly attired' or sell by short measure, and even he insisted that a wife must usually obey an ungodly husband.[48]

Adoption of a militant and embattled faith allowed women exceptional scope for missionary activity within the family, whether in co-operation with, or, sometimes, in opposition to, their husbands, for the leaders of proselytising minorities were readier than established Churches to use the services of normally subordinate members of society. Women played a vital part in communicating Lollard beliefs to children, servants and, on occasion, to their menfolk. A number of women owned Lollard books and lent or passed them on to other people. Contemporaries, including Bishop Pecock of Chichester (d. c. 1460) noted the presumptuous confidence in their own learning which Bible reading inspired in women. Some Lollards even thought women capable of the priesthood. In emergent English Protestantism, too, women played an important part. Two queens, Anne Boleyn and Catherine Parr, provided protection or patronage. Anne Askew in 1546, and a number of other married women under Mary I, died as witnesses to the Protestant faith either in defiance of, or without a lead from, their husbands. In some parishes, such as Stoke-by-Nayland in Suffolk, women played a vital part in keeping congregations alive during the Marian persecution. On both sides the importance of the female contribution was recognised: Bishop Bonner's commissary emphasised in 1556 the need to compel men to bring their wives to church, while the martyrs themselves addressed a large proportion of their letters to women.[49]

In Elizabeth I's reign, women assisted in both the survival and the rejuvenation of the old faith. Their power in the kitchen enabled conservative women to maintain the Catholic regime of fast and feast. Priests often chose to work through wives; John Gerard discussed with Sir Everard Digby's wife 'the best way of catching her husband in St Peter's net'. The phrase captures admirably the atmosphere of loyal conspiracy in which a solicitous wife joined for the sake of her husband's soul. Catholic mothers sometimes secured their children for the Church in face of the apathy or hostility of their husbands. Many women kept the faith alive in their households while their husbands attended the services of the established Church, until the spread of the practice of compounding for recusancy fines in the seventeenth century removed the major incentive for the continuance of this practice.[50]

It was in membership or even leadership of the radical sects of the mid-seventeenth century that women achieved the most striking expression of their religious feelings. The principle that the individual's admission to the congregation depended on his or her spiritual fitness enhanced their position in relation to their menfolk in many of the sects. Women helped to found many separatist congregations and were often numerically preponderant among their members. Among the Quakers, women were in many places the first preachers, fulfilling Joel's forecast that the daughters of Israel would prophesy. Other women engaged in polemical writing, composed ecstatic verses or even claimed to be able to perform miracles. Many disobeyed or abandoned ungodly husbands. Less spectacular but far more widespread was the heightened individual religious consciousness diffused among ordinary people. John Bunyan's chance encounter, during his daily work, with 'three or four poor women sitting at a door in the sun, and talking about the things of God' was a milestone on his road to conversion.[51]

One may question whether female attitudes to dissident religion underwent a major qualitative change during this period. The scale of the mid-seventeenth-century response and the extravagance of some of its manifestations were due to the intensity of the upheaval which had shaken English society and the collapse of normal controls rather than to a fundamental change in female attitudes. Even among the minority which experienced female religious radicalism it did not bring about a major redistribution of power within the family. Women unable to gain their husbands' co-operation or at least tolerance repeatedly had to seek fulfilment outside it. Rigid patriarchy reasserted itself in the later history of some of the sects. In the long run this period's assertion of women's intellectual equality was to be a more important legacy to feminism than its religious radicalism.[52]

The breakdown of marriage

Marital disharmony and unhappiness were very widespread according to contemporary observers, indeed commoner than mutual affection or contentment in the view of some. Among the readers at whom William Whateley aimed his *Bride Bush* (1617) were those who found marriage 'a little hell'. *The Homily of the State of Matrimony* remarked how few marriages there were 'without chidings, brawlings, tauntings, repentings, bitter cursings, and fightings'. Such strife was a major cause of anxiety, especially to women, among the patients of Richard Napier in the early seventeenth century. Matrimonial unhappiness was often attributed either to child matches and the effects of wardship, or, more commonly, to rash, impulsive choices, frequently inspired by physical infatuation, made without thought for the future. But most important of all, the foolish appetite for domination, the 'wicked vice of stubborn will and self love' and failure to adapt to partners' characters and temperaments or to make sufficient allowance for their failings were most frequently blamed in analyses of open discord. Marriage was hard work, and breaches were to be avoided only by mutual consideration, patience and self-restraint.[53] Diaries often reveal husbands' worries about the deterioration of their relations with their wives and their efforts to check the process. In December 1588 Richard Rogers was concerned about 'some abateing of the affection which had been' even 'though it was no such thing as was noted of any, or so much as betwixt our selves' and reproached himself for waiting a week or more before doing anything about it. Another minister, Henry Newcome, driven to his wits' end by his wife's bad temper, wrote in July 1652 that after four years of marriage he did not know how to humour her. 'When she is patient', he wrote, 'peace is so sweet to me that I dare not speak lest I should lose it.' The marital difficulties recorded in 1647–49 by Adam Eyre, a childless Yorkshire yeoman, seem to have been exacerbated by his wife's temper, sharpened by her ailments, and by his drinking and indebtedness, from which she refused to extricate him. Eyre was tempted to separate from her. But on New Year's Day 1648, he promised her 'to become a good husband to her for the tyme to come', though his prayer that they should leave off all their old contentions was, alas, not fulfilled.[54]

A very small minority of married people broke their bonds. Annulments, which only the church courts could grant, were rare. A pre-contract with another person was the commonest ground. The prohibited degrees of kinship (reduced in 1540) at no stage offered an easy way out of marriage, contrary to what has often been supposed. Surprisingly few annulments or renunciations of matches made by force or under the age of consent were recorded in the diocesan courts which served the majority of people of middling rank. In Tudor times they seem to have been commoner in the north than elsewhere, and especially in the sprawling north-western diocese of Chester. Some Protestant clergy thought that England should follow the example of the continental reformed churches and grant divorce for adultery, allowing the innocent party to remarry. In 1552, when reform of the ecclesiastical law was in prospect, the marquess of Northampton, who had been granted a separation on account of his first wife's adultery, secured an Act of parliament upholding his second marriage. Others acted without official sanction, and in 1595 such unauthorised second marriages were said to be common. But canon 107 of 1604 made the Church's hostility towards these unions quite clear, and the ecclesiastical divorce law was never reformed during this period. Not until 1670 was another Act ratifying a peer's second marriage passed, not until 1698 the first true divorce by Act of parliament.[55]

In the absence of divorce in the modern sense, the Church could only offer separation from bed and board, in the hope of ultimate reconciliation, on the grounds of adultery, cruelty or continual quarrels. But even these were relatively rare. In two years between 1553 and 1555, the consistory court of the bishop of London handled only about seven suits of this type. If a judge decreed a separation, he might order the division of the couple's goods or the payment to an innocent wife of alimony, usually a third, or at least a quarter of the annual value of the husband's estate.[56]

Adultery was widely held to be a much more serious offence in the wife than it was in the husband. This 'double standard' influenced the common law, which condemned the eloping wife to lose her dower or jointure, while providing no comparable penalty for the errant husband. The commonest explanation offered by contemporaries was that wifely adultery created a risk of inheritance by a bastard. Not content with this, subsequent writers have found the underlying motivation either in an awareness that lust and love are more closely associated in women than they are in men, or in a deep-seated male desire for absolute property in women. Neither the Protestant nor the Catholic Church ever accepted the double standard. Many authors held that the woman sinned more in respect of the effects on family life, both sexes sinned equally in respect of conjugal fidelity, while the man sinned more in respect of the responsibility to be expected of the individual. Belonging to the stronger sex, he was better equipped to resist temptation. During the seventeenth century, the double standard was a target of feminist polemic. Samuel Pepys, a jealous but ultimately unfaithful husabnd, effectively conceded its injustice in the secrecy of his diary.[57]

Patience and forgiveness were recommended to the wronged partner in some literary explorations of the theme of infidelity. This advice was, not surprisingly, addressed to wives in particular, but, by the later sixteenth century, husbandly forbearance was being depicted too, notably in Robert Greene's *Conversion of an English Courtezan* (1592). The husband portrayed by Greene, discovering his wife's adultery with his closest friend, set out, not to avenge himself, but to recover both his friend and his wife. His final reproach for her betrayal of a marriage in which they had shared 'coequal favours . . . as true loves' was delivered more in sorrow than in anger.[58]

How common adultery was among different social classes and how it was regarded in practice it is difficult to say. Something of its extent among the nobility may be gleaned from the incidence of illegitimacy in their offspring, though this is a somewhat crude and unreliable pointer, since some of these could have been conceived before their marriages. John Smyth could find only one recognised bastard in the history of the Berkeley family, begotten by Maurice Lord Berkeley when he was lieutenant of Calais Castle under Henry VIII. Even though Maurice never allowed his illegitimate son to come to England during his lifetime, Smyth commended his wife for her discreet forbearance. A number of mid-Tudor peers kept mistresses and provided for bastard children in their wills. There was a sharp fall in the proportion of known illegitimate children of the British nobility in the first half of the seventeenth century, which perhaps reflected the growing influence of a strongly Protestant piety, or at least a reluctance to flout its standards openly. After the middle of the century there was a renewed relaxation of sexual morality among the aristocracy, especially at about the time of the Restoration. In the upper classes, the rigour with which the double standard was applied in practice depended among other things upon the husband's own behaviour and the strength of family feeling in favour of the wife. In 1617, Sir Thomas Wentworth wrote to his cousin Christopher Danby on hearing that the latter had disowned his wife's last child. Most people, he pointed out, believed Danby's wife innocent of the adultery with which he charged her. However plainly the matter were proved, men would condemn Danby both for his own lapses and for refusing her the 'rites of marriage'.[59]

The incidence of adultery lower down the social scale is even more difficult to chart than it is among the nobility. Adulterous acts were supposed to be presented in the church courts, but large numbers of offences almost certainly went unreported, even if they came to light within the community. Neighbours sometimes tried to dissipate damaging rumours and keep couples together. Alternatively, they humiliated with their own informal punishments those who too openly flouted official standards of morality. Since law and opinion alike made it difficult for the married man to disown his wife's children, unmarried women, whose children might become a burden on the community, were more likely to be presented to the courts. Depositions taken during court proceedings give the impression that the reactions of individual husbands and wives to their partners' adultery varied very greatly. Some men, either through fear or indifference, turned a blind eye to their wives' infidelities. Women for their part sometimes sought judicial separations for adultery as well as men, although far less often. Thomas Harman's fictional account (1566) of how a woman's gossips helped her punish her errant husband with a severe beating probably reflected a real and widespread female refusal to accept the double standard.[60]

Physical violence was the other major ground for judicial separation, though in assessing its severity much seems to have been left to judges'discretion. The common law allowed the husband to chastise his wife, and wife-beating was the subject of much crude popular verse and anecdote. But it was generally condemned as shameful by the writers of Christian counsel save as a last response to extreme provocation, and checked or punished in individual cases by church courts and some municipal tribunals. And, whatever happened within the house, depositions make it clear that neighbours or passers-by felt it necessary to restrain an angry husband when he tried to attack his wife in street or shop. It is only fair to add that some women were capable of giving as good as they got. Husbands occasionally complained to the courts of the violence and other ill treatment they had suffered at their wives' hands.[61]

Privately agreed separations were thought to be very common in the later sixteenth and early seventeenth centuries, and may well have outnumbered those decreed by the courts. Subsequent litigation sometimes brought such private agreements to light. It was probably in the 1560s, for example, that Thomas Bennett of All Cannings (Wilts.) left his wife 'for that they colde not agree and for that she wolde not be obediente', after drawing up certain covenants concerning their separation. Lower down the social scale, men sometimes sold their wives. One man was summoned to answer for this offence as early as 1486, and a trickle of cases has been traced in the later sixteenth and seventeenth centuries, but the practice seems to have much commoner, or at least more widely reported, in the eighteenth.[62]

For the poor, desertion was the simplest escape route from marital responsibilities, though one much more readily open to men than to women. Over $8\frac{1}{2}$ per cent of the married women covered by a survey of the poor inhabitants of the city of Norwich in about 1570 had been abandoned by their husbands. Economic crises swelled the stream of desertions. The gradually tightening administration of the Poor Law in the early seventeenth century and the growing reluctance of parishes to allow a settlement to immigrants forced some of the married poor to live apart. Desperate and broken men went to fill the ranks of vagrants and petty criminals, of whose liaisons, contemporaries agreed, barely one in a hundred had been celebrated in church. Such unions were readily dissolved with or without mutual consent. Parliament recognised, though hardly began to tackle, the problem of unstable marriages when it passed in 1604 a statute imposing the death penalty on bigamists who, it said, ran out of one county into another, or into places where they were not known, before remarrying.[63]

Conclusion

In the official image of marriage sustained by a male-dominated society, woman was the subordinate partner. The Scriptures and subsequent Christian teaching emphasised her duty of obedience, while also stressing the husbandly obligation of tender consideration. Woman was thought to be man's inferior in intellect and virtue. This notion was challenged, but with limited practical consequences. The common law vested control of matrimonial property in the husband, though dower, inheritance and settlements gave many wives in the propertied classes some safeguards, bargaining power or even a degree of independence. In practice the real distribution of power within marriage was very often determined to a great extent by personal character, and actual partnerships could be much less patriarchal than ideal images might suggest.

Mutual affection was generally recognised to be desirable or even essential in marriage, and there is plenty of evidence of its existence in letters, diaries, autobiographies and epitaphs. Christian thought assigned the husband a superior role in it, but in literature and secular analysis it was more freely recognised as a force which modified male supremacy in marriage or even made the husband in some sense subject to his wife.

The wife was conventionally supposed to occupy a separate but subordinate sphere in the family economy. Yet although the tasks performed by husband and wife were largely separate, the overlap between their responsibilities was often large, and their co-operation very close, especially on the farm. The separation of spheres became more marked with the growth of wage- and salary-earning groups. At every social level man and wife shared much of their leisure.

Established Churches upheld the husband's supremacy in household religion, while assigning the wife some share in his responsibilities, especially after the Reformation. Protestants also emphasised the importance of the private prayers of the married couple. The unprecedented religious upheavals of this period encouraged all sorts of subordinate groups in society, including wives, to espouse a different faith and to take proselytising initiatives. But when husbands and wives came into conflict in this area, the result was not usually to alter the distribution of power within the family. Rather did the wife have to seek her religious fulfilment outside it.

For many, marriage was unhappy. Sixteenth- and seventeenth-century pastoral analysis blamed avoidable failures in mutual adjustment. Expectations appear to have been higher than historians sometimes allow. Yet there was for most of this period no divorce in the modern sense. Perhaps this fact weighed most heavily on wives. The common law allowed a man to beat his wife; it punished her adultery but not his. Yet the Church's remedy of judicial separation was available to both and it is wrong to think that contemporary opinion readily condoned the behaviour of the violent or flagrantly unfaithful husband. Marriage was, finally, an unequal partnership, but less unequal, and less different from marriage today, than might at first sight appear.

Notes and references

1.   **P. H. Barnum** (ed.), *Dives and Pauper*, Vol. 1, *Early English Text Society*, **275, 280** (1976, 1980), Pt. 2, 60–2, 65–7; **W. Harrington**, *In This*

Boke are conteyned the Cōmendacions of Matrymony, sig. Aii^v–iii, dated to between 1512 and 1515 by **D. Ramage** in *The Durham Philobiblon*, **1** (1949–55), 69; **L. L. Schücking**, *The Puritan Family: A Social Study from the Literary Sources*, Routledge & Kegan Paul, London, 1969, pp. 20–5; **C. H.** and **K. George**, *The Protestant Mind of the English Reformation*, Princeton UP, 1961, pp. 257–75; **K. M. Davies**, 'Continuity and Change in Literary Advice on Marriage', in **R. B. Outhwaite** (ed.), *Marriage and Society: Studies in the Social History of Marriage*, Europa Publications, London, 1981, pp. 62–3; **M. M. Knappen** (ed.), *Two Elizabethan Puritan Diaries*, American Society of Church History, Chicago, 1933, p. 57; *Certain Sermons or Homilies appointed to be read in Churches in the time of Queen Elizabeth of Famous Memory*, London, 1864, p. 140; **J. C. H. Aveling**, 'Catholic Households in Yorkshire, 1580–1603', *Northern History*, **16** (1980), 100, fn. 35, cites a number of works by famous Protestant divines. 'They all insist that the "gift of continency", though rare, is higher and more desirable than matrimony.'

2. Ephesians 5:22–4; **I. Maclean**, *The Renaissance Notion of Woman: A Study in the Fortunes of Scholasticism and Medical Science in European Intellectual Life*, Cambridge UP, 1980, pp. 7–14, 30–1, 42–4; **C. S. Kenny**, *The History of the Law of England as to the Effects of Marriage on Property and on the Wife's Legal Capacity*, London, 1879, esp. pp. 71–88; **F. J. Furnivall** (ed.), *Early English Meals and Manners*, *Early English Text Society*, orig. ser., **32** (1868), 185.

3. **T. Gataker**, *Marriage Dvties briefely covched togither; Ovt of Colossians, 3. 18, 19*, London, 1620, pp. 5–17, esp. 11 and 27–30; **S. Clarke**, *A Collection of the Lives of Ten Eminent Divines*, London, 1662, pp. 443–4; W. Gouge, *Of Domesticall Duties, Eight Treatises*, London, 1622, pp. 319–23; **T. Fuller**, *The Holy State and the Profane State*, **M. G. Walten** (ed.), Columbia UP, New York, 1938, Vol. II, pp. 1–2.

4. I Peter 3:7; Gouge, *op. cit.*, epistle dedicatory and pp. 368–9, 373–83; **W. Whateley**, *A Bride Bvsh or, A Direction for Married Persons. Plainely describing the duties common to both, and peculiar to each of them. By performing of which, Marriage shall proove a great helpe to such, as now for want of performing them, doe find it a little hell*, London, 1623 (first edn, 1617), pp. 129–73.

5. Barnum, *op. cit.*, Vol. I, Pt. 2, p. 67; **H. Smith**, *A Preparatiue to Mariage. The summe whereof was spoken at a Contract, and inlarged after*, London, 1591, p. 68; **R. Cawdrey**, *A Godlie Forme of Hovseholde Gouernment: for the Ordering of Private Families, according to the Direction of God's Word*, London, 1600 (first edn 1598), pp. 162–70, 179; **J. Pratt** (ed.), *The Acts and Monuments of John Foxe*, The Religious Tract Society, London, 1877, Vol. VIII, p. 197, **D. Rogers**, *Matrimoniall Honour: or the Mutuall Crowne and comfort of godly, loyall, and chaste Marriage*, London, 1642, pp. 244–51; Whateley, *op. cit.*, pp. 129–30; **T. Becon**, *The Catechism . . . with other pieces written by him in the Reign of King Edward the Sixth*, **J. Ayre** (ed.), *Parker Society*, **11** (1844) 337–9; **C. D'Evelyn** (ed.), *Peter Idley's Instructions to his Son*, Modern Language Association of America, Boston, 1935, p. 102.

6. Barnum, *op. cit.*, Vol. I, Pt. 2, p. 66; Gouge, *op. cit.*, p. 356; Rogers,

op. cit., pp. 264–5; D'Evelyn, *op. cit.*, p. 89; Becon, *op. cit.*, p. 339; Cawdrey, *op. cit.*, p. 88; Gataker, *op. cit.*, pp. 15–16.

7. Cf. Davies, *op. cit.*

8. *The Colloquies of Erasmus*, trans. **C. R. Thompson**, Univ. of Chicago Press, 1965, pp. 218–23, 270–1; **B. Castiglione**, *The Book of the Courtier*, J. M. Dent & Sons, London, 1928, pp. 176–236; **L. B. Wright**, *Middle-Class Culture in Elizabethan England*, U. of N. Carolina Press, Chapel Hill, 1935, Ch. xiii, 'The Popular Controversy over Woman'; **C. Camden**, *The Elizabethan Woman: A Panorama of English Womanhood, 1540–1640*, Cleaver Hume Press, London, 1952, Ch. ix, 'Certain Controversies over Women'; Maclean, *op. cit.*, pp. 85–6, 89; Wright and Camden describe works published under the names of Ester Sowernam and Rachel Speght.

9. Barnum, *op. cit.*, Vol. I, Pt. 2, pp. 92–3; Maclean, *op. cit.*, pp. 20–7, 55–7.

10. **M. Astell**, *A Serious Proposal to the Ladies, for the Advancement of their True and Greatest Interest*, London, 1697, Vol. I, pp. 12–32; Vol. II, pp. 192, 209–11; **J. Locke**, *The Second Treatise of Government and a Letter Concerning Toleration*, **J. W. Gough** (ed.), Basil Blackwell, Oxford, 1956, p. 41; **Halifax**, *Complete Works*, **J. P. Kenyon**, (ed.), Penguin Books, Harmondsworth, 1969, pp. 277–9.

11. **Sir F. Pollock** and **F. W. Maitland**, *The History of English Law before the Time of Edward I*, reprint of 2nd edn of 1898, Cambridge UP, 1968, Vol. II, pp. 299–300, 404–5, 407–13; Kenny, *op. cit.*, pp. 51, 71–82, 85–7; Anon., *The Lawes Resolutions of Womens Rights*, London, 1632, pp. 147–51, 154–82; Taunton, Somerset Record Office, Phelips MSS DD/PH/224/34; **M. Bateson**, *Borough Customs*, *II*, *Selden Society*, **21** (1906), civ; **V. Sackville-West** (ed.), *The Diary of the Lady Anne Clifford*, W. Heinemann, London, 1923, *passim*: **J. O. Halliwell** (ed.), *The Autobiography and Correspondence of Sir Simonds D'Ewes, Bart.*, London, 1845, Vol. I, pp. 43, 55; **J. M. Shuttleworth** (ed.), *The Life of Edward, First Lord Herbert of Cherbury, written by himself*, Oxford UP, 1976, pp. 40–1.

12. **J. Smyth**, *The Berkeley Manuscripts*, **J. Maclean** (ed.), Bristol and Gloucestershire Archaeological Society, Gloucester, 1883, Vol. II, pp. 142–3; **C. Richmond**, *John Hopton, a Fifteenth Century Suffolk Gentleman*, Cambridge UP, 1981, pp. 117–18; **E. W. Ives**, '"Agaynst taking awaye of Women"; the Inception and Operation of the Abduction Act of 1487', **E. W. Ives, R. J. Knecht** and **S. J. Scarisbrick** (eds), *Wealth and Power in Tudor England: Essays presented to S. T. Bindoff*, Athlone Press, London, 1978, p. 27; Kenny, *op. cit.*, pp. 99–102, 116; **L. Stone**, *The Crisis of the Aristocracy, 1558–1641*, Clarendon Press, Oxford, 1965, p. 635; **G. Davies** (ed.), *Autobiography of Thomas Raymond, and Memoirs of the Family of Guise of Elmore, Gloucestershire, Camden Society*, 3rd ser., **28** (1917), 152–3; **A. Clark**, *Working Life of Women in the Seventeenth Century*, George Routledge & Sons, London, 1919, pp. 151–3; London, Public Record Office, REQ 2/124/56; B. Winchester, *Tudor Family Portrait*, Jonathan Cape, London, 1955, pp. 138–9; **M. E. Finch**, *The Wealth of Five Northants. Families, 1540–1640, Northants. Record Society*, **19** (1956), 26; **R. A. Houlbrooke**, *Church Courts and the People during the English Refor-*

mation, Oxford UP, 1979, pp. 69–70; Harrington, *op. cit.*, sig. d ii^v; Smith, *op. cit.*, pp. 66–7; Whateley, *op. cit.*, pp. 82–3; Gouge, *op. cit.*, pp. 253–5, 291, 299–305 (Gouge, however, stated the common law quite clearly).

13. **N. Davies** (ed.) *Paston Letters and Papers of the Fifteenth Century*, Clarendon Press, Oxford, 1971, 1976, Vol. I, pp. xxxvii–xxxviii, lxxix, 215–329; **M. St Clare Byrne** (ed.), *The Lisle Letters*, Univ. of Chicago Press, 1981, Vol. I, pp. 55–68; **C. L. Kingsford** (ed.), *Stonor Letters and Papers, 1290–1483, Camden Society*, 3rd ser., **29–30** (1919), Vol. I, p. 110, *c*. 1470 ('lowly' address, somewhat rebarbative subsequent remarks); Winchester, *op. cit.*, pp. 83–4: **D. M. Meads** (ed.), *Diary of Lady Margaret Hoby, 1599–1605*, George Routledge & Sons, London, 1930, p. 268; Gouge, *op. cit.*, pp. 283–4.

14. Fuller, *op. cit.*, Vol. II, p. 8; Gouge, *op. cit.*, pp. 281–2, 286; Whateley, *op. cit.*, pp. 194–200; **T. Wright** (ed.), *Songs and Carols, now first printed, from a Manuscript of the Fifteenth Century, Percy Society*, **73** (1847), 26, 86–7; **J. C. D. Smith**, *A Guide to Church Woodcarvings: Misericords and Bench-Ends*, David & Charles, Newton Abbot, 1974, p. 50.

15. **P. Laslett**, *Family Life and Illicit Love in Earlier Generations: Essays in Historical Sociology*, Cambridge UP, 1977, p. 13; **T. H. Hollingsworth**, 'The Demography of the British Peerage', Supplement to *Population Studies*, **18** (1964), 11; **S. L. Thrupp**, *The Merchant Class of Medieval London, 1300–1500*, Univ. of Chicago Press, 1948, pp. 193, 196; Thompson, *op. cit.*, pp. 115, 120–2; cf. **G. A. Guarino** (ed.), *The Albertis of Florence: Leon Battista Albert's Della Famiglia*, Bucknell UP, Lewisburg, 1971, pp. 216–235.

16. *The 'Summa Theologica' of St Thomas Aquinas literally translated by Fathers of the English Dominican Province*, Burns, Oates & Washbourne, London, 1921–23, Vol. XVI, pp. 38–9; Harrington, *op. cit.*, sig. c vi; Barnum, *op. cit.*, Vol. I, Pt. 2, p. 66; Smith, *op. cit.*, p. 56.

17. Gataker, *op. cit.*, p. 5; Rogers, *op. cit.*, pp. 152–3.

18. Maclean, *op. cit.*, pp. 24–5; **T. Smith**, *De Republica Anglorum. The Maner of Gouernement or policie of the Realme of England*, London, 1583, p. 13.

19. Harrington, *op. cit.*, sig. A vi, D ii; Barnum, *op. cit.*, Vol. I, Pt. 2, 58–60, 66; **J. T. Noonan**, *Contraception*, Belknap Press, Cambridge (Mass.), 1966, pp. 246–57, 284–95, 303–12; **St Thomas Aquinas**, *Philosophical Texts*, **T. Gilby** (ed.), Oxford UP, 1951, p. 374; **H. A. Kelly**, *Love and Marriage in the Age of Chaucer*, Cornell UP, Ithaca, pp. 262, 269–73; Thompson, *op. cit.*, pp. 95–6; 124; Gouge, *op. cit.*, pp. 222–3; Whateley, *op. cit.*, pp. 15–26; **J. Taylor**, *The Rule and Exercises of Holy Living*, Longmans, Green & Co., London, 1926, pp. 70–1; **A. V. Judges** (ed.), *The Elizabethan Underworld*, G. Routledge & Sons, London, 1930, pp. 238–9.

20. Davis, *op. cit.*, Vol. I, pp. 134–5, 140, 218–9, 254, 665–6; Kingsford, *op. cit.*, Vol. I, p. 97; Vol. II, pp. 10–11, 14–16, 18, 22, 41, 45, 140; St Clare Byrne, *op. cit.*, Vol. I, pp. 26, 34; Vol. II, p. 353; Vol. V, pp. 272–326, 652–5; Winchester, *op. cit.*, pp. 67–75; **D. Townshend**, *Life and Letters of Mr Endymion Porter: Sometime Gentleman of the Bedchamber to King Charles the First*, T. Fisher Unwin, London, 1897, pp. 17–25, 29, 42, 48–62, 66–9, 74–8, 123–4, 199–200; **B. Schofield**

(ed.), *The Knyvett Letters, 1620–1644, Norfolk Record Society*, **20** (1949), 23, 55, 58, 60, 64, 67, 74, 75, 86, 93, 94, 98, 111, 162.

21. **R. Latham** and **W. Matthews** (eds.), *The Diary of Samuel Pepys: a New and Complete Transcription*, G. Bell & Sons, London, 1970–, Vol. III, p. 234, Vol. IV, pp. 186, 218, 435; Vol. V, pp. 150, 233–4, 307; for account of Pepys's infidelities, see L. Stone, *Family, Sex and Marriage, in England, 1500–1800*, Weidenfeld & Nicolson, London, 1977, pp. 552–61.

22. **J. Horsfall Turner** (ed.), *The Rev. Oliver Heywood, B. A., 1630–1702: his Autobiography, Diaries, Anecdote and Event books*, Brighouse, 1881–85, Vol. I, p. 62; **W. D. Christie**, *A Life of Anthony Ashley Cooper, First Earl of Shaftesbury, 1621–1683*, London, 1871, Vol. I, p. lii.

23. **L. Hutchinson**, *Memoirs of the Life of Colonel Hutchinson, with the fragment of an autobiography of Mrs Hutchinson*, **J. Sutherland** (ed.), Oxford UP, 1973, pp. 10, 32; **H. C. Fanshawe** (ed.), *The Memoirs of Ann Lady Fanshawe*, John Lane, London, 1907, pp. 3, 4, 5, 34–7, 63–4.

24. **B. Lubbock** (ed.), *Barlow's Journal of his life at sea*, Hurst and Blackett, London, 1934, Vol. II, pp. 309–10; **R. Gough**, *The History of Myddle*, **David Hey** (ed.), Penguin Books, Harmondsworth, 1981, pp. 169, 204.

25. Hundreds of such inscriptions survive from this period. For a selection from one county, see **H. T. Morley**, *Monumental Brasses of Berkshire*, Electric Press, Reading, 1924, pp. 55, 103, 129, 133, 137, 167, 169, 187, 199, 203, 213, 223, 245; cf. **R. Lattimore**, *Themes in Greek and Latin Epitaphs*, Univ. of Illinois Press, Urbana, 1942, pp. 271–80.

26. **M. Astell**, *Reflections upon Marriage*, 5th edn, Dublin, 1730 (first edn 1706), pp. 24–5, cited by **M. George**, 'From "Goodwife" to "Mistress": the Transformation of the Female in Bourgeois Culture', *Science and Society*, **37** (1973), 175.

27. Smith, *De Republica Anglorum*, p. 12.

28. Meads, *op. cit.*, summary on p. 48 and *passim*; Davis, *op. cit.*, Vol. I, pp. 126–45, 244, 251, 292–308, 309–324; **T. Stapleton** (ed.), *Plumpton Correspondence, Camden Society*, old ser., **4** (1839) cx–cxi, cxiii, 70–2, 167–9, 171, 184–5, 186–7; Winchester, *op. cit.*, pp. 70–1, 83–4, 94–5, 138, 178, 197; Smyth, *op. cit.*, Vol. II, pp. 63, 195–6, 253, 334–5, 337, 383–7; **W. C.** and **C. E. Trevelyan** (eds), *Trevelyan Papers*, Vol. III, *Camden Society*, old ser., **105** (1872) 22–3.

29. Schofield, *op. cit.*, p. 110; **F. P.** and **M. M. Verney**, *Memoirs of the Verney Family during the Seventeenth Century*, Longmans, Green & Co., 2nd edn, London, 1907, Vol. I, pp. 343–398; Townshend, *op. cit.*, p. 235.

30. **A.** (really J.) **Fitzherbert**, *The Book of Husbandry, 1534*, **W. W. Skeat**, (ed.), *English Dialect Society*, **13** (1882), 93–8. The first edition, which Skeat had not seen, was published in 1523 (*ibid.*,xx).

31. **J. D. Marshall** (ed.), *The Autobiography of William Stout of Lancaster 1665–1752, Chetham Society*, 3rd ser., **14** (1967) 68–9; **H. J. Carpenter** (ed.), 'Furse of Moreshead. A Family Record of the Sixteenth Century', *Report and Transactions of the Devonshire Association*, **26** (1894), 174–5, 177, 179; Gough, *op. cit.*, pp. 112, 198–9, 201, 204, 221, 222, 226, 230, 244; **M. Campbell**, *The English Yeoman under Elizabeth and the Early Stuarts*, Yale UP, New Haven, 1942, pp. 207, 255. Campbell also quotes from Tusser (p. 221) the lines

> Some respit to husbands the weather may send,
> But huswives affaires have never an end.

32. Clark, *op. cit.*, pp. 100, 106; Campbell, *op. cit.*, p. 165; **N. Lowe**, *The Lancashire Textile Industry in the Sixteenth Century, Chetham Society*, 3rd ser., **20** (1972), 27–31.

33. Clark, *op. cit.*, pp. 87–92, 111–18; **P. Laslett**, *The World We Have Lost*, Methuen, London, 1965, pp. 15–16; **A. Everitt**, 'Farm Labourers', in *The Agrarian History of England and Wales*, Vol. IV, *1500–1640*, pp. 425–6, 434; **R. Parkinson** (ed.), *The Autobiography of Henry Newcome, M.A., Chetham Society*, old ser., **26–7** (1852), I, 82–6; **M. Roberts**, 'Sickles and Scythes: Women's Work and Men's Work at Harvest Time', *History Workshop Journal*, **7** (1979), 3–28.

34. Judges, *op. cit.*, pp. 69, 71, 73, 79, 80, 92, 94, 186–9, 195–6.

35. Thrupp, *op. cit.*, pp. 169–72; **V. B. Elliott**, 'Single Women in the London Marriage Market: Age, Status and Mobility, 1598–1619', in Outhwaite, *op. cit.*, p. 91 (not one woman among 8,000 apprentices registered by 15 London companies between 1580 and 1640); Clark, *op. cit.*, pp. 102–6, 138–97; **C. Phythian–Adams**, *Desolation of a City: Coventry and the Urban Crisis of the Late Middle Ages*, Cambridge UP, 1979, pp. 87–8, 91–2; **M. Prior**, 'Women and Trade in Oxford 1500–1800'. (I am grateful to Mrs Prior for permission to cite this unpublished paper delivered at the Open University Women's Studies Committee Seminar 26 May 1981.)

36. Clark, *op. cit.*, pp. 197–234; Phythian–Adams, *op. cit.*, p. 88.

37. Phythian–Adams, *loc. cit.*; **J. F. Pound** (ed.), *The Norwich Census of the Poor, 1570, Norfolk Record Society*, **40** (1971), 16.

38. Latham and Matthews, *op. cit.*, Vol. V, p. 65.

39. **F. J. Furnivall** (ed.), *Harrison's Description of England in Shakspere's Youth*, London, 1877, Vol. I, p. 33; Clarke, *op. cit.*, pp. 31–2, 100, 139; Knappen, *op. cit.*, p. 74; **A. Jessopp** (ed.), *The Autobiography of the Hon. Roger North*, David Nutt, London, 1887, p. 9; Taunton, Somerset Record Office, D/D/Cd 36, 31 Oct. 1604, Williams c. Poole; 15 May 1605, Ecclestone c. Huishe.

40. Judges, *op. cit.*, pp. 102–5, 146–8; Rogers, *op. cit.*, pp. 250–1, 290; **W. B. Rye** (ed.), *England as seen by Foreigners in the Days of Elizabeth and James I*, London, 1865, p. 72; Wright, *Songs and Carols*, pp. 91–5.

41. Campbell, *op. cit.*, pp. 261, 310; **M. St Clare Byrne**, *The Elizabethan Home discovered in Two Dialogues by Claudius Hollyband and Peter Erondell*, F. Etchells & H. Macdonald, London, 1925, pp. 25–40, 84; Gough, *op. cit.*, p. 198; Thrupp, *op. cit.*, p. 173; Smyth, *op. cit.*, Vol. II, pp. 285, 337; St Clare Byrne, *Lisle Letters*, Vol. I, pp. 29, 92, 94; Camden, *op. cit.*, Ch. vi; Latham and Matthews, *op. cit.*, Vol. VI, pp. 320–1; Sackville-West, *op. cit.*, pp. 18, 43, 45, 57, 59, 76, 110–12; **J. M. Osborn** (ed.), *The Autobiography of Thomas Whythorne*, Clarendon Press, Oxford, 1961, p. 93; **D. M. Stenton**, *The English Woman in History*, George Allen & Unwin, London, 1957, pp. 212–14.

42. Thrupp, *op. cit.*, p. 48; Meads, *op. cit.*, pp. 62, 64, 66, 70, 72, 77, 89, 92, 93, 110, 118, 123, 128, 135, 136, 137 (going out together); 89, 93, 94, 97, 99–101, 103, 106, 108, 121, 135 (talking or keeping company); 97, 99, 107, 113, (reading); Camden, *op. cit.*, p. 111, citing Greene's *Perimedes the Blacksmith*; Latham and Matthews, *op. cit.*, Vols III, IV, *passim*.

43. Barnum, *op. cit.*, Vol. I, Pt. 1, pp. 327–8; **W. A. Pantin**, 'Instructions for a Devout and Literate Layman', in **J. J. G. Alexander** and **M. T. Gibson** (eds), *Medieval Learning and Literature: Essays presented to Richard Hunt*, Clarendon Press, Oxford, 1976, pp. 398–400.

44. **M. Todd**, 'Humanists, Puritans and the Spiritualized Household'. *Church History*, **49** (1980), 29–31; Becon, *op. cit.*, pp. 337, 340; Gouge, *op. cit.*, pp. 235–43; Rogers, *op. cit.*, pp. 128–46.

45. Knappen, *op. cit.*, p. 83; Horsfall Turner, *op. cit.*, Vol. II, pp. 58, 107.

46. Gouge, *op. cit.*, p. 260; Rogers, *op. cit.*, pp. 267–9.

47. **P. Collinson**, 'The Rôle of Women in the English Reformation illustrated by the Life and Friendships of Anne Locke', *Studies in Church History*, **2** (1965), 267–70; Meads, *op. cit.*, pp. 88, 94, 100, 104, 116, 121, 151, 154, 159, 166, 170; cf. Clarke, *op. cit.*, pp. 416–17; Verney and Verney, *op. cit.*, Vol. I, p. 500; Gouge, *op. cit.*, ff. 3ᵛ–4; **C. Cross**, '"Great Reasoners in Scripture"; the Activities of Women Lollards 1380–1530', in *Medieval Women, Studies in Church History, Subsidia*, **1** (1978), 359–80.

48. I Peter 3: 1–2; Davies, 'Continuity and Change in Advice on Marriage', pp. 68–70; Gouge, *op. cit.*, p. 329.

49. **Cross**, *op. cit.*, pp. 363–80; **R. Pecock**, *The Repressor of Over Much Blaming of the Clergy*, **C. Babington** (ed.), *Rolls Series*, **19** (1860), I, 123; **W. P. Haugaard**, 'Katherine Parr: the Religious Convictions of a Renaissance Queen', *Renaissance Quarterly*, **22** (1969), 350–3 (which however suggests that her support has been exaggerated); Pratt, *op. cit.*, Vol. V, pp. 60, 260, 537–50; Vol. VII, pp. 227–35, 237–8, 244–8, 250–1, 255, 693–6, 699–706; Vol. VIII, pp. 306, 493, 497–501, 505, 548–9, 556–7.

50. **J. Bossy**, *The English Catholic Community, 1570–1850*, Darton, Longman and Todd, London, 1975, pp. 112, 152–60; *John Gerard: The Autobiography of an Elizabethan*, trans. **P. Caraman**, Longmans, Green & Co., London, 1951, p. 166.

51. **K. V. Thomas**, 'Women and the Civil War Sects', *Past and Present*, **13** (1958), 42–57; Joel 2: 28; **J. Bunyan**, *Grace Abounding to the Chief of Sinners*, **R. Sharrock** (ed.), Clarendon Press, Oxford, 1962, p. 14.

52. Thomas, *op. cit.*, pp. 56–7.

53. Whateley, *op. cit.*, title page; **M. Macdonald**, *Mystical Bedlam: Madness, Anxiety and Healing in Seventeenth-Century England*, Cambridge UP, 1981, pp. 99–100; *Certain Sermons or Homilies*, pp. 535–6; Gouge, *op. cit.*, pp. 237–8; Smith, *Preparatiue to Mariage*, pp. 59–61.

54. Knappen, *op. cit.*, p. 82; Parkinson, *op. cit.*, Vol. II, pp. 295–6; **C. Jackson** and **H. J. Morehouse** (eds), *Yorkshire Diaries and Autobiographies in the Seventeenth and Eighteenth Centuries*, Surtees Society, **65** (1877), 36, 39, 43, 51, 53, 54, 65, 66, 68, 80, 84, 99, 105, 111, 115, 117.

55. **R. A. Houlbrooke**, *Church Courts and the People during the English Reformation*, Oxford UP, 1979, pp. 71–5; **R. H. Helmholz**, *Marriage Litigation in Medieval England*, Cambridge UP, 1974, pp. 74–100; **C. Haigh**, *Reformation and Resistance in Tudor Lancashire*, Cambridge UP, 1975, pp. 47–8; **L. Dibdin** and **C. E. H. Chadwyck Healey**, *English Church Law and Divorce*, John Murray, London, 1912, *passim*; **E. Bunny**, *Of Divorce for Advlterie, and Marrying againe: that there is no sufficient warrant so to do*, Oxford, 1610, preface, sig.** 2; **E. Cardwell**

(ed.), *Synodalia: A Collection of Articles of Religion, Canons and Proceedings of Convocations*, Oxford, 1842, Vol. I, pp. 307–8; **H. Couch**, 'The Evolution of Parliamentary Divorce in England', *Tulane Law Review*, **52** (1977–78), 513–40.

56. Houlbrooke, *op. cit.*, p. 68–9, 85–6; Greater London Record Office, DL/C/additional, 1553–55; Helmholz, *op. cit.*, pp. 100–7; **J. Ayliffe**, *Parergon Juris Canonici Anglicani*, London, 1726, pp. 58–60.

57. *The Lawes Resolutions of Womens Rights*, pp. 144–7; **K. V. Thomas**, 'The Double Standard', *Journal of the History of Ideas*, **20** (1959), 195–216; Barnum, *op. cit.*, Vol. I, Pt. 2, pp. 67–71; Gouge, *op. cit.*, pp. 218–21; Taylor, *op. cit.*, pp. 66–7 Wright, *Middle-Class Culture*, pp. 484–5, 505; Latham and Matthews, *op. cit.*, Vol. IV, p. 140, 15–16 May 1663.

58. D'Evelyn, *op. cit.*, p. 137; Judges, *op. cit.*, pp. 237–9.

59. Smyth, *op. cit.*, Vol. II, pp. 212, 214; Stone, *Crisis of the Aristocracy*, pp. 662–4; Hollingsworth, *op. cit.*, pp. 47–9; **J. Cooper** (ed.), *Wentworth Papers, 1597–1628, Camden Society*, 4th ser., **12** (1973), 94–6.

60. **R. A. Houlbrooke**, 'Church Courts and People in the Diocese of Norwich, 1519–1570', Oxford University D. Phil. thesis, 1970, p. 162; **M. J. Ingram**, 'Ecclesiastical Justice in Wiltshire, 1600–1640, with special reference to cases concerning sex and marriage', Oxford University D. Phil. thesis, 1976, pp. 218–23; Trowbridge, Wilts. County Record Office, Bishop's Dep. Bk. 16, ff. 48, 110; **G. R. Quaife**, *Wanton Wenches and Wayward Wives: Peasants and Illicit Sex in Early Seventeenth-Century England*, Croom Helm, London, 1979 pp. 65, 124–42; Osborn, *op. cit.*, p. 26; **T. Harman**, *A Caveat for Common Cursitors*, in Judges, *op. cit.*, pp. 102–5.

61. Stone, *Family, Sex and Marriage*, p. 326; Helmholz, *op. cit.*, pp. 100–107; **I.** and **P. Opie** (eds), *The Oxford Dictionary of Nursery Rhymes*, Clarendon Press, Oxford, 1951, pp. 410–11; Davies, 'Continuity and Change in Advice on Marriage', p. 68; *Certain Sermons or Homilies*, pp. 545–7; Smith, *Preparatiue to Mariage*, pp. 69–74; Gouge, *op. cit.*, pp. 389–93; Whateley, *op. cit.*, pp. 106–9, 169–72; **W. L. Sachse** (ed.), *Minutes of the Norwich Court of Mayoralty, 1630–1631, Norfolk Record Society*, **15** (1942), 86, 104, 187; Greater London Record Office, DL/C/207, ff. 2, 83, 96; **E. M. Elvey** (ed.), *The Courts of the Archdeaconry of Buckingham, 1483–1523, Bucks. Record Society*, **19** (1975) 144, 176.

62. *Certain Sermons or Homilies*, p. 132; Rogers, *op. cit.*, p. 13; Trowbridge, Wilts. County Record Office, Bishop's Dep. Bk. 5, f. 127ᵛ; Smyth, *op. cit.*, Vol. II, pp. 255, 402–3; Elvey, *op. cit.*, p. 41; **S. P. Menefee**, *Wives for Sale: An Ethnographic Study of British Popular Divorce*, Basil Blackwell, Oxford, 1981, esp. pp. 211–13.

63. Macdonald, *op. cit.*, p. 101; Pound, *op. cit.*, p. 95; Clark, *op. cit.*, pp. 80, 86, 118–20; Judges, *op. cit.*, pp. 55, 94; 2 James I, c. 11.

Chapter 6

Parents and children: infancy and childhood

Birth

The Church's teaching that the procreation of children was one of the major purposes of marriage harmonised to a varying extent with the economic strategies and personal needs of individual couples. To have too many children, or a large number of girls, might be burdensome, but childlessness was widely regarded as the worse plight. The labour of children and adolescents played an important part in the family economies of many craftsmen and husbandmen. Children were seen by many as an important potential source of help and comfort in old age. To all save those engaged in the most brutal struggle for mere survival, they were probably a source of psychological satisfaction which varied in depth according to individual character. They were pledges of their parents' love in whom the flesh of father and mother was united. The notion that parents lived in their offspring after their own deaths was a familiar one, and the theme of renewal through procreation inspired some of Shakespeare's finest sonnets.[1] The heir to a great line who failed to continue it was at best unfortunate, at worst shamefully negligent.

Marital fertility is influenced by a number of factors. First, there are big variations in the capacity to beget and conceive children between individual men and women. These variations are in part innate, in part the result of differences in diet, health and conditions of life and work. Second, female fecundity may decline with age; a woman's chances of conceiving in her thirties are probably substantially smaller than they are in her twenties.[2] Third, the duration of a marriage is a major determinant of the numbers of children born within it. The longer marriage is postponed, the shorter the fecund period will be, and the effect of late marriage is compounded by declining fecundity. Marriage may also be curtailed by the death of husband or wife before the onset of the menopause. Fourth, the length of the intervals between births within marriage is influenced by whether or not a mother feeds her babies herself. Stimulation of a nursing mother's nipple brings about production of the hormone prolactin which prevents the ovaries from maintaining ovulation.

Today the ! Kung women of the Kalahari desert typically bear children at intervals of about forty-four months. Short but frequent feeds throughout the twenty-four hours maintain a high level of prolactin production. In the eighteenth and nineteenth centuries, mean intervals between births were about thirty months in a village in Friesland (N. Germany) where long breastfeeding was customary, eight or nine months shorter in three villages in Bavaria where it was proscribed. In Chesham (Bucks.) between 1578 and 1601, known wet-nurses experienced intervals similar to those discovered in Friesland when feeding their own children and could double their length by taking a nurse child in succession to their own. The contraceptive effectiveness of breastfeeding is reduced by not feeding on demand and by early supplementation with pap, a widely practised feature of early modern infant feeding regimes.[3] Fifth, not all conceptions result in live births because of miscarriages and still births. Miscarriages were very rarely systematically recorded in our period save in the most thorough diaries and autobiographies. But the experience of Mrs Jane Josselin (1621–93), who miscarried in a third of her pregnancies, concentrated in the latter part of her child-bearing period, was by no means unique in the seventeenth century. Poor diet and heavy work may have helped to cause miscarriages. The parish registers of Hawkshead (Lancs.) were exceptional in recording abortive births between 1581 and 1710. There, the rate of still births per thousand live births fluctuated in the seventeenth century between twenty-nine and ninety-six per decade, reaching its highest point in the 1690s. John Graunt, writing in 1662, put the rate in London at about fifty per thousand. These figures may be compared with rates of ten to twenty per thousand in Europe today.[4] Finally, it was well known throughout our period that it was possible to prevent conceptions or births deliberately, by means of spermicides, abortifacients and above all by the practice of *coitus interruptus*.[5]

The major determinants of fertility changes in England between the sixteenth and nineteenth centuries were the age and incidence of marriage. Though some deliberate limitation of births within marriage took place, there is disagreement over its importance, and it may well have been more widely practised in certain communities or socio-economic groups than in others. But the latest and most authoritative study of English population history concludes that it did little to change overall fertility rates in the course of time.[6] The connections between social class and marital fertility remain obscure. Wealthy women tended to marry earlier than their social inferiors, were probably better fed, and generally employed wet-nurses. They probably had more children than the majority of women who married later than they did and fed their own children. Yet, despite the experience of some gentlewomen who bore children practically every year for a large part of their married lives, there is as yet little evidence to show that the fertility of the upper classes was substantially higher than that of the rest of the population. In the case of wives who experienced twenty-five years of marriage, the mean size of groups of children born was very similar in a sample of twelve parishes to that found among the offspring of the British nobility. In both cases it was roughly six or seven in the second half of our period.[7] Perhaps the deliberate limitation of births was more widespread among the upper classes, though this has yet to be demonstrated.[8] Another recently suggested possibility is that the straitlacing dictated by fashion adversely affected not only the health of gentlewomen but also their pleasure in intercourse and their capacity to conceive and bear children.[9]

Normal childbirth may have been very little more dangerous in our period than it is today, but even small complications and abnormalities introduced very much greater risks. When allowance is made for those mothers who died undelivered or in childbed of stillborn children, an overall maternal mortality rate of twenty-five per thousand birth events seems plausible for the sixteenth and seventeenth centuries. By contrast, the maternal mortality rate arising from complications of pregnancy, childbirth and puerperium recorded in Britain in 1979 was 0.12 per thousand births. It was widely believed during our period that the poor bore their children more easily than the rich. They were thought to be hardier, and among the upper classes, where elaborate preparations were made for the lying-in, childbirth was more likely to be perceived as a 'painful, dramatic, and dangerous process'. Although pregnancy was a source of some broad humour among the letter-writing classes, there was a strong undercurrent of anxiety on the part of both spouses. Pious wives often prepared for death.[10]

The supervision of birth usually lay within the female sphere. A dozen neighbours or kinswomen might attend, but the most important participant was the midwife. Midwives underwent no proper training. Such skill as they possessed they owed to experience and inherited lore. It is doubtful whether the obstetric handbooks of the period influenced midwives' practice before they were out of date. During the seventeenth century, physicians and man-midwives were coming to be called in during difficult cases. Though their ministrations doubtless had little effect on the overall level of maternal mortality, the best of them made considerable advances in the treatment of abnormal births.[11]

Husbands were often close at hand during labour, though much contemporary testimony does not make clear whether they were present at the bedside or confined to a neighbouring room. Certainly at least one seventeenth-century author thought that the husband's presence at his wife's side could be useful if she desired it.[12] William Gouge believed some men so insensitive that they thought 'but lightly' of their wives' anguish, but that many, including Gouge himself, were seared by the experience is beyond doubt. God offered the best hope of succour, prayer the relief of positive action, at a time when a man could give so little material help. 'What shall I do?' one distraught husband asked the godly minister John Carter (1554–1635), 'My wife is entring into her Travel, and I think she will die with very fear.' Carter told him to let her know that he himself would pray for her immediately. The conversion to Catholicism of Philip Wodehouse, one of the first achieved by the Jesuit John Gerard, was largely due to his wife's sudden and inexplicable recovery when she had received extreme unction after a dangerous birth. His wife's relief from premature labour pangs, apparently in response to his secret prayers, restored John Bunyan's faltering belief in God. Women's deaths in childbirth, sometimes recorded in funeral inscriptions from the fifteenth century onwards, inspired some of the most poignant monuments of the early seventeenth century.[13]

Happy messages took the news of safe and welcome births along the family network. 'Also, fadyr', wrote William Stonor in about 1473, 'my Suster Cotymore ys delyveryd of a feyre sun, and both don welle, blessed be Jhesu.'[14] His words were echoed in countless letters of the same type over the next two centuries. Letters of congratulation mingled vigorously expressed pleasure with pious hopes for God's blessing upon the newly born child.

Baptism marked the baby's reception into the Christian community and, held to be essential to salvation by the Catholic Church, took place in the later Middle Ages as soon as possible after birth. It changed in character after the Reformation. Some symbolic elements in the rite disappeared in 1552, though in both its Catholic and its Protestant forms it contained the godparents' renunciation of the devil and declaration of faith on the child's behalf as well as its naming and immersion. More important was the fact that the performance of baptism ceased to be regarded, officially at any rate, as absolutely essential to salvation. Thomas Becon explained in his *Catechism* (1560) that the baptism of water was only a seal or confirmation of the fact that God had already received the child of Christian parents into his glory. Only those who contemptuously refused it were excluded from heaven. The Book of Common Prayer, while still permitting immediate baptism if it seemed that the baby would die, recommended its performance upon a Sunday or holy day when the congregation might welcome the infant. The uneducated may have continued to look upon christening as a quasi-magical rite essential to the child's welfare, but a gradual relaxation of attitudes towards baptism was the natural consequence of this important shift in the Church's teaching. By the end of the seventeenth century it was common for half the baptisms in a parish to have been postponed for a week or more after birth, although there were big variations in practice from one parish to another.[15]

A christening was usually made an occasion for celebration by those who could afford it. The alehouse hostess could be sure at a christening '. . . to be rid of two or three dozen of cakes and ale by gossiping neighbours'. To the christening, the godparents brought their gifts: apostle spoons, porringers, bowls and mounted coral for the baby to cut his teeth on and to protect him from witchcraft.[16]

The choice of godparents was used to strengthen friendship, reinforce kinship and encourage the goodwill of actual or prospective patrons or employers. In theory their main duty was the elementary religious instruction of the child, but how far this was fulfilled in practice it is hard to tell. Some people certainly bore it in mind, however, In James I's reign, Dorothy Leigh advised her sons to seek from any person who asked them to act as godparents a solemn undertaking that the child would be taught to read the Bible as soon as possible. Adam Martindale recalled that his impoverished godmother gave him his first ABC when he was five as a result of her determination to perform her baptismal promise.[17] Some godchildren benefited from the connection materially, if not spiritually. They were often mentioned in wills, especially before the Reformation. In 1648 the Yorkshire yeoman Adam Eyre promised to provide his godson with clothes for a year to enable him to go to school in Leeds, and then to help find him a calling. In some communities, godparenthood may have withered under the hostile influence of puritan clergy who could see no Scriptural warrant for the institution, disliked the giving of pledges on the child's behalf, and felt that the duty of religious instruction belonged to parents. Elsewhere it probably continued to flourish.[18]

The choice of names for children, as well as the character of the baptismal rite, was influenced by Protestantism during this period. The privilege of bestowing a name, usually his or her own, was widely held to belong to one of the godparents, though saints' names, especially that of the saint on whose day the child had been born, were also immensely popular. These customs often led in practice to the bestowal of the same name on more than one sibling. In 1568, when Simon D'Ewes's father was christened, his two godfathers could not agree which of them should give him his name. As a result of their 'idle altercation and striving . . . at the font' the minister christened him Paul, after the saint on whose day he had been born, even though his elder brother had also been named Paul. Protestant hostility towards certain saints associated with popery, puritan suspicion of godparenthood, and a positive feeling that names should be chosen from Scripture, commemorate a divine mercy or symbolise a good intention, all weakened inherited custom.[19]

The new ideas never triumphed completely, however. The greater variety of opinion about the bestowal of names which prevailed after the Reformation gave parents more freedom to follow their own inclinations. One result was that the bestowal of the same name on more than one living child became much less frequent from the sixteenth century onwards. But in many cases parents continued to give babies the same name as older siblings who had died. Two seventeenth-century mothers, Catherine Danby and Lady Ann Fanshawe, and probably many others, intended in this way to preserve the memory of well-loved children whom they had lost. The decline of the practice of giving more than one child in a family the same name should not be attributed to a dawning awareness of the individuality of each child. Such awareness was far from new. Rather should it be explained in terms of a weakening of customary restraints and obligations and the availability of a wider choice of suitable names.[20]

Infant care: swaddling and feeding

In our period infant care was governed by customs and lore passed down from one generation of women to the next. In June 1647, Sir Ralph Verney, writing to his wife Mary about their baby son, asserted that midwives and old women knew better than any physician how to treat infants. The inherited regime was designed to maintain a womb-like environment for the newly born baby. It was to be kept out of bright light to avoid damage to its sight; rocked and sung to to encourage the sleep necessary for digestion. The aim was furthered by the swaddling bands which, wound round the child in a protective cocoon, were meant to help its limbs to grow straight and to prevent its scratching itself or going down on all fours like an animal. This first phase was short. Swaddling for a year or more might be recommended in handbooks, but some seventeenth-century English evidence suggests that children were transferred to 'coats' between one and three months after birth.[21]

Breastfeeding, the other major element of the infant's regime, lasted a good deal longer. Much medical opinion from antiquity onwards was strongly in favour of maternal feeding. The child was supposed to imbibe with his milk the characteristics of the woman who fed him, and if entrusted to a wet-nurse might grow up with a disposition entirely different from his mother's. A natural affection grew up between the child and the woman who suckled him, and his love would be focused on the wet-nurse if the mother refused the task. The Church, too, regarded breastfeeding as the mother's duty. During the sixteenth and early seventeenth centuries, maternal breastfeeding found forceful advocates among humanists (especially Erasmus), paediatricians and reforming clerics both Catholic and Protestant. Yet there were differences of opinion on the subject even among the supposedly expert. The long-established custom of employing wet-nurses, widespread among the upper classes in particular, proved strongly resistant to change. According to William Gouge there were many reasons why individual women were reluctant to suckle their own children. Many feared that it would spoil their looks and make them age more rapidly. Feeding also interfered with the social round; it interrupted the sleep of both husband and wife. (They may also have been influenced by the belief that coitus during the period of feeding was undesirable because it could cause a new conception which would divert nourishment from the child at the breast.) Some women claimed that they lacked the necessary skill, that they had no milk, that feeding made their breasts sore, or that they were not well enough to undertake' it. Nursing might force a woman to neglect her trade or the management of the household, and in such a case her husband could save money by paying a nurse. But however weighty any of these reasons may have appeared in individual cases, it seems likely that the long continuance of the practice of wet-nursing should be attributed above all to the strength of what Erasmus called 'tyrant custom'.[22]

It is true that some women in the upper and middle ranks of society, influenced by the arguments of humanists, paediatricians and reformers, felt bound to perform their duty or emboldened to follow their own inclinations. In the seventeenth century a number of ladies suckled their own children, some of them of high rank. But the very fact that their having done so should occasionally have been mentioned with special pride on their tombstones suggests that they remained a small minority. The proportion of suckling mothers was probably higher among the wives of godly ministers, who for the most part came from a more plebeian social background and were probably more responsive to the argument of Christian duty.[23]

The chances of survival of infants entrusted to wet-nurses were worse than of those suckled by their own mothers. In the second half of our period, about one in five baby boys born to the British nobility, died in the first year of life, but only approximately one in seven of those born in reconstitutable families in twelve provincial parishes. The likelihood that a far higher proportion of the former group were wet-nursed seems the most obvious reason for the difference between their experiences.[24]

Yet the biggest contrast in the quality of care and consequent effects on the infant's prospects lay not between maternal and wet-nursing but between good and bad wet-nursing. Those who took care in their choice of nurses could expect to bring most of their offspring home again. Paediatric handbooks set out detailed criteria of selection, of which the most important were the nurse's health, the quality of her milk, and her character. People of substance often picked nurses for their children on the basis of personal recommendation by trusted friends or relatives. The gentry commonly entrusted their infants to women living near their country houses, thus making supervision possible, while the very well-off could often afford to keep a nurse under their own roof. But hard-working parents who employed nurses for the economic reasons sketched by Gouge, and parish overseers arranging for the nursing of foundlings, were less discriminating. The worst sort of wet-nursing had lethal consequences. In the seventeenth century it was claimed by at least two writers that the great majority of the infants put out to nurse in the villages immediately round London never returned to their parents. The overworked poor country women who were commonly chosen to be nurses were forced to let the child lie and cry 'many times till it burst againe' thought William Gouge.[25]

Wet-nursing has sometimes been condemned for its supposed effects on the character of the child as well as its chances of survival. The individual, it has been argued, might suffer lasting psychological damage when removed from the woman to whom he had become attached during the first year or two of life. But modern studies of 'maternal deprivation' during infancy have been based on situations quite unlike that of the child coming home in former times after his period with a wet-nurse. The proper assessment of maternal deprivation depends upon the minute examination of the child's experience before, during and after separation. In some families, the services of wet-nurses were remembered with gratitude, sometimes generously rewarded, and they came nearer to being treated like kinsfolk than any other servants. Under these circumstances, wet-nurses could retain a share in their former charges' affections. Sir Walter Raleigh, however, believed that his son had easily transferred his affection from his wet-nurse and in the end forgotten her. For others the experience of severance from the wet-nurse may have been painful, but if so it is curious that even the frankest and least inhibited of seventeenth-century autobiographers should have failed to mention the fact.[26]

Breastfeeding was probably terminated in the majority of cases at some point in the second year of the infant's life, though sometimes before this and sometimes long afterwards. But supplementation of breast milk with pap and pre-chewed bread or vegetables began long before final withdrawal from the nipple. One consequence of this practice was of course to reduce the potential contraceptive effects of maternal feeding.[27]

Parental love and the loss of children

Writers on familial duties before and during this period generally regarded the tie between parents and their young children as one of the closest of human bonds. But parental love was far stronger than filial. It rose like the sap in a tree; it ran down like falling water; it shone down like sun on a wall calling forth only a relatively feeble reflected heat. According to William Gouge, it was the natural love fast fixed in their hearts by God which made many parents think no pains, cost or care too great to undergo for their children. Parental love, thought Thomas Gataker, grew with time; 'the longer they have them, the more they affect them, and the loather they are to leaue and forgoe them'; in this respect it provided a pattern for conjugal love. In part the strength of parental affection was due to the sense of possession, as Gataker saw: parents delighted in their children, not primarily because of their good qualities, but because they were theirs. Thus, according to Peter Idley, writing in the fifteenth century, the mere report that his wife has borne him a child is sufficient to kindle a man's love for it.[28]

However strong paternal affection, maternal love was held to be naturally stronger, at least at first. Every man knew, claimed Dorothy Leigh, that a mother's love for her children was 'hardly contained within the bounds of reason'. In the thirteenth century, Bartholomaeus Anglicus had described how the mother loved her child tenderly, kissed him and busied herself in feeding him. Daniel Rogers described the loving drudgery of the nursing mother in a passage which probably owed its vividness to personal observation. What man, he asked,

> were able to endure that clamor, annoiance, and clutter which she goes through without complaint among poore nurslines, clothing, feeding, dressing and undressing, picking and clensing them; what is it save the instinct of love which enableth her hereto?

A mother could of course love her baby even if she was not involved in all the 'annoiance' of its daily care. In an imaginary dialogue of Elizabeth's reign, we find a convincing portrayal of a wealthy mother's delight in her infant. On entering the nursery, after preliminary anxious enquiries as to possible ailments or teething pains, she commands the nurse to unswaddle, feed and wash him in her presence:

> O my little hart! God blesse thee . . . His little cheekes are wet, I beleeve you did leave him alone to crye and weepe . . . What a faire necke he hath! Pull off his shirt, thou art pretty [and] fat my little darling, wash his armepits . . . How he spreadeth his small fingers!

The dialogue concludes with the mother's careful instructions for the baby's cleaning and dressing. Included in a textbook designed to teach everyday French, it probably caught the flavour of countless female conversations which have left hardly a trace in the written record.[29]

But letters show that fathers, too, took an affectionate interest in infants. In July 1623 the duchess of Buckingham sent a most detailed description of her daughter's antics to her husband, impatient to read 'perticulers of our pretty mall'. Set upright, she reacted in a different way to each dance tune that was played, and would cry 'hah hah' when they danced her. Laid down, she would kick her legs over her head. 'I wood you were here but to see her for you wood take much delight in her now shee is so full of pretye playe and tricks . . .' In 1624, Thomas Wentworth caught in an epistolary snapshot his little godson 'laughinge, gapeinge and dauncinge in his father's armes to a piper that was playinge, to the great joie and comfort of the spectators, especially his father . . .' Endymion Porter's letters to his wife were full of enquiries about his little sons Charles and George. He asked his wife to send George's picture and himself sent the boy six little glass bottles with silver chains, sure that he would 'keep a terrible stir with them'.[30]

As some of these letters suggest, children's antics pleased their parents not only because they were charming in themselves but also because the development of the budding personality and intelligence were manifest in them. A number of parents recorded their children's learning to walk. Descriptions of mothers and nurses encouraging little children to speak with baby-talk and lullabies (some of which survive today) have come down to us from periods as far back as the Middle Ages. Humanists often celebrated parental delight in children's first utterances, which occasionally found their way into recorded reminiscences. Adam Martindale was very proud of his two-year-old son John, who drove back a lively calf, with a stick in his hand, 'crying *caw, caw*, meaning he had beaten the calfe'.[31]

Supposedly high rates of infant and child mortality have led some to question the quality of parental love in this period. More than a fifth of all the children born under Elizabeth I, about a quarter of those born under the Stuarts, probably died before reaching their tenth birthday. It has been argued that children's deaths were so common that parents could only ensure their own emotional stability by avoiding the investment of much affection in their offspring, or that the high rates themselves were in large part due to parental neglect.[32]

Not all child deaths can be expected to have an equal impact on parents, yet much discussion of bereavement during this period is vitiated by failure to take this simple fact into account. The deaths of babies, painful though they often are, are easier to come to terms with than those of older children. Parental love often takes time to grow. When they first held their babies, 40 per cent of the women covered by a recent survey allegedly experienced 'detachment or indifference–blank, deadened, neutral emotional reactions'. A further 11 per cent had mixed feelings. The Johnson correspondence in the sixteenth century, the case books of Napier, the diary of Ralph Josselin and the autobiography of Alice Thornton in the seventeenth, all show that the deaths of babies might be either intensely painful or expected to be so. Yet that solicitous father Ralph Josselin explained that he and his wife were able after initial grief to resign themselves to the death of a ten-day-old son because he was 'the youngest, and our affections not so wonted unto it'.[33] One might expect the experience of a modern parent to be similar. The fact that so high a proportion of child deaths occurred very early on probably meant that their emotional impact was much smaller than it would have been had they been spread more evenly through childhood. Of the deaths which occurred in the first decade of life, well over half, indeed almost two-thirds in Elizabeth's reign, probably took place in the first year. Of the latter, over half were concentrated in the first month.[34]

The risk of loss diminished sharply after the first year, even though mortality remained far higher than today throughout childhood. Grief tended to become more intense as the relationship between parent and child developed a new depth and fullness with the growth of the child's personality and its acquisition of particular skills, especially verbal communication. One of the most poignant of all testimonies of parental grief is Ben Jonson's farewell to his seven-year-old first son, whom he addressed as 'thou child of my right hand, and joy' and described as 'his best piece of *poetrie*'. But the loss of children seems to have been as devastating to the relatively humble patients of Richard Napier, who left no personal record of their grief, as it was to such autobiographers as John Evelyn, Adam Martindale and Lady Fanshawe.[35]

Christian theology offered powerful consolation for the deaths of children. In Catholic belief the baptised child who died innocent was assured of a swift passage to eternal bliss. This point was effectively made in the fourteenth-century poem *Pearl*, in which a girl who died when not yet two years old appeared before her grieving father in a vision. She had been crowned a queen in heaven although she had never even learnt her creed or prayers while on earth. John Wyclif, orthodox in this respect at least, castigated those mothers who gave way to grief when they lost their children. It was a great mercy on God's part to take a child out of the world.[36]

Renaissance humanism and Baroque sensibility encouraged the expression, especially in funerary art, of feelings whose commemoration would have been futile in the eyes of the medieval Church. The simple pathos of parental sorrow stands out from a number of monuments which record the deaths of children. After Sir Henry Montague's son had drowned at the age of three in 1625 while trying to retrieve an orange from a well, 'his unhappy Father' described him as a 'worthie and hopefull child, tender and Deare in the sight of his Parents' (Barnwell, Northants.). But grief was commonly mixed with a note of confidence or gratitude. Thus James I's daughter, Princess Sophia, who died the day after her birth in June 1606, was described on her tomb in Westminster Abbey as 'a royal rosebud plucked from her parents by death to bloom afresh in the garden of Christ'. The practice of depicting children upon their parents' memorial brasses had grown rapidly in the fifteenth century, and though at that time there had been little attempt to distinguish various children according to their ages, some late medieval brasses clearly depicted infants in the earliest months of life, occasionally on their own monuments. The portrayal of children on funeral monuments certainly grew much more lifelike from the late sixteenth century onwards, but this was part of the wider development of realism in representational art. It is unnecessary to attribute it to a new readiness to recognise the individuality of each child.[37]

To show that parental love for children was common is not the same as demonstrating that it was universal. The love of some parents for their children could have coexisted with widespread indifference and neglect. But there is no good evidence that such behaviour was typical and no need to use it as an explanation for patterns of infant (i.e. in the first year of life) and child mortality. Family reconstitution studies based on parish registers suggest that about one in seven babies may have died in the first year of life in the period 1550–1700. The collective experience of twelve parishes, covering various provincial villages and market towns, but none of the most unhealthy places, may have been rather better than that of the nation as a whole, but it seems unlikely to have been markedly different. It compared favourably with that of other countries during the same period and seems to have been similar to that of England as a whole in the second half of the nineteenth century, despite the major advances in the understanding of disease which had been made in the interval.[38]

Infant mortality was very largely due to things beyond parental understanding or control. As much as half of it may have been due to such 'endogenous' causes as the effects of difficult births and congenital defects. A pilot study of Ludlow (Shrops.) between 1577 and 1619 suggests that infants were highly vulnerable to certain winter infections but were largely protected by breastfeeding from such summer diseases as dysentery which carried off many older children. In twelve parishes, the mean level of infant mortality rose only very slightly between Elizabethan and later Stuart times, and indeed fell between the second half of the sixteenth and the first half of the seventeenth century. But child mortality (1–9) rose sharply, probably because of the spread of new sorts of infection, largely due to the growth of contacts with the extra-European world. To these, infants still at the breast may not have been so vulnerable. In the later Middle Ages, child mortality may have been greater than it was in the first two centuries of the parish register era because of the higher incidence of plague, believed to have been a particularly lethal scourge of the young.[39]

The geographical variations in mortality which parish registers reveal are also attributable in large part to the differential impact of disease. Infant mortality was far higher in towns and the notoriously unhealthy Fens than it was in a remote part of the north Devon coast. The worst rates were recorded in poor London parishes. In one, St Botolph without Aldgate, not far short of one in three of the baptised infants died within a year even in the comparatively healthy first half of Elizabeth's reign. By 1700, London infant mortality rates were probably far worse.[40]

The existence of widespread culpable neglect and infanticide has so far proved difficult to demonstrate. We would expect them to leave tell-tale traces in the demographic record such as higher mortality among baby girls (possibly regarded as less useful and more burdensome than boys) or among later-born children. Yet mortality was usually, though not always, higher among males than among females, as is also the case today.[41] Among the reconstitutable families of Terling in Essex, first-born children were more likely to die in their first year than second or third children, and 'severe birth trauma due to maternal inexperience' has been suggested as a possible reason for this state of affairs. Here the infant mortality rate among fourth and later children rose once more, but at 172 per thousand it was still well below the 186 per thousand calculated for first-born children. As a group they may have been rather less well looked after than those born in second and third place, but to claim that they were neglected would be going too far.[42]

The character of accidental deaths may provide another pointer to the practice of infanticide. Overlaying (i.e. suffocating a child by lying too close to, or on top of it, in bed), may have been the easiest and commonest way of killing a baby unobtrusively. The medieval Church issued repeated warnings against it; it was the second commonest specified cause of 'accidental' death in early modern London. Death may often have been intended, but in the majority of cases it was probably unintentional. Overlaying by servants was either suspected or narrowly averted by some conscientious parents, while in 1655 Oliver Heywood's nephew was overlaid by the child's own mother. Further down the social scale poor heating and over-crowding were probably the commonest causes. The latter obviously played a part in the large numbers of deaths by burning which occurred in the late medieval countryside when animals knocked embers into cradles. Toddlers suffered accidents from a wide range of hazards including stairs, wet floors, fires, boiling water, sharp edges, pits, ponds, dung heaps, animals' hooves and falling objects. Some of these still cause fatalities today, despite big improvements in living conditions, work patterns and devices for the prevention of accidents. Furthermore, in the face of immediate danger to their children's lives, the parents of late medieval and early modern England often made the most determined efforts to save them and showed the profoundest relief and gratitude when they were successful.[43]

Although it is impossible to measure the extent of infanticide, some have argued that there was a growing intolerance of the crime. The argument rests above all on the fact that the medieval secular courts appear in most cases to have left the punishment of those responsible for the deaths of infants to the church courts, which imposed penances, not capital punishment, whereas by the later sixteenth century they were executing much larger numbers of people convicted of infanticide. Yet the medieval church courts had dealt with married couples and often punished parents whose children's deaths had been due to negligence or bad luck rather than evil intent, while later on the lay courts seem to have been almost exclusively concerned with the killing of bastard children by their mothers, which was also the subject of a statute passed in 1624. It certainly cannot be maintained that Tudor and Stuart secular courts were actuated by a greater concern for the infant than the medieval church courts had been; in certain respects the latter had cast their net wider.[44]

Changes in the physical environment, in living conditions, and in the incidence and virulence of disease were almost certainly more important than developments in attitudes in determining the level of infant and child mortality. Mothers probably discharged their responsibilities well if indeed they succeeded in bringing six out of seven children through the dangerous first year of life. It seems likely that in most places the great majority of children were cherished and as well cared for as the age's primitive understanding of hygiene and disease and the economic pressures upon families would allow. The offspring of the unmarried, the vagrant poor and the inhabitants of the fetid slums of the big cities fared far worse. Between the sixteenth and the eighteenth centuries the expansion of towns was creating larger areas whose environments were inimical to infant and child life. On the other hand, the origins of modern paediatrics, to which Englishmen like Daniel Whistler and Walter Harris contributed, can be traced to the seventeenth century. In the era of the Scientific Revolution a new confidence was dawning that solutions could be found for all sorts of ills hitherto regarded as inescapable parts of the providential scheme. In the field of child care, rising mortality made the quest more urgent. There was also a growing readiness to challenge and discard inherited practices: John Locke, for example, questioned the usefulness of swaddling. Many mistakes were made, but ultimately there would be solid achievements. It was to be the children of the upper classes who would, especially in the second half of the eighteenth century, be the first to benefit.[45]

Discipline and indulgence

Parental affection was believed to be natural, instinctive and deep-rooted. But it was for a long time held undesirable to allow it untrammelled expression. Conventional wisdom laid much emphasis on the dangers attendant on parental indulgence. 'Spoiling' children meant making them physically and morally soft, prone to sickness and vices. It was the truly solicitous parent's responsibility to make sure that his offspring were not pampered, but strictly controlled for the good of their bodies and souls. The staple merchant John Johnson shared with his wife Sabine a love for their small children which was betrayed by their affectionate references to 'my two jewels', 'our brats' and 'my little maiden'. But when in 1545 his little daughter went to stay with an uncle, John Johnson earnestly asked him that she be kept in awe and not allowed to eat too much meat. Discipline and restraint were central elements in the task of upbringing as it was envisaged by the conscientious Tudor parent.[46]

This view had already been established for centuries. 'He that spareth his rod hateth his son' was of all Scriptural texts probably the one which bulked largest in discussions of the upbringing of children between the high Middle Ages and the reign of Elizabeth. The more the father loved his child, Bartholomaeus Anglicus had written in the thirteenth century, the more busily he taught him, chastised him and held him strictly under. Because he beat him so often, it seemed indeed that he did not love him. A son must be kept as close as a bird in a cage, advised Peter Idley.

Laugh not with them, but keep them low; show them no merry cheer
Lest thou do weep with them also; but bring them up in fear.

Thus the Marian martyr Robert Smith, paraphrasing Ecclesiasticus.[47]

But much personal testimony demonstrates that parents found chastisement a distasteful task. The kind mother, 'having seen her child do some witty unhappy trick, stands in doubt whether she shall laugh at him and let him escape, or frown at him and correct him'. Many parents, thought William Gouge, could not endure to hear their children cry. But fathers showed a greater ability to curb natural affection for their children's good, and resembled God more closely in the loving correction they administered, than did mothers, who were more likely to spoil and 'cocker' their children, or even to hinder their correction. St Paul had said that God offered himself to those who endured chastisement as unto sons. Just as God prepared individuals through sickness and other sufferings for their departure to a more glorious life, so, suggested Jeremy Taylor, paternal austerity prepared children for adulthood, while mothers softened and spoilt them.[48]

A pessimistic view of the child's nature, rooted in the Old Testament, but developed by Paul and Augustine, underlay the correctional approach to upbringing so widely expounded in the advice given to parents in the later Middle Ages and the era of the Reformation. Although the child was normally incapable of mortal sin before the age of seven, its innate depravity began to manifest itself long before then. Only the curbing of its essentially vicious impulses by God's grace, using parental discipline as its instrument, could give the child some prospect of escape from perdition. Any underlying tension which there may have been between the generally optimistic assumptions concerning the fate of the soul of the young child and the rather pessimistic assumptions which governed traditional advice on upbringing was not apparent in the texts in which the latter was set out.

Theoretical justification for a more indulgent mode of upbringing which would harmonise more closely with the feelings of those many parents who allegedly hated the duty of correction was to be found in the work of pagan classical writers. Galen (AD 129?–99), one of the most influential medical authors of late antiquity, had written that the normal child needed protection from corruption rather than correction of manners. Quintilian (AD b. *c.* 30–35) had held the infant's character to be morally neutral but innately capable of a positive response to education, and his ideas strongly influenced the educational writings of Erasmus. A number of humanists tended to place greater emphasis on the preservation of innocence than the correction of sin and believed that natural inclinations could be exploited rather than curbed in the educational process. His gentle upbringing of his children was remembered with pride by Sir Thomas More. In the *Gouernour* (1531) Sir Thomas Elyot insisted on the crucial part played by example and imitation in children's education. He like other writers deprecated the delight shown by 'lewd' parents in their children's oaths and dirty language.[49]

Contrary wise we beholde some chyldren, knelynge in theyr game before images, and holdyng up theyr lytell whyte handes, do moue theyr praty mouthes, as they were prayeng: other goynge and syngynge as hit were in procession: wherby they do expresse theyr disposition to the imitation of those thynges, be they good or iuell, whiche they usually do se or here.

Such an overt expression of delight in the ways of small children, cloyingly familiar to us, was most unusual at this time. Children's hearts and brains must, Elyot believed, be protected from corruption by the 'pestiferous dewe of vice'. A generation later Roger Ascham likenend 'the pure cleane witte of a sweete yong babe' to new wax ready to receive the best printing or a new unused silver dish fit to keep clean any good thing put into it. (That the young resembled wax in their pliability was a notion current in Chaucer's time if not before, but humanist educational theory gave it greater prominence.) If children were innocent or malleable, harsh punishment seemed inappropriate, and Ascham stoutly opposed needless beating. In the seventeenth century, an indulgent mode of upbringing was to be urged with confidence. Dorothy Leigh claimed in *The Mother's Blessing* (1616 and several later editions) that whatever children's disposition, gentleness would soonest bring them to virtue. The marquess of Halifax, in his *Advice to a Daughter* (1688), saw children's love as the root of their obedience.

You must deny them as seldom as you can, and when there is no avoiding it you must do it gently; you must flatter away their ill humour and take the next opportunity of pleasing them in some other things before they either ask or look for it. This will strengthen your authority, by making it soft to them, and confirm their obedience, by making it their interest.

Halifax had moved a very long way from medieval ideals. Instead of seeking to break their children's wills, parents were advised to avoid conflict wherever possible and to build their authority not on fear but on a love strengthened by the ready gratification of desire. Child management was to be guided by expediency, rather than Scriptural precept.[50]

A less pessimistic view of the child's nature made parental indulgence and a more demonstrative affection permissible, even commendable. From about the 1590s, such qualities were mentioned with grateful appreciation in epitaphs, and a little later in personal reminiscence. The inscription to Anne Theobald (d. 1594) at Faversham (Kent) recalls her 'maternal sweetness', while one at Stoke-by-Nayland (Suffolk) describes Anne Lady Windsor as an indulgent and most tender mother (1615). In 1620, Sir Thomas Wentworth called a kinsman 'an indulgent and louinge father'. The duchess of Newcastle (b. *c.* 1624) remembered how in her tender upbringing of herself and her sisters her mother had 'naturally' tried to please and delight them instead of thwarting or frightening them.[51]

The corrective emphasis of the advice on upbringing given in works of Christian counsel was somewhat softened during the Renaissance and Reformation. Writers laid more stress on the need for moderation in corporal punishment and on the importance of approaching this task in the right frame of mind. Some, such as Robert Cawdrey and William Gouge, thought that it should be used sparingly, or only as a last resort. The Pauline injunction 'Fathers, provoke not your children to anger, lest they be discouraged' (Colossians 3:21) attracted more comment than hitherto. When parents were 'wayward, hasty and churlish, ever brawling and chiding' remarked William Tyndale, they made their children 'heartless, and apt for nothing'. William Gouge sought to discourage 'too much austeritie in cariage, sowrenesse in countenance, threatning and reuiling in words, too hard handling, too seuere correction, too much restraint of libertie, too small allowance of things needfull, with the like', in his own comments on the text.[52]

In England, as in Germany, there seems often to have been some tension between Protestant writers' pessimistic premises concerning human nature and their relatively liberal practical advice concerning upbringing, influenced by classical and humanist precepts. An author like Robert Cawdrey, who wrote of the child in the cradle as altogether inclined to evil, could elsewhere use the metaphors of moist wax, new vessels, and fair, white, undefiled wool to describe it.[53]

The blending of humanist ideas with the corrective precepts

emphasised in the literature of Christian duty encouraged parents to avoid the extremes of severity and indulgence and to pursue the classical ideal of moderation in all things. Lord Burghley believed that 'the foolish cockering of some parents and the over-stern carriage of others causeth more men and women to take evil courses than naturally their own vicious inclinations'. In Roger North's vivid description of his mid-seventeenth century childhood his mother is represented as following the mean in child management with outstanding success. She was flexible, even indulgent, in some things. She appreciated that instruction was most effective when a child's attention had already been aroused. Accepting that her children's appetites were in general the best indication of what was good for them, she allowed them to drink from a bottle of small beer kept in their quarters when they wanted. But she maintained her authority inflexibly and crushed open rebellion with the rod. In some important respects her practice anticipated recommendations made by John Locke, the great exponent of the mean way in the upbringing of children. Like a true disciple of Quintilian, he wanted to exploit children's own inclinations to the full in the educational process. But he also believed that 'the Principle of all Vertue and Excellency' lay in a rational self-control which had to develop out of the restraints imposed upon the individual from his earliest years. Locke advised that, contrary to what he believed to be the 'ordinary way', children should be made to 'go without their Longings, even *from their very Cradles*', and should, when they were very little, learn perfect compliance with their parents' wills. Though in general Locke condemned corporal punishment, he nevertheless conceded that it should be used to curb '*Obstinacy or Rebellion*'. Excessive repression, however, jeopardised the success of the educational process. The man who had found 'how to keep up a Child's Spirit, easy, active, and free' while also drawing him to unpalatable tasks had in Locke's opinion 'got the true Secret of Education'.[54]

This period saw not only a gradual change in assumptions concerning the nature of children and the goals of early upbringing but also alterations in accepted patterns of comportment and modes of address between parents and their offspring. Outward and inward reverence towards parents were traditionally held to be enjoined by the commandment 'Honour thy father and thy mother, that thy days may be long in the land which the Lord thy God giveth thee' which prefaced all discussions of filial duty. The service done to parents and other superiors set over us was to be thought of as done to the Lord (Ephesians 6:7). According to *Dives and Pauper* the duty of honour comprised humility, respect, obedience, succour in need and good living. William Tyndale insisted that it was[55]

not to be understood in bowing the knee, and putting off the cap only, but that thou love them with all thine heart; and fear and dread them, and wait on their commandments; and seek their worship, pleasure, will and profit in all things; and give thy life for them, . . . remembering that thou art their good and possession, and that thou owest unto them thine own self and all that thou art able, yea, and more than thou art able to do.

Traditional etiquette underlined the child's subject status, but nowhere more clearly than in the ritual of the parental blessing, or parental invocation of God's blessing, which powerfully expressed the idea that the parent was God's representative. Potent though the ritual was in conveying an assurance of fundamental love and good-will, it was even more important in making the child act the role of subject and suppliant. Solemn requests for parental blessings are common in the great fifteenth-century letter collections. On the eve of the Reformation Richard Whytforde advised mothers and fathers to teach children to seek their blessing on their knees every night before they went to bed. The particularly solemn words and gestures recommended by Whytforde, including the sign of the Cross and a Latin invocation of the Trinity, would have emphasised the quasi-sacerdotal character of parental authority. After the Reformation, Protestant writers continued to recommend the ritual. Thomas Becon thought that children should be accustomed to humble themselves in this way both morning and evening. Correspondence, and some personal reminiscences, suggest that during the seventeenth century the blessing was coming to be bestowed more informally, with a bedtime kiss, for example, or restricted to solemn occasions, even though it remained a strictly observed part of family routine in some households, such as that into which John Wesley was born in 1703. William Gouge had to defend the practice against two principal objections: that it seemed to give even wicked parents a means of tapping divine benevolence, and that to kneel before parents was to accord them a reverence properly reserved to God. With the gradual decline of the formal blessing there disappeared the most potent ritual expression of the direct link between divine and parental authority.[56]

In any period it was probably only conscientious and literate parents who attempted to follow the pattern set out in the literature of counsel in their management of their children. Writers from Peter Idley in the mid-fifteenth century to John Locke in the late seven-teenth repeatedly contrasted the actual behaviour of parents with their recommendations. Some pampered and indulged their children while others oppressed theirs harshly. Ideal types of upbringing called for parental suppression of natural impulses, whether to show excessive fondness and affection, to shirk the task of correction, or to yield to sudden anger. In all periods it is likely that the behaviour of parents in the lower reaches of society differed fairly radically from that depicted in the literature of counsel or the reminiscences of gentlefolk.

Early training and education

By long-established convention the upbringing of young children belonged primarily to their mothers. Yet the nature of fatal childhood accidents recorded in late medieval coroners' rolls suggests that children in the countryside began to follow parents of their own sex about their work at a very early age, and this pattern probably continued to hold good during our period. Among children of two or three, for example, a much higher percentage of boys fell into water, a sign that they were more likely to venture away from the house, while the percentage of girls succumbing to mishaps involving pots and cauldrons was twice as high as that of boys who met their deaths in this way. Higher up the social scale, paternal participation in the upbringing of small children was doubtless limited, though reformers and humanists stressed its importance, and the progress of their little sons and daughters was a source of great interest and delight for many fathers. Roger North, who recalled that his childhood had passed 'as usuall, under the Mother's government' also remembered that his father had sometimes 'condescended to entertein the little credulous Impertinents . . . with an agreable as well as moral Effect . . .'. Charles Hoole described in 1660 how one father, after watching his two-year-old son making a collection of shells and sticks, devised for him a toy which enabled him to learn all the letters of the alphabet in eleven days. Of all fathers the clergy were in some ways the best qualified, and had the best reasons and opportunities, to share in the tasks of upbringing, and the close interest of one, Ralph Josselin, is apparent from his diary. But a man who took seriously his duty to begin the education of his children betimes could nevertheless find the experience a frustrating one. 'What a deale of patience is requisite to beare any converse with our little children,' remarked that solicitous father, Henry Newcome, 'How peevish and foolish are they!'[57]

Among the upper classes, the early education of children was a task largely delegated to servants. Whatever the care taken in their choice by conscientious parents, there were frequent complaints of negligence in this regard. Writers on education such as Sir Thomas Elyot called for discriminating selection. Concern to prevent children's corruption by bad example led to their segregation from the rougher and more uncouth domestic servants. Grace Sherrington (b. 1552) remembered how her governess advised the girls in her charge to avoid the company of serving men 'whose ribald talk and ydle gestures and evill suggestions were dangerous for' their 'chaste ears and eyes to hear and behold'. Her father had scourged a young man 'for making but a showe and countenance of a saucie and unreverent behaviour' towards his children, and dismissed him from his service.[58]

Of all educational tasks, the earliest to begin in the middle and upper ranks of society was the inculcation of 'good manners'. In a society in which service was the most important avenue of advancement at all levels, one of the most essential skills was the ability to make oneself acceptable to superiors. The good manners which were the prerequisite of social success grew naturally out of the marks of respect shown to parents. Proper physical deportment (upright bearing, control of head, eyes, eyebrows and hands) expressed reliability and deference. Marks of respect to be shown in conversation with superiors included baring the head, dropping the right knee, keeping silence till spoken to, listening carefully and answering sensibly and shortly. Compliance with commands was to be immediate, response to praise heartily grateful. At table, precedence was to be observed in seating and serving, and food was to be eaten with due decorum.[59]

Our glimpses of the process of early socialisation are rare. But in an imaginary dialogue of Claudius Hollyband's we possess a vivid picture of a dinner of 1573 in a middle-class London household. Reproofs for supposed lapses from good manners figure prominently in the parents'conversation with their children. The guests are much more indulgent towards the children than the anxious father. Their subordinate status is made clear not only by the reproofs given them but also by the bantering tone in which they are addressed and their being placed at their own table, which they are expected to leave early to attend on the adults. Parental concern with the deportment both of the small child and the adolescent is evident in reminiscence and correspondence. In 1639, on his first appearance in company, Edmund Verney's father and grandfather took unfavourable notice of his shyness and awkwardness, though his great-grandmother thought her son would have had more sense than to expect a child who was not yet three to acquire social ease immediately. Early social success, on the other hand, was a source of parental pleasure. Lady Anne Clifford noted proudly that her daughter was commended by all the company on making her first visit at the age of two and a half. In later childhood Lady Jane Grey claimed that every smallest activity she performed in her parents' presence had to be done perfectly if she was not to suffer taunts, threats or punishment.[60]

Reverence towards God was closely bound up with deference towards earthly superiors, and the well-nurtured late medieval child grew into a religion of gesture and observance at the same time as he acquired good manners. Early religious education was a parental responsibility. William Harrington and Richard Whytforde both thought that parents should teach their children the Lord's Prayer, Ave, Creed and Ten Commandments. Whytforde recommended that this instruction begin as soon as they could speak, and set out a much more detailed programme. The greater emphasis on inward understanding evident in Whytforde's work, written on the very eve of the Reformation, was further amplified in Protestant expositions of the parental duty of religious instruction. The Scriptures, from which children might in Thomas Becon's phrase 'drink in the knowledge of godliness from their young and tender years', bulked large in the programme.[61]

Parents capable of effective religious instruction must always have been a small minority. Pious parents who attempted to fulfil their duties were nevertheless widely scattered through the upper and middle ranks of society. Mothers played the biggest part in early religious instruction. As it increased in complexity during the Reformation and the subsequent era of confessional strife, some writers came to regard it as their most important and exacting responsibility. It was moreover one which could help to give useful purpose to the lives of those well-educated wives of gentlemen, merchants and professional men who lacked a major economic role.

Our direct evidence of maternal religious instruction dates from the time of the Reformation onwards. Towards the end of Henry VIII's reign, the wife of Sir William Lock, an alderman of London, secretly read to her three daughters out of Protestant books privately sent from overseas by her husband's factors. Under Elizabeth, many boys were drawn to the Catholic faith by their mothers, often in the face of paternal hostility or indifference. The mother of Oliver Heywood (b. 1630), a Lancashire yeoman's wife, pressed upon her children's consciences the 'undenyable maximes of christianity',took good care that they should learn the catechism, and encouraged them to read the Scriptures and other good books. She also taught them how to pray. Lady Alice Bramston (d. 1647) taught her children the Lord's Prayer, the Commandments and the Creed (which she heard them say every morning) and some psalms and chapters selected from both testaments. Roger North recalled the skill with which his mother had in her children's religious education turned to advantage their appetite for stories. This reminiscence underlines the importance of adapting the instruction given to children's capacities and needs. At first the lessons learnt had to be simple ones. We are told that one of the daughters of the godly Mrs Margaret Corbet (1629–57), who could not yet speak distinctly, was so impressed by her mother's teaching that she told her father that God would not bless those who told fibs, and that 'she had rather dye than tell a Fibb'.[62]

Lack of close and effective parental guidance, or over-zealous cultivation of children's awareness of sin and mortality could however sow the seeds of scepticism or deep anxiety. Children encouraged to make the Bible their first reading were likely to find in it incomprehensible or frightening things. Richard Norwood (b. 1590), son of a gentleman of declining fortunes, recalled how, when he was at most seven years old, astonished by Scriptural passages about the resurrection of the dead, he showed them to his father and mother, who seemed to smile at his childishness:

Upon which and the like occasions I often doubted whether things were really so as I conceived them or whether elder people did not know them to be otherwise, only they were willing that we children should be so persuaded of them, that we might follow our books the better and be kept in from play.

On the other hand John Hutchinson (b. 1615), whose religious instruction had been left to his nurse, and John Bunyan (b. 1628) both experienced terrifying childhood fears of the consequences of sin. In the 1660s the efforts of the widowed minister Oliver Heywood to inculcate a sense of sin in his son John more than once made the boy weep bitterly. In 1560 Thomas Becon had urged that 'learn to die' be among the earliest sentences taught to children, and death was a central theme of the juvenile religious literature of the seventeenth century. In his *Spiritual Counsel* (1694), John Norris told his children to imagine themselves in their deathbeds, their coffins and their graves.[63]

John Locke cogently expressed what were probably by his time widespread doubts about the value of methods commonly used to introduce children to religion. The child should begin his reading with Aesop's *Fables* rather than the Bible, whose indiscriminate perusal could only produce an odd jumble of thoughts in his head. He implicitly condemned the aims and approach of much juvenile religious literature when he insisted that God be presented to the child as the 'Supreme Being, Author and Maker of all Things, from whom we receive all our Good, who loves us, and gives us all Things' and warned that premature talk of spirits, or efforts 'to make him understand the incomprehensible Nature of that infinite Being' would simply mislead or confuse him.[64]

The ability to read was regarded, especially by the pious, as first and foremost the gateway to religious knowledge, and the Bible was often used as the first reading book. Several seventeenth-century autobiographers began to read between the ages of three and six, often at the mother's or nurse's knee. (In 1397 ABC books had been bought for the daughters of the earl of Derby, later Henry IV, when they were aged two and four respectively.) Four was widely recognised, from the later Middle Ages onwards, as the age at which formal instruction might usefully commence. By 1660 it could be assumed that children started school in cities and bigger towns at four or five, in the countryside, where there were fewer opportunities, at six or seven. Yet the early seventeenth-century schoolmaster John Brinsley claimed that those who sent their children to school at six usually did so more to keep them from getting in the way at home and in order to prevent accidents than from any great hope or desire that they learn something.[65]

Later childhood

According to the commonest conventional scheme inherited from antiquity, childhood comprised two phases, up to the age of seven and from seven to puberty respectively. Close and gentle care were thought appropriate in the first phase: at baptism the parents were charged to guard the child from fire, water and other perils up to the age of seven. The seventh year was held to be a milestone in physical and mental development. It was then that the second set of teeth began to emerge, then, it was believed, that the child could tell right from wrong and became capable of mortal sin and crime. Some educationalists thought that boys should now pass from the tutelage of women to that of men. Many modern writers on childhood also believe that the years between six and eight mark an important stage in the physical, intellectual and social development of the child.[66]

When they were six or seven, boys adopted adult dress. Before the introduction of doublet and hose in the fourteenth century, small boys had been dressed like adults. The long gown had probably been retained for children among other groups because it was felt to be more seemly and decorous than the new styles. The difference between younger boys in their 'coats' (gowns) and aprons, and the older ones in their doublet and hose is immediately apparent in Pieter Bruegel's *Children's Games* (1560). Little boys would often go to their first schools in coats, as did Richard Norwood in the 1590s.[67]

Formal education began in or near the home, typically given by tutor or chaplain to the children of the upper classes, by priest, parish clerk or the keeper of a petty school to those of humbler birth. But in later childhood the continued pursuit of education was much more likely to take the individual further afield. Its cost and physical accessibility severely limited the numbers of older children of the poorer classes who were able to take advantage of it.

In the upper and middle ranks of society children were commonly sent away from home to another household or to board in or near a school of good repute. Parents increasingly embraced the latter alternative, especially during the 'educational revolution' of the later sixteenth and early seventeenth centuries, when new schools were founded in large numbers.[68] Girls were less likely to be sent away than their brothers, and, despite an undoubted increase in the number of girls' schools, the pattern of household education persisted far longer in their case. It was there that the housewife's essential skills were best learnt, though reading, writing and accounts might also be taught.[69] A classical education was generally felt to be unsuitable for girls on account of their intellectual inferiority, even though many parents realised that in practice girls could learn as quickly as their brothers when they were given the same advantages.[70]

It was thought desirable to send children to school not only to inform their minds but also to form their characters. The two motives are intertwined in the mid-Tudor interlude *The Disobedient Child*. It tells the sad story of a boy kept at home by his doting father, a rich man, who, through giving way to his son's wishes, finds it increasingly difficult to insist upon obedience. The father weakly gives way to his son's protests against being sent to school, though not without fears that the untaught boy will end up like the poor knaves who scour latrines. Parents must subdue their children in time or see them go to the bad.

> And let us them thruste alwaye to the schole,
> Wherby at their bookes they maye be kept under:
> And so we shall shortely their courage coole,
> And brynge them to honestie, vertue and nurture.

If children became more difficult to control the longer they stayed at home, as *The Disobedient Child* suggested, it was probably best to send them away before adolescence, while they were still tractable. Stern but anxious fathers hoped, as their letters show, that their sons would be 'kept short' or 'kept under' in other households and at school. Nathaniel Bacon pointed out around 1570 that those parents who loved their children best sought to set them for a time in a 'good place' away from home, where they usually had everything they wanted. This was the way to teach them self-knowledge and how to forgo their desires, lessons best learnt early.[71]

Positive benefits were expected of the interaction between the older child and his peers. In 1537, Lady Lisle was advised to send her ten-year-old son James to college rather than give him private tuition because 'a child of a good nature' was 'pricked to learn' by competition, and because he would have companions 'of his own sort, both of birth and age'. Being 'on the playne ground' without advantages of birth, thought Christopher Guise, recalling his own departure for school at the age of nine or ten (*c*. 1628), enabled a boy to assess 'his owne price in the markett' of his contemporaries' opinion. The friendships, factions, intrigues, fights and ridicule of the free school, concluded Roger North, taught boys to be men at little cost.[72]

There is abundant evidence of parental interest in children's welfare and progress while at school, whether in the neighbourhood or further afield. Physical absence did not end parental concern any more than it does today. Nor was such solicitude new in our period. It is implicit in the detailed report on his young son's recovery from illness which Edmund Stonor received in about 1380. The boy was happy and healthy, had remembered himself to his mother and father without being reminded, and had begun to learn Latin at a not too taxing pace. The master and his wife wanted some of the boy's clothes sent back home – fewer would be enough and they might get torn or dirtied by accident. Active concern for her absent children's well-being is evident in the correspondence of Lady Lisle in the

1530s. Some fathers' solicitude for their sons' moral welfare was coupled with a traditional belief in the value of early physical correction. In *The French Littleton* (1576) Claudius Hollyband imagined an anxious father parting from his son's new schoolmaster with an injunction to correct, chasten and amend the boy's faults. But John Brinsley thought it the wise father's wish that his son 'get the best learning, in the shortest time, and with the least severitie'; in the second half of our period in particular, complaints about school masters' brutality, especially from the 'meaner sort' of parents, were allegedly frequent, and 'verbal, legal or even physical retaliation by aggrieved parents was very common'.[73]

Many parents understandably wished to see their children's schooling yield tangible and measurable results, and took an interest in their progress in learning. Such an interest is a recurrent theme of Hollyband's imaginary dialogues. John Brinsley, urging the grammar schools to set their house in order some fifty years later, imagined one father complaining that his son had been at school six or seven years without learning to read English well, another that his son's writing was so bad that he was unfit for trade or any other employment in which he would use his pen. The private schools had perforce to develop syllabuses better suited to pupils' needs and their parents' expectations. Sir Balthasar Gerbier, seeking to publicise the academy he founded at Bethnal Green during the Interregnum, provided free public lectures 'where not onely the Fathers of Families, but also the Mothers (mutually interested in the good educations of their Sonnes) could be more frequently informed of its method'. After the Restoration, Adam Martindale, a deprived minister turned teacher of mathematics, gave a practical demonstration of his pupils' skill in land surveying at their parents' request.[74]

Dissatisfied parents removed their sons to other schools. In 1583, Peter Pett, a master shipwright of Deptford, decided to withdraw his son Phineas from the free school in Rochester because of his 'small profiting' there and place him at a private school in Greenwich, which prepared him for university in three years. In the early 1630s, Adam Martindale's father removed him from a free to a private school after his master had kept him below a gentleman's son, an 'arrant dunce'.[75]

In sending their children away from home, whether to enter another household or to go to school, parents acted in what they conceived to be their children's best interests. They sought to advance their education, wean them from excessive dependence upon themselves, and help them to find new friends and patrons. But an oft-quoted Italian observer of the English social scene towards the end of the fifteenth century gained a very different impression of the purposes of the custom. Nearly all English children, he claimed, were put out to hard service in other people's houses at seven years of age, or nine at the most, never to return. This was due to the lack of affection in the English, to their desire to enjoy all their comforts themselves and the fact that they were better served by strangers than they would have been by their own children. Perhaps there was some truth in this last remark, but we have no reason to doubt the explanation, reported with scepticism by the Italian observer, that children were sent away from home to learn better manners, though this was only one of the aims of the practice. Traditional educational wisdom, as we have seen, demanded that children be subjected to fairly harsh discipline for their own benefit. Yet the strength of emotional bonds within the nuclear family made the task of necessary correction, increasingly important in later childhood, painful to mother and father. It was much easier for comparative strangers with whom children had no emotional ties. Alberti's *Della Famiglia* suggests that Italian patrician fathers could in their efforts to control their children count on the support of the elders of their kindred to an extent unknown in England. If indeed comparatively close-knit extended families were common among the Italian upper classes these may have made the task of discipline and socialisation easier to accomplish than it was in England. They may have provided the means of making a much smoother and more gradual transition from childhood to adulthood. In another respect, too, the observer's remarks are misleading. His reference to older children as 'apprentices' suggests that he had urban families in mind. Yet although the sons of merchants and tradesmen may have entered service or apprenticeship rather earlier in the late fifteenth century than they did in the second half of our period, it seems unlikely that they did so in large numbers when they were as young as nine. Entry into another household before ten was probably much commoner among the nobility and gentry, who still today despatch their offspring to preparatory schools at the age of eight.[76]

The economic contribution of children

Thus far our discussion of later childhood has centred on the comparatively privileged members of society. The majority were expected to begin to contribute to the household economy during these years. Every poor man that had brought up children to the age of twelve then expected their help, John Paston I thought in 1465, but children's gradual entry into work probably began in most poor households long before this. From about the age of eight onwards children were employed to weed, pick stones, gather wood, scare birds, mind babies, guard sheep, cast the seed in the furrow and help with harvest work. Children whose parents had no jobs for them to do would go to seek daywork from neighbours. In the seventeenth century, parents began to withdraw children from school as soon as they could make a useful economic contribution. The timing of the process largely depended upon the farmer's wealth; the greater a man's substance the longer he could leave his children there. Josiah Langdale (b. 1673) was not taken away till his father's death some time before he was nine. Then, a strong boy for his age, he was put to leading harrows, learning to plough and keeping the horse and oxen. William Stout (b. 1665) remembered how he and his brothers had begun to work rather later than his elder sister, who was soon needed to help her mother look after the younger children and to knit, sew and spin. As they reached ten or twelve, he and his brothers were taken from school, especially in spring and summer, to look after the sheep, help with the plough, go with the cart for turves, make hay and take part in shearing.[77]

In certain industries children began to work even earlier than in agriculture. In textile manufacture this was partly because the work could readily be performed under parental supervision and did not demand much physical strength. Thomas Wilson, writing in 1601, observed that in English towns children were, from the age of six or seven, 'forced to some art', whereby they maintained themselves and earned something for their parents and masters. In Norwich alone, so he claimed, children aged between six and ten had gained £12,000 a year, besides their keep, chiefly by knitting fine jersey stockings. In the early 1720s, Daniel Defoe, whose satisfaction concerning the employment of children resembled Wilson's, put the lower age limit of gainful employment of the properly taught child in textile areas at five around Taunton and Colchester, four or five around Norwich, and at four in the West Riding. But the 1570 Norwich census of the poor suggests that girls were much more readily fitted into the domestic economy of a textile town than were boys. Among those children aged between six and twelve still living with parents or other relatives whose age and sex were specified, over four-fifths of the girls were working, compared with less than a third of the boys. About a third of the boys were still at school. Lacking as yet the strength to play a useful part in male work, only a minority of these boys were entrusted with female work such as spinning and knitting which employed a substantial majority of the girls.[78]

A large proportion of the growing number of poor people were unable to maintain or employ their children themselves or find them employment through their own efforts. An Act of 1536 provided that all begging children above the age of five be put to service by local authorities. Acts of 1598 and 1601, covering all children whose parents were unable to maintain them, specified no minimum age for parish apprenticeship, but in practice it seems to have been seven. When in the 1630s a serious effort was made to improve the working of the parish apprenticeship system, the lower age limit chosen by the justices seems to have varied in different areas between seven and ten. In seventeenth-century Cambridgeshire, while bastards were commonly apprenticed at seven or eight, the age at which other children were bound ranged between nine and fifteen. Parents of younger children could be given some financial help in order to maintain them at home. There were repeated complaints that the system did not work properly: that the parish overseers of the poor did not enforce the statutory provisions; that parents did not wish to part with their children; that many of the householders chosen as masters proved unwilling to take the poor children billetted upon them, and, if forced to do so, treated them so badly that they ran away. Poor parents, then, might have to part with their children earlier than their more prosperous neighbours. The community's representatives might in theory assume the responsibilities which such parents had proved unable to meet, but they discharged them in a manner which vouchsafed such children only a bleak future. It is true that some masters, such as William Stout, the Quaker merchant of Lancaster, did their best for the parish apprentices entrusted to them, and some local authorities supervised the operation of parish apprenticeship fairly carefully, but most of these apprentices had little prospect of rising from the very bottom of the social scale.[79]

From the mid-sixteenth century onwards, special municipal institutions were developed in order to cope with the problem of the orphan, vagrant or uncontrollable child. But inadequate capacity, managerial inefficiency and lack of co-operation from parents or overseers led to the collapse of the more ambitious institutional projects, the modification of their original aims, or the deterioration of conditions within them. Entry into an institution placed an unenviable stamp upon the orphan, bastard or abandoned child. Parish apprenticeship, for all its shortcomings, provided at least a simulacrum of the service or apprenticeship into which the majority of children would enter.[80]

Conclusion

The Middle Ages passed on an ideal picture of the relationship between parents and their offspring. Children were welcome gifts from God. Parental love was the most deeply rooted of all human instincts, and showed itself especially in the mother's tender and loving care of the helpless baby. But it was futile to grieve in the face of infant deaths. Rather should the truly Christian mother be glad that God had taken her child to himself. The child which died before seven, the age of reason, was normally incapable of mortal sin and assured of paradise. Yet the child inherited original sin, which began to manifest itself even in infantile greed and rage, and the inborn propensity grew with intelligence. So it was the duty of the solicitous parent to correct his child with the rod. Successful parenthood largely depended upon the ability to curb one's natural inclinations, and those who did not want their children to become soft, truculent and good-for-nothing were wise to put them out in late childhood to undergo further discipline and training at the hands of strangers.

Much of the inherited picture survived throughout this period, but it changed in important respects. The Protestant reformers took over an emphasis on original sin and the parents' corrective responsibility. They also laid greater emphasis on the parents' part in early and thorough religious education. The humanists, on the other hand, believing as they did in the child's capacity for good and the moral neutrality of its impulses, sought to protect innocence and prevent deterioration rather than to correct inborn vices. To show natural parental affection seemed less dangerous than hitherto. Humanist readiness to give expression to natural pleasures and sorrows made more acceptable the display of delight in children in letters and of a qualified grief at their loss in memorial inscriptions. From the sixteenth century onwards there was a greater variety of patterns of upbringing. Yet the fusion of Christian and humanist ideas encouraged a 'middle way' in upbringing, between the extremes of severity and indulgence. It enhanced the complexity of the task of nurture, and consequently of fine judgement on the part of those who undertook it.

Actual experience and practice often stood in contrast with ideals. Children were not always welcome. Some birth control was practised, and the danger of infanticide was widely recognised. Yet despite the ease with which infanticidal practices could be masked within families, parish registers suggest that infant and child mortality were relatively low and very largely explicable in terms of environment and disease. There is much direct evidence of the reality of loving care in some families and of parental grief in face of the loss of children. Women of the upper classes did not generally suckle their own children, though humanist and Protestant propaganda may have persuaded a minority to do so. But this did not preclude care and solicitude in the choice and supervision of wet-nurses. Differences between the life patterns of socio-economic groups had many other effects on the child's prospects. The offspring of the urban poor, rapidly growing in numbers during this period, always had the poorest chances of surviving infancy. It was the poorer groups in society who had to exploit their children's labour in the struggle for survival at the earliest point. Only fathers and mothers who enjoyed the advantages conferred by economic means, education and a certain amount of leisure were able to approach the ideal of intensive parenthood set out in the literature of counsel, carefully polishing their children's manners, inculcating the principles of religion and laying the foundations of literacy. Such instruction for life as most children had from their parents was probably gained in byre and field, at spinning-wheel and oven. But the quality of parenthood was not of course determined by material circumstances alone, very important though these were. The unquantifiable and still only partially understood elements of individual character were crucial in this period as they still are today.

Notes and references

1. **A. Niccholes**, *A Discourse of Marriage and Wiving, and of the greatest Mystery therein contained: How to choose a good Wife from a bad*, London, 1615, p. 5; **W. Gouge**, *Of Domestical Duties Eight Treatises*, London, 1622, p. 210; *The Colloquies of Erasmus*, trans. **C. R. Thompson**, Univ. of Chicago Press, 1965, p. 284; of Shakespeare's sonnets, see e.g. i–iv, vi–xiii, xv–xvii.

2. 'New Study shows Risk of Delay in starting a Family', *The Times*, 19 Feb. 1982, 24a.

3. 'Physiology: Natural Contraception', *The Times*, 27 Feb. 1980; **A. Smith**, 'Breast-feeding and Pregnancy: Some Truth in the Old Wives' Tale', *The Times*, 21 Oct. 1981, 10f; **J. Knodel**, 'Espacement des naissances et planification familiale: une critique de la méthode Dûpaquier–Lachiver', *Annales, Economies, Sociétés, Civilisations*, **36** (1981), 480–3; **D. McLaren**, 'Nature's Contraceptive. Wet-nursing and Prolonged Lactation: The Case of Chesham, Buckinghamshire, 1578–1601', *Medical History*, **23** (1979), esp. 432; **G. F. Still**, *The History of Paediatrics*, Oxford UP, 1931, pp. 154, 376, 380, 424, 456.

4. **A. Macfarlane**, *The Family Life of Ralph Josselin, a Seventeenth-Century Clergyman: An Essay in Historical Anthropology*, Cambridge UP, 1970, pp. 199–202; **R. S. Schofield**, 'Perinatal Mortality in Hawkshead, Lancashire, 1581–1710', *Local Population Studies*, **4** (1970). 11–16.

5. **J. T. Noonan**, *Contraception*, Belknap Press, Cambridge (Mass.), 1966, pp. 200–30; **R. V. Schnucker**, 'Elizabethan Birth Control and Puritan Attitudes', *Journal of Interdisciplinary History*, **5** (1974–75), 655–60; **G. R. Quaife**, *Wanton Wenches and Wayward Wives: Peasants and Illicit Sex in Early Seventeenth Century England*, Croom Helm, London, 1979, pp. 133–4; **N. Culpeper**, *A Directory for Midwives*, London, 1675–76, Vol. I, pp. 70, 76–8; *The Ladies 'Dictionary*, London, 1694, p. 225.

6. **E. A. Wrigley** and **R. S. Schofield**, *The Population History of England, 1541–1871. A Reconstruction*, Edward Arnold, London. 1981, pp. 254–5; Professor Wrigley once believed that deliberate family limitation played a major part in reducing marital fertility in Colyton (Devon) during the seventeenth century, but subsequently concluded that its practice was probably becoming more evident in the register rather than more common; in a period when clandestine marriage was particularly common, family limitation may have been most widespread among the families whose marriages are recorded in the register. See **E. A. Wrigley**, 'Family Limitation in Pre-industrial England', *Economic History Review*, 2nd ser., **19** (1966), 82–109, and 'Marital Fertility in Seventeenth-Century Colyton: A Note', *Economic History Review*, 2nd ser., **31** (1978), 433–4. But for another historical demographer's continued belief in the contribution made by deliberate family limitation to declining marital fertility in the seventeenth century, see **K. Wrightson** and **D. Levine**, *Poverty and Piety in an English Village: Terling, 1525–1700*, Academic Press, London, 1979, p. 65.

7. Compare cumulative marital fertility 20–44 (means of twelve reconstitution studies) in Wrigley and Schofield, *op. cit*, p. 254, with computed

size of families after different periods of marriage in **T. H. Hollingsworth**, 'A Demographic Study of the British Peerage', supplement to *Population Studies*, **18** (1964), 40. See also **R. Finlay**, *Population and Metropolis: The Demography of London*, 1580–1650, Cambridge UP, 1981, pp. 135, 142: mean length of birth intervals between first and sixth child 23 months in two wealthy parishes, 27 in two poor ones.

8. **P. Laslett**, 'Mean Household Size in England since the Sixteenth Century', in **P. Laslett** and **R. Wall** (eds), *Household and Family in Past Time*, Cambridge UP, 1972, p. 155; **T. C. Croker** (ed.), *Autobiography of Mary, Countess of Warwick*, Percy Society, **76** (1848), 32–3.

9. **M. Davies**, 'Corsets and Conception: Fashion and Demographic Trends in the Nineteenth Century', *Comparative Studies in Society and History*, **24** (1982), 611–41.

10. **A. Eccles**, *Obstetrics and Gynaecology in Tudor and Stuart England*, Croom Helm, London, 1982, pp. 86, 125, 130; **T. H. Forbes**, 'By What Disease or Casualty: the Changing Face of Death in London', in **C. Webster** (ed.), *Health, Medicine and Mortality in the Sixteenth Century*, Cambridge UP, 1979, p. 128; Wrightson and Levine, *op. cit.*, p. 58; *Mortality Statistics, Childhood and Maternity. Review of the Registrar General on Deaths in England and Wales, 1979*. HMSO, London, 1981, p. 95.

11. Eccles, *op. cit.*, pp. 87–93, 101–8, 115–18, 123–4, 141; midwife's certificate of *c.* 1541 printed in **R. A. Houlbrooke**, *Church Courts and the People during the English Reformation*. Oxford UP, 1979, p. 77.

12. **B. Winchester**, *Tudor Family Portrait*, Jonathan Cape, London, 1955, p. 101; **D. Townshend**, *Life and Letters of Mr Endymion Porter: Sometime Gentleman of the Bedchamber to King Charles the First*, T. Fisher Unwin, London, 1897, p. 22; Macfarlane, *op. cit.*, p. 85; Eccles, *op. cit.*, p. 91, citing **N. Sudell**, *Mulierum Amicus, or the woman's friend*, 1666.

13. Gouge, *op. cit.*, pp. 400–2; **S. Clarke**, *A Collection of the Lives of Ten Eminent Divines*, London, 1662, pp. 10–11; *John Gerard: The Autobiography of an Elizabethan*, trans. **P. Caraman**, Longmans, Green & Co., London, 1951, p. 20; **J. Bunyan**, *Grace Abounding to the Chief of Sinners*, **R. Sharrock** (ed.), Clarendon Press, Oxford, 1962, p. 75; **J. Page-Phillips**, *Children on Brasses*, George Allen & Unwin, London, 1970. Figs. 53, 54.

14. **C. L. Kingsford** (ed.), *Stonor Letters and Papers*, 1290–1483. *Camden Society*, 3rd ser., **29–30** (1919), I, 133.

15. **J. Mirk**, *Instructions for Parish Priests*, **G. Kristensson**. (ed.), *Lund Studies in English*, **49** (1974), 72, 75; *Manuale ad Vsum Percelebris Ecclesie Sarisburiensis*, **A. J. Collins**, (ed.), *Henry Bradshaw Society*, **91** (1960), 35–44; *The First and Second Prayer Books of Edward VI*, J. M. Dent & Sons., London, 1910, pp. 394–9; **T. Becon**, *The Catechism . . . with other pieces written by him in the Reign of King Edward the Sixth*, **T. Ayre** (ed.), *Parker Society*, **11** (1844), 208, 214–17; **J. Pratt** (ed.), *The Acts and Monuments of John Foxe*, The Religious Tract Society, London, 1877, Vol. VIII, pp. 356–9; Gouge, *op. cit.*, pp. 60–6, **W. Tyndale**, *The Obedience of a Christen Man* in *Doctrinal Treatises and Introductions to Different Portions of the Holy Scriptures*, H. Walter (ed.). *Parker Society*, **42** (1848), 276–7; **B. M. Berry** and **R. S.**

Schofield, 'Age at Baptism in Pre-industrial England', *Population Studies*, **25** (1971), 456.

16. **P. Clark**, 'The Alehouse and the Alternative Society', in **D. Pennington** and **K. Thomas** (eds), *Puritans and Revolutionaries. Essays in Seventeenth-Century History presented to Christopher Hill*, Clarendon Press, Oxford, 1978, p. 63; **C. Hole**, *English Home-life, 1500 to 1800*, Batsford, London, 1947, pp. 41–2; **W. L. Sachse** (ed.), *The Diary of Roger Lowe of Ashton-in-Makerfield, Lancs., 1663–74*, Longmans, Green & Co., London, 1938, pp. 26, 73, 75, 96.

17. Mirk, *op. cit.*, p. 128; **D. Leigh**, *The Mother's Blessing: or, the Godly Counsaile of a Gentle-Woman, not long since deceased, left behind her for her Children*, 10th edn, London, 1627, p. 25; **R. Parkinson** (ed.), *The Life of Adam Martindale, written by himself*, Chetham Society, old ser., **4** (1845), 5; but see complaint of ignorance of godparents in pre-Reformation Norfolk in Pratt, *op. cit.*, Vol. VIII, p. 126.

18. **C. Jackson** and **H. J. Morehouse** (eds), *Yorkshire Diaries and Autobiographies, in the Seventeenth and Eighteenth Centuries*, Surtees Society, **65** (1877), 112, 173, 354; Wrightson and Levine, *op. cit.*, p. 93; **P. Collinson**, *The Elizabethan Puritan Movement*, Jonathan Cape, London, 1967, p. 369; for the doubts of a pious lady about godparenthood, see **D. M. Meads** (ed.), *Diary of Lady Margaret Hoby*, George Routledge & Sons, London, 1930, p. 118 (6 May 1600).

19. **M. J. Bennett**, 'Spiritual Kinship and the Baptismal Name in Traditional European Society', in *Social History Society Newsletter*, **4** (1979), 2–3; **C. W. E. Bardsley**, *Curiosities of Puritan Nomenclature*, London, 1880, pp. 1–195; **J. O. Halliwell** (ed.), *The Autobiography and Correspondence of Sir Simonds D'Ewes, Bart.*, London, 1845, Vol. I, p. 8.

20. **C. Jackson** (ed.), *The Autobiography of Mrs Alice Thornton, of East Newton, in the County of York*, Surtees Society, **62** (1875), 50; **H. C. Fanshawe** (ed.), *The Memoirs of Ann Lady Fanshawe*, John Lane, London, 1907, pp. 84–5; **L. Stone**, *The Family, Sex and Marriage in England 1500–1800*, Weidenfeld & Nicolson, London, 1977, p. 409.

21. **F. P.** and **M. M. Verney**, *Memoirs of the Verney Family during the Seventeenth Century*, Longmans, Green & Co., 2nd edn, London, 1907, Vol. I, pp. 362, 380; **M. C. Seymour** (ed.), *On the Properties of Things: John Trevisa's Translation of Bartholomaeus Anglicus 'De Proprietatibus Rerum'. A Critical Text*, Clarendon Press, Oxford, 1975, Vol. I. p. 299; Culpeper, *op. cit.*, Vol. II, p. 229; **M. C. Rowsell**, *The Life Story of Charlotte de la Tremoille, Countess of Derby*, Kegan Paul, Trench, Trübner & Co., London, 1905, p. 38; Macfarlane, *op. cit.*, p. 90.

22. Seymour, *op. cit.*, Vol. I, pp. 154, 303; Still, *op. cit.*, pp. 12, 66, 155, 184–5, 305; Thompson, *op. cit.*, pp. 267, 272–85; **H. Smith**, *A Prepar-atiue to Mariage, The summe whereof was spoken at a Contract, and inlarged after*, London, 1591, pp. 99–100; **D. Rogers**, *Matrimoniall Honour: or the Mutuall Crowne and comfort of godly, loyall, and chaste Marriage*, London, 1642, pp. 279–80; Culpeper, *op. cit.*, Vol. I, pp. 152–3; Gouge, *op. cit.*, pp. 507–18.

23. **Elizabeth, Countess of Lincoln**, *The Countesse of Lincoln's Nurserie*, 1622, reprinted in *Harleian Miscellany*, London, 1808–13, Vol. IV, pp. 27–33; **S. Clarke**, *The Lives of Sundry Eminent Persons*, London, 1683, Vol. II, p. 155; Fanshawe, *op. cit.*, p. 18: **L. Hutchinson**, *Memoirs*

of the Life of Colonel Hutchinson, with the fragment of an autobiography of Mrs Hutchinson, **J. Sutherland** (ed.), Oxford UP, 1973, pp. 287, 289; **R. Parkinson** (ed.), *The Autobiography of Henry Newcome, M. A.*, Chetham Society, old ser., 26–7 (1852), I, 13, 69; Jackson, *op. cit.*, pp. 92, 94, 124, 148, 166; Macfarlane, *op. cit.*, pp. 86–7; Stone, *op. cit.*, p. 428.

24. Hollingsworth, *op. cit.*, p. 67; Wrigley and Schofield, *op. cit.*, p. 249.

25. **F. Lebrun**, *La Vie Conjugale sous l'Ancien Régime*, Armand Colin, Paris, 1975, pp. 128–9, **T. Phaire**, *The Boke of Chyldren*, **A. V. Neale** and **H. R. E. Wallis**, (eds), E. & S. Livingstone Ltd, Edinburgh and London, 1955, pp. 18–9; Culpeper, *op. cit.*, Vol. I, p. 155; **E. M. Symonds** (ed.), 'The Diary of John Greene', *English Historical Review*, **43** (1928), 599–604, **44** (1929), 107–16; **A. H. Smith**, **G. M. Baker** and **R. W. Kenny** (eds), *The Papers of Nathaniel Bacon of Stiffkey*, Vol. I, *1556–1577, Norfolk Record Society*, **46** (1979) 87; Verney and Verney, *op. cit.*, Vol. I, pp. 361, 380, 513; **D. Gardiner** (ed.), *The Oxinden Letters, 1607–1642*, Constable & Co., London, 1933, pp. 112–3; Still, *op. cit.*, p. 381; *The Works of Dr John Tillotson, late Archbishop of Canterbury*, London, 1720, Vol. I, p. 524; Gouge, *op. cit.*, p. 512

26. **J. Bowlby**, *Child Care and the Growth of Love*, Penguin Books, Harmondsworth, 2nd edn, 1965, pp. 9–74; see esp. p. 45 for warning of need to pay 'minute attention' to all the characteristics and circumstances of maternal derpivation; **J. Smyth**, *The Berkeley Manuscripts*, **J. Maclean** (ed.), Bristol and Gloucestershire Archaeological Society, Gloucester, 1883, Vol. II, p. 77; Townshend, *op. cit.*, p. 126; **L. B. Wright** (ed.), *Advice to a Son: Precepts of Lord Burghley, Sir Walter Raleigh, and Francis Osborne*, Cornell UP, Ithaca,1962, p. 21.

27. Duration of breastfeeding discussed in Macfarlane, *op. cit.*, p. 87; **L. de Mause** (ed.), *The History of Childhood*, Souvenir Press (Educational & Academic) Ltd, London, 1976, pp. 35–6.

28. **P. H. Barnum** (ed.), *Dives and Pauper*, Vol. I, *Early English Text Society*, **275, 280** (1976, 1980), Pt. 1, 314–5; **T. Cobbet**, *A Fruitfull and Usefull Discourse tovching the Honour due from Children to Parents, and the duty of Parents towards their Children*, London, 1656, pp. 82–3; Gouge , *op. cit.*, pp. 149, 429, 499–500; **T. Gataker**, *Marriage Dvties briefely covched togither, Ovt of Colossians, 3. 18, 19*, London, 1620, pp. 37–8, 44; **C. D'Evelyn** (ed.), *Peter Idley's Instructions to his Son*, Modern Language Association of America, Boston, 1935, p. 99.

29. Leigh, *op. cit.*, p. 12; Seymour, *op. cit.*, Vol. I, 303; Rogers, *op. cit.*, p. 161; **M. St Clare Byrne**, *The Elizabethan Home discovered in two Dialogues by Claudius Hollyband and Peter Erondell*, F. Etchells & H. MacDonald, London, 1925, pp. 55–6.

30. British Library, Harleian MSS, 6987, f. 64 (I owe this reference to Keith Thomas); **J. P. Cooper** (ed.), *Wentworth Papers 1597–1628, Camden Society*, 4th ser., 12 (1973), 214: Townshend, *op. cit.*, pp. 36, 43, 51, 55. 57, 68, 80, 91, 92; Taunton, Somerset Record Office, Trevelyan MSS, DD/WO/57.

31. Macfarlane, *op. cit.*, p. 90; **V. Sackville-West** (ed.), *The Diary of the Lady Anne Clifford*, W. Heinemann, London, 1923, p. 66; Seymour, *op. cit.*, Vol. I, p. 304; **G. A. Guarino** (ed.),*The Albertis of Florence: Leon Battista Alberti's Della Famiglia*, Bucknell UP, Lewisburg, 1971, p. 55; **I. and P. Opie** (eds), *Oxford Dictionary of Nursery Rhymes*, Clar-

endon Press, Oxford, 1951, pp. 18–19; Parkinson, *Life of Martindale*, p. 154.

32. Wrigley and Schofield, *op. cit.*, p. 249; **P. Ariès**, *Centuries of Childhood*, Jonathan Cape, London, 1962 (trans. from French edn 1960), pp. 38–40; Stone, *op. cit.*, pp. 68–70.

33. 'Maternal Affection at Birth', *The Times*, 1 May 1980, 18d; **G. Gorer**, *Death, Grief and Mourning in Contemporary Britain*, Cresset Press, London, 1965, p. 109; Macfarlane, *op. cit.*, pp. 100, 165; Winchester, *op. cit.*, p. 102; Jackson, *op. cit.*, pp. 124–7.

34. Wrigley and Schofield, *loc. cit.*; **R. Schofield** and **E. A. Wrigley**, 'Infant and Child Mortality in England in the Late Tudor and Early Stuart Period', in Webster, *op. cit.*, p. 75.

35. **B. Jonson**, *The Poems*, **B. H. Newdigate**, (ed.), Basil Blackwell, Oxford, 1936, p. 15, (see also p. 8, 'On My First Daughter', who died at six months; the contrast in tone is marked); **M. Macdonald**, *Mystical Bedlam: Madness, Anxiety, and Healing in Seventeenth-Century England*, Cambridge UP, 1981, p. 82; **E. S. de Beer** (ed.), *The Diary of John Evelyn*, Clarendon Press, Oxford, 1955, Vol. III, pp. 206–10; Parkinson, *Life of Martindale*, pp. 108–9; Fanshawe, *op. cit.*, p. 84.

36. **E. V. Gordon** (ed.), *Pearl*, Clarendon Press, Oxford, 1953, pp. xi–xiii, xviii–xxv; **T. Arnold** (ed.), *Select English Works of John Wyclif*, Oxford, 1869–71, Vol. III, p. 199.

37. Page-Phillips, *op. cit.*, pp. 14–17 and Figs. 29, 30; Stone, *op. cit.*, pp. 408–9. In the development of my ideas on this subject I am much indebted to discussions with Mr David Missen and to his Reading University dissertation, 'The Portrayal of Children on Church Monuments, 1500–1700', 1979.

38. Wrigley and Schofield, *op. cit.*, p. 249; Schofield and Wrigley, *op. cit.*, p. 79; **A. F. Sillitoe**, *Britain in Figures: A Handbook of Social Statistics*, Penguin Books, Harmondsworth, 2nd edn, 1973, p. 33.

39. Schofield and Wrigley, *op. cit.*, pp. 69, 78, 89–90; Wrigley and Schofield, *op. cit.*, p. 249; **Z. Razi**, *Life, Marriage and Death in a Medieval Parish: Economy, Society and Demography in Halesowen 1270–1400*, Cambridge UP, 1980, pp. 129, 151.

40. Wrigley and Schofield, *loc. cit.*; Forbes, *op. cit.*, p. 139; **F. West**, 'Infant Mortality in the East Fen Parishes of Leake and Wrangle', *Local Population Studies*, **13** (1974), 43–4; Stone, *op. cit.*, p. 697, fn. 67.

41. For some parishes where the majority of infant deaths were of females, see **G. Reynolds**, 'Infant Mortality and Sex Ratios at Baptism as shown by Reconstruction of Willingham, a Parish at the Edge of the Fens in Cambridgeshire', *Local Population Studies*, **22** (1979), 31–7; **R. Wall**, 'Inferring Differential Neglect of Females from Mortality Data', *Annales de Démographie Historique*, (1981), 119–40, esp. 136 (I owe this reference to Olwen Hufton).

42. Wrightson and Levine, *op. cit.*, p. 57.

43. **R. H. Helmholz**, 'Infanticide in the Province of Canterbury during the Fifteenth Century', *History of Childhood Quarterly*, **2** (1975), 381, 387, fn. 2; Mirk, *op. cit.*, p. 76; Forbes, *op. cit.*, p. 133; Jackson, *op. cit.*, pp. 3–4, 91, 122, 129–30, 133–4, 170; de Beer, *op. cit.*, Vol. III, pp. 145, 371; **J. Horsfall Turner** (ed.). *The Rev. Oliver Heywood, B. A., 1630–1702: his Autobiography, Diaries, Anecdote and Event books*, Brighouse, 1881–85, Vol. I, pp. 34–5; **B. A. Hanawalt**, 'Childrearing among

the Lower Classes of Late Medieval England', *Journal of Interdisciplinary History*, **8** (1977), 8–13, 20–1; Parkinson, *Life of Martindale*, pp. 3–5; Halliwell, *op. cit.*, Vol. I, pp. 24–32.

44. Stone, *op. cit.*, p. 474; **B. A. Kellum**, 'Infanticide in England in the Later Middle Ages', *History of Childhood Quarterly*, **1** (1973–74), 367–88; Seymour, *op. cit.*, Vol. I, p. 296; Helmholz, *op. cit.*, pp. 381–2; **K. Wrightson**, 'Infanticide in Earlier Seventeenth-Century England', *Local Population Studies*, **15** (1975), 10–22; **P. E. H. Hair**, 'Homicide, Infanticide and Child Assault in Late Tudor Middlesex', *Local Population Studies*, **9** (1972), 43–6; 21 James I, *c.* 27.

45. Still, *op. cit.*, pp. 199–203, 235–6, 238, 276–81, 282–4, 295–8, 324–5, 376–86, 453–63; **J. E. Illick**, 'Child-Rearing in Seventeenth-Century England and America', in de Mause, *op. cit.*, p. 318; **R. Trumbach**, *The Rise of the Egalitarian Family: Aristocratic Kinship and Domestic Relations in Eighteenth-Century England*, Academic Press, London, 1978, pp. 187–208, 224–9.

46. Winchester, *op. cit.*, pp. 107–8.

47. Seymour, *op. cit.*, Vol. I, p. 311; D'Evelyn, *op. cit.*, p. 179; Pratt, *op. cit.*, Vol. VII, p. 358.

48. **A. V. Judges** (ed.), *The Elizabethan Underworld*, G. Routledge & Sons, London, 1930, p. 456; Gouge, *op. cit.*, p. 557; **J. Taylor**, *The Rule and Exercises of Holy Dying*, Longmans, Green & Co., London, 1929, p. 83.

49. Still *op. cit.*, p. 33; **G. Strauss**, *Luther's House of Learning: Indoctrination of the Young in the German Reformation*, Johns Hopkins UP, London, 1978, Chs 2 and 3, esp. pp. 34–5, 50–4, 58–61; Stone, *op. cit.*, p. 166; **Sir T. Elyot**, *The Boke Named the Gouernour*, J. M. Dent & Co., London, 1907, pp. 19–20.

50. **R. Ascham**, *The Scholemaster, Or plaine and perfite way of teachyng children to vnderstand, write, and speake, the Latin tong* . . . in *English Works*, **W. A. Wright** (ed.), Cambridge UP, 1904, pp. 175–7, 182–4, 187–8, 200; **G. Chaucer**, *The Merchant's Tale*, lines 1429–30; Leigh, *op. cit.*, pp. 45–7; **Halifax**, *Complete Works*, **J. P. Kenyon** (ed.), Penguin Books, Harmondsworth, 1969, pp. 290–1.

51. Cooper, *op. cit.*, p. 134; **Margaret, Duchess of Newcastle**, *The Life of William Cavendish, Duke of Newcastle, to which is added the True Relation of My Birth, Breeding, and Life*, **C. H. Firth** (ed.), John C. Nimmo, London, 1886, p. 278.

52. **Robert Cawdrey**, *A Godlie Forme of Hovseholde Gouernment: for the Ordering of Private Families, according to the Direction of God's Word*, London, 1600 (first edn 1598), pp. 50–1, 54–6; Gouge, *op. cit.*, pp. 155–6, 550–1, 556–7; Tyndale, *op. cit.*, p. 199.

53. Strauss, *op. cit.*, pp. 34–41; Cawdrey, *op. cit.*, pp. 268, 294.

54. Wright, *Advice to a Son*, p. 10; **A. Jessopp** (ed.), *The Autobiography of the Hon. Roger North*, David Nutt, London, 1887, pp. 1–7; **J. Locke**, *Some Thoughts Concerning Education*. 1693, in *The Educational Writings of John Locke*, J. Axtell (ed.), Cambridge UP, 1968, pp. 143, 145, 148–9, 158–60, 173–4, 177.

55. Barnum, *op. cit.*, Vol. I, Pt. 1, pp. 304–24; Tyndale, *op. cit.*, p. 168.

56. **R. Whytforde**, *A Werke for Housholders*, 1530, sig. Div^v–Ei; Becon, *op. cit.*, p. 350; Jackson, *op. cit.*, p. 64; Gouge, *op. cit.*, pp. 437–41; *A briefe and true report of two most cruel, unnaturall, and inhumane murders, don in Lincolnshire, by twoo husbands upon their wives*, in

Murder Narratives, **J. O. Halliwell** (ed.), London, 1860, p. 46 (I owe this reference to Dr J. A. Sharpe).

57. Hanawalt, *op. cit.*, pp. 8, 10–13, 16; Jessopp, *op.cit.*, pp. 1–2; **J. W. Adamson**, *Pioneers of Modern Education, 1600–1700*, Cambridge UP, 1905, p. 161; Macfarlane, *op. cit.*, p. 91; **T. Heywood** (ed.), *The Diary of the Rev. Henry Newcome, from September 30, 1661, to September 29, 1663, Chetham Society*, old ser., **18** (1849), 16.

58. Elyot, *op. cit.*, pp. 19, 23–5; **R. Weigall** (ed.), 'An Elizabethan Gentlewoman. The Journal of Lady Mildmay, circa 1570–1617', *Quarterly Review*, **215** (1911), 120, 122; cf. Hutchinson, *op. cit.*, p. 22; Duchess of Newcastle, *op. cit.*, p. 279.

59. **F. J. Furnivall** (ed.), *Early English Meals and Manners, Early English Text Society*, orig. ser., **32** (1868), 209–14, 230–1, 235–6, 252–6, 262–78.

60. St Clare Byrne, *op. cit.*, pp. 26–39; Verney and Verney, *op. cit.*, Vol. I, pp. 216–7; Sackville-West, *op. cit.*, pp. 44–5; Ascham, *op. cit.*, pp. 201–2.

61. Furnivall, *op. cit.*, pp. 225, 266–8; Elyot, *op. cit.*, p. 20; Barnum, *op. cit.*, Vol. I, Pt. 1, p. 327; **W. Harrington,** *In This Boke are conteyned the Cōmendacions of Matrymony*, sig. Dii^v, dated to between 1512 and 1515 by D. Ramage in *The Durham Philobiblon*, **1** (1949–55), 69; Whytforde , *op. cit.*, sig. B ii–C i; Becon, *op. cit.*, pp. 348, 350–5.

62. **J. Shakespeare** and **M. Dowling** (eds), 'Religion and Politics in Mid-Tudor England through the Eyes of an English Protestant Woman: the Recollections of Rose Hickman', *Bulletin of the Institute of Historical Research*, **55** (1982), 97; **A. Kenny** (ed.), *Responsa Scholarum of the English College, Rome. Part One*: 1598–1621, *Catholic Record Society*, **54** (1962), 75, 107, 119, 142, 154, 187–8, 242, 244, 305, 306, 316; Horsfall Turner, *op. cit.*, Vol. I, pp. 50–1; **Lord Braybrooke** (ed.), *The Autobiography of Sir John Bramston, K.B., of Skreens, in the Hundred of Chelmsford, Camden Society*, old ser., **32** (1845), 111; Jessopp, *op. cit.*, p. 5; Clarke, *Ten Eminent Divines*, pp. 506–7.

63. **W. F. Craven** and **W. B. Hayward** (eds), *The Journal of Richard Norwood, Surveyor of Bermuda*, Scholars' Fascimiles and Reprints, New York, 1945 p. 8; Hutchinson, *op. cit.*, p. 21; **J. Bunyan**, *Grace Abounding to the Chief of Sinners*, **R. Sharrock** (ed.), Clarendon Press, Oxford, 1962, p. 6; Horsfall Turner, *op. cit.*, Vol. I, pp. 205, 233; Becon, *op. cit.*, 348; **I. Pinchbeck** and **M. Hewitt**, *Children in English Society: From Tudor Times to the Eighteenth Century*, Routledge & Kegan Paul, London, 1969, p. 269.

64. Locke, *op. cit.*, pp. 241, 259–61.

65. **T. T. Lewis** (ed.), *Letters of the Lady Brilliana Harley, Camden Society*, old ser., **58** (1853), 5; **M. Spufford**, 'First steps in Literacy: the Reading and Writing Experiences of the Humblest Seventeenth-Century Spiritual Biographers', *Social History*, **4** (1979) 410–11; Hutchinson, *op. cit.*, p. 288; **K. B. McFarlane**, *The Nobility of Later Medieval England*, Clarendon Press, Oxford, 1973, p. 244; **L. Stone**, *The Crisis of the Aristocracy, 1558–1641*, Clarendon Press, Oxford, 1965, p. 677; **D. Cressy**, *Education in Tudor and Stuart England*, Edward Arnold, London, 1975, pp. 71, 95; *idem, Literacy and the Social Order. Reading and Writing in Tudor and Stuart England*, Cambridge UP, 1980, pp. 27–8; **J. Brinsley**, *Lvdvs Literarivs: or, the Grammar Schoole*, London, 1627, p. 9.

66. Seymour, *op. cit.*, Vol. I, pp. 291, 300; Collins, *op. cit.*, p. 37; Elyot, *op. cit.*, pp. 21–3; **J. A. Hadfield**, *Childhood and Adolescence*, Penguin Books, Harmondsworth, 1962, pp. 159–71; **E. B. Hurlock**, *Child Development*, McGraw-Hill, New York, 6th edn, 1978, p. 355.

67. **P. Cunnington** and **A. Buck**, *Children's Costume in England from the Fourteenth to the End of the Nineteenth Century*, Adam and Charles Black, London, 1972, pp. 14–25; Ariès, *op. cit.*, pp. 50–7; Craven and Hayward, *op. cit.*, p. 6.

68. **L. Stone**, 'The Educational Revolution in England, 1560–1640', *Past and Present*, **28** (1964), 41–80; *idem*, *Crisis of the Aristocracy*, pp. 684–5.

69. Smith et al., *op. cit.*, Vol. I, p. 24.

70. Verney and Verney, *op. cit.*, pp. 500–2; Hutchinson, *op. cit.*, p. 288; **M. Blundell** (ed.), *Cavalier: Letters of William Blundell to his Friends, 1620–98*, Longmans, Creen & Co. ,London, 1933, p. 247.

71. **T. Ingelend**, *The Disobedient Child*, **J. O. Halliwell** (ed.), *Percy Society*, **75** (1848), 8–15; Smith et al., *op. cit.*, Vol. I, p. 12; **M. St Clare Byrne**, *The Lisle Letters*, Univ. of Chicago Press, 1981, Vol. III, p. 19; Winchester, *op. cit.*, p. 225.

72. St Clare Byrne , *Lisle Letters*, Vol. IV, p. 481; **G. Davies** (ed.), *Autobiography of Thomas Raymond, and Memoirs of the Family of Guise of Elmore, Gloucestershire, Camden Society*, 3rd ser., 28 (1917), 115; Jessopp , *op. cit.*, p. 12.

73. Kingsford, *op. cit.*, Vol. I, p. 21; St Clare Byrne, *Lisle Letters*, Vol. I, pp. 87–9; *idem*, *Elizabethan Home*, p. 5; **J. Brinsley**. *A Consolation for our Grammar Schooles*, London, 1622, p. 40; **K. V. Thomas**, *Rule and Misrule in the Schools of Early Modern England: The Stenton Lecture, 1975*, University of Reading, 1976, pp. 10–11.

74. St Clare Byrne, *Elizabethan Home*, pp. 3–5, 38–9; Brinsley, *Consolation*, pp. 42–3; Adamson, *op. cit.*, p. 186; Parkinson, *Life of Martindale*, pp. 176–7.

75. **W. G. Perrin** (ed.), *The Autobiography of Phineas Pett*, Navy Records Society, **51** (1918), 2; Parkinson, *Life of Martindale*, p. 13.

76. **C. A. Sneyd** (trans.), *A Relation, or rather a True Account, of the Island of England . . . about the Year 1500, Camden Society*, old ser., **37** (1847), 24–5; Guarino, *op. cit.*, pp. 43–4, 50, 52, 56, 165.

77. **N. Davis** (ed.), *Paston Letters and Papers of the Fifteenth Century*, Clarendon Press, Oxford, 1971, 1976, Vol. I, p. 132; Hanawalt, *op. cit.*, 18–9; **A.** (really **J.**) **Fitzherbert**, *The Book of Husbandry, 1534*, **W. M. Skeat** (ed.), *English Dialect Society*, **13** (1882), 40; Spufford, *op. cit.*, 425; **A. Kussmaul**, *Servants in Husbandry in Early Modern England*, Cambridge UP, 1981, p. 72; **B. Lubbock** (ed.), *Barlow's Journal of his life at sea*, Hurst & Blackett, London, 1934, Vol. I, p. 15; **J. D. Marshall** (ed.), *The Autobiography of William Stout of Lancaster 1665–1752, Chetham Society*, 3rd ser., **14** (1967), 68–70.

78. **F. J. Fisher** (ed.), *The State of England anno dom. 1600, by Thomas Wilson, Camden Society*, 3rd ser., **52** (1936), 20; **D. Defoe**, *A Tour Through the Whole Island of Great Britain*, Dent, London, 1962, Vol. I, pp. 62, 266; Vol. II, p. 195; **J. F. Pound** (ed.), *The Norwich Census of the Poor, 1570, Norfolk Record Society*, 40 (1971), *passim*.

79. 27 Henry VIII. *c.* 25; 39 Elizabeth I, c. 3; 43 Elizabeth I, c. 2; **E. M. Leonard**, *The Early History of English Poor Relief*, Cambridge UP,

1900, pp. 175, 244, 247, 342; **E. M. Hampson**, *The Treatment of Poverty in Cambridgeshire, 1597–1834*, Cambridge UP, 1934, pp. 49–50, 154, 156–7, 159–60; Pinchbeck and Hewitt, *op. cit.*, pp. 101, 237, 239–40; **A. J. Fletcher**, *A County Community in Peace and War: Sussex 1600–1660*, Longman, London, 1975, p. 158; Marshall, *op. cit.*, p. 154. The children of the poor did not necessarily or always leave home earlier than those of other social groups, as is shown by Alan Macfarlane's analysis of a 1695 listing of Kirkby Lonsdale (West-morland) in *Family Life of Josselin*, p. 210.

80. Best survey of institutional developments in Pinchbeck and Hewitt, *op. cit.*, Ch. 7.

Chapter 7

Parents and children: adolescence and beyond

The duration of adolescence

The concept of adolescence, a long period when the individual has ceased in some respects to be a child, but has not yet achieved full adulthood, has been indispensable since antiquity. It has always been held to begin with puberty, but its termination has been more difficult to fix, because full maturity of body and judgement have been held to come at different times. But all the more important schemes of 'ages of life' devised in antiquity and the Middle Ages put the achievement of full adulthood in the middle or later twenties. The people of the sixteenth and seventeenth centuries regarded adolescents as children in some respects, adults in others, as we still do today. Thus in the early seventeenth century James Allyn, a Somerset youth, was variously described as 'simple young man working as a daye laborer' and 'a simple young boye, being scarce xx^ty yeares old'. But people of his age were perhaps more commonly described in terms appropriate to children. In 1596, a witness in the Exeter consistory court described a young man and woman, the elder of whom was not above twenty, as 'nothing reckoned of amongst them that knowe them, vnlesse it be amongst boyes and gerles suche as they are'.[1]

Perhaps the most important characteristics of male adulthood were the ability to control property and to earn the living of an independent householder. Upon these in turn depended the ability to make one's own marriage. (The normal minimum ages of full marriage in ecclesiastical law, twelve for females and fourteen for males, had been fixed at what was theoretically the beginning of what was thought of as the long process of puberty. But in our period teenage marriages were very often, perhaps usually, arranged by others rather than initiated by the parties.) Twenty-one was the age at which the male tenant by knight service came out of wardship, and during the Middle Ages the 'knightly majority' had gradually become the majority of the common law, the age below which the 'infant' of legal parlance could not alienate his lands, make a deed or most sorts of contract. The Church's canons of 1604 insisted that those marrying under the age of twenty-one should have their parents' or guardian's consent. The age at which sons in the property-owning classes actually attained economic independence largely depended upon how long their parents survived and the extent to which the latter used their wills to delay the transfer of property or attach conditions to it. It could in practice be some years after legal majority. Apprenticeship had become by 1450 by far the commonest means of entry to skilled trades and crafts in towns. By the early years of our period, the companies of higher status were insisting upon terms of seven to ten years. These, together with a typical age of admission of fourteen or sixteen meant that an apprentice could not acquire the freedom before his early or middle twenties, and the ability to set up shop was commonly delayed some years beyond this. The Statute of Artificers (1563) laid down that apprenticeship must last till twenty-four in corporate towns, twenty-one in husbandry. The provisions relating to apprenticeship in husbandry remained very largely a dead letter, and the ability to earn a man's wage in agri-culture some time before the age of twenty-one was often recognised in justices' assessments. But since service combined opportunities to save for eventual marriage with a higher standard of living than could be expected outside it, many young people may have been in no hurry to leave it. Entry into the professions demanded a long period of training. The age of entry to university was rising very slowly during this period: at Oxford the median age went up from sixteen and a half in 1600 to eighteen and a half in 1800, in other words by about a year a century. Youthful rashness, intemperance and lack of judgement were used by contemporaries as justifications for the prolongation of the period of adolescent tutelage. But in the case of apprenticeship, demographic and economic reasons may have been more important. Efforts to postpone entry into trades and crafts were one response to increased competition for places within them at a time of rising population. In the countryside, however, rising population tended in the long run to have a very different effect, for by making labour cheaper it reduced the incentive to keep servants and made it more advantageous to hire labourers when they were needed.[2]

Parental authority

Writers of the literature of Christian counsel sought to instil in young people the duty of obedience and respect towards their parents and those who stood in their place. This duty they based above all upon the fourth or fifth commandment. Obedience was also enjoined in some other texts, notably Ephesians 6: 1: 'Children obey your parents in the Lord; for this is right.' Respect and obedience were not to terminate upon the achievement of majority. The good child showed his respect for his parents throughout their lives, above all, in the first half of our period, by seeking their blessing. In 1468 John Paston III, then about twenty-four, sent his mother a humble request to remember to give him her blessing once a day. Sir Thomas More was allegedly prompt, even after his elevation to the chancellorship, to seek a blessing from his aged father whenever he met him. But how far did the duty of obedience extend? How long did it last? Many writers appeared reluctant to give clear answers to these question.[3]

Apart from individual force of character, parental power depended above all upon the possession of property and the successful inculcation of the duty of obedience within both household and community. In our period, both the extent of the duty of obedience and its Scriptural basis were to be called in questions.

In the eyes of contemporaries, religious divisions posed the most fundamental threat to the unity of the family as of the state. Confessional strife introduced new opportunities, and for many a new need, to make choices. Early Protestantism was often pictured by its opponents as a religion which drew a disproportionate amount of support from dissident youth, and young people's espousal of it sometimes led to bitter intra-familial conflicts. Later, a number of the converts to Catholic recusancy were to be the offspring of Protestant parents, and some suffered disinheritance as a result. The breakdown of religious unity during the civil war and the subsequent proliferation of sects magnified the ideological pressures upon parental authority. Children who chose their own course in religion could no longer see their parents as God's representatives in the most important area of life. The Marian martyr Julius Palmer was not only disinherited but also cursed by his mother on account of his conversion, but his staunch Protestant faith enabled him to bear this most formidable of all parental sanctions with equanimity, and he told his mother that though she might give him her curse, which he had not deserved, she could not give him God's. Many young people must have argued, as did Thomas Ellwood, the son of a minor Oxford-shire gentleman who became a Quaker in 1659, at the age of twenty, that matters of conscience lay outside the bounds of paternal power. Ephesians 6: 1 did indeed enjoin obedience to parents, but with the vital qualification *in the Lord*: God's claim upon the individual's obedience had priority over that of any earthly father.[4]

Lord Clarendon believed that parental authority had been seriously weakened by the upheavals of the civil war and the Interregnum:

. . . Parents had no Manner of Authority over their Children, nor Children any Obedience or Submission to their Parents; but every one did that which was good in his own Eyes.[5]

Perhaps he was guilty of pessimistic exaggeration. Although the political and religious division of families was a frequent occurrence, it was experienced by only a minority of the population. After the century of intermittent ideological turbulence which followed the Reformation, religion ceased to be a major cause of intra-familial conflict. Yet the re-examination of the basis of authority in family as well as state which was prompted by ideological division left an enduring legacy in the secularisation of political thought. The great political theorists either bypassed Scripture or sought to demonstrate that it would not bear the weight of long-accepted interpretations.

John Locke drew a clear distinction between the necessary obedience of children and the duty of respect laid upon them by the fifth commandment. (It was a fundamental assumption of the patriarchal political theory which Locke was concerned to refute that children's duty of obedience was a permanent one.) During childhood, according to Locke, God gave parents power over their offspring for the latter's own good:

The subjection of a minor places in the father a temporary government, which terminates with the minority of the child; and the honour due from a child places in the parents a perpetual right to respect, reverence, support, and compliance, too, more or less, as the father's care, cost and kindness in his education has been more or less.

The honour mentioned in the fifth commandment was thus very different from the necessary obedience of children, and the extent of the consideration which individuals were entitled to receive from their adult offspring depended upon the love and diligence with which they had discharged the parental responsibilities with which God had entrusted them. Locke thus blew away from parental authority the sacred mist with which earlier commentators had surrounded it.[6]

In practice, however, the wealthy man might continue to exercise considerable power over his children long after the legal age of majority, while the poor man who could neither maintain nor employ them lost it long before. Locke implicitly recognised this when he wrote that it was commonly in the father's power to bestow his property 'with a more sparing or liberal hand, according as the behaviour of this or that child hath comported with his will and humour'.[7] (But there had always been obstacles to the disinheritance of the heir, and the development of family settlements in the seventeenth century made it more difficult. A father's ability to break the entail upon the estate and resettle it was often dependent upon his heir's cooperation, which may have made it necessary for landed fathers to manage their eldest sons with greater skill and circumspection.)

This period witnessed not only some questioning of the extent of parental authority but also some relaxation of the rules governing filial comportment. John Aubrey, looking back in 1670, thought that this had been most marked during the Interregnum. Formerly, he claimed, even gentlemen of thirty or forty had had to stand 'like great mutes and fools bare headed' in their parents' presence. But the origins of more informal epistolary styles among the propertied classes can be traced back beyond the seventeenth century. The elaborately deferential opening salutations of the fifteenth century were discarded during the sixteenth, and forms of address gradually became more affectionate. By the early seventeenth, some sons could begin their letters 'Dear and Loving Father', or, in the manner which has remained common down to the present day, 'Dear Father'. Letters could become fuller and more intimate records of pleasures and preoccupations. The correspondence between Thomas More and his daughter Margaret hints at the part which humanism may have played in the process. His salutations and endearments (all in Latin) strike a note new in English letters from parents to children: 'My most sweet child', 'My dear Margaret', 'My darling Margaret'. John Veysey praised a letter from Margaret to her father in the highest terms, not only for its scholarly qualities but also for its 'expressions of tender affection'.[8]

There was also in this period a real but partial and very gradual relaxation among the propertied classes of parental control over the choice of marriage partners and callings, though in both areas this was accompanied by a good deal of conflict. As we have already seen, the diminution of external pressures upon the family in the shape of endemic disorder and (later) fiscal feudalism encouraged the gentry to allow their children more say in the choice of marriage partners. The selection of a child's future calling was traditionally regarded as a parental responsibility. Family strategies, birth order and fathers' determination that sons follow their own callings all militated against individual freedom of choice. But humanists like Ascham thought that the choice of calling should be based upon a thorough assessment of a child's aptitudes, and this point of view influenced what Protestant writers on domestic duties had to say about the subject. Children, wrote Thomas Becon, were to be set to such occupations as they were most inclined and apt to. 'For by striving against nature nothing cometh well and fortunately to pass.' Thomas Fuller concluded that 'parents who cross the current of their children's genius (if running in no vicious channells) tempt them to take worse courses to themselves'.[9]

In practice parents and guardians varied in their readiness to take children's preferences into account. At one end of the spectrum stood the childless priest, uncle to Thomas Whythorne (b. 1528) who, having made a disinterested decision to further his young nephew's education, gave Thomas the fullest freedom, putting a wide range of alternatives before him. Thomas Beveridge (b. 1584), was offered by his father, a man of middle rank, a choice between a domestic, an academic and a mercantile career (though he disliked all three, and ultimately decided to enter the English College in Rome). Sir William Wentworth, writing in 1613, wished his heir to consider 'their naturall desposition and their owne desire' in advising his three youngest brothers what profession to pursue. Among seventeenth-century yeomen, a group heavily influenced by hard practical considerations, some fathers took their sons' aptitudes and wishes into account, though not always to begin with, while others simply expected their sons to follow them on the land.[10]

New opportunities for the enterprising and adventurous were created by the development of an integrated national economy, the astonishing growth of London, the commercial revolution and the demand for labour in English settlements beyond the seas. What were believed to be the opportunities for rapid advancement in London lured young people to it from all over the country. Jane Martindale, a Lancashire girl, was fired by desire to go up and enter service there after talking to people who had come to stay in the country during an attack of plague, probably in 1625. She persisted in her plan despite the best efforts of her parents and others to dissuade her. Robinson Crusoe was not alone in embarking on a career of adventure at sea in the face of his father's alternative plans. Richard Norwood, a Bermuda pioneer, recalled how at first his father strongly opposed his going because he 'was altogether ignorant of that course of life, and thought it the worst of all others, none of our kindred nor acquaintance taking that course'. Edward Barlow, son of a poor Lancashire husbandman, threw over in 1656 an uncongenial apprenticeship his father had arranged for him, sought work in London and ultimately went to sea. His description of the eagerness with which he had as a boy listened to stories of travels and strange things in other countries gives a vivid impression of the way in which the broadening of horizons affected the outlook of even relatively humble people.[11]

Service, apprenticeship and higher education

By late adolescence, a substantial proportion of young people, perhaps most of them, had left home finally or for a long period. We have seen that many of the poor had to part with their offspring in late childhood, while the upper classes commonly sent theirs away from home at that time for what they considered to be their own good. The reasons for sending children away in adolescence were similarly both positive and negative. Service, apprenticeship and higher education were necessary paths to advancement. On the other hand most parents could not employ or maintain their children at home, and even if they could, found them difficult to control. Robert Cawdrey, writing towards the end of Elizabeth's reign, found fault with parents of his generation for their reluctance to reprimand their children when they reached fifteen or sixteen, and imagined their answering him 'oh then they be growne to mens and womens estate, they may not be reprehended, they may not be disgraced'. During the Interregnum, Thomas Cobbet, a minister in New England, complained that there children commonly treated their parents with gross and open disrespect. The latter were 'commonly put more to it, to make use of their childrens hands and help', presumably because of the shortage of labour in America, and children's consciousness of their parents' dependence upon them made them insolent. In the very different conditions of England, parents who needed labour could hire servants, who were probably psychologically easier to punish than their own children.[12]

It would however be a mistake to assume that English parents did not employ their own children. Autobiographical details in church court depositions show that many young people helped their parents for some years before their departure into service or after their return from it, and some described themselves as their parents' servants. Autobiographers such as William Stout, Josiah Langdale and John Cannon recalled the work they had done on their parents' farms. Both types of source reveal that two or three sons were sometimes employed; it was not the heir alone, waiting to step into his father's shoes, who helped run the farm. But the labour of children was available for only part of a family's life cycle, and this fact was a major element in the demand for servants.[13]

The great majority of the adolescent population probably entered some form of service or apprenticeship. The large mass of co-resident employees hired by the year for domestic and agricultural work (the majority of whom were adolescents), were called servants, though apprentices, too, were often so described. But 'apprenticeship' denoted a fairly long period of service in which the adolescent would learn the skills of his future calling, though it embraced arrangements which varied enormously in their formality, duration, cost and value to the entrant and his family, from the training of the goldsmith or merchant to the compulsory parish apprenticeship of the pauper child. Voluntary apprenticeships in husbandry were sometimes agreed, but annual service was far commoner.[14] Adolescents of both sexes went to work in other people's households, but the employment opportunities for members of each sex depended upon the character of the local economy. Farmers and craftsmen generally needed more young men than young women. Within agriculture, there were more opportunities for girls in pastoral than in arable husbandry. Domestic service offered increasing opportunities for girls as the household staffs of the nobility and gentry, predominantly male in the fifteenth century, became predominantly female by the end of the seventeenth. 'As to Maid Servants', observed Gregory King in 1695, 'All great Towns require more than Men Servants, the country otherwise.' When he wrote, this was probably true of London as well as of Lichfield, the town which inspired his remark, though it had not been true of early seventeenth-century London.[15]

The level of demand for servants and apprentices changed over time and varied from place to place. Farmers were keen to take on servants if they needed to be sure of having labour available all the year round or if it was in relatively scarce or uncertain supply. The importance of servants to the farmer was greatest in pastoral areas of scattered settlement and in times of stagnant population such as the later seventeenth century. Rising population increased and cheapened the supply of labour, making it more sensible for a man who did not need help all the year round to hire labourers as and when he needed them rather than feed and house servants. In industry, apprenticeship declined in the long term together with craft organisation and the growth of new occupations in which it had never been enforced; wage labour grew increasingly important. In London, the proportion of the population made up of apprentices probably fell during the seventeenth century from 15 per cent to under 5 per cent. It is impossible to say what proportion of the country's population was in service or apprenticeship at any one time. Only a few detailed local censuses are available. Among these, the highest proportions in service, about a quarter in each case, were to be found in Coventry (1523) and Ealing (1599). The proportions among those covered by later censuses were generally considerably lower. At Swindon in 1697 over two-thirds of those in the 15–19 age-group were living with their parents, about half of those in their early twenties. How far the differences which censuses reveal were due to the distinctive characters of local economies, how far to long-term changes in patterns of adolescent employment, is not yet entirely clear. In this field there is still much to be learnt.[16]

Servants tended to move from poorer households to richer ones. Only a minority of households contained them, for example 34 per cent at Ealing in 1599, 31 per cent at Goodnestone in 1676. In the communities covered by sufficiently informative pre-industrial censuses, 84.1 per cent of gentry households contained them, 71.9 per cent of yeoman households. But only 46.8 per cent of the households of husbandmen did so, 2.2 per cent of those of labourers.[17]

The age of entry into apprenticeship and service may have risen in the course of time. Twelve may have been the commonest age of entry into service in early Tudor Coventry, but seventeenth-century urban censuses reveal few servants that young. One result of efforts to restrict numbers coming into crafts was perhaps to raise the age of entry into apprenticeship as well as departure from it. But long apprenticeships and an early age of entry were common in poorer crafts. The mid-teens were probably the years in which the largest numbers of adolescents entered service in husbandry. At Ealing (1599) the proportions in service were highest in the age-group 15–19 (72%) and 20–24 (78%). But as many as 15 per cent of the 10–14-year-olds were in service, a far higher percentage than in communities covered by seventeenth-century censuses.[18]

Such were the characteristics of service and apprenticeship which were most important in the context of household and family. Three major topics will be touched on in the discussion which follows: the role of parents in placing their children in service or apprenticeship, continuing contacts between the servant or apprentice and his or her parents and, finally, the extent to which the master assumed the functions of a parent.

Parental support was particularly important in securing apprenticeships to crafts and trades of high repute. Masters exacted substantial premiums in return for the skills and other long-term advantages which these positions were expected to confer. Parents' responsibility to find the best possible masters for their sons was stressed by such writers as Robert Cawdrey, who believed that too many concerned themselves with the physical well-being of their children during apprenticeship at the expense of the moral. The terms of the indenture by which the apprentice bound himself to serve his master in return for instruction were to some extent a matter for negotiation between the master and the boy's parent or other sponsor. The master might be prepared to receive a smaller premium in return for a longer period of service, or give undertakings concerning the apprentice's advancement beyond those usually entered into. But the poorer a father was the less discriminating he could afford to be. In 1656, when Edward Barlow became a burden to his parents, his father 'hearing of a man of a reasonably good trade that was willing to take an apprentice', decided to bind Edward if he was willing. Barlow agreed to the proposal more out of fear of being turned out of doors than for any love he had for the trade.[19]

Parental support could be important to the adolescent seeking short-term service. A prospective employer might demand a 'passport' or testimonial from the servant's father. In 1542 William Howham of Peterborough took the initiative in offering one, writing to describe his daughter to John Johnson as a girl of good charater, familiar with all sorts of women's work after three or four years in service. A master might, like the Yorkshire yeoman Adam Eyre, ask known and trusted acquaintances if their children were available to serve. But another Yorkshireman, Henry Best, advised prospective masters 'neaver to hyre such as are too neare theire friends', and it seems likely that as the years went by most servants would come increasingly to rely in finding employment upon their own efforts and their success in selling themselves at the statute sessions or hiring fair.[20]

After their children had left home, thought Robert Cawdrey, parents should visit them as often as they could, see how they were getting on, and give them good advice. A number of autobiographies show that parents, especially mothers, did not want their children to travel too far when they left home, lest they lose touch with them. A substantial minority of apprentices went a long way to be bound, but in the case of the majority, fairly frequent contact was probably not hard to maintain. Of the apprentices enrolled at Gloucester between 1595 and 1640, for instance, 31 per cent had been born in the city and 44 per cent had come from the county of Gloucester. Parental concern for apprentices' and servants' physical or moral welfare is apparent in some surviving correspondence. Scattered through the archives of various courts are the records of suits undertaken by parents against masters who had maltreated their children, wasted their time, made them do unsuitably menial work or failed to provide them with adequate food and clothing according to their covenants. Servants in husbandry commonly spent two or three days with their relatives at the end of their contracted year and the period of service may often have been broken or followed by a spell of help at home.[21]

Ideally the master stood in the parent's place and assumed some of the parental responsibilities. It was often asserted that the positions of children and servants were similar or even the same. But the short duration of most terms of service clearly militated against the establishment of a very close bond between masters and servants. The apprentice's standard term was seven years and was often longer, but most other servants stayed in one place for a very much shorter time. Of farm servants, the most numerous of all, a half or more commonly left after a year's service. Some masters thought it sensible to part with servants before too long because they were most diligent when they first arrived; others encouraged mobility in order to prevent servants gaining settlements and the right to poor relief. But it seems clear that servants themselves were often glad to leave or careless of their employers' displeasure.[22]

The master was legally bound to provide for his servants' physical needs and to look after them when ill. Their spiritual welfare was his moral responsibility, one conscientiously discharged by such pious employers as Lady Margaret Hoby and John Bruen. But William Gouge claimed that servants frequently muttered against the religious exercises imposed by the godly; it was a common complaint, he said, that profane, worldly masters were better served than religious ones. Most masters were unwilling to give proper religious instruction; many even kept their servants at work upon the Sabbath itself. The master also shared the parent's duty of correction, which was ideally to be moderate and reasonable. But the fact that Thomas Becon had to warn masters not to fall out with their servants and not to 'curse, and lame them, cast dishes and pots at their heads, beat them, put them in danger of their life' suggests that the conduct of many masters diverged markedly from the ideal. In Elizabethan and Stuart Essex, indeed, men accused at the assizes of killing their servants greatly outnumbered those accused of killing their children, though a far smaller proportion of them appear to have been convicted. The good master gave his departing servant some help towards his 'setting out in the world'. John Bruen helped his servants to get married. In 1654, John Evelyn bound his lackey apprentice to a carpenter, giving with him £5 and new clothing. He throve and became rich. Pepys and his wife obtained a marriage licence for his apprentice clerk and her chamber-maid and gave them £40 each. But the Pepyses' relations with their servants far more often ended in mutual dissatisfaction. Far from helping their apprentices to establish themselves, many masters, so it was claimed, deliberately neglected their training for fear of future competition or even drove them into running away.[23]

It is true that the relationships built up between the most conscientious masters and their longest employed or most deeply trusted servants sometimes resembled those between parents and children, especially when masters had no children of their own. John Johnson's sonless master, Anthony Cave, enhanced John's father's legacy by judicious investment, lent him money and gave him wise advice on his ventures. In 1545, John's brother Otwell held a dying apprentice in his arms. Some apprentices married their masters' daughters. Some domestic servants, too, were cherished with a quasi-parental affection. In 1675 the pious Quaker John Banks wrote to urge his servants James and Mary to live in true love and subjection to their mistress and to set his children a good example. When Oliver Heywood's servant Martha left him in 1674 after a stay of sixteen years, he wrote that he 'loved her as a child'.[24]

These were nevertheless exceptional cases. The contractual basis and limited duration of the relationship between master and servant differentiated it from that between parent and child. William Gouge stressed that servants' places were inferior to children's. They were not to expect the same privileges. Fear necessarily played a greater part in securing obedience to masters, because there were 'not those motiues to stirre vp loue in seruants to their masters, as in children to their parents', as Gouge recognised. Service and apprenticeship usually contained an element of calculation on both sides. In larger households there was an increasing tendency to segregate children and servants, for fear the latter might set the former a bad example. Humbler masters probably maintained the sort of distinction which Edward Barlow immediately noticed in his prospective employer's household when he went a-liking (i.e. for a probationary period) in 1656. The apprentices sat at the same table as their master and his wife and children, but at the lower end, and they had pudding without suet or plums, and meat of poorer quality. By such small but very tangible distinctions it was made clear to apprentices and servants that they did not belong to their employer's family, in the sense in which we use the word.[25]

Education of the adolescent through service in another household began to decline among the upper classes sooner than it did further down the social scale, but this decline was a long drawn out process, and throughout this period the great household continued to play some part in the education of the children, particularly the daughters, of the gentry and yeomanry. In order to place their sons and daughters in households of high repute, parents made strenuous efforts, and exploited the influence of kin and friends to the full. Once they had been placed, solicitous parents expected to receive regular bulletins concerning the well-being and progress of their children, and especially their success in pleasing their master and mistress. Continuing parental support and influence remained important to the adolescent's advancement after the departure from home. In Henry VII's reign, for example, Dorothy Plumpton, then in Lady Darcy's household, begged her father Sir Robert to show by his fatherly kindness that she was indeed his child and to still the tongues of those who, in the absence of answers to her repeated messages, believed that he bore her little favour. The reception given to adolescent sojourners clearly varied greatly. Some were receiving an education for which their parents were paying, while others received wages. Letters from the voluminous correspondence of Lady Lisle show that in 1539 her daughter Katharine was made as welcome by one great lady as if she were her own daughter, whereas she expected to be regarded by another 'but as her woman'.[26]

A small minority of young men, at its largest in the early seventeenth century, entered the universities and the Inns of Court. Preparation for a career was only one of the functions of these institutions. London and the two universities gave the student opportunities to pursue a rich variety of extra-curricular subjects and to acquire or perfect valuable social skills. The broadening of one's circle of useful acquaintance was another major purpose of higher education. Whatever aim was uppermost in parents' minds, many of them no doubt hoped that the student would emerge better equipped to serve his family as well as himself. The young Christopher Trevelyan told his 'Deare and most careful Parentes' in a letter written in September 1605:

. . . I will intermitte no paines or diligence through which I may increase my learning and knowledge, always aiming at the ende wherfore I am placed in this University; that at length I may be a comfort to my parentes, and a joy and a healpe to my frendes and kindred.[27]

Many parents took steps to ensure that their sons should not waste their time or succumb to temptation during this most dangerous period of life. When her sixteen-year-old son Walter went to Oxford in 1473, Margaret Paston wanted him 'sette in good and sad rewle'. One fifteenth-century parent seeking the help of a friend in the oversight of a son about to enter Lincoln's Inn stipulated 'yn especialle' that he was to be kept from the company of women. Care was taken in the selection of tutors by parents of widely differing social station, such as Lady Lisle in the sixteenth century and Richard

Heywood and Richard Evelyn in the seventeenth. The last-named apparently decided not to entrust his son John to his elder brother's Oxford tutor because he felt that he had been 'more zelous in his life then industrious with his Pupils'. Many parents expected tutors to send them regular reports, which ranged from the tactfully euphemistic to the shrewdly penetrating. When her eldest son John was studying law in London in 1535, Lady Lisle received news of him both from the servant attending on him and from her husband's London agent. Such solicitous seventeenth-century parents as William Trumbull and Lady Brilliana Harley expected their sons to send them their own full and regular reports on their studies and welfare.[28]

But parents naturally varied widely in the amount of interest they showed in their absent children, as we should indeed expect in the light of today's experience. Christopher Guise remembered his Oxford contemporaries before the civil war passing their time in drinking and flirtations with tavern girls. In his Inn, though he took pleasure in 'poetry, some mathematickes, and a little history', he learnt no law. Christopher's father, having given him 'all the aditions of breeding' usually available to young gentlemen, and with other children to look after, then left him to his own devices, giving him only 'the example of a country gentleman and a good huntsman'.[29]

Relationships between parents and children during and after adolescence

It may seem paradoxical that we have more copious and intimate evidence bearing on the relations between parents and children in the phase of adolescence, when most of the young were poised to leave the nest or had already done so, than in childhood, when they had been under much closer parental supervision. But the fact is not really surprising. The absence of children generated correspondence; their launching in the world aroused parental anxieties which were often recorded in diaries and autobiographies as well as letters. Adolescence, when many individuals first began to live an autonomous intellectual and spiritual life and to view their parents with a new clarity and detachment, was often the first stage of life vividly recorded by autobiographers, and their conflicts with their parents were frequently the most important and fully recorded events of this phase. The evidence bearing on the quality and development of the emotional bonds between the generations in this phase of the family's life cycle is particularly rich, but it suffers nevertheless from major shortcomings. It relates preponderantly to the most highly literate social groups, the gentry and the clergy, and to the second half of our period. It defies quantification, and can only be used by way of cautious impressionistic generalisation and illustrative example to suggest the range of the possible rather than to demonstrate what was typical. The following discussion will focus in turn upon four relationships: those between father and son, mother and son, father and daughter and mother and daughter, and will attempt to take social status and (to some extent) birth order into account.

In the landed classes, a father's hopes and fears centred on the eldest son who would inherit his house and estate and carry on his line after his death. Ideally, the relationship between father and eldest son was a particularly close one. The father was supposed to prepare his heir for his responsibilities by gradually taking him into his confidence. In 1472 Thomas Mull wrote his brother-in-law Thomas Stonor a letter which reveals his feeling that Stonor's relationship with his son William, then in his early twenties, was not as close as it should have been. He urged him to call William forth when they were at home together, to let the young man walk with him, give him 'wordes of good comforte' and show him that he was indeed his 'good ffader'. Mull thought this especially necessary in order to break William's disposition to be a 'musyr and a studyer'. A special token of the bond between a man and his heir was the carefully prepared letter of counsel or the last message written on the eve of death, in which the fullest and most intimate advice was usually directed to the eldest son. It was to him that his father directed strict injunctions to take care of his younger brothers and sisters and to love and obey his mother.[30]

The strength of the tie between father and heir nevertheless varied greatly. The relationship between Sir Edmund Verney and his son Ralph (b. 1613), was a particularly close and affectionate one, as is demonstrated by the remarkably frank, relaxed and solicitous tone of their letters. But the fact that it was a source of great pleasure to a friend, who told Sir Edmund that she thought there could not be a better young man, suggests that it may have been somewhat exceptional. A father's high expectations of his eldest son could be a source of tension between them. In 1465, John Paston I went so far as to exclude his son John from his house. Answering his wife's plea that he take John back into his grace, Paston told her that his son's presumptuous and indiscreet demeanour had set his other servants a bad example. Obviously weary of remaining under his father's roof, he had nevertheless found no other place to go. But, the elder Paston continued, it had been his son's failure to help himself or use his opportunities, his drone-like idleness and dependence on the labours of others which had grieved him most. Other fathers perhaps suspected that their heirs were waiting impatiently for their own deaths. John Locke criticised those fathers who kept their sons ignorant of their estates and concerns 'as if they were guarding a secret of State from a Spy, or an Enemy'. The relationship could be a bitter and acrimonious one. The quarrel between James Lord Berkeley (d. 1463) and his unpleasant son William could only be ended by a formal agreement in which William undertook among other things not to trouble his father and to support him in his lawsuits; James for his part undertook to receive him 'as his son and heire to his favor and good faderhood' only after he had entered a bond of £1,000 for the observation of the agreement. In other cases attachment was tenuous. Sir George Courthop was sent away from home after his mother's death, when he was only four. His father remained a stranger to him for many years, and when he died on the eve of the civil war, the business of mourning had to give way to what Courthop saw as the much more pressing necessity of securing his father's office in the face of expected competition.[31]

Primogeniture tended to reinforce the bond between fathers and their eldest sons, but this did not mean that fathers were indifferent to the welfare of their younger offspring. The good father should, as Thomas Fuller put it in the seventeenth century, observe gavelkind, i.e. equal sharing, in dividing his affections, though not his estate. Thomas Fanshawe (d. 1601) urged his three eldest sons to be 'natural, loving and careful' towards their younger brothers and sisters, who were, he said, as dear to him as any of them were. Strong paternal affection for more than one son is clearly evident in the seventeenth-century correspondence of such gentry families as the Knyvetts and Verneys. The fact that fathers were so much less bound by law and custom in their relationship with their younger sons could permit more spontaneity than was possible in that of father and heir. Indeed, men often loved a younger son or sons better than the heir, as had been recognised as long ago as the twelfth century. Youngest sons were sometimes particularly well loved or trusted. The frank and forthright way in which Robert Carey warned his father, Lord Hunsdon, of Queen Elizabeth's displeasure, points to a high degree of mutual confidence. He wrote of Hunsdon with a reticence typical of the period, but the 'great content' he derived from Hunsdon's acceptance of his marriage, which had offended the queen and most of his best friends, speaks volumes for their relationship. Robert Boyle, youngest son of the earl of Cork (d. 1643), believed that he had always been his father's favourite, either because of the physical and mental resemblance between them, or (which he considered more likely) because he had not had as much time to disappoint him with bad behaviour as his elder brothers had had. Some observers of the modern family believe that whereas first-born children receive the most attention and are the foci of the highest expectations, the last born usually enjoy the most relaxed relationships with their parents.[32]

Apart from the gentry, the group to have left most evidence concerning relationships between fathers and sons were the pious married clergy of the seventeenth century. It is in this group that we find the most intense brooding over boys' moral development, though they also worried about early accidents and illnesses. Less restricted by primogeniture, moved by their sense of duty, such fathers almost certainly divided their interest and solicitude more evenly among their sons than did the gentry. The four best-documented godly ministers, Ralph Josselin, Adam Martindale, Henry Newcome and Oliver Heywood, each had trouble with an undutiful or disobedient son. In the case of Newcome the experience may have been especially painful, for it was his favourite son Daniel, whom he already regarded as his 'finest boy' when he was only five, who tried his father throughout his life. In most of these cases the misbehaviour was fairly serious by the standards of any period. This bitter experience may have been in part due to a filial reaction against the heavy emotional demands which their beliefs led these fathers to make of their sons. Yet all were extremely reluctant to impose the penalties to which their belief in the sacred character of paternal authority laid their sons open. They shrank from the possibility that God had excluded one of their children from his grace. Perhaps they feared that he had judged them through their offspring, whose failures reflected their own. 'Lord,' asked Oliver Heywood, 'is there no difference betwixt covenanted children and such as are out of covenant? Shall children of so many prayers and teares miscarry?' Josselin, Martindale and Newcome forgave errant sons their failed careers and the marriages they had made without their knowledge. They continued to hope for repentance and amendment.[33]

Merchants were another social group free of primogeniture, even though many of them sought in practice to establish their eldest sons on the land. This freedom made it easier for a father to reward application and ability. The staple merchant Richard Cely (d. 1482) transferred his love and trust from his incompetent son Robert, probably his eldest, to George and Richard, the sons best able to promote the family business. The strength of his attachment to George is evident from the anxiety he suffered when he heard that his twenty-one-year-old son had fallen ill on a business trip to Bruges in 1479. He urged him to be as cheerful as he could, to cosset himself and to obey his physicians. He would rather wait for his money than have his son delay his recovery. The way in which inherited skills and interests could strengthen the bond between father and son is also evident in the autobiography of Phineas Pett (1570–1647), a craftsman, not a merchant, but one whose standing as a naval master shipwright was as high as that of many merchants. With his eldest surviving son, Peter, who continued the family tradition, Phineas worked in close co-operation during the naval expansion of the 1630s, and his references to this 'loving son', laconic though they are, suggest pride, affection and trust. An only son might carry a particularly large burden of parental expectations. John Tupholme, mayor of Boston, writing in 1548 to his son William, whom he had apprenticed to the staple merchant John Johnson, told him that the chief care he had in his mind was to see him do well. 'Ho! What a pleasure it is for a man for to see his child go forward to be praised of his master! It is above a great deal of riches!'[34]

The majority of the farmers who formed one of the biggest occupational groups probably hoped to pass on a holding to at least one son and to draw on the labour of more than one before death or retirement. But the most vivid available evidence of the quality of relationships between farmers and their sons comes from the writings of men whose bent took them away from the path their fathers had trodden, since the yeoman and husbandmen of our period have left little in the way of reminiscence or correspondence. Prosperous yeomen were often glad to give one son or more a good school education or apprenticeship. Taking into account the boy's bent, the prospects of advancement, and the possible benefits to the family accruing from his skills and new acquaintance, they may well have judged the investment well made. Hugh Latimer remembered with respect and gratitude the yeoman father whose keeping him at school had made possible his career in the Church, and recalled how, as a lad of about twelve, he had buckled on his father's armour before the older Latimer went to fight for the king at Blackheath in 1497. Some seventeenth-century autobiographers described paternal sympathy and insight in the assessment of their aptitudes. Others had come into conflict with their fathers or proved unable to comply with their plans. This did not however always destroy the affection between them. William Lilly's unsuccessful yeoman father had no patience with his son's dislike of agricultural tasks, told him he was good-for-nothing and was allegedly glad to be rid of him. But when Edward Barlow threw over the apprenticeship arranged for him, he set off for London with a paternal blessing, and tears in his eyes. Four years later, his father managed to visit him. Subsequently, Barlow sent back to his family money saved from his hard-earned seaman's wages whenever he could, and in 1669, just paid off after a voyage, went to stay with them for three months. John Cannon, frustrated by his father's refusal to allow him to study, turned out a hopelessly unreliable farm-hand, and his younger brother finally assumed the position of farm manager to their father which would have been John's for the taking. Yet Cannon remained in touch after his entry into the Excise service, and his father twice travelled over 100 miles to see him. Cannon associated his recovery from smallpox with the arrival of his sixty-three-year-old father, the sound of whose voice 'administered great Comfort' to him. Taking hold of his son's hand, the old man blessed him and thanked God he had found him alive.[35]

Maternal influence in the early years of boys' lives was commonly reckoned to be strong, and it is clear from personal testimony that the bond between mother and son was often a very durable one. Mothers were pictured as being more indulgent than fathers. Many autobiographers dwelt longer on their mothers or remembered them with greater affection. In many gentry families, maternal love and expectations may have been less heavily concentrated upon the heir than were paternal. When a mother was an heiress, her property was often used to endow a younger son or sons.

Among the gentry were some outstanding female correspondents whose letters throw a great deal of light on their relations with their sons. Margaret Paston secretly kept in touch with her son John II when he left home without permission in 1463, despite the risk of her husband's displeasure. In 1464–65 she did her best to assuage his anger towards his eldest son. When he had succeeded his father, her fondness for him survived the irritation and worry which his prodigality and negligence caused her. John had cause to call her his 'most tender and kind mother'. Margaret and her cheerful and competent second son John III shared a warm affection, and she even confided in him her worries about her eldest son's wastefulness and failure to write to her. Relations were not always so cordial: in 1472 Margaret was finding it hard to put up with the presence of the twenty-eight-year-old John and his younger brother Edmund in her house. But five years later, she made John III's marriage possible through her readiness to settle property of hers upon him. Margaret watched over her fourth son Walter's moral welfare and application to his books. She wanted him to enter the Church but explained that 'I will loue hym bettere to be a good seculare man þan [than] to be a lewit [lewd] prest'. Anxious concern for her sons' physical health runs through her letters. She nursed John II through sickness, and urged him to take good care of his inexperienced younger brothers when they left for Calais with Edward IV's army in 1475. 'God saue yow all', she wrote, 'and send me good tythynges off yow all.'[36]

A particularly strong blend of maternal love and pious vigilance is evident in the letters which Lady Brilliana Harley wrote from her Herefordshire home to her eldest son Ned after he went up to Oxford in 1638. Many of them contained some expression of affection in the shape of a wish to be with Ned, to share his experience, happy or unhappy, or an assurance that he was the comfort of her life. A stream of delicious eatables and other presents accompanied her letters. 'Deare Ned,' she wrote, summing up her two first preoccupations, 'be carefull of your health, and aboue all, of keeping your hart cloos with your God.' She wanted to know what books he was reading, and, particularly when he was in London, to discuss politics with him. Lady Harley's concern for her younger sons, real though it undoubtedly was, seems pale in comparison with her feelings for Ned, who probably benefited not only from being the first-born, but also from the existence of a strong personal affinity between himself and his mother. His brothers Robert and Tom continued to waste their time at home until they were well into their teens, but their mother seems to have seen comparatively little of them and to have regarded it as her husband's responsibility to 'thinke of some course for them'. She nevertheless often alluded to his brothers' health and progress or lack of it in her letters to Ned. She found her second son Robert somewhat stubborn, touchy and reserved and urged Ned to write to him to avoid hurting his feelings. Tom on the other hand she found much more like Ned, and when he was thirteen his interest in what was going on in parliament contrasted strongly with Robert's political apathy. Evidence of Tom's affection for Ned gave their mother particular pleasure.[37]

Maternal love and solicitude are vividly described in some auto-biographies of the sons of seventeenth-century yeomen and husbandmen. A uniquely poignant drawing by Edward Barlow records the moment of his hurried and somewhat furtive departure for London, while his forlorn mother stands at their cottage door, vainly calling him back. William Stout's mother 'was always a tender, carefull and provident mother . . . , and tooke great pains to improve her children'. At this social level, too, shared piety could strengthen the bond between mother and son and help it to survive their physical separation. After his entry into the ministry, Oliver Heywood continued to draw strength from the affection and support of the mother to whom he owed his early religious education. One Sunday afternoon he suddenly 'found a ful tide' of extraordinary divine assistance, and later discovered that his mother had been praying in secret at that very moment.[38]

Maternal affection was not always matched by reciprocal filial sentiments. Samuel Pepys recorded that his old mother was so over-joyed to see him when he visited her in October 1664 that she was ready to weep every time she set eyes on him. Yet when she came to London the following May he coldly recorded her weakness of judgement and 'doting' discourse. He refused the 'poor wretch's' parting plea that he forgive his brother John, despite the distress this caused her. John Cannon's mother was sorry to see him leave the neighbourhood of his home, and wept tears of joy when he visited her in 1714 not long before her death. In his eyes, however, she remained the woman who had frustrated his adolescent ambitions, favoured his brother and sister at his expense, and frequently beaten him when his brother bore tales against him. His bare record of her death shows hardly a trace of emotion.[39]

Over-protective mothers were sometimes blamed for stunting the individual's development and denying him opportunities.[40] But men rarely complained that their mothers had never felt affection for them. Simon Forman the astrologer was quite exceptional in claiming that his widowed mother sent him off to live with an aunt when he was still a child because she never loved him and begrudged his being at home.[41] Those who suffered from maternal coldness or indiffer-ence usually masked the fact in decent silence. On the other hand, men's memories of their mothers were much less often scarred by the major conflicts of adolescence and young adulthood over their marriages, callings and religious or political opinions, in which fathers frequently assumed the role of major adversary. Mothers seldom appeared in this light unless they were widows, when they had to make decisions affecting their children for which husbands normally assumed ultimate responsibility. Widows' property rights, too, were sometimes a source of resentment. But the deepest and most lasting bitterness resulted from remarriage and having to share a mother with strangers.

Men were seldom directly involved in the upbringing of their daughters. But there is plenty of evidence of paternal desire to have daughters educated in 'swete maners and vertuouse custome', of care to advance them through service and marriage, of pride in their good looks and accomplishments and of concern for the preservation of their honour and good name. It was his sense of responsibility for the well-beloved daughters of whom he saw so little that impelled the Chevalier de la Tour Landry to write, round about 1371, that 'litil book' of good advice which was to become one of the most widely translated of all European conduct books.[42] Girls were often a source of delight to their fathers and of all their children the ones they were readiest to indulge. Lear may have been exceptional in his gullibility, but certainly not in his need for his daughters' love. Many men grew increasingly dependent upon the affection and company of unmarried daughters as old age crept upon them.[43]

A father's straightforward affectionate pleasure in his daughters is vividly expressed in the references which the Norfolk squire Thomas Knyvett made in his letters to his daughters Elizabeth and Muriel ('Buss and Muss', 'my bonny Girles' or 'my brace of Girles'). They reflect his pleasure in Muriel's improved deportment, his solicitude for Elizabeth's health, his desire for the company of both girls. From confinement in Cambridge at the height of the civil war in 1643 he wrote:

I must not forget to thanke my deer Buss for her rare composuer of her crums of comfort to her poor father: 't made me almost cry' like Pig' hogg, god Bless her sweet face.[44]

Interest in a daughter's education and shared personal piety could strengthen the relationship between father and daughter and add to its significance. Delight in favourite daughters' learned accomplishments strengthened the paternal love of such fathers as Thomas More and John Evelyn, but the importance of piety was more widespread. The love between Thomas More and his eldest daughter Margaret, who was also the closest to him, was tested and refined by his imprisonment and the prospect of his death. A common sense of divine purpose deepened the human relationship between father and daughter, and Margaret's love helped More meet his ordeal, as his last letter shows.

I never liked your manner toward me better, than when you kissed me last.
For I love when daughterly love and dear charity hath no leisure to look to
worldly courtesy.

Farewell my dear child, and pray for me, and I shall for you and all your
friends, that we may merrily meet in heaven.[45]

It seems likely that relatively few fathers and daughters shared
moments of such emotional intensity. But More was far from being
the only man whose fatherly solicitude was strengthened by his
religious convictions. In the seventeenth century, pious and affectionate concern are evident alike in the letters of the Lancashire
recusant squire William Blundell at one end of the religious spectrum
and of the Quaker John Banks at the other. Blundell, who had
sacrificed so much for his religion, knew what trials his daughters
would face in the convent, but counted the ultimate goal more than
worth the cost. Writing in 1659 to Jane, the first of his daughters to
enter religion, Blundell likened the 'sundry sorts of temptations,
great dryness in devotion, and weariness in the exercise of religion'
encountered in the monastic life to the accidents and delays she had
experienced on her way from Lancashire to Rouen. For his daughter
Frances, he later wrote, he was arranging a marriage on the other
side of the sea with a spouse who would neither die nor displease
her. John Banks wrote as her 'tender and affectionate father' to his
daughter Sarah on her entry into service in London in 1682,
reminding her of his love towards her since her birth and his concern
for her salvation. In this letter to Sarah, and in the lines written to
his three younger daughters from prison in 1684, his advice was carefully tailored to the age, needs, circumstances and understanding of
each girl.[46]

Relations between fathers and daughters should not however be
painted in a uniformly rosy hue. Of all relationships within the
family, this was the one whose harmony depended most heavily on
the child's compliance. Fathers in the property-owning classes were
much slower to yield the initiative in marriage to their daughters
than they were to their sons. The assumption that it belonged to
them underlay both the anger of the Buckinghamshire father who in
1521 told his daughter 'Voyde harlot owte of my sight' when he found
out about her marriage plans and the pained shock of John Evelyn
in face of his well-loved daughter Elizabeth's elopement over a
century and a half later.[47] The problem of how to marry a large
number of daughters was often a worrying and irksome one which
placed considerable strain on the relations between fathers and
daughters. William Blundell, for example, was an affectionate father
who no doubt persuaded himself that he was acting for the best in
consigning most of his girls to the convent. Yet it is also clear that
this course of action was a convenient one for a father who would

otherwise have felt bound to make a time-consuming search for suitable husbands among his beleaguered co-religionists. There is evidence that some of these daughters felt lonely and neglected. Some men perhaps left their girls unmarried because they were reluctant to lose them. And how many fathers resembled John Milton in their readiness to make their daughters drudges to lighten the burdens of their old age and incapacity?[48]

In modern England, sociologists consider the bond between mother and daughter to be commonly the strongest and most enduring of those between members of the nuclear family. This is largely because in child care and household management one generation of women has much to give the next by way of help and advice, whereas a man will very often follow a calling different from his father's.[49] Despite the fact that occupational succession was then much commoner than it now is, the same was true, though to a lesser extent, of the centuries before 1770.

The upbringing of daughters, unlike that of sons, remained the responsibility of one parent throughout childhood. In the farmer's household economy, a capable adolescent girl could play a vital part as her mother's chief domestic assistant, as the references to his sister Elin in William Stout's autobiography make clear. A daughter's placement in another household was a matter of particular concern to her mother, and it was to her mother, once she had left home, that a girl was probably most likely to direct her complaints of homesickness and requests for guidance. Although in theory the ultimate control of children's marriages might lie with their father, the mother was often first to be consulted, and might even take the initiative in the making of a match. 'He that would the daughter win, must with the mother first begin.' Among the upper classes and the middling sort, women often went to their mothers' houses for their lying in, or were visited by them. How warmly this support might be appreciated we can see from a letter sent by Anne Bacon to her mother not long before her delivery in 1573. 'I wish with all my hart my fortune were so good as to have yow ther.' A mother might continue to send her married daughter intimate advice. In 1633, Lady Mary Peyton charged her eldest daughter Anne to love, honour and obey her husband, but added that she would desire nothing unreasonable. Anne knew, she continued, obviously referring to her own marital experience, what she had suffered herself.[50]

Mothers' responsibilities in the advancement of adolescent girls often lay heavy on them, especially when, as widows, they had to carry them alone. Two generations of Paston mothers were haunted by fears that their daughters would make unsuitable marriages. Agnes kept Elizabeth in near imprisonment and subjected her to physical bullying when she was trying to arrange her marriage to a much older man. Margaret and her daughters got on each others' nerves when they were at home together. Margery's marriage to the family's bailiff was not forgiven her, and the fear that her sister Anne might make a similar match preyed on her mother's mind. Anne Murray, recalling her childhood before the civil war, described her mother as a conscientious parent who 'spared noe expence' in her daughters' education and took particular care of their religious instruction. But when in 1644 Anne received addresses from a young man whom her mother judged an unsuitable match for her, her mother responded by withholding her blessing for fourteen months.[51]

Adolescence was a phase during which, while pushing their offspring from the nest, parents sought to retain authority over them and to influence their future course. There was tension between these two objectives, and conflict between adolescent children and their parents was common. Yet parental love survived both strife and physical separation. 'This is the nature of parents to hope well of their children, how bad soever', wrote Richard Norwood, reflecting on the joy with which, in about 1610, his father had greeted what looked like the return of a repentant prodigal son. His father, he realised, loved him, despite the earlier sharpness and austerity with which, after the age of seven or eight, he had prepared his son for his departure from home, and the conflict between them over his choice of calling. His long absence, the apprehension of his final loss, had sharpened the edge of his father's joy.[52]

The death of a child in adolescence or young adulthood struck parents a bitter and sometimes fatal blow. Such a death destroyed the hopes and expectations which had developed over several years and wiped out both material and emotional investment. Both types of loss were inextricably bound up in the feelings of the bereaved. The shipwright Phineas Pett's record of the death of his 'dear beloved' son Richard in 1629 is the most poignant in his terse auto-biography. The deep paternal satisfaction Pett had derived from the successful transmission of his skill is suggested by his description of Richard as a 'very hopeful young man, and for his years an excellent artist, being trained by me to that purpose for making of ships'. In July 1658, Henry Newcome, hearing that an acquaintance's son had died at Cambridge, reflected that 'there is now an end of a deal of money, good education, fine parts, many expectations'. The physical manifestations of the malady of grief were often particularly acute in such cases. After the countess of Warwick had lost her only son, then on the verge of manhood, she suffered what she described as a 'great pain I had got constantly at my heart'; when her husband heard the news, 'he cried out so terribly that his cry was heard a great way; and he was the saddest afflicted person could possibly be'. The blow they had suffered often brought death to parents who had lost a child in youth. We need not disbelieve Richard Cely's warning, given to his brother George in 1480, that his capture or slaying would be death to both their parents.[53]

The old and their children

One of the widely acknowledged purposes of the procreation of children was to provide the married couple with a source of comfort in old age. The child's duty to help his parents in need was stressed by all those writers who discussed the Ten Commandments, though many of them claimed that it was often neglected.

Their unmarried children were perhaps the most important single source of assistance for the old. This at least is what the fullest and most informative local censuses suggest. In six communities between 1599 and 1796, 48 per cent of the married elderly (i.e. those aged sixty and over), 28 per cent of the widowed and single, had unmarried children living with them. The earliest of these censuses, drawn up at Ealing in 1599, shows that in this community the majority of the elderly married people of both sexes were thus placed. Four facts help to explain these percentages. First, marriage was late. Second, women commonly went on bearing children until the late thirties or early forties. Third, a high proportion of the old compared with today survived only into the early years of old age. Fourth, the widowed often found second partners a good deal younger than themselves, who might already have, or later bear, children.[54]

Girls in particular may have been encouraged to stay at home or to return thither from service in order to look after parents in their old age. A Somerset woman, Margaret White, described in about 1594 how she had lived with her father. She had 'guided him and his howsehowlde, and was continuallye with him in his sicknes vntill his deathe . . .'. In 1695 the minister Henry Newcome expressed in his will his confidence that his daughter Rose would stay with his wife after his death. Ultimately, he wished 60 per cent of his goods to go to her

in consideration that she hath denied herself and spent her time, and strength in painful, tender attendance upon us both in our old age and great infirmities . . . .

In 1702, Thomas Greene, a seventy-four-year-old grocer and draper of Lancaster, sent for his two daughters, then living with relatives in London, 'in hopes and expectation that they might be assistant to him and their mother in his trade and otherways in their old age'.[55]

Community lists and censuses suggest that elderly married people comparatively rarely lived in the same household with their married children. Of those listed in six English censuses taken between 1599 and 1796 only just over 5 per cent did so and in most cases they were still the nominal heads, or joint heads, of the household.[56] Only the comparatively wealthy had estates or holdings big enough to support two married couples. Households containing them were commonest among the upper classes. The co-residence of two couples under one roof was contrary to conventional wisdom, and could give rise to tension whether effective control remained in the older generation or passed to the younger. A father's dissatisfaction with the management of a son hitherto subject to him is vividly suggested by the reported words of John Webb the elder of Backwell (Somerset) to his kinsman Walter Webb in 1601. Walter had come as a guest to a banquet. The elder Webb told Walter

Yow are like to haue but a shorte feast heere, but I praye if yow haue not good cheere blame my sonne John Webb and not me, for of my troth I haue made him master of all, payinge me x^{li} by the yeare and finding me and my wyfe sufficient meate and drinke and all other maintenance and to discharge all rentes and dutyes whatsoever.

Walter expressed surprise that the elder Webb should have been so generous to a man so young and so recently married before seeing how good a manager he would be. Webb answered that he was making trial of his son's abilities because he himself was old and his labour was done. But father and son had agreed that if the younger John did not turn out to be a good manager, his father would take back the holding and the stock into his own hands at the end of the year.[57]

There was an old and deep-rooted belief that it was foolish for the old to put themselves into the power of their children, expressed in an ancient story. A man who handed over his estate to his son was gradually demoted from a place of honour at the top of the table to a couch behind the door where he died miserably, covered in sackcloth. In a variant of the tale, the aged father managed before it was too late to deceive his son into believing that he had a chest full of money under his bed, thereby ensuring proper treatment for the rest of his days. It was more seemly, thought the author of *Dives and Pauper*, for parents to put themselves in their children's keeping than in that of strangers. But however much they trusted them, they should always retain ultimate control of their estates and thus 'kepyn her [their] childryn in her daunger [danger]'. No prison, warned Daniel Rogers nearly two and a half centuries later, could be more irksome than a son's or a daughter's house, and he urged parents not to trust their children:

Love must descend, not ascend: its not naturall (saith *Paul*) for children to provide for parents, but for parents to provide for them, therefore invert not providence . . . be sure to hold stroake sufficient in your hand, for the securing of love and duty from your children.[58]

It was in order to hold 'stroake sufficient' that parents with property to pass on often entered into detailed and legally enforceable agreements providing for maintenance and houseroom or equivalent cash payments. Enormous numbers of such agreements are to be found on medieval manor court rolls. Succession to businesses as well as farms and holdings could be regulated in this manner.[59]

Early censuses suggest that whether through preference, custom or economic circumstances, elderly married couples were far more likely to live on their own than with their married children. Some of these elderly couples may have received payments from children under the terms of retirement agreements stipulating that they should have separate accommodation. But the physical strength and skills which were the major or only assets of a growing proportion of the population could not be exchanged with children for maintenance and support. How many of the poor received some financial help, however meagre, from offspring who had left home it is impossible to say. The will to help may have been there, but the resources were, in most cases, probably lacking. The sailor Edward Barlow sent or gave various sums of money to his parents, whom he considered 'ancient and poor people', but not all of it reached them, and his gifts were in any case irregular and relatively small.[60]

The widowed elderly were far more likely than the married to live with married children. Widows were much readier than widowers to enter households headed by their children or children-in-law, but even for widows the transition was by no means always easy. William Stout's mother, widowed in 1681, maintained her own household till her youngest son had grown up. She then remained with her eldest son Josias until shortly after his marriage in 1710, with which she seemed well satisfied at first. But her daughter-in-law, who had kept house for her father, would not allow Mrs Stout as much say in housekeeping as the old lady expected, which made her uneasy. In a year's time, Josias asked his bachelor brother William to take her in.[61]

Even though their help could not be counted upon, children probably constituted one major source of assistance and support in their parents' old age. Children probably helped above all as unmarried residents within parental households, secondly by offering the widowed elderly a haven within their own households. But a substantial minority of the elderly who had brought up children did not live under the same roof with offspring, whether they continued to maintain their own households, lodged with others or lived in institutions. The poor were the least able either to keep their children at home or to find shelter under their roofs. A census of the poor of Norwich drawn up in 1570 shows for example that the proportion of elderly women living with a child in the same household was less than half as large as it was in the six early listings already referred to.[62]

Enfeebled elderly people and widows constituted a large proportion of the recipients of the relief provided for in the Elizabethan Poor Laws. Since nearly all the early censuses were drawn up after the introduction of the Poor Laws, it is possible that important changes in the residential situation of the elderly occurring between the first and second halves of this period are not reflected in them. Legislation of 1598 laid down that the children of 'poor, old, blind, lame and impotent' people should maintain them if they were of sufficient ability. In practice, overseers may have been fairly generous in their assessment of 'ability' and ready to relieve many of the elderly in their own homes. It is possible that by underpinning the viability of their independent households, the Poor Laws actually made the poor less dependent on their children. But the extent to which, in the absence of organised poor relief, the elderly lived with their children before the late sixteenth century has yet to be investigated. The only early sixteenth-century census so far thoroughly analysed, covering Coventry in 1523, shows that there households of three generations were far rarer, not more numerous, than they were in later pre-industrial England. In part this was due to a relatively low adult life expectation. But even when parents lived to see their children married, they seem to have lived near, rather than with them.[63]

Grandparents

A minority of parents, probably largest at the upper levels of the social scale, lived to be grandparents. In households of three generations, comparatively rare in England, grandparents no doubt played some part in the care and supervision of young children. The yeoman's son John Cannon, whose father had lived close to his own father's house, remembered how the latter had kept order among his quarrelling grandchildren by means of genial threats of disembowelment or bribes of 'apples and toyes of small value'. Children were commonly sent to stay with grandparents who lived some distance away. Gentlewomen often entrusted one or more members of their broods to grandparents, usually, perhaps, to their own parents. In the 1630s the Somerset gentleman Amias Bampfield and his wife Anne sent three and perhaps five of their children to Anne's parents' house at Payhembury (Devon). The yeoman's son Richard Baxter was sent to stay with his grandfather; the Essex clergyman Ralph Josselin received his daughters' children. Grandchildren's sojourns were often long ones. Among both the poor of Norwich in 1570 and the people covered by a sample of later pre-industrial censuses, nearly 5 per cent of the elderly had grandchildren living in their households without their parents.[64]

Old people often seem to have adopted a more relaxed attitude towards the upbringing of children than their parents did. Perhaps the responsibility for the moulding of character weighed less heavily and less directly upon them, while the diminished obligations of old age left them more time to enjoy small children's company. According to John Locke, mothers in upper-class families often looked forward impatiently to their sons' marrying and producing grandchildren for them to play with. But old men, too, enjoyed their grandchildren.

From a letter which Thomas Phelips wrote to his son Edward in 1588, it seems that his grandson 'lyttle Robben yo[u]r worldly ioye' was the apple of his eye. This grandson, later Sir Robert (1586–1638), was, in writing to his own son Edward in the 1630s to describe the latter's daughter as 'My little jewell . . . and my good companion'. 'Betty is very well and is my fyne gyrle though wee fall owt twenty tymes a daye' he reported in about 1636. Endymion Porter's mother told him she wished he could see her sitting at table flanked by his children, her 'little chickens'. No occupation in all her life had given her so much content as seeing them in bed at night or getting them up in the morning.[65]

Grandchildren who represented the main hope of continuing a family line were often regarded with particular affection. But such attachment was not limited to members of the male line: some grandfathers looked to daughters' sons to perpetuate their names. Simonds D'Ewes, son of an only daughter, was named after the maternal grandfather in or near whose house he spent his childhood. D'Ewes loved him 'most tenderly above any other person in the world' on account of the indulgent upbringing he had given him. Sir Anthony Ashley bestowed both his Christian name and his surname upon his only daughter's son, later earl of Shaftesbury. But his decision to settle all his property so that it should come to his grandson was, according to the latter, due not only to dynastic feeling but also to his growing personal fondness for him, 'being a prating boy and very observant of him'.[66]

The relationship between grandparents and grandchildren was often a source of mutual pleasure and affection, but it could be more than that, for some grandfathers took a close interest in their grandchildren's education. The conviction that it was possible to educate without harshness which Ascham took as his starting-point in *The Scholemaster* was shared by Sir Richard Sackville and other privy councillors to Queen Elizabeth. Sackville recalled how a harsh master had made him dislike learning, but he was determined to turn this mishap to the benefit of his little grandson. Perhaps no man took a closer interest in the education of his grandsons than William Blundell, the seventeenth-century Lancashire recusant squire, whose daughter's sons Edmund and Richard Butler spent long periods in his house at Crosby. Writing to his son-in-law about Edmund's progress in 1677, Blundell told him how the boy might be beating in the brambles to start a hare within an hour or two after being 'up to the ears in Plutarch, in a hot dispute whether Alexander the Great or Caesar was the braver man'. In the education of his grandsons, Blundell displayed a happy empathy, a shrewd judgement of character, above all a lively enjoyment. Solicitous though he was of his grandsons' moral as well as physical welfare, critical though he was of their shortcomings. Blundell seems in bringing them up to have been largely free of that burden of anxiety about their children's development which restrained the outward expression of affection in many conscientious parents. As his grandsons grew to adulthood, Blundell remained their closest confidant.[67]

Conclusion

The adolescent contribution to the English economy between the fifteenth and eighteenth centuries was proportionately far higher than it is today. The law bore far more heavily upon youthful delinquents. Yet the achievement of full adulthood and independence was longer postponed. Youth was recognised as a dangerous time during which prolonged tutelage and close control were felt to be necessary. In this respect, attitudes did not change much during the period under review. Yet there was a perceptible relaxation, in the upper and middle social ranks, of marks of subordination. Ideological divisions, economic diversification and the opening of a wider world somewhat enhanced the choices and opportunities open to the young.

A period of education, training or service away from the parental home was felt to be salutary for the individual. But parental support commonly remained important during this phase of his life. The best opportunities for advancement were only to be secured through the investment of time, money or influence on the part of parents or other close relatives. Parental interest in the absent adolescent very often remained keen. The master was expected to assume some parental responsibilities, and the relationship between him and his servant or apprentice could become a close one. But in its basis, duration and intensity it was quite different from that between parent and child.

The bond between adolescents and their parents typically remained a strong one despite long periods of separation. The death of a child was often hardest to bear in adolescence or young adulthood, representing as it did the maximum loss of emotional and material investment. The strength of attachment varied a great deal, and it is impossible to generalise with confidence about something which depended so much upon individual character and circumstances. Property, skills, social roles and piety: the inheritance of any one or a combination of these might strengthen the relationship between parent and child. But the high expectations which were invested in an heir or developed from close personal involvement in a child's upbringing and training could place a heavy burden on a relationship. Affection sometimes developed more easily between parents and their younger offspring or children of the opposite sex. The potential sources of conflict between adolescents and their parents were many. But parental love often survived repeated disappointments.

The coming of puberty did not herald the final departure of all children. Some may never have left home. Others returned at intervals during and after service. In many cases adolescents made a far from negligible contribution to the economy of the parental household. Children were widely looked upon as a possible source of help and support in old age despite the existence of a long tradition of cautionary tales warning parents not to depend on them. Especially in the early years of old age, a large proportion of the elderly presided over households which still contained unmarried offspring. Although few elderly couples, save in the upper ranks of society, lived in the same household with their married children, many of the widowed elderly, especially women, found refuge under a filial roof. As grandparents, the old in turn often proved a useful source of assistance in child care. Grandparenthood could be a source of comfort and satisfaction both to old people and to the third generation; in many cases, one suspects, it may have helped to maintain and strengthen the links between the old and their children.

Notes and references

1. **M. C. Seymour** (ed.), *On the Properties of Things: John Trevisa's Translation of Bartholomaeus Anglicus 'De Proprietatibus Rerum'. A Critical Text*, Clarendon Press, Oxford, 1975, Vol. I, pp. 291–2; **W. Gouge**, *Of Domesticall Duties Eight Treatises*, London, 1622, pp. 525–6; **G. F. Still**, *The History of Paediatrics*, Oxford UP, 1931, p, 6; **S. L. Thrupp**, *The Merchant Class of Medieval London, 1300–1500*, Univ. of Chicago Press, 1948, p. 195; **G. Strauss**, *Luther's House of Learning: Indoctrination of the Young in the German Reformation*, Johns Hopkins UP, London, 1978, p. 336; Taunton, Somerset Record Office, D/D/Cd 36, Salter c. Bucklebridge; Exeter, Devon Record Office, Chanter 864, f. 477. The best discussion of concepts of adolescence is in **K. V. Thomas**, 'Age and Authority in Early Modern England', *Proceedings of the British Academy*, **62** (1976), 214–32, though it perhaps exaggerates the strength of *new* deliberate 'pressure to subordinate the young' during this period.
2. Thomas, *op. cit.*, 216–7, 221–6, 228, 230; **O. J. Dunlop** and **R. D. Denman**, *English Apprenticeship and Child Labour: A History*, Fisher Unwin, London, 1912, Chs 1–3, 5, 7; **A. Kussmaul**, *Servants in Husbandry in Early Modern England*, Cambridge UP, 1981, pp. 37–8, 100–1.
3. **P. H. Barnum** (ed.), *Dives and Pauper*, Vol. I, *Early English Text Society*, **275**, **280** (1976, 1980), Pt. I, 304–24; **N. Davis** (ed.), *Paston Letters and Papers of the Fifteenth Century*, Clarendon Press, Oxford, 1971, 1976, Vol. I, p. 540; **T. Stapleton**, *The Life and Illustrious Martyrdom of Sir Thomas More*, trans. **P. E. Hallett**, Burns, Oates & Washbourne, London, 1928, p. 3; Gouge, *op. cit.*, p. 493.
4. **S. Brigden**, 'Youth and the English Reformation', *Past and Present*, 95 (1982), 51–67; **A. Kenny** (ed.), *Responsa Scholarum of the English College, Rome, Part One: 1598–1621, Catholic Record Society*, **54** (1962), 66, 122, 126, 128, 132, 145, 147, 156, 159, 161, 168, 174, 188, 228, 230,

261, 265, 266, 295, 296, 299, 323, 330, 343, 345; **J. Pratt** (ed.), *The Acts and Monuments, of John Foxe*, The Religious Tract Society, London, 1877, Vol. VIII, p. 209; **C. G. Crump** (ed.), *The History of the Life of Thomas Ellwood . . . written by his own hand*, Methuen, London, 1900, p. 34.

5. Quoted by **C. Hill**, *Puritanism and Revolution: Studies in Interpretation of the English Revolution of the 17th Century*, Secker & Warburg, London, 1965, p. 210.

6. **J. Locke**, *The Second Treatise of Government, and a Letter Concerning Toleration*, **J. W. Gough** (ed.), Basil Blackwell, Oxford, 1956, pp. 32–6.

7. *Ibid.*, pp. 36–7.

8. **O. L. Dick** (ed.), *Aubrey's Brief Lives*, Penguin Books, Harmondsworth, 1962, p. 26; Stapleton, *op. cit.*, pp. 108–17.

9. **C. D'Evelyn** (ed.), *Peter Idley's Instructions to his Son*, Modern Language Association of America, Boston, 1935, p. 83; **R. Ascham**, *The Scholemaster, Or plaine and perfite way of teachyng children, to vnderstand, write, and speake, the Latin tong . . .* in *English Works*, **W. A. Wright** (ed.), Cambridge UP, 1904, pp. 189–95; **T. Becon**, *The Catechism . . . with other pieces written by him in the Reign of King Edward the Sixth*, **J. Ayre** (ed.), *Parker Society*, **11** (1844), 355; **T. Fuller**, *History of the Worthies of England*, **J. G. Nichols** (ed.), London, Edinburgh and Perth, 1811, Vol. I, p. 167.

10. **J. M. Osborn** (ed.), *The Autobiography of Thomas Whythorne*, Clarendon Press, Oxford, 1961, pp. 10–11; Kenny, *op. cit.*, Vol. I, pp. 73–4; **J. P. Cooper** (ed.), *Wentworth Papers 1597–1628, Camden Society*, 4th ser., **12** (1973), 55; **R. Parkinson** (ed.), *The Life of Adam Martindale, written by himself*, *Chetham Society*, old ser., **4** (1845), 24; **J. Cannon**, χρονεχα *Seu Annales or Memoirs of the Birth Education Life and Death of Mr Iohn Cannon Sometime Officer of the Excise and Writing Master at Mere Glastonbury & West Lydford in the County of Somersett*, n.d., MS in the Somerset Record Office, Taunton, pp. 30, 34; **J. Horsfall Turner** (ed.), *The Rev. Oliver Heywood, B. A., 1630–1702: his Autobiography, Diaries, Anecdote and Event books*, Brighouse, 1881–85, Vol. I, p. 157; **J. D. Marshall** (ed.), *The Autobiography of William Stout of Lancaster 1665–1752*, *Chetham Society*, 3rd ser., **14** (1967), 70–1; *The Lives of those Eminent Antiquaries Elias Ashmole Esq., and Mr William Lilly, written by themselves*, London, 1774, pp. 9–10.

11. Parkinson, *op. cit.*, pp. 6–7; **W. F. Craven** and **W. B. Hayward** (eds), *The Journal of Richard Norwood, Surveyor of Bermuda*, Scholars' Facsimiles and Reprints, New York, 1945, p. 31; **B. Lubbock** (ed.), *Barlow's Journal of his life at sea*, Hurst & Blackett, London, 1934, Vol. I, pp. 15–22.

12. **R. Cawdrey**, *A Godlie Forme of Hovseholde Gouernment: for the Ordering of Private Families, according to the Direction of God's Word*, London, 1600, p. 292; T. Cobbett, *A fruitfull and Usefull Discourse-tovching the Honour due from Children to Parents, and the duty of Parents towards their Children*, London, 1656, pp. 11, 93–5; excellent discussion 'Children and Servants: the Problem of Adolescence' in **A Macfarlane**, *The Family Life of Ralph Josselin, a Seventeenth-Century Clergyman: An Essay in Historical Anthropology*, Cambridge UP, 1970, pp. 205–10.

13. Trowbridge, Wilts. Record Office, Bishop's Dep. Bk. 16, f. 110; Bishop's Dep. Bk. 61, ff. 29, 142^v–3, 208, 239^v–40; Taunton, Somerset Record Office, D/D/Cd 20, f. 76^v; D/D/Cd 95, deposition by Thomas Langfield, 30 May 1678, in Chaffie et Chaffie c. Chaffie et Chaffie; Marshall, *op. cit.*, 70, 75–6; **M. Spufford**, 'First Steps in Literacy: the Reading and Writing Experiences of the Humblest Seventeenth-Century Spiritual Autobiographers, *Social History*, **4** (1979), 425–6; Cannon, *op. cit.*, p. 33; Kussmaul, *op. cit.*, p. 24.

14. *Ibid.*, pp. 5–7; but for an apprenticeship in husbandry, see **A. H. Smith**, **G. M. Baker** and **R. W. Kenny** (eds), The *papers of Nathaniel Bacon of Stiffkey, Vol. I, 1556–1577, Norfolk Record Society*, **46** (1979), 273.

15. Kussmaul, *op. cit.*, pp. 14–16, 34–5; **M. Girouard**, *Life in the English Country House: A Social and Architectural History*, Yale UP, London, 1978, pp. 27–8, 142; **D. V. Glass**, 'Two Papers on Gregory King', in **D. V. Glass** and **D. E. C. Eversley** (eds), *Population in History: Essays in Historical Demography*, Edward Arnold, London, 1965, pp. 205–6; **R. Finlay**, *Population and Metropolis: The Demography of London 1580–1650*, Cambridge UP, 1981, pp. 140–1; **R. Thompson**, *Women in Stuart England and America: A Comparative Study*, Routledge & Kegan Paul, London, 1974, pp. 31–5. For the high proportion of female servants in Coventry in 1523, see **C. Phythian–Adams**, *Desolation of a City: Coventry and the Urban Crisis of the Late Middle Ages*, Cambridge UP, 1979, pp. 206–11.

16. Kussmaul, *op. cit.*, pp. 22–4, 97–105; Dunlop and Denman, *op. cit.*, pp. 94–101, 112–33; Finlay, *op. cit.*, pp. 66–7; **P. Laslett**, *Family Life and Illicit Love in Earlier Generations: Essays in Historical Sociology*, Cambridge UP, 1977, pp. 32, 34, 44, 90; **R. Wall**, 'The Age at Leaving Home', *Journal of Family History*, **3** (1978), 189–90, 195, 200.

17. Macfarlane, *op. cit.*, pp. 209–10; **P. Laslett**, 'Mean Household Size in England since the Sixteenth Century', in **P. Laslett** and **R. Wall** (eds), *Household and Family in Past Time*, Cambridge UP, 1972, p. 154 (mean proportions).

18. Phythian–Adams, *op. cit.*, p. 83. For a possibly orphaned boy accepted into service at twelve before being apprenticed at fourteen (1559) see **R. W. Hudson** and **J. C. Tingey** (eds), *The Records of the City of Norwich*, Jarrold and Sons, Norwich and London, 1910, Vol. II, p. 177; for very early apprenticeship in some poorer trades, see Dunlop and Denman, *op. cit.*, pp. 98–9; Laslett, *Family Life and Illicit Love*, p. 44.

19. Cawdrey, *op. cit.*, pp. 258, 273; **S. R. Smith**, 'The London Apprentices as Seventeenth-Century Adolescents', *Past and Present*, **61** (1973), 150; Lubbock, *op. cit.*, Vol. I, p. 16. Gouge, *op. cit.*, p. 446, complained of children who bound themselves without parental consent, but the trades concerned must have been poor ones. For possibly exceptional paternal care in choosing a master, see **R. Parkinson** (ed.), *The Autobiography of Henry Newcome, M.A., Chetham Society*, old ser., **26–7** (1852), I, 170–9.

20. Taunton, Somerset Record Office, D/D/Cd 12, deposition of John Hodges in Tyther c, Fludd (*c.* Jan. 1568?); **B. Winchester**, *Tudor Family Portrait*, Jonathan Cape, London, 1955, p. 120; **C. Jackson** and **H. J. Morehouse** (eds), *Yorkshire Diaries and Autobiographies in the Seventeenth and Eighteenth Centuries, Surtees Society*, **65** (1877), 31, 87;

C. B. Robinson (ed.), *Rural Economy in Yorkshire in 1641, being the Farming and Account Books of Henry Best, of Elmswell in the East Riding, Surtees Society*, **33** (1857), 134.

21. Cawdrey, *op. cit.*, p. 274; Parkinson, *Life of Martindale*, p. 6; Lubbock, *op. cit.*, Vol. I, pp. 20–1; Cannon, *op. cit.*, p. 58; **P. Clark**, '"The Ramoth–Gilead of the Good": Urban Change and Political Radicalism at Gloucester 1540–1640', in **P. Clark, A. G. R. Smith** and **N. Tyacke** (eds), *The English Commonwealth 1547–1640: Essays in Politics and Society presented to Joel Hurstfield*, Leicester UP, 1979, p. 169; Winchester, *op. cit.*, pp. 129–30, 225–7; **D. Gardiner** (ed.), *The Oxinden Letters, 1607–1642*, Constable & Co., London, 1933, pp. 210–1; London, Public Record Office, REQ 2, 46/12, 113/18, 95/54; **W. L. Sachse** (ed.), *Minutes of the Norwich Court of Mayoralty, 1630–31, Norfolk Record Society*, **15** (1942), 76; **R. H. Hilton**, *The English Peasantry in the Later Middle Ages*, Clarendon Press, Oxford, 1975, pp. 51–2; Robinson, *op. cit.*, p. 135; Laslett, *Family Life and Illicit Love*, p. 34.

22. Gouge, *op. cit.*, pp. 442, 602–3, 606–7, 613–14, 621–2, 675; Kussmaul, *op. cit.*, pp. 52–3.

23. **D. M. Meads** (ed.), *Diary of Lady Margaret Hoby, 1599–1605*, George Routledge & Sons, London, 1930, pp. 62, 66, 67, 109, 120, 130; **S. Clarke**, *The Second Part of the Marrow of Ecclesiastical History*, 2nd edn, London, 1675, Vol. II, p. 86; Gouge, *op. cit.*, pp. 610–11, 666–8, 674–5, 680, 688; Becon, *op. cit.*, pp. 362–3; **J. A. Sharpe**, 'Domestic Homicide in Early Modern England', *Historical Journal*, **24** (1981), 37–41; **E. S. de Beer** (ed.), *The Diary of John Evelyn*, Clarendon Press, Oxford, 1955, Vol. III, p. 95; **R. Latham** and **W. Matthews** (eds), *The Diary of Samuel Pepys: a New and Complete Transcription*, G. Bell & Sons, London, 1970–, Vol. IX, pp. 493, 526; Vol. XI, pp. 259–60. I am indebted to the analysis of relations between the Pepyses and their servants in **C. Croydon**, 'Domestic Servants of the Later Seventeenth Century with Particular Reference to the Servants of Samuel Pepys', Reading University dissertation, 1978.

24. Winchester, *op. cit.*, pp. 26, 28, 55; *A Journal of the Life, Labours, Travels &c of John Banks, Friends' Library*, **9** (1834), 293; Horsfall Turner, *op. cit.*, Vol. III, pp. 137–8.

25. Gouge, *op. cit.*, pp. 168, 616; Lubbock, *op. cit.*, Vol. I, p. 18.

26. Meads, *op. cit.*, pp. 7, 22–5, 166, 200, 201, 202, 267; **M. St Clare Byrne** (ed.), *The Lisle Letters*, Univ. of Chicago Press, 1981, Vol. III, pp. 8–9, 12–17, 133–218, 442; Vol. IV, pp. 109, 112–14, 119, 123, 128–31, 144, 163–5, 174, 183; Vol. V, pp. 448–9, 453, 730; **T. Stapleton** (ed.), *Plumpton Correspondence, Camden Society*, old ser., **4** (1839), 202–3, 231–2.

27. **W. C.** and **C. E. Trevelyan** (eds), *Trevelyan Papers, Vol. III, Camden Society*, old ser., **105** (1872), 79.

28. Davis, *op. cit.*, Vol. I, p. 370; Thrupp, *op. cit.*, p. 231; Horsfall Turner, *op. cit.*, Vol. I, pp. 159–60; de Beer, *op. cit.*, Vol. II, pp. 16–17; **B. Schofield** (ed.), *The Knyvett Letters 1620–1644, Norfolk Record Society*, **20** (1949), 19–20; St Clare Byrne, *op. cit.*, Vol. IV, pp. 12–20, 25–35; Reading, Berks. Record Office, Trumbull Correspondence, Misc. Corr. L; **T. T. Lewis** (ed.), *Letters of the Lady Brilliana Harley, Camden Society*, old ser., **58** (1853), 8, 11, 19, 42, 136.

29. **G. Davies** (ed.), *Autobiography of Thomas Raymond, and Memoirs of the Family of Guise of Elmore, Gloucestershire, Camden Society*, 3rd ser., **28** (1917), 116–20.

30. **C. L. Kingsford** (ed.), *Stonor Letters and Papers, 1290–1483, Camden Society*, 3rd ser., **29–30** (1919), I, 128. Paternal counsel can be found in both personal and more elaborately literary forms from the very beginning of the period onwards. See the letter of 30 April 1450 from the duke of Suffolk in **J. Gairdner** (ed.), *The Paston Letters, 1422–1509 A. D.*, John Grant, Edinburgh, 1910, Vol. I, p. 121, and D'Evelyn, *op. cit.*,

31. **F. P.** and **M. M. Verney**, *Memoirs of the Verney Family during the Seventeenth Century*, Longmans, Green & Co., 2nd edn, London. 1907, Vol. I, pp. 77–8; Davis, *op. cit.*, Vol. I, pp. 127–8; **J. Locke**, *Some Thoughts Concerning Education*, 1693, in *The Educational Writings of John Locke*, **J. Axtell** (ed.), Cambridge UP, 1968, p. 202; **J. Smyth**, *The Berkeley Manuscripts*, **J. Maclean** (ed.), Bristol and Gloucestershire Archaeological Society, Gloucester, 1883, Vol. II, pp. 75–6; **S. C. Lomas** (ed.), *The Memoirs of Sir George Courthop, 1616–1685*, in *The Camden Miscellany*, **11**, *Camden Society*, 3rd ser., **13** (1907), 103–4, 137.

32. **T. Fuller**, *The Holy State and the Profane State*, **M. G. Walten** (ed.), Columbia UP, New York, 1938, Vol. II, pp. 12–13; **H. C. Fanshawe** (ed.), *The Memoirs of Ann Lady Fanshawe*, John Lane, London, 1907, p. 283; Schofield, *op. cit.*, esp. pp. 149–50; Verney and Verney, *op cit.*, Vol. I, p. 102; **T. F. T. Plucknett**, *A Concise History of the Common Law*, Butterworth, London, 5th edn, 1956, p. 526; **F. H. Mares** (ed.), *Memoirs of Robert Carey*, Clarendon Press, Oxford, 1972, pp. xiv–xv, 4, 26; **T. Birch**, *The Life of the Honourable Robert Boyle*, London, 1744, pp. 21, 29–30; 'How Middle Children in Families bear the Brunt', *The Times*, 22 Feb. 1982, 1d.

33. Macfarlane, *op. cit.*, pp. 120–3; Parkinson, *Life of Martindale*, pp. 211–13, 215; *idem, Newcome's Autobiography*, Vol. I, pp. 97, 181, 182; Vol. II, pp. 215, 229, 234, 245, 253; Horsfall Turner, *op. cit.*, Vol. I, pp. 319–21, 340; Vol. II, pp. 202–4, 205–7.

34. **A. Hanham** (ed.), *The Cely Letters, 1472–1488, Early English Text Society*, **273** (1975), x, 64–5, 261; **W. G. Perrin** (ed.), *The Autobiography of Phineas Pett, Navy Records Society*, **51** (1918), 149, 150–4, 160; Winchester, *op. cit.*, pp. 225–7.

35. *Sermons by Hugh Latimer sometime Bishop of Worchester*, J. M. Dent & Co., London, 1906, p. 85; *Lives of Ashmole and Lilly*, pp. 9–10 (see n. 10 above); Lubbock, *op. cit.*, Vol. I, pp. 21, 48, 50, 139, 174–7, 252; Cannon, *op. cit.*, pp. 30–3, 54, 85, 87–8, 101–2.

36. Davis, *op. cit.*, Vol. I, pp. 127–8, 287–90, 293, 353, 358–61, 370, 372, 375–6, 379–80, 474–8, 576–7, 609.

37. Lewis, *op. cit.*, 8, 9, 11, 19, 26, 30–1, 37, 39, 42–3, 46–7, 55, 61, 65, 69, 80, 91, 93, 101, 112, 115, 117–21, 126, 128, 135, 136, 170, 175, 200.

38. Lubbock, *op. cit.*, picture facing Vol. I, p. 20; Marshall, *op. cit.*, p. 175; Horsfall Turner, *op. cit.*, Vol. I, pp. 47, 155–6.

39. Latham and Matthews, *op. cit.*, Vol. V, p. 298; Vol. VI, pp. 99, 112, 133–4; Cannon, *op. cit.*, pp. 23, 30, 40, 41, 58, 111, 114.

40. Smyth, *op. cit.*, Vol. II, pp. 253, 394; *Life of Lord Herbert*, p. 35; Verney and Verney, *op. cit.*, Vol. I, p. 151.

41. **A. L. Rowse**, *Simon Forman: Sex and Society in Shakespeare's Age*, Weidenfeld & Nicolson, London. 1974, p. 271.
42. **Sir T. Elyot**, *The Boke Named the Gouernour*, J. M. Dent & Co., London, 1907, p. 20; **H. Paget**, 'The Youth of Anne Boleyn', *Bulletin of the Institute of Historical Research*, **54** (1981), 162–70; Davis, *op. cit.*, Vol. II, p. 413; **C. Jackson** (ed.), *The Autobiography of Mrs Alice Thornton, of East Newton, in the County of York*, Surtees Society, **62** (1875), 8; **L. Hutchinson**, *Memoirs of the Life of Colonel Hutchinson, with the fragment of an autobiography of Mrs Hutchinson*, **J. Sutherland** (ed.), Oxford UP, 1973, p. 288; **A. Browning** (ed.), *Memoirs of Sir John Reresby: the complete text and a selection from his letters*, Jackson, Son & Co., Glasgow, 1936, pp. 227, 406; **M. Y. Offord** (ed.), *The Book of the Knight of the Tower, Early English Text Society*, supplementary ser., **2** (1971), 12–13.
43. London, Public Record Office, REQ 2/83/44; Lomas, *op. cit.*, p. 145; **Lord Braybrooke** (ed.), *The Autobiography of Sir John Bramston K.B., of Skreens, in the Hundred of Chelmsford, Camden Society*, old ser., **32** (1845), 380.
44. Schofield, *op. cit.*, pp. 97, 104, 113, 117, 119, 122, 125, 136–7, 140, 142.
45. De Beer, *op. cit.*, Vol. IV, pp. 421–4; Stapleton, *Life of More*, p. 203.
46. **M. Blundell** (ed.), *Cavalier: Letters of William Blundell to his Friends, 1620–98*, Longmans, Green & Co., London, 1933, pp. 76–8, 138; *Journal of Banks*, pp. 332–6, 361–4.
47. **E. M. Elvey** (ed.), *The Courts of the Archdeaconry of Buckingham, 1483–1523, Bucks. Record Society*, **19** (1975), 310; de Beer, *op. cit.*, Vol. IV, pp. 460–2.
48. Blundell, *op. cit.*, pp. 170–1; **W. R. Parker**, *Milton. A Biography*, Clarendon Press, Oxford, 1968, Vol. I, pp. 585–6.
49. **M. Young** and **P. Willmott**, *Family and Kinship in East London*, Penguin Books, Harmondsworth, 1962, p. 188; **P. Willmott** and **M. Young**, *Family and Class in a London Suburb*, The New English Library, London, 1967, pp. 69–70.
50. Marshall, *op. cit.*, pp. 68–9, 76; Kingsford, *op. cit.*, Vol. I, p. 123; **A. J. Fletcher**, *A County Community in Peace and War: Sussex 1600–1660*, Longman, London, 1975, p. 38; Smith et al., *op. cit.*, Vol. I, pp. 24, 75; **D. Gardiner** (ed.), *The Oxinden Letters, 1607–1642*, Constable & Co., London, 1933, p. 87.
51. Davis, *op. cit.*, Vol. I, pp. 30–1, 339, 343, 348; Vol. II, p. 32; **J. G. Nichols** (ed.), *The Autobiography of Anne Lady Halkett, Camden Society*, new ser., **13** (1875), 2–14.
52. **W. F. Craven** and **W. B. Hayward** (eds.), *The Journal of Richard Norwood, Surveyor of Bermuda*, Scholars' Facsimiles and Reprints, New York, 1945, pp. 8, 31–2.
53. Perrin, *op. cit.*, p. 143; Parkinson, *Newcome's Autobiography*, Vol. I, p. 96; **T. C. Croker** (ed.), *Autobiography of Mary, Countess of Warwick, Percy Society*, **76** (1848), 30–1; Stapleton, *Plumpton Correspondence*, p. 197n; de Beer, *op. cit.*, Vol. II, p. 12; Latham and Matthews, *op. cit.*, Vol. III, p. 213; Hanham, *op. cit.*, p. 100.
54. Laslett, *Family Life and Illicit Love*, pp. 201 (where only five places are named in the description of the data), 203–4; **K. J. Allison**, 'An Elizabethan Village "Census"', *Bulletin of the Institute of Historical Research*, **36** (1963), 91–103.

55. Taunton, Somerset Record Office, D/D/Cd 18, f. 2: Parkinson, *Newcome's Autobiography*, Vol. II, pp. 284–5; Marshall, *op. cit.*, 140–2.

56. Laslett, *Family Life and Illicit Love*, p. 201, and above, n. 54.

57. Taunton, Somerset Record Office, D/D/Cd 36, 10 July 1605, deposition by Walter Webb in Jenkins c. Webb.

58. Barnum, *op. cit.*, Vol. I, Pt. 1, pp. 310–2; Thomas, *op. cit.*, p. 238; **D. Rogers**, *Matrimoniall Honour: or the Mutuall Crowne and comfort of godly, loyall, and chaste Marriage*, London, 1642, pp. 92–3.

59. **A. Macfarlane**, *The Origins of English Individualism: The Family, Property and Social Transition*, Basil Blackwell, Oxford, 1978, pp. 136–8. But **Z. Razi**, in 'Family, Land and the Village Community in Later Medieval England', *Past and Present*, **93** (1981), 7–8 has claimed that in Halesowen between 1270 and 1348, the great majority of retiring property holders trusted their children sufficiently not to feel the need to enter into legally binding agreements with them. Cf. Thrupp, *op. cit.*, p. 151.

60. Laslett, *Family Life and Illicit Love*, p. 180; Lubbock, *op. cit.*, Vol. I, p. 139.

61. Laslett, *Family Life and Illicit Love*, p. 201, Marshall, *op. cit.*, pp. 159, 175.

62. Estimate based on my own analysis of *Norwich Census of the Poor*, **J. F. Pound** (ed.), *Norfolk Record Society*, 40 (1971).

63. 39 Elizabeth I, c. 3; **R. M. Smith**, 'Fertility, Economy and Household Formation in England over Three Centuries', *Population and Development Review*, **7** (1981), 610; Phythian–Adams, *op. cit.*, pp. 94–5, 154–6.

64. Cannon, *op. cit.*, 11–12; Amias and Ann Bampfield to John Willoughby, 28 Nov. 1637, Taunton, Somerset Record Office, Trevelyan Papers DD/WO/57; de Beer, *op. cit.*, Vol. II, p. 7; Davies, *op. cit.*, pp. 112–13; **J. M. Lloyd Thomas** (ed.), *The Autobiography of Richard Baxter, being the Reliquiae Baxterianae abridged from the folio (1696)*, J. M. Dent & Sons, London, 1931, p. 3; Macfarlane, *Family Life of Josselin*, pp. 115–16; Laslett, *Family Life and Illicit Love*, p. 201; Pound, *op. cit*

65. Locke, *Some Thoughts Concerning Education*, p. 324; Taunton, Somerset Record Office, DD/PH/224/1, 15, 16, 18, 21, 26, 29, 31; **D. Townshend**, *Life and Letters of Mr Endymion Porter: Sometime Gentleman of the Bedchamber to King Charles the First*, T. Fisher Unwin, London, 1897, pp. 84–5.

66. **J. O. Halliwell** (ed.), *The Autobiography and Correspondence of Sir Simonds D'Ewes, Bart.*, London, 1845, Vol. I, pp. 2–4, 25–33, 37–8; **W. D. Christie**, *A Life of Anthony Ashley Cooper, First Earl of Shaftesbury, 1621–1683*, London, 1871, Vol. I, pp. iv–vi.

67. **R. Ascham**, *The Scholemaster, Or plaine and perfite way of teachyng children, to vnderstand, write, and speake, the Latin tong . . . in English Works*, **W. A. Wright** (ed.), Cambridge UP, 1904, p. 177; Blundell, *op. cit.*, pp. 125, 151–2, 176–81, 223–4, 227, 229, 231–2, 238–40, 246–7, 264–8.

Chapter 8

Death and the broken family

Death and bereavement

Death was in this period the constant companion of life. A husband's or wife's chances of losing his or her partner before old age, a child's prospects of losing one or both parents before he had achieved adulthood, were far higher than they are today. A far larger proportion of deaths took place in the early and middle decades of adulthood than occurred in old age, whereas the reverse is true today. During epidemics, deaths multiplied, commonly striking down many members of the same household. Their devastating effects are vividly conveyed by the testimony of an eyewitness recorded by the biographer of Ignatius Jurdaine, a great Exeter merchant. During the plague of 1625

he had seen morning after morning coming to his [i.e. Jurdaine's] door, sometimes thirty, sometimes forty, yea fifty, or sixty, or more, wringing their hands; some crying that their husbands were dead; Others that their wives were dead: Others that their children were dead, and that they had not any thing wherewithall to bury them.

Death itself was far more likely to be the moment of parting between an individual and his family than it is today. To the family belonged not only the physical care of the dying, now so largely taken over by the hospital, but also the responsibility for helping the individual to make a good end. Self-interest, too, dictated the attendance at the deathbed of a number of close relatives, because it was typically there that wills were made or amended, especially by those with relatively little property. Prospective beneficiaries gathered round the deathbed, not only to bear witness to the dying man's wishes, but also, if need be, to attempt to sway him in their favour.[1]

In pious households, those around the bedside helped the dying person to make a good end. The drastic simplification during the Reformation of the last rites administered by the clergy may have made the help given by members of the family more important. Simonds D'Ewes, recalling his mother's death in 1618, remembered how he had 'assisted at her pallet-side, kneeling, weeping, and

praying with others, a great part of the time she lay drawing on
. . .'. When his first wife lay dying in 1622, Sir Thomas Wentworth
read the Bible to her, repeated psalms together with her, and joined
in her prayers. During the last night of her life, Mrs Margaret Ducke
(d. 1646) sent for her husband and the rest of her family to be roused
from their beds to pray with her.[2]

The dying, central figures in this culminating drama of their lives,
often played their part by making declarations of faith and by giving
parental blessings and godly exhortations to their children to live in
love and concord. During the long period of excruciating pain which
preceded the death of Alice Thornton's mother in December 1659
she 'putt forth her selfe . . . in good instructions, severe reproofes
for all sins in generall, with a contineuall prayeing to God . . .'. Two
days before her death, having sent for Alice and her grandchildren
to take a last farewell, she kissed each of them, pouring out prayers
and blessings. Readiness to die and a serene confidence in his or her
future in the next world could be immensely valuable to the individual's friends and kinsmen, helping them to come to terms with
their bereavement. The Yorkshire recusant squire Thomas Meynell
wrote that the 'happie and exquisite end' of his 'most loving wife' in
1604 made him very confident that he would meet her again in
heaven. His aged aunt Dorothy Scrope 'did make a very Happie End,
most comfortable to us her Friends and Hopefull of salvation which
Jesus graunt to her and us all'. The 'sweet frame of mind and melody
of heart and soul' of William Stout's father just before his death in
1681 greatly comforted his wife and children and assured them of his
future happiness and peace with God.[3]

To very many, however, it was not given to die well. Intriguing
or distraught wives and children gave them no help. Sickness or
delirium all too often prevented men from making a good end.
Earthly concerns frequently filled the last moments of consciousness.
At this time the future welfare of their dependents must often have
occupied men's thoughts. Oliver Heywood told a pathetic story of
his attendance upon a bibulous young widower who had suffered a
fatal accident on his way home one Saturday night. He tried in vain
to focus the young man's mind on his salvation. Nothing troubled
him except the prospect of leaving his little son.[4]

The interval between death and burial allowed friends and kindred
to pay their personal respects to the laid-out corpse. The sight of the
body forced the bereaved to confront the finality of death and
separation, and might precipitate or accelerate a healthy process of
mourning. The godly minister John Carter (d. 1635) left instructions
that his body should not be put in a coffin before the arrival of his
son, who had been unable to be present at his deathbed. Upon his
arrival, his son 'fell upon his face and kissed him, and lift up his voice
and wept, and so took his last leave of him till they should meet in
a better world'.[5]

Demonstration of the esteem of friends and kindred for the dead person was one of the main purposes of the funeral rites. A large gathering was a measure of his 'worship' and expressed for a moment the solidarity of his house and its allies, at least in the upper ranks of society. The funeral feast was a last demonstration of the dead man's liberality, exercised through his surviving representatives. Many, even among the pious, judged generosity on this occasion to be essential to preserve the good name of the deceased and his family. Adam Martindale, for instance, recalled that his yeoman father (d. 1658) had left the amount to be spent upon his funeral wholly to the discretion of his children.

But considering how good a father he had beene, and how fashionably he (in the time of his prosperity) had lived among his neighbours, we thought it convenient to bring him home handsomely out of his owne, and soe we did. For all that came to the house to fetch his corpse thence (beggars not excepted) were entertained with good meat, piping hote, and strong ale in great plentie.

A further rich dinner accompanied by plenty of wine and strong drink took place in a tavern after the burial. Martindale was sure that some funerals, though twice as expensive, had not been so creditable to those who had paid for them.[6]

The funeral service underwent a fundamental change in the course of this period. Catholic ritual provided for sustained intercession on behalf of the dead man's soul before, during and after the interment of his body. In 1552, however, the last traces of intercession were removed from the burial service, in liturgical recognition of the Protestant conviction that prayers for the dead were useless. No longer could the living do anything to help those whom they had lost. The trental of masses sung for the soul of the departed and the services which customarily took place a month and a year after his death had served to give the bereaved a sense of constructive activity. The continuing value of Catholic doctrine and practices to bereaved members of the recusant community is vividly illustrated by two incidents recounted by the Jesuit John Gerard. A Staffordshire widow saw a light in her room every night after her husband's death. Her spiritual adviser concluded that her husband's soul, on its way to heaven, still needed prayers to help it, and suggested that mass should be offered for him on thirty successive days 'according to the old custom of the country'. The widow was able to help by going to communion several times with the same intention. On the night following the last mass of the trental, three lights appeared in the room instead of the usual one, and all eventually mounted heavenwards. This showed the widow that her husband had been taken thither by two angels, and left her in great comfort of soul. Gerard himself assuaged the grief of the recently widowed Lady Vaux by telling her that a single prayer for her husband would do him more good than many tears.[7]

Tombs or gravestones marked the burial places of many people of substance. One of the purposes of the late medieval funeral inscription was to assist the salvation of the dead man's soul by beseeching God's mercy and requesting the prayers of passers-by. This function disappeared before the cold wind of Protestant doctrine, leaving others to develop and burgeon after the Reformation.

Commemoration had always been a primary purpose of funeral monuments. By the close of the Middle Ages, the memorial commonly served the family as well as the individual, showing husband and wife, often with their children, whose numbers demonstrated the fruitfulness of their union. The display of the wife's coat of arms and rehearsal of her parents' names reminded the onlooker how honourable the couple's marriage had been, how illustrious their connections. These commemorative purposes were fulfilled in the century following the Reformation by some of the most massive and grandiose tombs ever set up in England. Now, however, funeral inscriptions began to lay increasing stress on the personal qualities of the deceased, seldom mentioned in the Middle Ages. In this respect they betrayed the influence of Renaissance humanism, which itself bore the strong imprint of classical antiquity. The domestic virtues gradually gained a more prominent place. One purpose of these inscriptions, like that of the funeral sermons preached in large numbers after the Reformation, was didactic: to set patterns of virtue before the reader. But the enumeration of such qualities as parental indulgence or steadfast wifely love also gave some measure of the bereaved person's sense of loss.

Grief had been a prominent theme of pagan classical inscriptions, but had become somewhat incongruous in the context of Christian funeral art. When it reappeared in memorial inscriptions in the course of the English Renaissance, it did so in lines imbued with the spirit of classical antiquity. But grief was christianised and made acceptable even to the pious. Inscriptions told how their faith enabled the bereaved to overcome their sorrow, or pointed out that their loss was the dead man's gain. In this way, those left behind were able to testify not only to their affection and sense of loss but also to their Christian faith and fortitude.

The development of the funeral monument's form facilitated the fulfilment of its new purposes. On the finer monuments the dead were portrayed with greater realism and in postures which brought them into closer rapport with the onlooker. More important in the long run, however, was the fact that inscriptions gradually moved from a peripheral to a central place, till by the later seventeenth century by far the commonest type of memorial was the inscribed stone. A well-phrased epitaph could convey more personal feeling than any but the best sculpture, which was very expensive. The increasing popularity of the inscription was due in large part to the diffusion of humanist culture among the educated élite and the growth of literacy in the middling ranks of society. The comparative cheapness of a commemorative inscription put a gravestone within reach of a growing minority of the population. In the second half of our period, headstones began to sprout in churchyards hitherto almost bare of permanent monuments. Gravestones could become objects of personal pilgrimages like that paid by the young Lancashire apprentice Roger Lowe and his sister to their parents' grave in 1665.[8]

A formal period of mourning gave the bereaved time in which to come to terms with loss. The Christian scheme accepted the individual's need to grieve, while offering him consolation and the possibility of constructive action. No death was a meaningless accident; each fitted into the divine plan and was directly attributable to God's will. The prospect of salvation allowed the bereaved to believe that his loss was gain for the person he had loved. The Catholic Church provided, as we have seen, for positive intercessory action. In the eyes of both Catholics and Protestants, God also sought through death to bring the survivor closer to himself. In 1469, Margaret Paston wrote to remind her son John II that he had lost two useful acquaintances within a year:

God wysythyt [visiteth] ȝow as yt plesythe hym jn sundery wyses. He woold ȝe xuld knowe hym and serue hym better þan ȝe haue do before thys tyme, and þan he wule send ȝow þe more grace to do wele in alle others thynggys. And fore Goddys loue, remembyreyt rythe welle and takeyt pacyentely, and thanke God of hys vysitacyon . . . .

Excessive sorrow was a bad thing, but a just measure of natural grief made the individual more malleable, more responsive to the divine purpose. In this respect, some Protestant teachers may have allowed a more positive role to natural affections than they had usually been assigned in the Middle Ages. The characteristic prayer of pious Protestants was that God would 'sanctify' their loss in order to bring them closer to him. Oliver Heywood recalled eleven occasions up to August 1663 when his heart had been 'abundantly melted and inlarged'; of these his return from his first wife's burial 'through rich grace . . . exceeded any other time before mentioned . . .'.[9]

The individual's need to mourn those to whom he is most closely attached is a fundamental one. A common pattern in individual reactions to bereavement has been observed in a recent study. After passing through the initial shock, the bereaved person typically goes through a phase of 'violent grief and disorganisation' before the inception of a longer period of adjustment and reorganisation.[10] The ritual phasing of mourning greatly aided the process of ultimate readjustment. Funeral and mourning customs in the centuries before 1700 allowed the bereaved to 'work through' and overcome grief. The funeral, which took place in the time of deepest sorrow, dramatised the loss and allowed the bereaved to give rein to their feelings. Both during the funeral itself and to varying degrees during the subsequent period of mourning, they were supported by the outward manifestations of respect for the dead in which kinsfolk participated. The period of mourning allowed the individual to offer a continuing tribute to the dead while lightening the burden of social obligations.

Widowhood

Marriages varied greatly in emotional strength and depth. Contemporary writers on family duties believed that husbands and wives were often glad to be rid of unloved partners. Enough testimony survives, however, to demonstrate that loss of husband or wife was for many people a most severe trial, for some a shattering experience. Self-control often broke down at the deathbed. To Mary Penington (*c*. 1625–82), the sight of her young husband in a mortal fever was a dreadful one; 'my very heart strings seemed to me to break', as she later recalled. Told that he could not die while she remained at the bedside, she let out a distraught cry 'die! die! must he die! I cannot go from him.'[11]

The shock experienced by the individual in the face of death was as familiar in this period as it is to modern observers. Breaking the news of a loved one's death gently and discreetly, postponing it till a suitable moment, was a precaution of which one reads repeatedly. Much evidence survives of the subsequent period of 'violent grief and disorganisation'. John Johnson, attempting to console his brother-in-law for the loss of his wife in 1545, referred to his making 'a great moan' and having a 'troubled heart'. In 1595, Lady Vaux was 'completely overwrought' by her husband's death. She hardly moved out of her room for a year afterwards, and proved unable to bring herself to enter the wing of the house in which he had died for at least another three years. The depression which often followed bereavement sometimes culminated in suicide. In 1681–82, Oliver Heywood recorded two cases, only just over a year apart, both of them committed by quite humble people.[12]

Those who had experienced the loss of a spouse commonly referred to it as the greatest they had ever suffered. Richard Napier's case notes and the direct testimony of autobiographers convey the same sense of devastation. '. . . I want her at every turne, every where, and in every worke', wrote Oliver Heywood after his own wife's death. 'Methinkes I am but halfe myselfe without her.' 'See me,' prayed the grief-stricken Lady Ann Fanshawe, 'with my soul divided, my glory and my guide taken from me, and in him all my comfort in this life.'[13] The lasting sense of loss experienced by husbands and wives deprived of their partners often found expression in funeral monuments after about the middle of the sixteenth century. Explicit references to grief, rare in the Middle Ages, now became common. Eager anticipation of future reunion and the continuing bond between partners separated by death, were frequent themes of inscriptions. Perhaps the most popular idea of all was that of the union in one grave of those hitherto bound together by the same love. In the seventeenth century such Baroque sculptors as Epiphanius Evesham and John Bushnell depicted bereaved spouses struggling to master their grief or falling, distraught, under its weight. Inscriptions sometimes matched the realism of sculpture in their vivid accounts of the physical symptoms of grief.[14]

The likelihood of losing one's spouse before old age was much higher between the fifteenth and seventeenth centuries than it is today. The frequency of early spousal bereavement must not however be exaggerated. More than half the first marriages contracted by the nobility between 1558 and 1641 lasted over twenty years, practically a third over thirty. In Colyton (Devon) the mean duration of marriages whose length could be traced in the parish register was over twenty years between 1550 and 1699, and about a fifth lasted thirty-five years or more between 1550 and 1649. For the majority of people who underwent the experience, marriage would have been the longest close association of their lives. There is abundant evidence that the death of a spouse was often a devastating experience; little that people consciously or unconsciously limited their emotional investment in their partners so as to lessen the impact of an expected bereavement. Lady Fanshawe, who described her husband as having lived with her '*but* twenty-three years and twenty-nine days' was clearly unaware that the duration of their marriage had almost certainly been longer than the average of her time. The ideal fate was to die together in old age. In 1623, John Hutchinson's grandfather died on the same day as his wife without being told of her death: 'Whether he perceiv'd and would not take notice, or whether some strange sympathy in love or nature tied up their lives in one, or whether God was pleas'd to exercise an unusuall providence towards them, preventing them both from that bitter sorrow which such seperations cause, it can be but conjectur'd.' Most people left no record of what they felt when they lost husband or wife. But enough evidence survives to show that the experience was commonly thought to be a harrowing one.[15]

At any one moment, a high proportion of the adult population was in a widowed state. The proportion of householders who were widowed in seventy communities listed between the late sixteenth and early nineteenth centuries was about one-fifth. (Among the seventy communities there were, however, considerable differences. At Clayworth (Notts.) in 1688 more than a quarter of householders were widowed people.) The proportion was probably similar at Coventry in 1523 to that among the seventy communities. No fifteenth-century local censuses are known to exist, but at Ombersley (Worcs.) in 1419, about 14 per cent of the manorial tenants were widows; presumably there were some widowers too. A substantial proportion of households, then, was based on 'broken' families lacking one of their leading partners. Only a minority of these widowed householders were 'solitaries'; the great majority had children living with them. Most widowed people are likely to have been householders, but a minority lived in children's households, as lodgers, or in institutions.[16]

Widowhood seems to have been experienced by many more women than men. In first marriages, the majority of women were younger than their husbands, and in the second half of our period tended to enjoy an equal or slightly higher life expectation soon after marriage. (This was not true of all periods or of all social groups. Among the peerage, for example, between 1558 and 1641, more first marriages were curtailed by the deaths of wives than by those of husbands.) Early censuses give the impression that at any one time widowhood was likely to be the lot of far higher numbers of women than of men. In sixty-one communities covered by surviving pre-industrial population listings, the total number of widows outnumbered that of widowers by over two to one. The surplus of widows was often especially marked in towns. In Coventry in 1523 there were nearly nine times as many widows as widowers among householders; in Lichfield in 1695 well over three times as many among the population at large.[17]

Widows not only greatly outnumbered widowers but were generally in a weaker legal and economic position, though this varied greatly according to the type of property held. Best placed were members of the landed classes. The common law gave the widow a right of dower in a third of her husband's lands, a right usually waived in return for a jointure agreed in the marriage settlement. The jointure of the loved and trusted wife could be increased after marriage. In the later Middle Ages, husbands' jointure settlements sometimes gave their widows a life interest in the greater part or even the whole of an estate. The later evolution of the marriage settlement restricted, but never entirely removed, the possibility of enhancing the jointure.[18] In addition to her jointure, the widow held any lands which had come to her as an heiress. The childless widowed heiress was uniquely independent. Widows with children very often had important responsibilities as guardians, to which a number proved fully equal. Such formidable Elizabethan widows as Bess of Hardwick and Lady Elizabeth Hoby, later Lady Russell, showed considerable vigour in litigation, estate management and the promotion of their children's interests. But the widow's extensive property rights and duties as guardian could be sources of friction between her and her children, especially the heir. The question of the younger children's maintenance, if not previously settled, or the widow's efforts to improve their endowment, could both give rise to resentment or dispute.[19]

By local custom, most notably in London and the ecclesiastical province of York, the widow was entitled to a third part of her husband's goods, or a half if he had no children, and the widow's part, unlike a jointure, was hers to dispose of exactly as she wished. The position of the widow of a rich merchant or financier with the bulk of his estate in movable goods could therefore be very favourable. But over most of England, the widow's third was probably a thing of the past by the close of the Middle Ages, and it was ultimately abolished in the province of York as well by a statute of 1692. Only in the division of intestates' estates did the allocation of a widow's part survive. Men who took the trouble to make a will could dispose of their movable goods as they wished. Surviving wills suggest, however, that testators were usually concerned to provide for their wives as well as they could. Wives were more likely than anybody else to be appointed executrices and guardians. Widows often took over the running of their husbands' businesses. But some towns or crafts may only have allowed them to do so as a stopgap measure, while others gave them full freedom to train apprentices on their own account.[20]

Local and manorial customs made a bewildering variety of provisions for widows. The proportion of her husband's land the widow was entitled to hold was a third in many places, a half, two-thirds, even the whole in others. Her widow's rights might last for her lifetime or terminate when her eldest son reached his majority. In some places widow's rights terminated on remarriage while in others they were unaffected by it. The arrangements made for widowhood by local custom therefore varied greatly in their security and duration.[21] The decline of customary tenures gradually reduced the numbers of widows who benefited from the sort of provision outlined above, but this development was far from complete in 1700, especially in the west of England. The position of the widows of the growing number of farmers holding on short non-customary leases was more precarious. Worse still was that of the partners left to fend for themselves by the deaths of cottagers, poor craftsmen and labourers.

The widower's position was in general far more favourable than the widow's. The common law made him tenant of his wife's lands for life 'by curtesy of England' provided only that they had had a child. The wife who predeceased her husband could not give away from him the goods which she had brought to the marriage or acquired during it. Local custom, too, was usually good to the widower. The gavelkind custom of Kent gave him only half his wife's inherited lands, and that only so long as he remained unmarried, but was more generous in allowing him curtesy whether he had begotten a child of her or not.[22]

Remarriage

Should the widowed remarry or remain as they were? Under different circumstances there were good reasons for both courses of action. Loyalty to the memory of a first spouse was highly commended. Margaret, duchess of Newcastle, recalled that her mother's grief for her father, Sir Thomas Lucas (d. 1649), had been so lasting that, though she often spoke of him, she never did so without tears and sighs; she had 'made her house her cloister'. Some husbands made the provisions for their widows which they included in their wills dependent on their remaining unmarried. In some cases it is quite clear that such testators' main concern was the well-being of their children. Sir Henry Fanshawe (d. 1616) expressed his confidence that his widow would abstain from remarriage for this reason. The widowed themselves often took the interests of their offspring into account. James Fretwell (b. 1699) recalled his widowed grandfather's solicitude for his three daughters. He had broken off negotiations with one woman 'upon account of some words she let drop concerning his children'. When a second woman to whom he made his addresses came over to see his house, he was careful to ask her how she liked them. Despite her hearty assurances, she turned out 'a very indifferent mother' to his considerable grief. Some people did not want to be stepparents. In 1532, the widow Katherine Andrews was said to have told her suitor, a Norwich widower, that if ever she married, she would marry him, except for one thing: 'I woll never be step moder, for I understand ye have children, and that shuld cause us never to agree. . . .' When remarriage was in prospect, we can sometimes see kinsfolk or 'friends' trying to protect children's interests. When in about 1566 the father of Elizabeth Watkins of Wells (Somerset) was contemplating remarriage, Elizabeth's suitor was advised to secure 'such things as the father wold geve to his daughter . . . before he weare married or els his second wife wold not suffre him to geve hir anie thing afterward . . .'. After the death of his first wife in 1640, Henry Oxinden of Barham (Kent) was pressed by his brother-in-law to show his affection for her memory and to satisfy her surviving relatives by settling an adequate income on his son and suitable portions on his daughters. Even while his daughter was still alive, William Blundell, the Lancashire recusant squire, concerned to further the marriage prospects of his beloved grandson Edmund, suggested that his son-in-law give up 'the power, or . . . the greatest part of a power' to settle a jointure upon another wife.[23]

A serious disincentive to remarriage was the fact that in many places a woman's customary rights lasted only so long as she remained a chaste widow. This was true of the gavelkind custom of Kent, as well as the most widespread custom in Dorset. The ancient customs of the manor of Taunton Deane (Somerset) were quite exceptional in making widows their husbands' heirs. This meant that they were completely free to remarry, and land could pass from Taunton Deane women to the children of the last marriages they made. Her rights made marriage with such a widow an exceptionally attractive proposition.[24]

There were a number of reasons for remarriage, as well as considerations militating against it. Emotional fulfilment was one, especially in the case of those whose first marriages had been arranged or made for economic reasons. After his master's death in 1627, the young William Lilly married his widow. Having twice been married to old men, she was 'now resolved to be couzened no more'. Second marriages, Daniel Rogers thought, were often made by people who sought 'jollity, and a braver and fuller life, then formerly they were content with'.[25]

Compelling economic reasons for remarriage may nevertheless have been more immediately important in the majority of cases. In the running of a farm, a husband or wife was often an indispensable partner whose blend of commitment, trustworthiness and complementary skills could not be found even in the best of servants. The craftsman's widow might well have to marry again in order to ensure the survival of her husband's business, and her choice might in practice be restricted to one of his craft. In the summer of 1593, Edmund Myll, visiting the widow Treglyne in Bodmin (Cornwall), asked her how she liked his companion John Morcombe, telling her 'he is one of thy husbandes occupation and therfore is best meete for thee', and she answered that she liked him very well.[26] In this sort of situation, one of her husband's apprentices might seem doubly attractive, as a partner who would perhaps allow her to bear some sway within the household while also holding out the prospect of effective support in old age. Such support was a major aim of remarriage, which helps to explain why the widowed so often chose partners younger and more vigorous than themselves. Such a strategy for old age was particularly important for the poor, heavily dependent as they were on physical strength and manual dexterity.

Need for help in the task of bringing up children was another important reason for remarriage. In Edward VI's reign, a Bridgnorth woman accepted a second husband because she was 'troubled as she said with certain unruly children of hers, and could not be quiet for them'; Gilbert Burnet, bishop of Salisbury, took a third wife in 1700 in order, he said, 'to provide a Mistris to my family and a mother to my children', and these reasons were no doubt important ones for many men humbler than he was. Remarriage was sometimes even intended to safeguard the interests of the children of the first marriage. In seventeenth-century Dorset, where the most widespread custom allowed a copyholder's widow to hold his tenement for her life provided she remained single, a number of elderly copyholders married young women, many of whom undertook to make payments to their husbands' children.[27]

Realising as they did that their spouses' remarriage might be necessary, some accepted the prospect with equanimity. Thomas Haukes, a gentleman burnt under Mary I for his Protestant beliefs, concluded his last message to his wife with the advice that she marry a God-fearing man who would love her and care for her. William Hunt of Cloford (Somerset), trying to console his distraught wife as he lay on his deathbed in 1633, told her that 'she might doe well enoughe'. He would give her all he had, and he 'advised her to be carefull of her selfe, [and] with home she marryed after his death, that he might not spend that which he he the said Hunt had gotten . . . .'.[28]

In general the prospects of remarriage were far better for men than they were for women, both because the laws and customs of property were more favourable to the former and because women so heavily outnumbered men among the widowed, especially in towns and among the poor. Among the listed poor of Norwich in 1570, for example, there were about twelve times as many widowed or unmarried women aged sixty-one or over as there were men. Of the men aged sixty-one or over 88 per cent were married, but only just over a quarter of the women. Furthermore, over two-thirds of these elderly married men allegedly had wives who were more than ten years younger than themselves, while only 13 per cent of the married men aged sixty or under were in this position. The fact that so many old men had wives much younger than themselves is probably attributable to the determination of widowers to guard against ultimate destitution and a lonely death by finding themselves young and active new wives. The same strategy may have been pursued by poor widows, though with less success, for only 32 per cent of the wives aged sixty-one or over had husbands more than ten years younger than themselves.[29]

But widows with substantial property were regarded as good matches. Some outstandingly successful mercantile careers, such as that of John Isham, mercer and merchant adventurer, married in 1552, ten years after the commencement of his apprenticeship, were built on London widows' portions and custody of their children's legacies. Marriage to a master's widow offered the apprentice or struggling young journeyman alluring prospects of early establishment. The widow of substance was well placed to please herself in choosing her second husband. She might, like Margaret Denton (b. 1612), widowed at twenty-five, assert her opinion that 'all the riches in the world without content is nothing', and insist upon her liberty to choose a man for whom she felt affection. But eyewitness accounts of courtship in the church courts suggest that widows, often independent, even forward, could also be determined to protect their own economic interests. The widow Yarmouth of Blundeston (Suffolk), asked in 1558 why she did not go forward with a projected match between herself and a young man, answered that it was his father's fault, because she had demanded £60 with him and his father would only give £40.[30]

Mourning for a spouse was supposed to last a year. Yet though such haste might provoke unfavourable comment, remarriage often took place long before the year was out. Discussion sometimes got under way almost as soon as the burial had taken place, in at least one case when the widow was still carrying her previous husband's child. Among a sample of remarried people traced in parish registers of the seventeenth and eighteenth centuries, 48 per cent of the men had married within a year of bereavement, 37 per cent of the women; the mean intervals for the two sexes were almost exactly two and three years respectively. The presence of children under fifteen tended to delay remarriage, not only in the case of women, whose interval of widowhood grew longer with the number of their children, but also in that of men, who tended to remarry later than average if they had two children or more. No doubt the ages of children and the amount of help that the eldest could give were important facts to consider when deciding whether or not to marry again.[31]

Remarriage was much commoner in this period than it is today. Over a third of the married children of British peers born in the third quarter of the sixteenth century married twice; the proportion dropped to less than a sixth among those born in the last quarter of the seventeenth. In the sixteenth century, 30 per cent of those marrying may have been widows or widowers, compared with little over one in ten in the mid-nineteenth century. Despite a long-term downward trend, the proportion of widowed people among the newly married could go up in the short term. In seventeenth-century Beccles (Suffolk) it rose from 22.7 per cent in the pre-war decades to 26.4 per cent in the years after the Restoration.[32]

In the long term, the fact that fewer marriages were cut short by death before old age reduced the extent of remarriage. The frequency of crises of mortality dropped sharply from the sixteenth century onwards. In the seventeenth century, however, there was a fall in expectation of life which helps to explain the increase in the incidence of remarriage at Beccles. In the fourteenth century, a much higher proportion of marriages of manorial tenants had involved widows before the catastrophic mortality of the Black Death than after it. This had drastically altered the relationship between people and resources, with two important consequences. First, adult expectation of life was improved, reducing the likelihood that marriage would be curtailed. Secondly, land became easier to obtain, and marriage to a widow less necessary in order to acquire it.[33]

Improved expectation of life will not explain by itself the rapid decline in remarriage among the children of peers. Greater readiness to take young people's wishes into account in arranging marriages may have made for better relations between husbands and wives and stronger loyalty to the memory of lost partners, but this seems to have been a very gradual development. Did the growing 'strictness' of marriage settlements make it harder to finance second unions?

Given the frequency of remarriage, the experience of living in a 'reconstructed' family must have been a common one. Such a description might be given to a large range of possible combinations, from the childless couple one of whom had previously been married to the family containing two or even more sets of children from previous marriages as well as the offspring of the remarried couple who formed its core. One of the very best of local censuses shows that in Clayworth in 1688 as many as 39 per cent of the couples resident in the village included at least one and sometimes two partners who had lost a previous spouse.[34]

Contemporary commentators believed that the experience of remarriage was often a difficult one. People whose earlier marriage had proved emotionally unsatisfactory often entered their new unions with dangerously high expectations whose subsequent frustration caused much misery. Others, happy in their previous marriages, could not readily transfer their affection to new partners. In many people, thought William Gouge, 'their loue of a former husband or wife departed is so fast fixed in their heart, as they can neuer againe so intirely loue any other'. The main reason, however, why subsequent marriages were 'seldome so comfortable and peaceable as the *first*' was the attitude of the children of earlier unions, who could not put up with stepparents. The inward contempt, grumbling and undutiful behaviour of most children towards stepparents brought much grief to natural parents and caused 'much discord and dissention' between natural and stepparents.[35] Children's resentment towards stepparents, which sometimes broke into abuse or even physical violence, is amply documented in wills and the records of litigation. The fact that the rupture and replacement of familial ties were accompanied by a great deal of bitterness and distress is of course difficult to square with the notion that emotional demands and fulfilment within the family during these centuries were relatively modest. In reality, the clearest evidence of the importance of familial bonds to the individual's emotional well-being and security stems from the loss of one of the two principal partners in the nuclear family and the efforts of the survivors to establish new relationships.

Orphanhood and parental deprivation

There is not nearly as much evidence of what children felt when they lost their parents as there is of spouses' reactions to the deaths of husbands and wives. Pre-adolescent children did not record their feelings in diaries or correspondence, or if they did such material has failed to survive. Autobiographers who looked back in later years upon the experience of childhood loss tended to be terse or reticent in their description of it. Sometimes the remarks of observers allow us a glimpse of it. In 1659, Henry Newcome recorded the burial of a dyer, a widower who left nine children behind him. 'The cries of the children at the funeral, moved most that were present.' There is much evidence that the death of a parent in adolescence or young adulthood could be a bitter blow. In 1482, one of George Cely's correspondents referred to his 'grett hevenes' after his father's death, and, reminding him that no man might set himself against God's will, urged him to take it patiently and not to hurt himself. In 1503, William Paston, then in his mid-twenties, received a similar message from William Warham. Lady Anne Clifford described the news of her mother's death in May 1616 as 'the greatest and most lamentable cross that could have befallen me'. As late as November 1617, so she confided to her diary, 'I wept extremely to remember my dear and blessed Mother.' William Cavendish, duke of Newcastle, allegedly loved his parents so much that he said he would willingly have survived by begging had God only allowed them to live. Evidence of lasting grief at a humbler level of society comes from the diary of the Lancashire apprentice Roger Lowe, who described it as his common custom to visit the churchyard to look at graves. He described how on 1 January 1665

Att noone my sister Ellin came to me in the church yard and we went, both of us, to my father and mother's grave and stayd awhile, and both wept.[36]

Funeral monuments could not only serve as a focus for children's memories of their parents, but also, from the late sixteenth century onwards, act as vehicles for the expression of filial love, gratitude and grief. Some of the very best funeral sculpture captures the experience of bereavement in poignant fashion. In the panels round the tomb of Sir Thomas Hawkins (1618) at Boughton-under-Blean (Kent), Epiphanius Evesham depicted his mourning sons and daughters. The former seem to be exercising a manly self-control, but the faces of the latter are contorted with grief. Among them, a little girl reaches up to her eldest sister for comfort.

The qualitative range of parent–child relationships was probably as great during these centuries as it is today. To suggest that all suffered bitterly when their parents died would be as foolish as to claim that our ancestors were incapable of strong personal attachments or deep grief in the face of bereavement. Many may have looked forward impatiently, as the fifteenth-century author of *Dives and Pauper* thought they did, to the parental deaths which would bring them their inheritances. Others may have greeted the loss of parents with indifference. Others again, once close to parents, but long emotionally and materially independent of them, could accept their deaths in old age as part of the natural order. The sailor Edward Barlow was grieved by the news of his father's death, but, he wrote in his journal, 'he was an ancient man of eighty-seven years, and I could not expect he should live long'.[37]

How common was the experience of parental deprivation in childhood and youth? A very rough estimate would be that at least half the people who reached the age of twenty-five had lost one of their parents. But variations from time to time and place to place would of course have been great. Sometimes the position was clearly worse than this: in a notoriously unhealthy period and environment, nearly 60 per cent of the surviving sons of a sample of London aldermen were under twenty-one when their fathers died in the years between 1318 and 1497. No source can be relied upon to give us a complete picture of the extent of parental deprivation even in one place. Early local censuses do not include those who had entered service in another community, and attempts to make allowances for their departure are bedevilled by the fact that those who had lost one parent or both were more likely than other children to be sent away from home. The counts of young children are the least likely to have been affected by these factors. Among children under ten, 21 per cent of those in Ealing in 1599 had lost at least one parent, 12.3 per cent of those in Lichfield in 1697.[38]

Early local censuses suggest that most of those who remained at home after losing father or mother lived with a widowed parent who had not remarried, only a small minority with stepparents. This was not always true: a majority lived with stepparents in Clayworth in 1688. In the parish of Ryton (Co. Durham), devastated by dearth and disease in the 1580s and 1590s, households of 'broken marriages, of children, step-children and foster children' are said to have been very common at the end of the sixteenth century, though this seems to be an impressionistic assertion based on the detailed analysis of very few households. Elsewhere the prevailing pattern at that time was quite different. The Ealing census of 1599 does not allow us to identify with complete confidence every child in the village who had lost a parent, but it seems to show that only a small minority of children lived with stepparents.[39]

If indeed the experience of living with stepparents was a comparatively rare one, this may have been in part because deliberate efforts were made to avoid it. We have already seen that children were sometimes viewed as obstacles to remarriage. But they may often have been sent away from home in order to avoid friction between them and stepparents. This was the course recommended by William Gouge to the man who found his new wife quite unable to get on with his children. Remarriage certainly led to the departure from home of such autobiographers as Arise Evans (at the early age of seven or eight), Lodowick Muggleton and Josiah Langdale; perhaps to that of Ralph Josselin too.[40]

Relations with stepparents were very often difficult. Most of them, thought William Gouge, sought to undermine their partners' natural affection for their children. Robert Cawdrey believed that women failed in their duty to stepchildren more often than men, 'by reason that their affections bee stronger then mens, and many times ouerrule them'. Children were in fact far likelier to lose their fathers before they reached adulthood than to lose their mothers, and many more lived with stepfathers than with stepmothers, a fact which seems reassuring in the light of this belief. Indeed relationships between men and their stepchildren were by no means always bad. William Stonor (d. 1494) and Thomas More were two men who earned the gratitude of stepdaughters through their conscientious discharge of their duties towards them. But much testimony, especially in the records of testamentary litigation, suggests that a mother's remarriage was likely to be just as prejudicial to a child's interests as a father's. The behaviour of one unscrupulous stepfather was simply described in a pathetic bill of complaint sent to the chancellor of the diocese of Winchester by Elizabeth Gambylfelde in 1539. Her father on his deathbed had left legacies to his five children, of whom she was now the only one left. His wife Joan, their mother and her husband's executrix, had subsequently married another man who, having got hold of all her previous husband's goods, now refused to pay a penny of the legacies due to his stepchild. The rivalries between the children of two marriages increased the strain on the reconstructed family. Repeatedly we read of bitter jealousies and resentments, even of efforts to get half-siblings disinherited. Rivalries between children who shared both parents were often fierce enough, but animosities between two broods had a sharper edge. John Hutchinson's experience had a common quality. Settling at his father's house after his return from the university, he 'enjoyed no greate delight, another brood of children springing up in the house, and the servants endeavouring with tales and flatteries to sow dissention on both sides'.[41]

Kin other than father and mother played at least some part in the care and support of those who had lost one or both parents. From 1601 the Poor Law laid the responsibility for helping poor children who were unable to work upon their grandparents 'being of sufficient ability' after their parents. For their part, grandparents, especially towards the lower end of the social scale, casting round for every possible source of support in their last years, may have had some material incentive to take such children in. Some people invested in their grandchildren the affection they had felt for children they had lost. This is clearly true of Henry Newcome, who looked after James, son of his undisciplined favourite son Daniel, after the latter's death. James became 'partly an idol' to his grandfather and 'the very darling of the family'. His death in 1695 helped precipitate Newcome's own. At least two other godly ministers, John Carter and Adam Martindale, brought up the children of dead sons.[42]

Uncles and aunts stood next to grandparents among those who had a moral obligation to assist orphans, though they were not usually legally bound to do so. When in June 1631 Elizabeth Dickens of St Mary's parish in Norwich agreed to keep her nephew Richard, a child under five years old, it was noted in the mayor's court book that she was to receive 10d. a week. It was probably their brothers or brothers-in-law to whom individuals most often entrusted the care of their children and the execution of their wills if they had neither spouse nor parents alive or equal to the task. Many of those to whom the care of orphans and their goods was granted in cases of intestacy were uncles. The rule that the guardian in socage was to be the closest relative to whom the child's property could not descend meant that in practice maternal uncles often filled this position. Among early diarists and autobiographers given important help by uncles after losing one or both parents were Ralph Josselin, Alice Thornton, Thomas Raymond and Marmaduke Rawdon, son of an alderman of York. But orphans brought up by close relatives often had cause for complaint. James Palmer of Shorewell (Isle of Wight), entrusted to the care of Thomas Palmer after his father's death in 1619, was kept at school for less than a year before being employed in turn in housework and as an unpaid assistant in Thomas's trade of tailor. In addition, Thomas spent a large part of the money due to James by his father's will. William Edmundson, a Quaker autobiographer (b. 1627), lost his mother when he was about four and his father when he was eight. He and his five brothers and sisters received harsh treatment at the hands of his maternal uncle, whom his eldest brother and brother-in-law ultimately sued for the children's portions and the 'injuries and wrongs' done them.[43]

It was to kinsfolk and to guardians chosen by their parents that the care of orphans belonged in the first place. Outside agencies (royal, manorial, municipal or ecclesiastical courts) seldom took an interest in their affairs unless they were heirs to property. Which court had jurisdiction depended upon the nature of the property in question.

Until 1646, the heirs to lands held by knight service and other military tenures whose fathers died during their minority passed into the wardship of the lord of the lands. The minority lasted till twenty-one in the case of boys, sixteen in that of girls. Wardship gave the guardian the right to take the profits of the portion of the heir's lands which came under his control, and, more importantly, to decide whom he should marry, The Crown's rights overrode those of all other lords even if the smallest portion of the tenant's lands was held of the king. The balance between the interests of mesne lords and the Crown tilted still further towards the latter under the Tudors, especially with the creation of new military tenants among the purchasers of church lands. The concentration of rights of wardship in the Crown and their much more vigorous exploitation enhanced their unpopularity.

It was the sale of wardships, carried on on a large scale since the thirteenth century, but greatly increased during the sixteenth, which was the most hated feature of the system. Faced with widespread hostility, the Crown showed greater readiness to take the wishes of fathers and kinsfolk into account. The proportion of wardships sold to mothers, kinsfolk, wards themselves, or trustees appointed by their fathers, grew from a fifth to a third between Edward VI's reign and the end of Elizabeth's. Reforms of 1603 and 1610 further facilitated the purchase of wardships by fathers, their nominees and other relatives. The proportion granted to strangers fell to well under a half by 1628–30, though a minority of families did not benefit from the reforms.[44]

The abolition in 1646 of the Court of Wards and of military tenures, confirmed in 1660, was one of the most important constitutional and legal changes in the history of the English landed classes. Henceforth, families could make constructive long-term plans to deal with the contingency of a minority. Prudent fathers commonly divided the responsibilities of guardianship between a number of people, including the widow, a business adviser and somebody who could supervise the management of the estates. The Court of Chancery assumed the supervision of the guardians and developed machinery for the scrutiny of their accounts. Minorities, hitherto periods when many families faced heavy fiscal burdens and the danger of mismanagement of their estates, now presented major opportunities for retrenchment and investment.[45]

Did the abolition of feudal wardship tend to weaken parental authority? The threat of feudal exploitation had been one of the most concrete and readily comprehensible reasons for submission to a father's wishes in marriage. Furthermore, since the feudal guardian stood in the father's place, the very existence of feudal wardship tended to buttress the idea that it was the father's right to marry his children. The diminution and removal of this external pressure may well have made young people less willing to comply with parental wishes in this and other matters. Sir John Reresby, born in 1634, and thus one of the first generation to reach manhood after the abolition of the Court of Wards, remembered with a hint of resentment how his mother had treated him like a ward despite the abolition of the institution of wardship. He, and others like him, now expected a slacker rein.[46]

A number of towns took care of the interests of the orphans of freemen. London had done so since the thirteenth century. Its orphans' court chose guardians when none had been named by will, and made sure that children received their due proportion of their father's goods whether the latter had made wills or not. Grants of custody were made conditional on the orphan's proper upbringing.

The guardian had either to enter a recognisance to pay the child his portion when it fell due, or pay the money to the city chamberlain for safe keeping. The interest paid on the deposited sum was used to meet the expenses of upbringing, but the guardian might with the court's permission dig into capital to meet such expenses as an apprenticeship premium. Until London's bankruptcy in 1682, which ushered in the swift decline of its orphans' court, the latter seems to have acted most effectively to safeguard the interests of its fatherless freemen's children. Study of the subsequent careers of children of London aldermen who died between 1586 and 1612 suggests that the orphans were as successful as the non-orphans. Many other towns exercised jurisdiction over orphans' affairs in the sixteenth and early seventeenth centuries, but London's court was probably uniquely well organised and effective.[47]

The church courts exercised what was perhaps the widest jurisdiction over orphans, though even they acted only when the orphan had an interest in property subject to probate. In the absence of a guardian appointed by will, the court chose one, to take care of the orphan's person till puberty, and his goods till the attainment of full majority. Guardians were ultimately liable to render account of their administration and could be removed for misconduct, but in practice the courts do not seem to have supervised their activities very closely.[48]

The fate of those orphans who had lost both parents and had no property rights or other close relatives, remains obscure. Many are probably not identifiable in local censuses and listings. In theory, no doubt, they were provided for by a growing number of institutions, and, from the sixteenth century onwards, by parish apprenticeship. But even in the best run institutions the outlook for inmates was comparatively bleak. In Christ's Hospital, founded in 1552 for the care of London orphans, the mortality rate in the 1–4 age-group was 283 per thousand between 1563 and 1583, compared with a mean of 65 per thousand among boys and 59 per thousand among girls in the same age-group in twelve English parishes between 1550 and 1599.[49] Much contemporary testimony points to the hard usage of parish apprentices by masters who were very often reluctant to take them in the first place. Before the child without parents or close kin yawned the pit of maltreatment, neglect and early death.

Conclusion

Historians have sometimes inferred from the stark facts of comparatively high mortality, frequent remarriage and widespread step-relationships the existence in late medieval times of an emotional climate fundamentally different from today's, in which death was accepted with resignation or even indifference and affection within the family was tepid. Certainly Christianity tried to teach people to accept the impermanence of earthly ties and to set it in the context of the divine scheme. Yet the Church also recognised the reality of bitter grief, and Catholics could do something constructive for their dead. Funeral monuments influenced by Renaissance humanism and more intimate and revealing private records bear witness to the pain of personal loss in the second half of our period. But the increasing evidence of pain was due not to a change in emotional climate but to the development of new vehicles of expression.

There were very often compelling economic reasons for remarriage, since without it the continued viability of holding or workshop could be impossible to ensure. Especially for those within sight of the frontier of destitution's grim domain, the chance to provide for old age by choosing a much younger second partner was one which it would have been foolish to waste. For young men, marriages to older women were often the unavoidable price to pay for economic independence. In general, however, the chances of remarriage were poorer for women than they were for men because of women's more limited property rights and the adverse sex ratio.

Remarriage and the creation of 'reconstructed' families were often accompanied in the view of contemporary observers by harsh regrets and much personal resentment and friction, which were worse when children were involved. Step-relationships were often full of bitterness and jealousy. Early censuses suggest that in many places few of those who had lost mother or father lived with stepparents. It may be that those who could afford to do so postponed remarriage if they had children while those determined to remarry sent their offspring away sooner than they otherwise would have done. The prospects for the fatherless or motherless child depended above all on the love and economic means of the surviving parent. Other kinsfolk had some part to play when both parents had died. A number of courts were concerned with heirs to property, but their efficiency in protecting orphans' interests varied greatly. For those with no interested kinsfolk and no property the prospects were slender.

Notes and references

1. **T. H. Forbes**, 'By What Disease or Casualty: the Changing Face of Death in London', in **C. Webster** (ed.), *Health, Medicine and Mortality in the Sixteenth Century*, Cambridge UP, 1979, p. 124; **S. Clarke**, *A Collection of the Lives of Ten Eminent Divines*, London, 1662, p. 472; **G. Gorer**, *Death, Grief and Mourning in Contemporary Britain*, Cresset Press, London, 1965, pp. 17–19.

2. **J. O. Halliwell** (ed.), *The Autobiography and Correspondence of Sir Simonds D'Ewes, Bart.*, London, 1845, Vol. I, p. 111; **C. V. Wedgewood**, *Thomas Wentworth, First Earl of Strafford, 1593–1641: A Revaluation*, Jonathan Cape, London, 1961, p. 43; Clarke, *op. cit.*, p. 499.

3.   **C. Jackson** (ed.), *The Autobiography of Mrs Alice Thornton, of East Newton, in the County of York, Surtees Society*, **62** (1875), 106–16; **J. H. Aveling** (ed.), *Recusancy Papers of the Meynell Family, Catholic Record Society*, **56** (1964), 8, 41; **J. D. Marshall** (ed.), *The Autobiography of William Stout of Lancaster, 1665–1752, Chetham Society*, 3rd ser., **14** (1967), 73.

4.   **J. Taylor**, *The Rule and Exercises of Holy Dying*, Longmans, Green & Co., London, 1929, p. 109; **J. Horsfall Turner** (ed.), *The Rev. Oliver Heywood, B. A., 1630–1702: his Autobiography, Diaries, Anecdote and Event books*, Brighouse, 1881–85, Vol. II, p. 251–2.

5.   Gorer, *op. cit.*, pp. 20, 73–6; Clarke, *op. cit.*, p. 19.

6.   **R. Parkinson** (ed.), *The Life of Adam Martindale, written by himself, Chetham Society*, old ser., **4** (1845), 119–20.

7.   *John Gerard: The Autobiography of an Elizabethan*, trans. **P. Caraman**, Longmans, Green & Co., London, 1951, pp. 38–9, 147.

8.   **K. A. Esdaile**, *English Church Monuments 1510–1840*, Batsford, London, 1946, pp. 46–51, 54–63, 130–9; **B. R. Kemp**, *English Church Monuments*, Batsford, London, 1980, pp. 65–83, 93–120; **F. Burgess**, *English Churchyard Memorials*, SPCK, London, 1979, pp. 27–8; **W. L. Sachse** (ed.), *The Diary of Roger Lowe of Ashton-in-Makerfield, Lancs., 1663–74*, Longmans, Green & Co., London, 1938, p. 77.

9.   **N. Davis** (ed.), *Paston Letters and Papers of the Fifteenth Century*, Clarendon Press, Oxford, 1971, 1976, Vol. I, p. 346; Horsfall Turner, *op. cit.*, Vol. I, pp. 209–10.

10. Gorer, *op. cit.*, pp. 126–32.

11. **M. Penington**, *A Brief Account of my Exercises from my Childhood*, Philadelphia, 1848, p. 33, cited by **P. Delany**, *British Autobiography in the Seventeenth Century*, Routledge & Kegan Paul, London, 1969, pp. 158–9.

12. **B. Winchester**, *Tudor Family Portrait*, Jonathan Cape, London, 1955, p. 82; Caraman, *op cit.*, p. 144; Horsfall Turner, *op. cit.*, Vol. II, pp. 173, 301.

13. *Ibid.*, Vol. I, p. 177; **H. C. Fanshawe** (ed.), *The Memoirs of Ann Lady Fanshawe*, John Lane, London, 1907, p. 195; **M. Macdonald**, *Mystical Bedlam: Madness, Anxiety and Healing in Seventeenth-Century England*, Cambridge UP, 1981, pp. 103–4.

14. For outstanding works by Evesham and Bushnell, see Kemp, *op. cit.*, pp. 107, 112; for vivid description of physical consequences of grief, see monument to Elizabeth Lady Rous (d. 1692) at Rous Lench (Worcs.).

15. **L. Stone**, *Crisis of the Aristocracy, 1558–1641*, Clarendon Press, Oxford, 1965, pp. 590, 787; **P. Laslett**, 'Philippe Ariès and *la famille*', *Encounter*, **46**, no. 3 (March, 1976), 81; Fanshawe, *op. cit.*, p. 13; **L. Hutchinson**, *Memoirs of the Life of Colonel Hutchinson, with the fragment of an autobiography of Mrs Hutchinson*, **J. Sutherland** (ed.), Oxford UP, 1973, p. 20.

16. **P. Laslett**, 'Mean Household Size in England since the Sixteenth Century', in **P. Laslett** and **R. Wall** (eds), *Household and Family in Past Time*, Cambridge UP, 1972, p. 147 and *Family Life and Illicit Love in Earlier Generations: Essays in Historical Sociology*, Cambridge UP, 1977, pp. 88, 95, 198; **C. Phythian-Adams**, *Desolation of a City: Coventry and the Urban Crisis of the Late Middle Ages*, Cambridge UP, 1979, p. 202; **R. H. Hilton**, *The English Peasantry in the Later Middle*

Ages, Clarendon Press, Oxford, 1975, p. 99. The presence of large numbers of people of indeterminate marital status in many community censuses, and especially in the 1523 lists for Coventry, means that precise percentages cannot be given.

17. **E. A. Wrigley** and **R. S. Schofield**, *The Population History of England, 1541–1871. A Reconstruction*, Edward Arnold, London, 1981, pp. 250, 255; Stone, *op. cit.*, p. 787; Laslett, *Family Life and Illicit Love*, p. 198; Phythian-Adams, *op. cit.*, p. 92; **D. V. Glass**, 'Two Papers on Gregory King', in **D. V. Glass** and **D. E. C. Eversley** (eds), *Population in History: Essays in Historical Demography*, E. Arnold, London, 1965, p. 209.

18. **J. Smyth**, *The Berkeley Manuscripts*, **J. Maclean** (ed.), Bristol and Gloucestershire Archaeological Society, Gloucester, 1883, Vol. II, pp. 91, 172–3; **P. Jefferies**, 'The Medieval Use as Family Law and Custom: the Berkshire Gentry in the Fourteenth and Fifteenth Centuries', *Southern History*, 1 (1979), 51–3; **R. Trumbach**, *The Rise of the Egalitarian Family: Aristocratic Kinship and Domestic Relations in Eighteenth-Century England*, Academic Press, London, 1978, p. 73.

19. Davis, *op. cit.*, Vol. I, pp. 298–9, 379–80, 451, 500–3; **J. P. Cooper** (ed.), *Wentworth Papers, 1597–1628, Camden Society*, 4th ser., 12 (1973), 29–31; **J. M. Shuttleworth** (ed.), *The Life of Edward, First Lord Herbert of Cherbury, written by himself*, Oxford UP, 1976, p. 36; **A. Browning** (ed.), *Memoirs of Sir John Reresby: the complete text and a selection from his letters*, Jackson, Son & Co., Glasgow, 1936, pp. 4–5, 26; London, Public Record Office, REQ 2/95/4.

20. **Sir F. Pollock** and **F. W. Maitland**, *The History of English Law before the Time of Edward I*, reprint of 2nd edn of 1898, Cambridge UP, 1968, Vol. II, pp. 348–56; Phythian-Adams, *op. cit.*, p. 92; **M. Prior**,'Women and Trade in Oxford 1500–1800' (unpublished paper), pp. 13–17; **A. Clark**, *Working Life of Women in the Seventeenth Century*, George Routledge & Sons, London, 1919, pp. 104, 154, 160–3, 167–73, 188.

21. Pollock and Maitland, *op. cit.*, pp. 421–2, 427; Hilton, *op. cit.*, p. 99; **W. Lambarde**, *A Perambulation of Kent*, Chatham, 1826, pp. 501–2; **J. H. Bettey**, 'Marriages of Convenience by Copyholders in Dorset during the Seventeenth Century', *Proceedings of the Dorset Natural History and Archaeological Society*, 98 (1976), 1–2; **M. Spufford**, *Contrasting Communities: English Villagers in the Sixteenth and Seventeenth Centuries*, Cambridge UP, 1974, pp. 88–90, 111–19, 161–4.

22. Lambarde, *op. cit.*, pp. 500–1.

23. **Margaret, Duchess of Newcastle**, *The Life of William Cavendish, Duke of Newcastle, to which is added the True Relation of my Birth, Breeding, and Life*, **C. H. Firth** (ed.), John C. Nimmo, London, 1886, p. 289; Fanshawe, *op. cit.*, p. 286; **C. Jackson** and **H. J. Morehouse** (eds), *Yorkshire Diaries and Autobiographies in the Seventeenth and Eighteenth Centuries, Surtees Society*, 65 (1877), 177; Norwich, Norfolk and Norwich Record Office, ACT 4B, f. 119ᵛ; Taunton, Somerset Record Office, D/D/Cd 12, answer to summary allegation of Elizabeth Watkins; **D. Gardiner** (ed.), *The Oxinden Letters, 1607–1642*, Constable & Co., London, 1933, pp. 179–80; **M. Blundell** (ed.), *Cavalier: Letters of William Blundell to his Friends, 1620–98*, Longmans, Green & Co., London, 1933, pp. 231–2.

24. Lambarde, *op. cit.*, p. 501; Bettey, *op. cit.*, p. 1; **W. A. Jones**, 'The

Customs of the Manor of Taunton Deane', *Somerset Archaeological and Natural History Society*, **18** (1872), 79–99.

25. *The Lives of those Eminent Antiquaries Elias Ashmole Esq., and Mr William Lilly*, written by themselves, London, 1774, p. 27; **D. Rogers**, *Matrimoniall Honour: or The Mutuall Crowne and comfort of godly, loyall, and chaste Marriage*, London, 1642, p. 45.

26. Exeter, Devon Record Office, Chanter 864, ff. 59ᵛ–60.

27. **J. Pratt** (ed.), *The Acts and Monuments of John Foxe*, The Religious Tract Society, London, 1877, Vol. VIII, p. 747; **H. C. Foxcroft** (ed.), *A Supplement to Burnet's History of my own Time*, Clarendon Press, Oxford, 1902, pp. 508–9; Bettey, *op. cit.*, pp. 2–5.

28. Pratt, *op. cit.*, Vol. VII, p. 117; Taunton, Somerset Record Office, D/D/Cd 77, deposition of E. Bowden in Hunt c. Pickford, 17 Sept. 1633. Hunt's brother-in-law was a broadweaver.

29. **J. F. Pound** (ed.), *The Norwich Census of the Poor, 1570*, Norfolk Record Society, **40** (1971), esp. p. 95; cf. Laslett, *Family Life and Illicit Love*, p. 208; **C. Carlton**, *The Court of Orphans*, Leicester UP, 1974, pp. 67–70.

30. **M. E. Finch**, *The Wealth of Five Northants. Families 1540–1640*, Northants Record Society, **19** (1956), pp. 6–7; **S. L. Thrupp**, *The Merchant Class of Medieval London, 1300–1500*, Univ. of Chicago Press, 1948, pp. 105–7; **F. P.** and **M. M. Verney**, *Memoirs of the Verney Family during the Seventeenth Century*, Longmans, Green & Co., 2nd edn, London, 1907, Vol. I, p. 166; Norwich, Norfolk and Norwich Record Office, DEP 6A, f. 272.

31. *Ibid.*, ff. 106–7; **R. S. Schofield** and **E. A. Wrigley**, 'Remarriage Intervals and the Effect of Marriage Order on Fertility', in **J. Dupâquier, E. Hélin, P. Laslett, M. Livi-Bacci** and **S. Sogner** (eds.), *Marriage and Remarriage in Populations of the Past*, Academic Press, London, 1981, pp. 213–19.

32. **T. H. Hollingsworth**, 'The Demography of the British Peerage', Supplement to *Population Studies*, **18** (1964), 21; Wrigley and Schofield, *op. cit.*, pp. 258–9.

33. **R. M. Smith**, 'Some Reflections on the Evidence for the Origins of the "European Marriage Pattern" in England', in **C. C. Harris** (ed.), *The Sociology of the Family: New Directions for Britain*, Sociological Review Monographs, 28, Keele, 1979, p. 94; **Z. Razi**, *Life, Marriage and Death in a Medieval Parish: Economy, Society and Demography in Halesowen 1270–1400*, Cambridge UP, 1980, pp. 63, 66, 130–1, 138.

34. Laslett, *Family Life and Illicit Love*, pp. 57–8. The social importance of the reconstructed family is emphasised by **M. Chaytor**, 'Household and Kinship: Ryton in the Late Sixteenth and Early Seventeenth Centuries', *History Workshop Journal*, **10** (1980), esp. 38.

35. **W. Gouge**, *Of Domesticall Duties Eight Treatises*, London, 1622, pp. 226–7, 488; cf. **R. Cawdrey**, *A Godlie Forme of Hovseholde Gouernment: for the Ordering of Private Families, according to the Direction of God's Word*, London, 1600 (1st edn 1598), pp. 240–2.

36. **R. Parkinson** (ed.), *The Autobiography of Henry Newcome, M. A.*, Chetham Society, old ser., **26–7** (1852), I, 101; **A. Hanham** (ed.), *The Cely Letters, 1472–1488*, Early English Text Society, **273** (1975), 128; **J. Gairdner** (ed.), *The Paston Letters, 1422–1509 A. D.*, John Grant,

Edinburgh, 1910, Vol. III, p. 401; **M. St Clare Byrne** (ed.), *The Lisle Letters*, Univ. of Chicago Press, 1981, Vol. II, p. 283; **V. Sackville-West** (ed.), *The Diary of the Lady Anne Clifford*, W. Heinemann, London, 1923, pp. 30, 32, 80; *Life of Newcastle*, p. 204; Sachse, *op. cit.*, p. 77.

37. **P. H. Barnum** (ed.), *Dives and Pauper*, Vol. I, *Early English Text Society*, **275, 280** (1976, 1980), Pt. I, 306; **B. Lubbock** (ed.), *Barlow's Journal of his life at sea*, Hurst & Blackett, London, 1934, Vol. II, p. 385.

38. Laslett, *Family Life and Illicit Love*, pp, 162–3, 170; Thrupp, *op. cit.*, p. 202.

39. Laslett, *Family Life and Illicit Love*, pp. 164, 166; Chaytor, *op. cit.*, esp. p. 38; **K. Wrightson**, 'Household and Kinship in Sixteenth Century England', *History Workshop Journal*, **12** (1981), 151–8, esp. 152; **K. J. Allison**, 'An Elizabethan Village "Census"', *Bulletin of the Institute of Historical Research*, **36** (1963), 96–103.

40. Gouge, *op. cit.*, p. 410; **A. Evans**, *An Eccho to the Voice from Heaven*, London, 1652, p. 6; Delany, *op. cit.*, p. 93; **A. Macfarlane**, *The Family Life of Ralph Josselin. a Seventeenth-Century Clergyman: An Essay in Historical Anthropology*, Cambridge UP, 1970, p. 16.

41. Gouge, *op. cit.*, p. 581, Cawdrey, *op. cit.*, pp. 241–2; Laslett, *Family Life and Illicit Love*, p. 166; **C. L. Kingsford** (ed.), *Stonor Letters and Papers, 1290–1483, Camden Society*, 3rd ser., **29–30** (1919), II, 55; **E. F. Rogers** (ed.), *The Correspondence of Sir Thomas More*, Princeton UP, 1947, pp. 249n, 517; **R. A. Houlbrooke**, *Church Courts and the People during the English Reformation*, Oxford UP, 1979, p. 106; Hutchinson, *op. cit.*, pp. 25, 90, 92, 283; cf. **G. Davies** (ed.), *Autobiography of Thomas Raymond, and Memoirs of the Family of Guise of Elmore, Gloucestershire, Camden Society*, 3rd ser., **28** (1917), 113–14; **W. G. Perrin** (ed.), *The Autobiography of Phineas Pett, Navy Records Society*, **51** (1918), 4, 12.

42. 43 Elizabeth I, c. 2; Pound, *op. cit.*, (esp. suggestive is pathetic entry re. Eme Stowe and her bastard grandson, *ibid.*, p. 36); Parkinson, *Newcome's Autobiography*, Vol. II, pp. 283–4, 293; Clarke, *op. cit.*, p. 13; Parkinson, *Life of Martindale*, p. 221.

43. **W. L. Sachse** (ed.), *Minutes of the Norwich Court of Mayoralty, 1630–31, Norfolk Record Society*, **15** (1942), 165; **K. Wrightson** and **D. Levine**, *Poverty and Piety in an English Village: Terling, 1525–1700*, Academic Press, London, 1979, pp. 93–4; **Sir E. Coke**, *The Compleate Copy-holder*, London, 1644, p. 26; **G. C. Homans**, *English Villagers of the Thirteenth Century*, reprint by W. W. Norton & Co. Inc., New York, 1975, pp. 191–3; above, Chapter 3 (for Josselin and Thornton); Davies, *op. cit.*, pp. 20, 25–35, 44; **R. Davies** (ed.), *The Life of Marmaduke Rawdon of York, Camden Society*, old ser., **85** (1863), 5–8; Winchester, Hants, Record Office, CB 116, pp. 19–20; *A Journal of the Life of William Edmundson, Friends' Library*, **4** (1833), 3.

44. **H. E. Bell**, *An Introduction to the History and Records of the Court of Wards and Liveries*, Cambridge UP, 1953, pp. 116–17.

45. **P. Roebuck**, 'Post-Restoration Landownership: The Impact of the Abolition of Wardship', *Journal of British Studies*, **18** (1978–79), 67–85.

46. Browning, *op. cit.*, pp. 4–5.

47. Carlton, *op. cit.*, esp. pp. 79–81.

48. **R. H. Helmholz**, 'The Roman Law of Guardianship in England, 1300–1600', *Tulane Law Review*, **52** (1977–78), 223–57; Houlbrooke, *op. cit.*, pp. 104–5.
49. **C. Cunningham**, 'Christ's Hospital: Infant and Child Mortality in the Sixteenth Century', *Local Population Studies*, **18** (1977), 39; Wrigley and Schofield, *op. cit.*, p. 249.

Chapter 9

Inheritance

Introduction

Any discussion of inheritance should take into account the whole process of transfer of resources from one generation to the next whether before death or, after it, by means of bequest[1] or succession. The process varied in scale and duration at different levels of society. The wealthy landowner would hope not only to educate all his children in a manner befitting their rank but to 'advance' them by marriage and endowment in such a way as to ensure that they would not have to work for their living. To this end he set in train a complex series of gifts and transfers which commonly began some time before his death and continued after it. In the middling ranks of society there were very many people whose advancement depended partly upon the portions their parents had bequeathed them or the money they had invested in their education, but partly too upon their own efforts and the favour of employers or patrons. A very poor man might be hard put to it even to bring up his children till they could earn their living by their own physical labour. For a growing proportion of the population, certainly a majority by the end of this period, individual resilience, strength and skill were assets more significant than inherited possessions.

One of the fullest and most valuable case studies of the process of transfer so far carried out concerns a member of the middle ranks of society. The seventeenth-century clergyman Ralph Josselin made such a study possible by leaving not only a will but a series of accounts. Nearly half the resources flowing from Josselin to his surviving children in the shape of land, goods and payments for education, apprenticeship and marriage portions had already been transferred before he made his will. He had enabled many of his children to marry or establish themselves long before his death.[2] This pattern was probably common among men of his economic standing. But the extent to which parents provided for their children in their own lifetimes clearly depended in large part on how long they lived and the ages of their children when they died. The proportion of an individual's resources which passed to his offspring after his death was highest when he died while they were still small children. Conversely, a man who reached advanced old age and saw all his children attain adulthood might have divested himself of nearly all his property beforehand.[3] But, as the foregoing survey of old age will have suggested, individual security and authority were often felt to depend on the continued control of resources. So men commonly held on to a substantial proportion of their property or made agreements or settlements which guaranteed their continued use of it until death ended their need.

Laws and customs of inheritance

Generally speaking there was very considerable freedom to dispose of possessions in accordance with individual wishes. But this freedom was restricted in certain respects. In order to understand these restrictions it will be as well to begin by setting out the rules which governed the succession to property when the individual owner failed to make any arrangements of his own. Then we shall see how far he could prevent their coming into operation. If a man made no will, portions of his goods were supposed to be allocated to his widow and children. The 1670 Statute of Distributions provided that one-third of an intestate's estate should go to the widow, two-thirds to his children.[4]

The most important rules governing succession to lands were those of the common law. Of these the principal was male primogeniture. Males excluded females of equal degree (e.g. a brother would exclude a sister). Among males of equal degree only the eldest inherited, but females inherited together as co-heiresses. A dead descendant was represented by his or her descendants. This rule overrode the preference for males, so that, for example, the daughter of a dead eldest son excluded a younger son. The widow had a right to dower, but for her life only. These rules applied to most of the lands held by 'free' tenures such as knight service and free socage which were directly subject to the supervision of the royal courts. They also governed the descent of most of the land held by 'copyhold of inheritance' in accordance with manorial custom. (The other main form of copyhold tenure was copyhold for lives, so called because grants were for the lives of certain named people.)[5]

Different customary rules governed the descent of land in various parts of the country. In Kent and some smaller areas free socage lands were largely subject to the custom of gavelkind by which they were divided equally among sons. Some copyholds of inheritance descended in gavelkind; others were partible among all children, male or female. Others again went to the youngest son or youngest daughter by the custom known as 'Borough English'.[6]

Freedom to bequeath goods by will had existed long before 1450, and leases for terms of years and tenements in many towns could be disposed of in the same way. In some places and areas, however, testamentary freedom was restricted by custom. Throughout the ecclesiastical province of York (until 1693), in London (until 1725) and in other towns, the testator was bound to leave one-third of his goods to his wife and another third to be divided equally among his children, taking into account such provision as had already been made for them. In London, the court of orphans upheld this tripartite scheme, adjusting, sometimes by substantial amounts, those wills which failed to take account of it.[7]

The medieval common law allowed a man to alienate his land during his lifetime, but not, with the major exceptions noticed above, to devise it by will. In the later Middle Ages, however, the development of feoffments to uses allowed a man to continue to enjoy the use of his lands during his own life and, in effect, dispose of them by his will, in which he could give instructions to his feoffees. The bitterly unpopular Statute of Uses (1536) was pushed through as a result of Henry VIII's determination to curb the evasion of feudal incidents by means of these feoffments. The Statute of Wills (1540) was a realistic compromise. Those who held lands by knight service were allowed to devise up to two-thirds of their lands by will. The remaining third passed to the heir, who became a ward of the Crown if he was still a minor at the time of his father's death. As for tenants in socage, they were allowed to devise all their lands by will, and this freedom was extended to all landowners on the final abolition of military tenures in 1660. (In each case the landowner's actual freedom of disposal was considerably less than the theoretical statutory maximum if he had a wife alive because of her dower or jointure rights.)

In the long run the law allowed increasing freedom to alienate land. But landowners often wanted some control over the future fate of their lands as well as freedom for themselves, and the law had to resolve the conflict between these two contradictory desires. The entail, invented in the thirteenth century, was the major means of control. Entailed land was given to the grantee and a specified class of his heirs; by a grant of land in tail male, the donor could limit its descent to males and therefore avoid the division among daughters provided for by the common law. Entails might preserve the inheritance, but they also imposed what were felt to be unacceptable limitations on the donor's descendants and allegedly undermined their parental authority. Between the fifteenth and early seventeenth centuries, lawyers, courts and parliament gave landowners the means of breaking entails, and new forms of perpetual entail which attempted to overcome these obstacles were nearly all judged invalid. In 1600 the inheritances of the realm were in Francis Bacon's vivid metaphor tossed upon a sea of legal uncertainty.[8]

Meanwhile, however, there developed other voluntarily accepted means of restricting freedom of alienation. In fifteenth-century marriage agreements and settlements, landowners, in order to secure good marriages for their heirs, increasingly often undertook to entail upon the latter most of their estates or a substantial proportion of them. The entail of land upon the bride and groom was a central feature of most sixteenth-century marriage settlements. This safeguarded the interests of the married pair. The next step was to protect those of their eldest son, the hoped-for grandson of the settlor. In the early seventeenth century another form of marriage settlement, hitherto little used, rapidly gained wide acceptance. This gave the bride and groom a joint life estate with a remainder in tail to their male heir. Later in the century it became increasingly common for grooms themselves, of whom an increasing proportion were married after the attainment of their majorities, to join in the making of marriage settlements. Whereas the idea of a perpetual entail represented a one-sided attempt by a landowner to bind his descendants, this type of settlement depended upon the consent of those involved to the orderly transmission of property from one generation to the next. A major technical advance of the 1640s greatly improved the machinery of the settlement. This was the invention of trustees 'to preserve contingent remainders', i.e. to safeguard estates in land dependent upon an event or condition which might not happen before a given time, as for example the birth of a grandson before the settlor's death. Additional remainders, to take effect if the marriage produced no male heir, could be specified in the settlement. The appointment of these trustees also enabled the settlor to make any provision out of the estate for younger children more secure; the arrangements for them were spelt out in the marriage settlement. It was this type of settlement which became known as the 'strict' settlement.[9]

Freedom of alienation had been established for manorial copyholders of inheritance before the start of this period. The customary course of inheritance could be avoided by surrender into the hand of the lord's representative for regrant to the tenant's nominee. By surrendering to the use of his will, the tenant could postpone the nomination of his successor till he was on his deathbed.[10]

There was a widespread individual desire for freedom in disposal of possessions. Men wanted such freedom, not because they wanted to leave their families unprovided for, or because they wished to depart radically from customary norms, but because they wanted more scope in choosing how to meet their familial and extra-familial obligations, and on what scale. They wanted to secure their parental authority and, we may suspect, to be in a position to reward aptitude, application and loyalty among their children. The law came to concede great freedom to the individual, but some significant legal customary obstacles remained.

Since individuals had considerable freedom to decide how and when to transfer possessions to the next generation, it seems appropriate to attempt to identify various parental or family strategies. Yet the concept of a 'strategy' has its dangers if it makes us think of inheritance as a controlled, tidy and carefully thought-out process. There were many reasons why this was frequently not the case. In the first place there were many parents who through profligacy, ineptitude, miscalculation and plain misfortune failed to make adequate provision for their children. In large families it was often impossible to provide as generously for youngest as for second sons. Unforeseen circumstances often made it impossible to carry out earlier plans.

Secondly, parental dissatisfaction might lead to diminished provision for children or even to their attempted disinheritance. It is true that there were substantial obstacles to disinheritance. A major objection against entails voiced by Thomas Starkey in the 1530s and against settlements on unmarried children made by Henry Oxinden and Heneage Lord Finch in the seventeenth century was that they weakened control over heirs.[11] Yet even in the upper ranks of society it was often the case that sufficient property remained at parental disposal to penalise a recalcitrant heir fairly severely. Children other than the heir were of course far more at the mercy of their parents. Strict settlements of the seventeenth century commonly made payments of daughters' portions conditional on their compliance with parental wishes. In the eighteenth century, it became common practice to specify a lump sum whose distribution among younger sons and daughters was left to parental discretion. In London from 1551 at latest, and probably in other towns, children could lawfully be disinherited for 'reasonable' cause.[12] Disinheritance or partial disendowment was no doubt much more often threatened than carried out: it was dangled over the heads of unsatisfactory heirs by parents as diverse in standing and outlook as Margaret Paston in the fifteenth century and Ralph Josselin in the seventeenth. Sometimes it certainly took place. In the sixteenth and seventeenth centuries religious differences led to the disinheritance of a number of gentlemen's sons. Richard Gough recorded a number of instances in the parish of Myddle of the disinheritance of children most of whom had married without their fathers' consent. Witnesses in testamentary litigation often described how testators saddened by children's absence or misbehaviour finally decided to cut them out of their wills or drastically to reduce the provision intended for them.[13]

A widespread tendency to leave the final settlement of the individual's affairs till shortly before death, whether through inertia, superstition or the fear of losing control over children, also militated against orderly transmission of property. Largely because of the Church's desire to uphold the declared wishes of a dead man wherever possible and thus avoid intestacy, necessary testamentary formalities were minimal. Wills of land were not made subject to adequate safeguards till 1677. The fact that wills could be made and indeed altered with very little formality encouraged would-be beneficiaries to attempt to manipulate the dying, sometimes going so far as to try to make a will out of a few broken utterances. In 1562 witnesses examined at Winchester described how John Palmer had been badgered on his deathbed by his mother Alice and his wife Katherine. Property was uppermost in both women's minds, their mutual mistrust obvious. When John told his mother that she should have the lease of his mill 'by and by' if he died, she said eagerly to her daughter-in-law, 'Lowe, Kateryn, we may make a will of this if he speke no more.' 'Nay mother,' Katherine answered, 'this is to no purpose. We will haue more of hym or we go.' William Roulston, lying sick in the house of his brother-in-law John Braye in Nymet Rowland (Devon) shortly before Christmas 1596, made Braye his executor and told the handful of people present that he wanted no more witnesses because if his brother John found out he would come and 'keepe a greate adoe' with him, but he would never have a penny of William's goods.[14]

Mountains of testimony set down by the scribes of various courts are suffused with the acrid odour of unedifying disputes over the property of the dead. Men's failure to set their affairs in order in good time or their neglect of due formalities often contributed to these disputes. Lying on his deathbed in 1444, William Paston concluded, somewhat late in the day, that the meagre provision he had made for his younger sons would force them to 'hold the plowe be the tayle'. He resolved to give them certain manors. He would not, he told his eldest son John, give so much to one that the rest should not have enough to live on. But after his father's death John ruthlessly prevented the implementation of these oral provisions. Early in Elizabeth's reign, Thomas Dixon, yeoman, held three yardlands of the manor of Ogbourne St George (Wilts.). Wishing 'lyke a good and naturall and loving father having a faithfull care and providence to advaunce euerye of his children according to his Abilitie with some small porcion of lyving or Substaunce' he leased two of them to his two younger sons for ninety-nine years. His eldest son, begrudging this generous provision, subsequently challenged it on the ground that leases of such length were against the custom of the manor. These two disputes were between brothers.[15] As bitter and possibly even more numerous were quarrels with stepparents and half-siblings. Many of these conflicts were settled, one suspects, by a process of adjustment or compromise whose final results may not have been all that close to the intentions of the dead.

Aims, practice and social consequences

The following discussion will be concerned with inheritance and succession among those socio-economic groups whose practice has so far received most attention from historians: the nobility and gentry, lesser landholders, farmer-craftsmen, townsmen, and one professional group, the clergy. In each case certain broad patterns or tendencies can be discerned. But no short survey can do justice to the immense variety of individual circumstances, aims and attitudes.

The nobility and gentry

Primogeniture was no doubt strongest towards the top of society, but a strong sentiment in its favour was to be found among the ambitious middling sort. Even clerical writers whose audience was probably drawn predominantly from townsmen and yeomen upheld and justified the favoured position of the first-born with references to nature and Scripture as well as law and custom. Maintenance of patrimonies was considered to be essential to the survival of the social hierarchy and the stability of the state. The attachment of the landed classes to primogeniture even in an area where it ran counter to local custom is shown by the way in which the gentry of Kent prevented the operation of gavelkind by will, settlement or disgavelling act of parliament from the late Middle Ages onwards. But the custom left a lasting imprint in the county's large numbers of branches of the same name and the continuing readiness of some families to use outlying or newly acquired properties to establish younger sons.[16]

Theoretical defence of primogeniture was often coupled with an insistence upon parents' moral obligation to provide for all their offspring. Indeed it was one justification of primogeniture that it encouraged parents to prepare their younger sons for callings profitable to a commonwealth.[17] In practice the prospects of the younger sons of the landed classes depended not only on parental affection and sense of duty but also on the resources available for their endowment, the legal machinery employed, the opportunities open to them and the demographic situation. There was a widespread, perhaps general desire among the landed gentry and nobility to endow younger sons as well as possible. But their interests had to be considered in conjunction with those of the heir, first provided for in the normal course of events, those of his future bride, often vigorously represented by her father, and those of good estate management.

Ability and readiness to endow younger sons with land depended upon the way in which it had come into a father's hands and the size of his estate. An old rule that inherited lands should be passed on intact while new acquisitions might be bestowed on younger sons was always influential; men who married heiresses were especially well placed to provide for them. William Cecil Lord Burghley and Sir Nicholas Bacon, both of whom owed their enormous wealth to their successful careers in the service of the Tudor Crown, each made generous provision for more than one son.[18] The holders of middle-sized and small estates, especially those who had made no new acquisitions, were much less ready than great landowners to use land to establish younger sons.

It has been argued that endowment of younger sons with land grew rarer in the course of time. Late medieval nobles had exploited the freedom conferred on them by the mechanism of feoffments to uses to make generous provision for younger sons, although even then the extent of permanent dispersal had been small because of their high mortality and the operation of entails. Thereafter, fewer younger sons had been given land. In the seventeenth century, so the argument continued, the mortgage became a much more attractive basis for long-term loans, and could be used as a means of financing portions or annuities. Then the advent of the strict settlement made the payment of portions more secure. Hitherto, fathers uncertain whether their heirs could be trusted to fulfil their intentions for younger sons had often provided for the latter with a grant of land either in tail or for a stipulated period. The strict settlement, embracing much or most of the estate, greatly reduced both their need and their ability to do this. But recent work indicates that the process of change was both more gradual and more complex than this argument might suggest. It has been shown that some great land-owners were still endowing younger sons with unsettled or newly acquired land even at the end of this period, while others had provided for them with rent charges and annuities in its first half. There are some signs of a movement away from endowment with land by the middling and smaller gentry of Kent and the north and west of England, but in such counties as Berkshire, Bedfordshire and Leicestershire the main aim of such men had been to pass on undivided estates even in the fourteenth and fifteenth centuries.[19]

The amount of suitable employment open to the younger sons of the landed classes fluctuated over time. Opportunities to serve the nobility shrank, especially in the seventeenth century, as the latter reduced the number of their gentlemen attendants and recruited a greater proportion of their servants from the humbler classes. A military life appealed to high-spirited but poorly endowed younger sons, but it remained arduous, hazardous and ill-paid even after the fitful but ultimately considerable expansion of the navy and the establishment of a standing army in the mid-seventeenth century. More secure was a career in royal administration or the court. The most dramatic expansion in the number of posts worth a gentleman's having took place under the Yorkists and early Tudors, reaching its climax in the reign of Henry VIII. Thereafter relatively few posts were created before the bureaucratic and fiscal innovations of the second half of the seventeenth century. Of the learned professions the most consistently attractive was the law, to whose rapid expansion a veritable explosion of litigation in the sixteenth century made an important contribution. The Reformation and the changes associated with it reduced the numbers, wealth and standing of the clergy. Only gradually thereafter did the better-endowed ecclesiastical benefices recover their desirability. A third profession, medicine, grew rapidly, but even so absorbed relatively few men. Trade always drew recruits from the gentry, though the great majority of them were the sons of 'mere' gentry below the rank of esquire. The influx grew markedly between the fifteenth and seventeenth centuries, encouraged by the expansion of trade and the enormous wealth and great prestige of the richest London merchants. But gentlemen's sons were often endowed with insufficient capital or lacked useful contacts or aptitude for business.[20]

The landowner with few younger children was better able to provide for them than he who had many. When the process of provision was not planned, especially if it had not been completed by the time of the father's death, or if unforeseen financial difficulties had arisen, those members of a large family who arrived last were likely to be the least well endowed. When it was planned, as in the more developed family settlements, the scale of provision for each son or daughter was frequently limited by their total number. Attempts to provide generously for large numbers of children often placed unacceptably large burdens on estates which contributed to the decline of families even in the era of the 'strict' settlement.[21]

Periods when there were fewest younger sons and daughters to be provided for were also ones when, other things being equal, their prospects were comparatively rosy. Broadly speaking, the upper classes were producing more children under Elizabeth and the early Stuarts than they were afterwards. Child mortality rose for most of the seventeenth century, so that fewer offspring reached adulthood. What was happening before the later years of Elizabeth's reign is more obscure, but the fifteenth century was a period of high mortality. When mortality was high, families were more likely to fail in the main line, leaving heiresses. The wealth and lands which the latter brought with them could be used either to establish a second son or to improve the prospects of more than one child. Lady Mary Verney had hoped, she told her husband in 1647, to keep enough of her land 'to have provided well for my toe younger boyes and my gerll . . .'.[22]

It is difficult to discern any strong or general trends in the fortunes of younger sons. Rather these fluctuated in accordance with the changing developments which have been outlined. One of the gloomiest assessments of the lot of younger sons was penned in 1601 by Thomas Wilson, who claimed that their state was 'of all stations for gentlemen most miserable'. Their plight was further deplored in John Ap Robert's frequently reprinted *Apology for a Younger Brother*, first published in 1618. These two authors were both writing at a time when high fertility and a dramatic expansion of the ranks of the gentry had sharpened competition for places of profit and honour whose numbers had almost certainly failed to expand at the same rate as demand. Perhaps, then, the situation of younger sons was worse at this time than it had been earlier or would be later. Their humiliating dependence on heirs' goodwill particularly irked Wilson. In so far as the strict settlement made their provision more secure, it may have brought about a lasting improvement in their position.[23]

The situations of younger sons are difficult to compare with those of non-inheriting daughters because there was a much greater variety in the types of provision made for sons. The costs of education were often much greater in the case of sons and are now largely hidden from view by lack of evidence. Some have thought that daughters were better endowed. But so far the fullest discussion of the subject has not supported this view. 'The fact that testators usually left the same amount for an unborn child, whatever its sex, suggests that equal treatment was the norm, or the minimum for sons, as it became in strict settlements.'[24] Different daughters were not always equally provided for, but Sir Thomas Brews, John Paston III's father-in-law, was probably expressing a widely held sentiment when he said that he would be loath to bestow so much on one daughter that her sisters should fare the worse. Most gentlemen of early seventeenth-century Sussex, we are told, 'looked for the contentment of a happy and respectable match for all their daughters, rather than bid for a grand match for the eldest girl'.[25]

The common law rules of descent gave a man's daughter priority over his brother or nephew and, when there was more than one daughter but no son, divided the land between them as co-heiresses. These rules could be circumvented by a gift or settlement in tail male. Some landowners thought it very important to maintain the unity of estates and their connection with the family name. But men were less likely to pursue these aims if it meant sacrificing the interests of their own children than if it was a matter of diverting the inheritance from more remote descendants. As a rule, the late medieval landowner put his daughter's interests above those of his brother or his brother's son. But the gradual elaboration of settlements, culminating in the strict settlement, in which provision was made for unborn descendants, favoured succession in tail male and reduced the prospects of females. The rise of the strict settlement was however offset, at least in the short term, by demographic developments. It seems probable that only a minority of substantial landowners born between 1625 and 1699 succeeded both in begetting a son and in surviving till that son was married. So land often came to people who were untrammelled by prior settlements, including men with daughters and heiresses themselves.[26]

The strict settlement was not the product of new attitudes or aspirations. Rather was it the best mechanism so far devised for the fulfilment and reconciliation of aims long cherished by landed men. Its perfection was no sudden invention but the culmination of deep-rooted legal developments, though the relaxation of the Crown's feudal grip and the birth of an efficient money market were prerequisites of its effective operation. It was primogeniture above all which benefited from the strict settlement. In so far as younger sons and daughters were concerned, the aim was more secure rather than more generous provision. Yet even the best institutional device for the maintenance of lineages and estates could not safeguard them against the worst consequences of individual extravagance or ineptitude. Nor could it guarantee that the line would not die out through failure of male heirs, especially since a high proportion of younger sons seem to have chosen not to marry.

Peasants, yeomen and husbandmen

The family strategies of landholders below the level of the gentry were much more strongly influenced by local inheritance customs. But custom was no strait-jacket: it was itself influenced by economic and demographic circumstances. It could be circumvented by individuals and changed by the agreements of communities. But in order to understand the complex changes of our period, it is necessary first to examine their medieval background, going back beyond the devastating epidemics of the fourteenth century, generally recognised as a watershed in medieval social history.

In one view, the most fundamental principle underlying the rules of inheritance of the medieval English peasantry was that 'family land belonged to the whole family; every member had a claim to support from it, from generation to generation'. Family rights limited very severely the individual's ability to alienate land held by custom. Very many transfers of land recorded in manorial court rolls at least as far back as the thirteenth century were simply leases, made by families at stages of their developmental cycle when they were unable, or did not need, to farm all their land themselves.[27] According to the opposite view, the customary landholder had complete freedom to sell or grant his holding away from his children and younger brothers had no right of maintenance. The operation of customary rules could be prevented; there was no such thing as 'family land'.[28]

One of the best documented and most thoroughly studied of medieval manors is Halesowen (Worcs.). Here, inequalities in holdings, already substantial in 1270, grew much greater before the Black Death. Each successive crisis, especially the terrible famines of 1315–17, forced poorer tenants to borrow seed corn and rent money from their richer neighbours, and, ultimately, to lease or sell their land. But accumulations of land by wealthier and middling tenants were not retained, for new acquisitions, indeed if necessary pieces of inherited holdings, were used to establish younger children, despite the fact that primogeniture was the custom of this manor. The wealthiest tenants were able to bring up the most children and had the greatest numbers to provide for. Economic and demographic circumstances exerted relentless downward pressures on the majority of the population. As successive crises impoverished and ultimately ruined those at the bottom of the social scale, so the less successful offspring of rich and middling tenants slipped down to replace them. On the one hand, then, there was an intense concern to establish offspring on the land, to which the most emphatic statements of individual rights of ownership and alienation give too little weight. On the other hand, there was an active land market, which quickened in times of agrarian crisis, when land flowed from the poor to the prosperous.[29]

The period of high mortality which began with the Black Death has long been thought to have weakened the ties between families and the land. There was a great increase in the proportion of land transfers which took place between people who were not apparently related to each other, 'whether because of the lack of heirs or because of the very considerable mobility of the peasant population'. Many families died out in the male line; the shortage of tenants and labourers on many manors created opportunities for enterprising immigrants. When, as at this time, land was relatively abundant, tenants had less cause to hang on to a particular holding, having improved prospects of exchanging it for something better. But historians may have failed fully to perceive the continuing importance of hereditary succession simply because it is not immediately visible in the records of the post-Black Death era. In Halesowen, and probably elsewhere, far more land now passed to females because of the relative paucity of male heirs. The many historians who have relied upon surnames to trace intra-familial land transfers may therefore have greatly underestimated their numbers in the period after the Black Death. During the sixteenth and seventeenth centuries there was what at first sight appears a marked increase in the proportion of land transfers between relatives. But this may have been due in large part to the fact that reduced mortality had improved the chances of male succession.[30]

The period of high mortality nevertheless had enduring consequences. First, it strengthened the tendency towards polarisation in rural society. The greater availability of land and a lower survival rate among children meant that richer peasants were much better placed to reconcile their twin aims of accumulation and adequate provision for their offspring than they had been before the Black Death. But the bulk of small and middling tenants lacked the resources substantially to increase their holdings, and the gap between the richest and poorest tenants widened. Secondly, there was almost certainly *some* weakening of custom. In order to attract tenants, much formerly customary land was rented on leases which though often long, and free from all taint of bondage, provided less security for lessees' descendants than the tenures they replaced.[31]

The rise of population between the early sixteenth and mid-seventeenth centuries, which perhaps made England as populous by 1650 as it had been over 300 years before, did not restore early fourteenth-century conditions. Trade, foreign and domestic, and industry, urban and rural, now became far more important in the English economy than they had ever been before the Black Death. The growing importance of the market was especially favourable to substantial farmers, many of them the descendants of men who had been able to build up big holdings during the 'drastic culling' of the population in the fourteenth and fifteenth centuries. Such men benefited from the sixteenth-century rise in agricultural prices and were able to accumulate cash surpluses to help endow non-inheriting children. They might be put towards the leasing or even the purchase of farms. But a growing number of farmers' sons could now enter trade, industry or the professions. Such opportunities were far more numerous than they had been in the less-developed economy of the fourteenth century.[32] Smaller farmers, especially in arable areas, were to fare less well in the new era. Benefiting from the expansion of the market much less or not at all, they had more children to provide for than their fifteenth-century forebears. Furthermore, demographic developments had tilted the balance in the landlords' favour. Increasing demand for holdings made it their interest to probe custom, and helped them to raise rents and dues. Poor and bad harvests, especially in the black 1590s, as in the early fourteenth century, drove countless small farmers into debt and ultimately forced many of them off the land.

The variety of provision for children and the changes of strategy which circumstances could bring about within a substantial farmer's family are well illustrated by the arrangements made by William Stout's parents in the later seventeenth century. Stout's father, a Lancashire yeoman, left his farm to his eldest son. He abandoned an early plan to set up William, his second son, on a farm as well, perhaps in the light of a revised assessment of his aptitudes, and apprenticed him instead. His third son's early inclination to husbandry was rewarded with a farm. Money accumulated for his two youngest sons, who later died, was used by his widow to buy additional land for the first and third sons. This land she charged with payments to William and his sister, who had also been left a money portion by her father. Various widely separated communities have yielded examples of yeomen who established more than one son on the land without dividing their main farms. In Myddle (Shrops.) some men owed their success in this respect to fortunate marriages. But it seems likely that land acquired for younger sons was usually smaller in extent and often held on less secure terms than that left to the eldest. As the national economy developed and diversified, an increasing proportion of younger sons of yeomen and husbandmen became craftsmen or traders. In Myddle during the seventeenth century such younger sons were exceedingly numerous. Their destinations ranged from London to the villages of the neighbourhood, their occupations from goldsmith and merchant tailor to tanner, shoemaker and glover. Urban records bear out the impression gained from reading of their experience. In 1551–53, the 'better-off peasantry' were the chief source of immigrant London freemen then registered. In 1630–60 the proportions of the recorded apprentices of seven London companies who came from families of yeomen, husbandmen and other agricultural workers ranged from 19 to 47 per cent. (Yeomen's sons were in the majority among these boys, especially in the better companies.) But only a few of the more substantial inhabitants of Myddle sent sons to university, and college admission books which give indications of status describe only a tiny proportion of entrants as the sons of yeomen or farmers. Most small and middling farmers were probably unable to forgo the labour of their adolescent children in order to give them the necessary schooling.[33]

Small farmers were the least able to accumulate cash portions to help give their children a start in life. They were the most likely to distribute among them the stock and equipment needed for their holdings' effective running or to burden them with the payment of disproportionately large sums after their deaths. Poignant evidence in wills points to the determination of even the smallest landholders, men who described themselves as labourers, to do what they could for all their children. But often the portions stipulated, even if they proved possible to pay, must have been at best a useful supplement to wages earned in service.[34]

Partible inheritance was the custom in some places. It is important not to make the distinction between partibility and impartibility too sharp. In seventeenth-century Kent, for example, the custom of gavelkind did not usually lead to the fragmentation of holdings, though it may have acted as a brake on their accumulation. Individual farms were usually preserved by agreements among brothers to join in selling the property or that one buy out the others. For one man to buy out his brothers was equivalent to his paying substantial portions. In other areas, even when primogeniture was the rule, holdings were sometimes so heavily burdened that the practical consequences were little different from those of gavelkind.[35]

The survival of partible inheritance customs has been attributed to relatively weak seigneurial control and to sparse population or abundant additional sources of livelihood. Such explanations have frequently been combined. Partible inheritance was sometimes found in pastoral areas, especially upland and woodland, where population was widely scattered and the typical unit of settlement was the hamlet or farmstead, making effective manorial control difficult to achieve.[36]

When population was increasing, partition would sooner or later produce holdings too small to support their tenants. Even communities with very rich or abundant pastures, extensive commons or wastes could not continue to practise partition indefinitely without risking some serious impoverishment. The abandonment of partibility occurred rather earlier, in general, in the lowland than in the highland zone, in areas of mixed farming than in pastoral districts, though there were many local variations on this general pattern. A change of custom in a community might depend on the lord's initiative or the presence within it of a group of landholders sufficiently influential to give a lead, or a mixture of the two. Practice could vary within as well as between communities. In Willingham (Cambs.), in the late sixteenth century, bigger farmers tried to keep their holdings intact and to provide for younger children with cash or land newly purchased or leased, but the smaller the holding, the more likely the occupier was to divide it among his sons. In this village the resources of the fen (extensive rights of pastures, fishing, fowling and reed-cutting) enabled men to survive on smaller and smaller plots, putting off much longer than elsewhere the final abandonment of a stake in the land.[37]

Rural craftsmen

In some communities, the continuance of partible inheritance was made possible only by the development of industrial by-employments. In the Weald of Kent such woodland by-employments as 'timber-felling and carpentry, wood-turning, charcoal-burning, and iron-smelting' developed as well as cloth-making. A cloth industry also developed in the valleys of Westmorland, while in Garsdale and Dentdale (Yorks.), so it was claimed in 1634, the division of tenements had proceeded so far that many families had become dependent on the local industry of knitting coarse stockings.[38]

A high proportion of farmers (nearly half, according to one estimate, in the seventeenth century) were also craftsmen.[39] Some rural craftsmen served their local communities first and foremost. Others were drawn into production for external markets of varying size. The most rapidly expanding markets provided the largest numbers of children with opportunities of occupational succession. But it was among those who served them that the hazards of dependence upon industry for a livelihood manifested themselves soonest.

Among the smiths, cobblers, carpenters and tailors of Myddle were founders of dynasties which survived in the parish for several generations, occasionally for well over a century. Sometimes the skill was inherited by a younger son, or more than one son took up the craft. A skill essential to the community, once acquired, was a particularly dependable resource, one less subject to waste or dissipation than most assets. In passing on skills to their sons, craftsmen may often have achieved particularly close and beneficial relationships with them. On the other hand, the market open to a local craftsman of this type was a limited one. Similar dynasties have been found among the Thames fishermen based at Oxford. Fisheries were limited in number and potential productivity, and younger sons had either to marry other fishermen's daughters or move into ancillary crafts.[40]

Various expanding industries depended upon the work of the independent craftsmen of the pastoral areas. They included the making of woodware and pottery, mining, metalworking, weaving, lace-making and stocking-knitting. The expansion of an industry might lead to the partition of holdings, even when no custom of gavelkind existed, so that more than one son might continue to combine craft and farm. But when the balance of dependence shifted too far from land to industry, the craftsman's position became increasingly precarious. This happened earliest in some of the textile areas. The cloth industries of the West Country and East Anglia came to be largely dominated by capitalists who 'put out' materials to cottagers. Slumps or interruptions of trade caused intermittent distress in some clothing areas from at least the 1520s onwards. The protracted crisis of the early seventeenth century cracked the fragile basis of the domestic economy in some of the old-established clothing areas and destroyed the prospects of craftsmen's children.[41]

Townsmen

As yet we know little about the extent of occupational succession among urban craftsmen. Many craftsmen certainly trained at least one son to follow them, but craft dynasties which lasted three generations seem to have been uncommon. Merchant dynasties, which have been more thoroughly studied, rarely held a leading position beyond the second generation in the male line.[42]

Various factors militated against the continued connection of name and business in towns, whether among craftsmen or merchants. The first of these was relatively high mortality, increasingly important the further one travelled down the social scale. The second was the availability of a much greater range of opportunities than existed in the countryside. If a man spread his sons between various crafts, trades and professions, and the one he had trained to succeed him died, there would be no one to carry on his business. Furthermore, many sons from both craft and merchant families in provincial towns moved on to bigger towns or to London.[43]

The division of movable goods and money among widow and children in conformity with urban inheritance customs had a deleterious effect on enterprises.[44] The widow's third, unlike a dower in land, was at her disposal, and might be conveyed to another husband. The widow, with the biggest share of the goods, was often the member of the family best placed to ensure the survival of the business. Urban dowers and portions might be inimical to the establishment of dynasties, but they also helped a number of young craftsmen and merchants to establish themselves.

In the case of the merchant class, the desire to acquire land, due to its social prestige, security as an investment, immunity from partible inheritance and usefulness as a retreat during epidemics, also militated against continuity. Although relatively few of the many merchants who purchased land actually retired into the countryside or succeeded in establishing a son as a gentleman, the money thus invested often constituted a significant drain on businesses. Daughters were far more likely than their brothers to rise out of the merchant class, carrying their portions with them, because gentry, while unwilling to marry their daughters to townsmen's sons, were often happy to accept merchants' girls as daughters-in-law for the sake of their dowries.[45]

The short-lived and precarious character of urban business success is vividly illustrated by the case histories of the families of Lancaster tradesmen and merchants written by William Stout, a successful businessman of the town who had in many cases acted as their executor or trustee. A sample of these accounts, from the years 1694–1712, covers the affairs of eight townsmen of very varied wealth who had sons. Only one business was carried on, for a short time, by a widow and son. Investment in real estate and the division of accumulated capital between widows and children militated against the survival of enterprises. In two cases the fathers' affairs had already gone downhill before their deaths. The fact that most of some eighteen sons left Lancaster was also important. Only two or three could be described as successful. Most of the boys died abroad or at sea in youth or early manhood or failed through their own negligence, incompetence, credulity or proneness to drink. All those who failed or died had been prepared for crafts, business, commerce or service at sea. Stout's narratives leave a sombre impression of the high risks attendant on a business career at the end of our period and the terrible price paid in death by disease or shipwreck by many of those who made England's commercial revolution. Business success, once attained, was precarious even in the first generation. Even when he prepared a son for a business career, a man could not make sure of endowing him with the qualities to which he had owed his own success. Thomas Greene, a wealthy Lancaster grocer and draper, kept one son, Richard, at work in his shop. He was 'very obliging to customers for 10 or 12 years, till he fell into company and came to decline'; eventually he died of drink before his father.[46]

Personal character, demography, economic fluctuations, social aspirations and inheritance customs: all these contributed to the high turnover of urban families. A partial and gradual change of aspirations among the London ruling class was accompanied by a change of custom. The richest men in London enjoyed an exceptional wealth, power and prestige. In the course of time the purchase of a large landed estate came to seem less necessary to many of these men as a means of acquiring gentility and security, though for the purposes of recreation, entertainment and the display of gentlemanly tastes the acquisition of a comparatively small one within easy reach of the capital remained desirable. In the later seventeenth century, an increasingly diverse range of secure investments offered itself, including mortgages, stocks, shares and government securities. As the goal of a transition to landed society lost some of its previous attraction, so too the customary division of movable capital became less acceptable. The statute of 1724 which abolished the custom alleged that great numbers of merchants and other wealthy persons active in London had refused to become freemen on account of it. Somewhat more favourable conditions now existed for the formation of urban dynasties. The proportion of London aldermen who had themselves originated there was by 1738–63 45 per cent, about twice as high as the early seventeenth century.[47]

Professional men: the clergy

Fathers among the professional classes commonly sought to provide for some of their offspring by encouraging them to follow in their own footsteps. Many were in a position to bequeath their practices or the purchasable reversions of their offices. Even those who were not often possessed valuable professional contacts, knew potential patrons or had an insider's knowledge of the educational avenues to be followed. If more than one son entered a thriving profession, an enduring attachment to it could develop in different branches of a family. Sir John Bramston (1611–1700), lawyer and son of a lawyer, mentioned in his account of his grandfather's descendants numerous kinsmen who had followed different sorts of legal career: the positions held ranged from a humble attorney's clerkship to a chief justiceship of the King's Bench.[48]

The clergy of the Church of England formed one of the largest professional groups. By the end of the sixteenth century the great majority of them were married. In later Stuart Leicestershire, at least a quarter of the beneficed clergymen were themselves the sons of men who had belonged to the same social group. Between a quarter and a third of the county's incumbents prepared at least one of their own sons for the ministry. The main reason why more did not do so was probably lack of financial means. In fact the majority of the wealthier clergy who had sons probably sent at least one of them into the ministry. Some sent two (as did those conscientious nonconformist ministers Oliver Heywood and Henry Newcome in the same period) or even three. In the middling ranks of the profession, it was probably the commonest single career choice for eldest sons, but the majority of sons had to follow other callings, most frequently trades and crafts. In this county, most of the poorer clergy could not afford the prolonged formal education necessary to fit a son for the ministry. The relative poverty of so large a proportion even of the beneficed clergy was then perhaps the most important single reason why the profession never developed into a practically closed hereditary caste. Others lay in personal character and demography. Many sons were unsuited to a clerical career; some men failed to beget sons or even to marry. But there were some clerical dynasties lasting more than two generations. Occasionally, when a family had purchased an advowson, it remained for a long time in the same parish.[49]

Conclusion

The advancement of his children according to his ability was held to be a central concern of the 'good and naturall and loving father' throughout this period. It was a process requiring care and forethought which typically began long before death. The man who reached the age of fifty without providing for his children's advancement was likened to him who sought corn in the fields at the end of September, according to Thomas Phelips (d. 1588). 'And', he concluded, 'who ys not carefull for his famely ys accompted worse then a heathen.'[50] Very many were unable to give their children material help, but numerous wills witness to an anxious concern, widespread even among the poor, that children should benefit from such meagre possessions as their parents were able to bequeath. But it would be naive to suppose that all parents were equally conscientious in this respect. Some were feckless or incompetent; others quarrelled with their children. Struggles over inheritance sometimes started before the deaths of property holders and continued long after them, frustrating their intentions.

Parental strategies in the advancement of children and the extent of their success were largely shaped by law and custom and by economic and demographic facts. Primogeniture had put down deep roots among the propertied classes. The preservation of a patrimony to pass down the line was not in theory incompatible with fairly generous provision for non-inheriting children, whose advancement was seen as a prime responsibility of owner and heir and a charge on the estate, except in so far as they could be provided for with new acquisitions. In every century individuals naturally varied greatly in the determination and efficiency with which they pursued these objectives. They did not change in the long term, but, among the upper classes, the means of realising them did. The rise of the strict settlement was the product not of a revolution in sentiments but of a long period of legal experiment and of changed political and economic circumstances. Partible inheritance customs also influenced parental strategies in the areas where they still prevailed. Legal and customary restrictions could be circumvented, customs themselves altered. But partible inheritance customs proved far more vulnerable than primogeniture.

Economic developments strongly influenced patterns of provision and helped to determine how far traditional customs remained viable. The growth of trade, industry and the professions created an increasing range of opportunities for younger sons which made primogeniture more acceptable to all those landowners or land-holders who had sufficient resources to pay for education or training. It was those who did not who were driven to forms of provision for their children which in their effects resembled gavelkind and which helped to make small farms more vulnerable. On the other hand abundant shared resources and the development of rural industry allowed the division of holdings to continue without destroying the basis of craftsmen-farmers' livelihood in certain wood-pasture, fenland and upland areas.

It was always easier to provide for few children than for many. Excessive fertility was an important source of economic difficulties for some families at every social level. Opportunities for younger sons were created by high mortality, whether in towns, leaving niches to be filled by immigrants, or in landed families, making available heiresses whose lands or dowries could be used to make more generous provision for children than would otherwise have been possible. A relatively low expectation of life among the upper classes during the seventeenth century reduced the chances for renewal of strict settlements during the first decades after their introduction.

Inheritance laws and customs had important economic and social consequences. Primogeniture, as it was intended to, helped to maintain the integrity of estates and holdings. It weakened the bonds of kinship and encouraged the flow of younger sons into trade and industry, helping to sustain the continued growth of urban populations. Partible inheritance stimulated the growth of certain rural industries and helped to prevent the establishment of urban dynasties. Laws and customs could be changed; given different laws and customs, the broad character of economic change might have been similar. But it is hard to believe that its pace and course would have been the same.

Notes and references

1. Some indications of proportions of population making wills in **R. T. Vann**, 'Wills and the Family in an English Town: Banbury, 1550–1800', *Journal of Family History*, **4** (1979), 352; **P. Slack**, 'Mortality Crises and Epidemic Disease in England 1485–1610', in **C. Webster** (ed.), *Health, Medicine and Mortality in the Sixteenth Century*, Cambridge UP, 1979, p. 12.

2. **A. Macfarlane**, *The Family Life of Ralph Josselin, a Seventeenth-Century Clergyman: An Essay in Historical Anthropology*, Cambridge UP, 1970, pp. 54, 64–7.

3. **M. Spufford**, 'Peasant Inheritance Customs and Land Distribution in Cambridgeshire from the Sixteenth to the Eighteenth Centuries', in **J. Goody, J. Thirsk** and **E. P. Thompson** (eds), *Family and Inheritance: Rural Society in Western Europe, 1200–1800*, Cambridge UP, 1976, pp. 171–3.

4. **T. F. T. Plucknett**, *A Concise History of the Common Law*, Butterworth, London, 5th edn, 1956, pp. 729–31; 22 & 23 Charles II, c. 10.

5. **Sir F. Pollock** and **F. W. Maitland**, *The History of English Law before the Time of Edward I*, reprint of 2nd edn of 1898, CUP, 1968, Vol. II, p. 260; **E. Kerridge**, *Agrarian Problems in the Sixteenth Century and After*, George Allen & Unwin, London, 1969, pp. 32–40.

6. *Ibid.*, pp. 34–5, 37–8.

7. Plucknett, *op. cit.*, p. 745; **C. Carlton**, *The Court of Orphans*, Leicester UP, 1974, pp. 73–6.

8. **K. B. McFarlane**, *The Nobility of Later Medieval England*, Clarendon Press, Oxford, 1973, pp. 63–4, 68–71, 80; **J. P. Cooper**, 'Patterns of Inheritance and Settlement by Great Landowners from the Fifteenth to the Eighteenth Centuries', in Goody et al., *op. cit.*, pp. 199–208; **B. Coward**, 'Disputed Inheritances: Some Difficulties of the Nobility in the Late Sixteenth and Early Seventeenth Centuries', *Bulletin of the Institute of Historical Research*, **44** (1971), 195–7.

9. McFarlane, *op. cit.*, pp. 81–2; **L. Bonfield**, 'Marriage Settlements, 1660–1740: The Adoption of the Strict Settlement in Kent and Northamptonshire', in **R. B. Outhwaite** (ed.), *Marriage and Society: Studies in the Social History of Marriage*, Europa Publications, London, 1981, pp. 102–8; **H. J. Habakkuk**, 'Marriage Settlements in the Eighteenth Century', *Transactions of the Royal Historical Society*, 4th ser., **32** (1950), 15–18; **R.Trumbach**, *The Rise of the Egalitarian Family: Aristocratic Kinship and Domestic Relations in Eighteenth-Century England*, Academic Press, London, 1978, pp. 72–4. (The co-operation of the bridegroom in ensuring the transmission of property to unborn heirs, later so important in the evolution of the strict settlement, appears in one draft indenture of marriage settlement as early as 1454. John Clopton promises and ensures by the faith of his body that he will leave lands to the yearly value of forty marks to his heirs and issue male of the body of Elizabeth Paston his prospective bride, besides the lands settled on the couple by his father, if the same issue male show proper filial obedience: **N. Davis** (ed.), *Paston Letters and Papers of the Fifteenth Century*, Clarendon Press, Oxford, 1971, 1976, Vol. I, pp. 40–1.

10. **E. Levett**, *Studies in Manorial History*, Clarendon Press, Oxford, 1938, pp. 208–23; **A. Macfarlane**, *The Origins of English Individualism: The Family, Property and Social Transition*, Basil Blackwell, Oxford, 1978, pp. 106–8; Kerridge, *op. cit.*, pp. 63–4.

11. **T. Starkey**, *A Dialogue between Reginald Pole and Thomas Lupset*, **K. M. Burton** (ed.), Chatto & Windus, London, 1948, p. 176; **D. Gardiner** (ed.), *The Oxinden Letters, 1607–1642*, Constable & Co., London, 1933, pp. 275–6; Bonfield, *op. cit.*, pp. 109–10.

12. Trumbach, *op. cit.*, pp. 102–3 (I am grateful to Professor Eileen Spring

for giving me her opinion on this point); Carlton, *op. cit.*, p. 75
(included marrying without father's consent, gross immorality, felony).
13. Davis, *op. cit.*, Vol. I, p. 379; Macfarlane, *Family Life of Josselin*,
pp. 121–3; *John Gerard: The Autobiography of an Elizabethan*, trans **P.
Caraman**, Longmans, Green & Co., London, 1951, pp. 21, 82–3; **A.
Kenny** (ed.), *Responsa Scholarum of the English College, Rome. Part
One: 1598–1621, Catholic Record Society*, **54** (1962), 122, 168, 188; **R.
Gough**, *The History of Myddle*, **David Hey** (ed.), Penguin Books,
Harmondsworth, 1981, pp. 90, 93, 101, 206, 224; Norwich, Norfolk and
Norwich Record Office, DEP 4A, ff. 204–9, 234; DEP 4B, ff. 287–8;
DEP 6A, f. 90, DEP 8, ff. 65–6; Trowbridge, Wilts. Record Office,
Bishop's Dep. Bk. 61, ff. 25, 28ᵛ; cf. Macfarlane, *Origins of English
Individualism*, pp. 92–3.
14. 29 Charles II, c. 3; **H. Swinburne**, *A Brief Treatise of Testaments and
Last Wills*, London, 1590, ff. 184–93, 263–72; Winchester, Hants.
Record Office, CB 13, ff. 220–1; Exeter, Devon Record Office, Chanter
864, ff. 389–90.
15. Davis, *op. it.*, Vol. I, pp. 44–8; London, Public Record Office, REQ
2/83/51.
16. **R. Cawdrey**, *A Godlie Forme of Hovseholde Gouernment: for the
Ordering of Private Families, according to the Direction of God's Word*,
London, 1600 (1st edn 1598), pp. 338–41; **W. Gouge**, *Of Domesticall
Duties Eight Treatises*, London, 1622, pp. 576–8; **F. R. H. Du Boulay**,
The Lordship of Canterbury: an Essay on Medieval Society, Nelson,
London, 1966, pp. 142–62; **C. W. Chalklin**, *Seventeenth-Century Kent:
A Social and Economic History*, Longmans, London, 1965, pp. 1, 55–7,
69, 194–6.
17. Gouge, *op. cit.*, pp. 577–8.
18. Cooper, *op. cit.*, p. 216.
19. McFarlane, *op. cit.*, p. 70; **L. Stone**, *The Crisis of the Aristocracy,
1558–1641*, Clarendon Press, Oxford, 1965, pp. 178–83; Habakkuk, *op.
cit.*, 15–18; Cooper, *op. cit.*, pp. 212–21, 229–30, 313–27; **P. Jefferies**,
'The Medieval Use as Family Law and Custom: the Berkshire Gentry
in the Fourteenth and Fifteenth Centuries', *Southern History*, **1** (1979),
pp. 57–60, 66; **K. S. Naughton**, *The Gentry of Bedfordshire in the Thirteenth and Fourteenth Centuries*, Leicester U. Department of English
Local History, *Occasional Papers*, 3rd ser., **2** (1976), 24–5. For information about Leicestershire I am indebted to Dr G. G. Astill.
20. **S. R. Smith**, 'The Social and Geographical Origins of the London
Apprentices, 1630–1660', *Guildhall Miscellany*, **4** (1971–73), 199–200;
R. Grassby, 'Social Mobility and Business Enterprise in Seventeenth-
century England', in **D. Pennington** and **K. Thomas** (eds), *Puritans and
Revolutionaries, Essays presented to Christopher Hill*, Clarendon Press,
Oxford , 1978, pp. 359–72.
21. Cooper, *op. cit.*, pp. 232–3; Kenny, *op. cit.*, Vol. I, p. 102; **Sir John
Habakkuk**, 'The Rise and Fall of English Landed Families, 1600–1800',
Transactions of the Royal Historical Society, 5th ser., **29** (1979), 199 and
preface to **M. E. Finch**, *The Wealth of Five Northants. Families, 1540–1640*,
Northants. Record Society, **19** (1956), xii–xiii.
22. **T. H. Hollingsworth**, 'The Demography of the British Peerage', supplement to *Population Studies*, **18** (1964),32–3, 60; McFarlane, *op. cit.*,
pp. 173–6; **J. Hatcher**, *Plague, Population and the English Economy*,

1348–1530, Macmillan, London, 1977, p. 27; **F. P. and M. M. Verney**, *Memoirs of the Verney Family during the Seventeenth Century*, Longmans, Green & Co., 2nd edn, London, 1907, Vol. I, pp. 364–5. But Cooper, *op. cit.*, p. 215, suggests that younger sons' chances of *marrying heiresses* probably declined with the ending of the sale of marriages without the consent of the wards' families.

23. **F. J. Fisher** (ed.), *The State of England, anno dom. 1600, by Thomas Wilson, Camden Society*, 3rd ser., **52** (1936), 24; **J. Thirsk**, 'Younger Sons in the Seventeenth Century', *History*, **54** (1969), 358–377; Habakkuk, 'Marriage Settlements in the Eighteenth Century', pp. 19–20. Yet if the lot of younger sons really was improving in general it is somewhat puzzling that so high a proportion of them should have remained unmarried in the seventeenth and eighteenth centuries, at least among the peerage families: see Hollingsworth, *op. cit.*, p. 20.

24. Cooper, *op. cit.*, p. 215.

25. Davis, *op. cit.*, Vol. II, p. 413; **A. J. Fletcher**, *A County Community in Peace and War: Sussex 1600–1660*, Longman, London, 1975, p. 39.

26. McFarlane, *op. cit.*, p. 73; Habakkuk, 'Rise and Fall of Landed Families', p. 190; **L. Bonfield**, 'Marriage Settlements and the "Rise of Great Estates": the Demographic Aspect', *Economic History Review*, 2nd ser., **32** (1979), 483–93; **C. Clay**, 'Marriage, Inheritance and the Rise of Large Estates in England, 1660–1815', *Economic History Review*, **21** (1968), 515–18. Some landowners tried to do justice to both daughters and heirs male, or even sacrificed the former: see Cooper, *op. cit.*, pp. 208–10.

27. **C. Howell**, 'Peasant Inheritance Customs in the Midlands 1280–1700' in Goody et al., *op. cit.*, pp. 113, 135–7.

28. Macfarlane, *Origins of English Individualism*, pp. 80–130.

29. **Z. Razi**, *Life, Marriage and Death in a Medieval Parish: Economy, Society and Demography in Halesowen 1270–1400*, Cambridge UP, 1980, pp. 52–7, 94–8.

30. **R. Faith**, 'Peasant Families and Inheritance Customs in Medieval England', *Agricultural History Review*, **14** (1966), 92; Howell, *op. cit.*, pp. 124–5, 130–2, 139; **A. Jones**, 'Land and People at Leighton Buzzard in the Later Fifteenth Century', *Economic History Review*, 2nd ser., **25** (1972), 18–27; Macfarlane, *Origins of English Individualism*, pp. 95–9; **R. Faith's** review of this work in *Journal of Peasant Studies*, **7** (1979–80), 387; **Z. Razi**, 'Family, Land and the Village Community in Later Medieval England', *Past and Present*, **93** (1981), 19–28.

31. Razi, *Life, Marriage and Death*, pp. 139–50; **R. H. Hilton**, *The Decline of Serfdom in Medieval England*, Macmillan, London, 1969, pp. 44–7.

32. Howell, *op. cit.*, pp. 138–9, 149–55; **M. Spufford**, *Contrasting Communities: English Villagers in the Sixteenth and Seventeenth Centuries*, Cambridge UP, 1974, pp. 85–6, 109; **K. Wrightson** and **D. Levine**, *Poverty and Piety in an English Village: Terling 1525–1700*, Academic Press, London, 1979, p. 98.

33. **J. D. Marshall** (ed.), *The Autobiography of William Stout of Lancaster 1665–1752, Chetham Society*, 3rd ser., **14** (1967), 70–3, 102–3 (Stout's father also left a little land to each of his two youngest sons and some 'out parcels' to William); Gough, *op. cit.*, pp. 77–249, *passim*; Thirsk, *op. cit.*, p. 361; **M. Campbell**, *The English Yeoman under Elizabeth and the Early Stuarts*, Yale UP, New Haven, 1942, p. 125; **G. D. Ramsay**,

'The Recruitment and Fortunes of Some London Freemen in the Mid-Sixteenth Century', *Economic History Review*, 2nd ser., **31** (1978), 531, 535–7 (many of the most successful freemen came from yeomen families); Smith, *op. cit.*, p. 205; **L. Stone**, 'The Educational Revolution in England 1560–1640', *Past and Present*, **28** (1964), 66; Spufford, *op. cit.*, pp. 171–81. The proportion of recruits to the better London companies who had a rural background was probably shrinking by 1700.

34. Howell, *op. cit*, p. 152; Spufford, *op. cit.*, pp. 87, 107–8, 159–61, 166; **A. Everitt**, 'Farm Labourers', in *The Agrarian History of England and Wales*, Vol. IV, *1500–1640*, Cambridge UP, 1967, p. 456.

35. Chalklin, *op. cit.*, pp. 56–7; Spufford, *op. cit.*, pp. 87, 106–8.

36. **J. Thirsk**, 'Farming Regions of England', in *Agrarian History*, Vol. IV, pp. 9–12 (see Everitt, note 34).

37. *Ibid.*, *loc. cit.*; Spufford, *op. cit.*, pp. 159–61.

38. **J. Thirsk**, 'Industries in the Countryside', in *Essays in the Economic and Social History of Tudor and Stuart England*, **F. J. Fisher**, (ed.), Cambridge UP, 1961, pp. 70, 78–84.

39. *Idem*, 'Seventeenth-Century Agriculture and Social Change', in **J. Thirsk** (ed.), *Land, Church and People: Essays presented to Professor H. P. R. Finberg, Agricultural History Review*, supplement (1970), 172.

40. Gough, *op. cit.*, esp. pp. 110, 224; **D. G. Hey**, *An English Rural Community: Myddle under the Tudors and Stuarts*, Leicester UP, 1974, pp. 143–62; **M. Prior**, *Fisher Row: Fishermen, Bargemen and Canal Boatmen in Oxford, 1500–1900*, Clarendon Press, Oxford, 1982, pp. 70–1.

41. Thirsk, 'Seventeenth-Century Agriculture and Social Change', pp.171–4; **D. C. Coleman**, *Industry in Tudor and Stuart England*, Macmillan, London, 1975, p. 27; **A. Clark**, *Working Life of Women in the Seventeenth Century*, George Routledge & Sons, London, 1919, pp. 118–9; **B. Sharp**, *In Contempt of All Authority: Rural Artisans and Riot in the West of England, 1586–1660*, Univ. of California Press, Berkeley, 1980, pp. 1, 156–74.

42. **M. G. Davies**, *The Enforcement of English Apprenticeship, 1563–1642*, Harvard UP, Cambridge (Mass.), 1956, p. 12; Ramsay, *op cit.*, pp. 528, 533; Smith, *op. cit.*, p. 204 (both suggesting relatively little continuity in the male line); **A. D. Dyer**, *The City of Worcester in the Sixteenth Century*, Leicester UP, 1973, pp. 154, 180; **D. M. Palliser**, *Tudor York*, Oxford UP, 1979, p. 154; **S. L. Thrupp**, *The Merchant Class of Medieval London, 1300–1500*, Univ. of Chicago Press, 1948, pp. 191, 223; **C. Phythian-Adams**, *Desolation of a City: Coventry and the Urban Crisis of the Late Middle Ages*, Cambridge UP, 1979, p. 142.

43. Dyer, *op. cit.*, p. 188; Smith, *op. cit.*, pp. 199, 202.

44. See esp. **W. G. Hoskins**, 'The Elizabethan Merchants of Exeter', in **S. T. Bindoff**, **J. Hurstfield** and **C. H. Williams** (eds), *Elizabethan Government and Society. Essays presented to Sir John Neale*, Athlone Press, London, 1961, pp. 185–6; Dyer, *op. cit.*, p. 180.

45. Thrupp, *op. cit.*, pp. 226–7, 279–87, **W. T. MacCaffrey**, *Exeter 1540–1640: The Growth of an English County Town*, Harvard UP, Cambridge (Mass.), 1958, pp.260–1; Carlton, *op. cit.*, p. 80.

46. Marshall, *op. cit.*, pp. 110–13, 125, 128–9, 132–6, 142–7, 151–2, 156–7, 166–8, 199–200.

47. **N. Rogers**, 'Money, Land and Lineage: The Big Bourgeoisie of Hanov-

erian London', *Social History*, **4** (1979), 442–454; Cooper, *op. cit.*,
p. 226; 11 George, I c. 18.

48. **Lord Braybrooke** (ed.), *The Autobiography of Sir John Bramston, K.B,
of Skreens, in the Hundred of Chelmsford*, Camden Society, old ser.,
32 (1845), esp. 4–34.

49. **J. H. Pruett**, *The Parish Clergy under the Later Stuarts: The Leicestershire Experience*, Univ. of Illinois Press, Urbana, 1978, pp. 32–7.

50. Taunton, Somerset County Record Office, DD/PH/224/5.

Chapter 10

Conclusion

Between the fifteenth and eighteenth centuries there was little change in familial forms and functions. The nuclear family was dominant and wider ties of kinship were relatively weak. Nuptiality may have fluctuated in response to economic opportunity, but it probably did so within the broad limits of the 'west European' marriage pattern, though how and when this pattern became established are still matters of controversy. Reproduction, the upbringing and advancement of offspring, mutual protection and material support, care in sickness and incapacity, remained the family's most important functions. Some of these were assumed by non-familial institutions if familial provision was inadequate or non-existent. But there is no evidence of a decline of familial functions during this period. It cannot be said, for example, that through the development of the Poor Laws in the sixteenth century the community undertook responsibilities previously discharged by the family. There were, however, considerable differences between social groups and geographical areas in the extent to which families conformed to the dominant form or fulfilled the prime functions. These differences far outweighed any changes which took place over time.

There was some change in ideals of family life, but this was both complex and gradual. Several contributory streams, of which law, Christian doctrines, classical and humanist thought and romantic literature are perhaps the most obvious, had joined and mingled over the centuries. The key notions of conjugal affection, husbandly and parental authority and responsibility and filial duty originated long before this period began. In the course of it, affection was gradually given more scope and increasing emphasis while the insistence on authority was somewhat lessened. The shift was a significant though not a fundamental one. But to what extent the behaviour of the majority of people reflected changing ideals remains extremely obscure.

The basic forms and functions of the family may have remained the same, its body of guiding ideals may have changed only gradually, but family life was nevertheless affected by major economic, institutional and social changes. To a substantial minority these may have brought benefits, particularly greater freedom of choice in marriage and other avenues of advancement. But the pressures towards downwards social mobility were strong. Social groups in which family life was vulnerable and precarious had long existed, but during this period they greatly increased in size. Poverty eroded the capacity to discharge the basic functions of support, upbringing and advancement. Some developments had mixed consequences. Urbanisation may have enhanced individual choices and opportunities, but it also lowered life expectation, especially in the vulnerable first year.

Changes in the emotional life of societies or social groups are exceptionally difficult for historians to assess. Even in today's world the factors which shape the immense variety of individual character are only imperfectly understood. Claims that this period saw a strengthening of attachments and a greater concentration of affection within the nuclear family are suspect except in so far as they relate to small and thoroughly studied social groups. Some historians have overestimated the influence of changing ideals. Psychohistorical methods involving a priori reasoning, the application of controversial psychological theories, comparisons between radically different societies and the wrenching of evidence out of context have led to unsound conclusions on such subjects as the effects of early modern methods of upbringing and of the premature deaths of parents, spouses and children. The vastly increased quantity and quality of the sources available from the sixteenth century onwards has led some to suppose that this period saw a revolution of sentiments and attitudes. They have tended to conclude that feelings of whose expression they could find no evidence simply did not exist.The personal life of the great majority remains for ever hidden from the historian's scrutiny. But the chance light cast by such largely unexplored records as judicial depositions show that passionate attachment and the anguish of bereavement could be as forcefully expressed in the fifteenth century as they are today. Among the thousands of patients of all classes save the poorest who visited the Buckinghamshire clergyman and psychiatric healer Richard Napier between 1597 and 1634, the commonest specified causes of stress were courtship troubles, marital problems and bereavement. 'All of the measures we can devise agree: The emotional lives of ordinary men and women were centered primarily within the nuclear family.'[1] There seems to be no good reason to believe that the same had not been true 200 years earlier.

Notes and references

1.   **M. MacDonald**, *Mystical Bedlam: Madness, Anxiety and Healing in Seventeenth-Century England*, Cambridge UP, 1981, p. 105.

Select bibliography of secondary works

Comments on several of the books listed here will be found in Chapter 1.

UP = University Press

General surveys of the history of the family in England and western Europe

1. **J.-L. Flandrin**, *Families in Former Times: Kinship, Household and Sexuality*, Cambridge UP, 1979.
2. **F. Lebrun**, *La Vie Conjugale sous l'Ancien Régime*, Armand Colin, Paris, 1975.
3. **M. Mitterauer** and **R. Sieder**, *The European Family: Patriarchy to Partnership from the Middle Ages to the Present*, Basil Blackwell, Oxford, 1982.
4. **E. Shorter**, *The Making of the Modern Family*, Collins, London, 1976.
5. **L. Stone**, *The Family, Sex and Marriage in England 1500–1800*, Weidenfeld & Nicolson, London, 1977.

Demography and social structure

Note: relevant demographic studies are so numerous that it is impossible to give a properly representative selection here without creating an imbalance in the bibliography. See the excellent bibliography in (23).

6. **J. D. Chambers**, *Population, Economy and Society in Pre-Industrial England*, Oxford UP, 1972. Still useful for clear and concise introductory discussion of major problems, though largely superseded by (23).
7. **A. Everitt**, 'Social Mobility in Early Modern England', *Past and Present*, **33** (1966).
8. **R. A. P. Finlay**, *Population and Metropolis: The Demography of London, 1580–1650*, Cambridge UP, 1981.

9.   **J. Hatcher**, *Plague, Population and the English Economy 1348–1530*, Macmillan, London, 1977.
10. **T. H. Hollingsworth**, 'A Demographic Study of the British Ducal Families', *Population Studies*, **11** (1957), reprinted in **D. V. Glass** and **D. E. C. Eversley** (eds), *Population in History: Essays in Historical Demography*, Edward Arnold, London, 1965.
11. **T. H. Hollingsworth**, 'The Demography of the British Peerage', supplement to *Population Studies*, **18** (1964).
12. **P. Laslett**, *The World We Have Lost*, Methuen, London, 1965; 2nd edn, 1971.
13. **P. Laslett**, *Family Life and Illicit Love in Earlier Generations: Essays in Historical Sociology*, Cambridge UP, 1977.
14. **P. Laslett** and **R. Wall** (eds), *Household and Family in Past Time*, Cambridge UP, 1972.
15. **A. Macfarlane**, *The Origins of English Individualism: The Family, Property and Social Transition*, Basil Blackwell, Oxford, 1978.
16. **R. M. Smith**, 'Population and its Geography in England, 1500–1730' in **R. A. Dodgshon** and **R. A. Butlin** (eds), *An Historical Geography of England and Wales*, Academic Press, London, 1978.
17. **L. Stone**, 'Social Mobility in England, 1500–1700', *Past and Present*, **33** (1966).
18. **R. Wall**, 'Regional and Temporal Variations in English Household Structure from 1650', in **J. Hobcraft** and **P. Rees** (eds), *Regional Demographic Development*, Croom Helm, London, 1977.
19. **K. Wrightson**, *English Society, 1580–1680*, Hutchinson, London, 1982.
20. **E. A. Wrigley** (ed.), *An Introduction to English Historical Demography*, Weidenfeld & Nicolson, London, 1966.
21. **E. A. Wrigley**, 'A Simple Model of London's Importance in changing English Society and Economy 1650–1750', *Past and Present*, **37** (1967).
22. **E. A. Wrigley**, 'Mortality in Pre-Industrial England: The Example of Colyton, Devon, over Three Centuries', *Daedalus*, **97** (1968).
23. **E. A. Wrigley** and **R. S. Schofield**, *The Population History of England 1541–1871. A Reconstruction*, Edward Arnold, London, 1981.

Some important accounts of social groups

24. **M. Campbell**, *The English Yeoman under Elizabeth and the Early Stuarts*, Yale UP, New Haven, 1942.

25. **A. Everitt**, 'Farm Labourers', in **J. Thirsk** (ed.), *The Agrarian History of England and Wales*, Vol. IV, *1500–1640*, Cambridge UP, 1967.
26. **M. E. Finch**, *The Wealth of Five Northamptonshire Families, 1540–1640, Northants. Record Society*, **19** (1956).
27. **R. H. Hilton**, *The English Peasantry in the Later Middle Ages*, Clarendon Press, Oxford, 1975.
28. **G. C. Homans**, *English Villagers of the Thirteenth Century*, Harvard UP, Cambridge, 1941.
29. **G. E. Mingay**, *The Gentry: The Rise and Fall of a Ruling Class*, Longman, London, 1976.
30. **B. Sharp**, *In Contempt of All Authority: Rural Artisans and Riot in the West of England, 1586–1660*, Univ. of California Press, Berkeley, 1980.
31. **L. Stone**, *The Crisis of the Aristocracy, 1558–1641*, Clarendon Press, Oxford, 1965.
32. **S. L. Thrupp**, *The Merchant Class of Medieval London, 1300–1500*, Univ. of Chicago Press, 1948.
33. **R. Trumbach**, *The Rise of the Egalitarian Family: Aristocratic Kinship and Domestic Relations in Eighteenth-Century England*, Academic Press, London, 1978.

Some studies of individual families

A tiny sample of the enormous literature. Those selected include some works partly or primarily designed as editions of correspondence which also contain copious and useful comment and discussion. In **Macfarlane's** hands an old genre is transformed by the employment of new approaches.

34. **H. S. Bennett**, *The Pastons and Their England*, Cambridge UP, 1932.
35. **M. Blundell** (ed.), *Cavalier: Letters of William Blundell to His Friends, 1620–98*, Longmans, Green & Co., London, 1933.
36. **M. St Clare Byrne** (ed.), *The Lisle Letters*, 6 vols, Univ. of Chicago Press, 1981.
37. **D. Gardiner** (ed.), *The Oxinden Letters, 1607–1642*, Constable & Co., London, 1933.
38. **A. Macfarlane**, *The Family Life of Ralph Josselin, a Seventeenth-Century Clergyman: An Essay in Historical Anthropology*, Cambridge UP, 1970.
39. **F. P.** and **M. M. Verney**, *Memoirs of the Verney Family during the Seventeenth Century*, 2nd edn abridged and corrected by **M. M. Verney**, 1904, reissue, 2 vols, Longmans, Green & Co., London, 1907.
40. **B. Winchester**, *Tudor Family Portrait*, Jonathan Cape, London, 1955.

Some important community studies

41. **D. G. Hey**, *An English Rural Community: Myddle under the Tudors and Stuarts*, Leicester UP, 1974.
42. **C. Phythian-Adams**, *Desolation of a City: Coventry and the Urban Crisis of the Late Middle Ages*, Cambridge UP, 1979.
43. **Z. Razi**, *Life, Marriage and Death in a Medieval Parish: Economy, Society and Demography in Halesowen 1270–1400*, Cambridge UP, 1980.
44. **V. Skipp**, *Crisis and Development: An Ecological Case Study of the Forest of Arden, 1570–1674*, Cambridge UP, 1978.
45. **M. Spufford**, *Contrasting Communities: English Villagers in the Sixteenth and Seventeenth Centuries*, Cambridge UP, 1974.
46. **K. Wrightson** and **D. Levine**, *Poverty and Piety in an English Village: Terling, 1525–1700*, Academic Press, London, 1979.
See also
47. **A. Macfarlane, S. Harrison** and **C. Jardine**, *Reconstructing Historical Communities*, Cambridge UP, 1977.

Family and kindred

See **Macfarlane** (15), (38), **Trumbach** (33), **Wrightson** (19).
48. **M. Anderson**, *Family Structure in Nineteenth Century Lancashire*, Cambridge UP, 1971.
49. **M. Chaytor**, 'Household and Kinship: Ryton in the Late Sixteenth and Early Seventeenth Centuries', *History Workshop Journal*, **10** (1980).
50. **Z. Razi**, 'Family, Land and the Village Community in Later Medieval England', *Past and Present*, **93** (1981).
51. **R. M. Smith**, 'Kin and Neighbors in a Thirteenth-Century Suffolk Community', *Journal of Family History*, **4** (1979).
52. **K. Wrightson**, 'Household and Kinship in Sixteenth Century England', *History Workshop Journal*, **12** (1981).

The making of marriage

See also **Laslett** (12), **Razi** (43), **Stone** (5), (31), **Wrigley** and **Schofield** (23).
53. **P. E. H. Hair**, 'Bridal Pregnancy in Rural England in Earlier Centuries', *Population Studies*, **20** (1966).
54. **P. E. H. Hair**, 'Bridal Pregnancy in Earlier Rural England further examined', *Population Studies*, **24** (1970).
55. **J. Hajnal**, 'European Marriage Patterns in Perspective' in Glass and Eversley (eds), *Population in History* (see (10)).
56. **R. H. Helmholz**, *Marriage Litigation in Medieval England*, Cambridge UP, 1974.

57. **G. E. Howard**, *A History of Matrimonial Institutions, chiefly in England and the United States*, Univ. of Chicago Press, 1904.
58. **P. Laslett, K. Oosterveen** and **R. M. Smith** (eds), *Bastardy and its Comparative History*, Edward Arnold, London, 1980.
59. **D. Levine**, *Family Formation in an Age of Nascent Capitalism*, Academic Press, London, 1977.
60. **R. B. Outhwaite**, 'Age at Marriage in England from the Late Seventeenth to the Nineteenth Century', *Transactions of the Royal Historical Society*, 5th ser., **23** (1973).
61. **R. B. Outhwaite** (ed.), *Marriage and Society: Studies in the Social History of Marriage*, Europa Publications, London, 1981.
62. **G. R. Quaife**, *Wanton Wenches and Wayward Wives: Peasants and Illicit Sex in Early Seventeenth Century England*, Croom Helm, London, 1979.
63. **M. Slater**, 'The Weightiest Business: Marriage in an Upper-Gentry Family in Seventeenth-Century England', *Past and Present*, **72** (1976).
64. **R. M. Smith**, 'Some Reflections on the Evidence for the Origins of the "European Marriage Pattern" in England', in **C. C. Harris** (ed.), *The Sociology of the Family: New Directions for Britain*, Sociological Review Monographs, 28, Keele, 1979.
65. **R. M. Smith**, 'Fertility, Economy and Household Formation in England over Three Centuries', *Population and Development Review*, **7** (1981).
66. **E. A. Wrigley**, 'Clandestine Marriage in Tetbury in the late Seventeenth Century', *Local Population Studies*, **10** (1973).

Husband and wife

See also **Phythian-Adams** (42), **Pollock** and **Maitland** (121), **Stone** (5), (31), **Wrightson**, (19).
67. **A. Clark**, *Working Life of Women in the Seventeenth Century*, George Routledge & Sons, London, 1919.
68. **K. M. Davies**, 'Continuity and Change in Literary Advice on Marriage', in Outhwaite (ed.), *Marriage and Society* (61).
69. **L. Dibdin** and **C. E. H. Chadwyck Healey**, *English Church Law and Divorce*, John Murray, London, 1912.
70. **C. S. Kenny**, *The History of the Law of England as to the Effects of Marriage on Property and on the Wife's Legal Capacity*, London, 1879.
71. **I. Maclean**, *The Renaissance Notion of Woman: A Study in the Fortunes of Scholasticism and Medical Science in European Intellectual Life*, Cambridge UP, 1980.
72. **L. L. Schücking**, *The Puritan Family: A Social Study from the*

Literary Sources, Routledge & Kegan Paul, London, 1969.

73. **D. M. Stenton**, *The English Woman in History*, Allen & Unwin, London, 1957.

74. **K. V. Thomas**, 'The Double Standard', *Journal of the History of Ideas*, **20** (1959).

75. **R. Thompson**, *Women in Stuart England and America: A Comparative Study*, Routledge & Kegan Paul, London, 1974.

76. **M. Todd**, 'Humanists, Puritans and the Spiritualized Household', *Church History*, **49** (1980).

Childhood

See also **Finlay** (8), **Macfarlane** (38), **Schücking** (72), **Stone** (5), **Trumbach** (33), **Wrightson** (19), **Wrightson** and **Levine** (46).

77. **P. Ariès**, *Centuries of Childhood*, Jonathan Cape, London, 1962.

78. **L. de Mause**, *The History of Childhood: The Evolution of Parent – Child Relationships as a Factor in History*, Souvenir Press (Educational & Academic), London, 1976.

79. **A. Eccles**, *Obstetrics and Gynaecology in Tudor and Stuart England*, Croom Helm, London, 1982.

80. **B. A. Hanawalt**, 'Childrearing among the Lower Classes of Late Medieval England', *Journal of Interdisciplinary History*, **8** (1977).

81. **R. H. Helmholz**, 'Infanticide in the Province of Canterbury during the Fifteenth Century', *History of Childhood Quarterly*, **2** (1975).

82. **J. Knodel** and **E. van de Walle**, 'Breast Feeding, Fertility and Infant Mortality: An Analysis of some Early German Data', *Population Studies*, **21** (1967).

83. **D. McLaren**, 'Nature's Contraceptive. Wet-nursing and Prolonged Lactation: The Case of Chesham, Buckinghamshire, 1578–1601', *Medical History*, **23** (1979).

84. **I. Pinchbeck** and **M. Hewitt**, *Children in English Society: From Tudor Times to the Eighteenth Century*, Routledge & Kegan Paul, London, 1969.

85. **J. H. Plumb**, 'The New World of Children in Eighteenth Century England', *Past and Present*, **67** (1975).

86. **R. S. Schofield**, 'Perinatal Mortality in Hawkshead, Lancashire, 1581–1710', *Local Population Studies*, **4** (1970).

87. **R. S. Schofield** and **E. A. Wrigley**, 'Infant and Child Mortality in England in the Late Tudor and Early Stuart Period', in **C. Webster** (ed.), *Health, Medicine and Mortality in the Sixteenth Century*, Cambridge UP, 1979.

88. **M. Spufford**, 'First Steps in Literacy: The Reading and Writing

Experiences of the Humblest Seventeenth-Century Spiritual Autobiographers', *Social History*, **4** (1979).
89. **G. F. Still**, *The History of Paediatrics*, Oxford UP, 1931.
90. **G. Strauss**, *Luther's House of Learning: Indoctrination of the Young in the German Reformation*, Johns Hopkins UP, London, 1978.
91. **K. Wrightson**, 'Infanticide in Earlier Seventeenth-Century England', *Local Population Studies*, **15** (1975).
92. **E. A. Wrigley**, 'Family Limitation in Pre-industrial England', *Economic History Review*, 2nd ser., **19** (1966).
93. **E. A. Wrigley**, 'Marital Fertility in Seventeenth-Century Colyton: A Note', *Economic History Review*, **31** (1978).

Adolescence

See also **Macfarlane** (38).
94. **M. H. Curtis**, 'Education and Apprenticeship', *Shakespeare Survey*, **17** (1964).
95. **O. J. Dunlop** and **R. D. Denman**, *English Apprenticeship and Child Labour: A History*, Fisher Unwin, London, 1912.
96. **A. Kussmaul**, *Servants in Husbandry in Early Modern England*, Cambridge UP, 1981.
97. **R. O'Day**, *Education and Society, 1500–1800: Social Foundations of Education in Early Modern Britain*, Longman, London, 1982.
98. **S. R. Smith**, 'London Apprentices as Seventeenth-century Adolescents', *Past and Present*, **61** (1973).
99. **K. V. Thomas**, 'Age and Authority in Early Modern England', *Proceedings of the British Academy*, **62** (1976).
100. **R. Wall**, 'The Age at Leaving Home', *Journal of Family History*, **3** (1978).

Old age

See also **Phythian-Adams** (42), **Thomas** (99).
101. **P. Laslett**, 'The History of Ageing and the Aged', in *Family Life and Illicit Love* (13).
102. **S. R. Smith**, 'Growing Old in Early Stuart England', *Albion*, **8** (1976).

Death and the broken family

See also **Laslett** (12), (13), **Phythian-Adams** (42), **Spufford** (45), **Stone** (5), (31).

103. **P. Ariès**, *Western Attitudes towards Death: From the Middle Ages to the Present*, Johns Hopkins UP, London, 1974.
104. **P. Ariès**, *The Hour of Our Death*, Allen Lane, London, 1981.
105. **J. H. Bettey**, 'Marriages of Convenience by Copyholders in Dorset during the Seventeenth Century', *Proceedings of the Dorset Natural History and Archaeological Society*, **98** (1976).
106. **C. Carlton**, *The Court of Orphans*, Leicester UP, 1974.
107. **R. H. Helmholz**, 'The Roman Law of Guardianship in England, 1300–1600', *Tulane Law Review*, **52** (1977–78).
108. **J. Hurstfield**, *The Queen's Wards: Wardship and Marriage under Elizabeth I*, Longmans, London, 1958.
109. **P. Laslett**, 'Parental Deprivation in the Past: A Note on Orphans and Stepparenthood in English History', in *Family Life and Illicit Love* (13).
110. **M. MacDonald**, *Mystical Bedlam: Madness, Anxiety and Healing in Seventeenth-Century England*, Cambridge UP, 1981.
111. **P. Roebuck**, 'Post-Restoration Landownership: The Impact of the Abolition of Wardship', *Journal of British Studies*, **18** (1978–79).
112. **R. Schofield** and **E. A. Wrigley**, 'Remarriage Intervals and the Effect of Marriage Order on Fertility' in **J. Dupâquier** et al., (eds), *Marriage and Remarriage in Populations of the Past*, Academic Press, London, 1981.

Inheritance

See also **Carlton** (106), **Finch** (26), **Hey** (41), **Macfarlane** (15), (38), **Razi** (43), **Spufford** (45), **Stone** (31), **Thrupp** (32).
113. **L. Bonfield**, 'Marriage Settlements, 1660–1740: The Adoption of the Strict Settlement in Kent and Northamptonshire', in Outhwaite (ed.), *Marriage and Society* (61).
114. **C. Clay**, 'Marriage, Inheritance, and the Rise of Large Estates in England, 1660–1815', *Economic History Review*, 2nd ser., **21** (1968).
115. **R. Faith**, 'Peasant Families and Inheritance Customs in Medieval England', *Agricultural History Review*, **14** (1966).
116. **J. Goody**, **J. Thirsk** and **E. P. Thompson**, (eds), *Family and Inheritance: Rural Society in Western Europe, 1200–1800*, Cambridge UP, 1976.
117. **H. J. Habakkuk**, 'Marriage Settlements in the Eighteenth Century', *Transactions of the Royal Historical Society*, 4th ser., **32** (1950).
118. **W. G. Hoskins**, 'The Elizabethan Merchants of Exeter', in **S. T. Bindoff**, **J. Hurstfield** and **C. H. Williams** (eds) '*Eliz-*

abethan Government and Society: Essays presented to Sir John Neale, Athlone Press, London, 1961.

119. **P. Jefferies**, 'The Medieval Use as Family Law and Custom: the Berkshire Gentry in the Fourteenth and Fifteenth Centuries', *Southern History*, **1** (1979).

120. **K. B. McFarlane**, *The Nobility of Later Medieval England*, Clarendon Press, Oxford, 1973.

121. **Sir F. Pollock** and **F. W. Maitland**, *The History of English Law before the Time of Edward I*, reprint of 2nd edn of 1898, Cambridge UP, 1968.

122. **J. Thirsk**, 'Industries in the Countryside', in *Essays in the Economic and Social History of Tudor and Stuart England*, **F. J. Fisher** (ed.), Cambridge UP, 1961.

123. **J. Thirsk**, 'Younger Sons in the Seventeenth Century', *History*, **54** (1969).

124. **R. T. Vann**, 'Wills and the Family in an English Town: Banbury, 1550–1800', *Journal of Family History*, **4** (1979).

Historiography

125. **M. Anderson**, *Approaches to the History of the Western Family, 1500–1914*, Macmillan, London and Basingstoke, 1980. The best available survey. Much stronger on the second half of its period than the first; concentrates on recent work.

126. **P. Laslett**, 'Introduction to the History of the Family' in Laslett and Wall (eds), *Household and Family in Past Time* (14). Excellent account of the development of interest in the family among historical sociologists.

127. **F. Mount**, *The Subversive Family: An Alternative History of Love and Marriage*, Jonathan Cape, London, 1982. Lively, stimulating, sometimes polemical; shrewd criticisms of the work of some overrated historians; anticipates some of the points made in this book.

Postcript

Some important work has appeared in 1983, too late for me to take account of it in my own text. Three books published by the Cambridge University Press demand particular mention. Lloyd Bonfield has supplied a full account of *Marriage Settlements, 1601–1740: The Adoption of the Strict Settlement*. His claim that provision for the division of estates among surviving daughters was increasingly common in the late seventeenth century calls in question my own conclusion, based on the work of previous writers, that 'It was primogeniture above all which benefited from the strict settlement' (above, p. 238).

Cicely Howell's discussion of inheritance strategies in *Land, Family and Inheritance in Transition: Kibworth Harcourt 1280–1700* contains a forceful re-statement of the conclusions of her article in item 116 of my bibliography. Jack Goody concludes that *The Development of the Family and Marriage in Europe* was strongly influenced by the Christian Church in late Antiquity and the Middle Ages. The rôle of the Protestant Reformation was comparatively small.

During the year I learnt of Dr. Hassell Smith's research on the household of Nathaniel Bacon at Stiffkey (Norfolk), the results of which have not so far been published. These suggest that at any rate in great households married servants and servants recruited from the immediate vicinity were, during the Tudor period, commoner than I have implied.

November 1983   R.A.H.

Index